Travel Discount Coupon

This coupon entitles you to special discounts when you book your trip through the

GLOBAL TRAVEL NETWORK® RESERVATION SERVICE

Hotels ♦ Airlines ♦ Car Rentals ♦ Cruises
All Your Travel Needs

Here's what you get: *

- ♦ A discount of $50 USD on a booking of $1,000** or more for two or more people!
- ♦ A discount of $25 USD on a booking of $500** or more for one person!
- ♦ Free membership for three years, and 1,000 free miles on enrollment in the unique Miles-to-Go™ frequent-traveler program. Earn one mile for every dollar spent through the program. Earn free hotel stays starting at 5,000 miles. Earn free roundtrip airline tickets starting at 25,000 miles.
- ♦ Personal help in planning your own, customized trip.
- ♦ Fast, confirmed reservations at any property recommended in this guide, subject to availability.***
- ♦ Special discounts on bookings in the U.S. and around the world.
- ♦ Low-cost visa and passport service.
- ♦ Reduced-rate cruise packages.

Visit our website at http://www.travnet.com/Frommer or call us globally at 201-567-8500, ext. 55. In the U.S., call toll-free at 1-888-940-5000, or fax 201-567-1838. In Canada, call toll-free at 1-800-883-9959, or fax 416-922-6053. In Asia, call 60-3-7191044, or fax 60-3-7185415.

* To qualify for these travel discounts, at least a portion of your trip must include destinations covered in this guide. No more than one coupon discount may be used in any 12-month period, for destinations covered in this guide. Cannot be combined with any other discount or program.

**These are U.S. dollars spent on commissionable bookings.

***A $10 USD fee, plus fax and/or phone charges, will be added to the cost of bookings at each hotel not linked to the reservation service. Customers must approve these fees in advance.

Valid until December 31, 1998. Terms and conditions of the Miles-to-Go™ program are available on request by calling 201-567-8500, ext 55.

ROM123

Frommer's®

Rome

by Darwin Porter
and Danforth Prince

Macmillan • USA

About the Authors

A native of North Carolina, **Darwin Porter** was a bureau chief for the *Miami Herald* when he was 21, and later worked in television advertising. A veteran travel writer, he wrote Frommer's first-ever guide to Italy, which launched what is today's Frommer's "Complete" series, and he has been a frequent traveler in Italy ever since. He's joined by **Danforth Prince,** formerly of the Paris bureau of the *New York Times,* who has lived and traveled in Italy extensively. This team writes a number of best-selling Frommer guides—notably to England, France, the Caribbean, and Germany.

MACMILLAN TRAVEL

A Simon & Schuster Macmillan Company
1633 Broadway
New York, NY 10019

Find us online at **http://www.mgr.com/travel**

ISBN 0–02–861208–6
ISSN 0899–319–X

Editor: Reid Bramblett
Production Editor: Lynn Northrup
Design by Michele Laseau
Digital Cartography by Ortelius Design and Roberta Stockwell
Page creation by Terri Sheehan, Joy Dean Lee, Deb Kincaid, Trudy Coler, Linda Quigley, and Karen Teo

Special Sales

Bulk purchases (10+ copies) of Frommer's and selected Macmillan travel guides are available to corporations, organizations, mail-order catalogs, institutions, and charities at special discounts, and can be customized to suit individual needs. For more information write to: Special Sales, Macmillan General Reference, 1633 Broadway, New York, NY 10019.

Manufactured in the United States of America

Contents

List of Maps

An Invitation to the Reader

In researching this book, we discovered many wonderful places—hotels, restaurants, shops, and more. We're sure you'll find others. Please tell us about them, so we can share the information with your fellow travelers in upcoming editions. If you were disappointed with a recommendation, we'd love to know that, too. Please write to:

Darwin Porter & Danforth Prince
Frommer's Rome, 11th Edition
Macmillan Travel
1633 Broadway
New York, NY 10019

An Additional Note

Please be advised that travel information is subject to change at any time—and this is especially true of prices. We therefore suggest that you write or call ahead for confirmation when making your travel plans. The authors, editors, and publisher cannot be held responsible for the experiences of readers while traveling. Your safety is important to us, however, so we encourage you to stay alert and be aware of your surroundings. Keep a close eye on cameras, purses, and wallets, all favorite targets of thieves and pickpockets.

What the Symbols Mean

✪ Frommer's Favorites

Hotels, restaurants, attractions, and entertainment you should not miss.

$ Super-Special Values

Hotels and restaurants that offer great value for your money.

The following abbreviations are used for credit cards:

AE American Express
CB Carte Blanche
DC Diners Club
DISC Discover
ER enRoute
EU Eurocard
JCB Japan Credit Bank
MC MasterCard
V Visa

The Road to Rome

1

Rome is a city of images, vivid and unforgettable. One of the most striking is dawn from Janiculum Hill as the city's silhouette, with its bell towers and cupolas, comes gradually into view.

Rome is also a city of sounds, beginning, early in the morning, with the peal of church bells calling the faithful to mass. As the city awakens and comes to life, the sounds multiply and merge into a kind of *sinfonia urbana*. The streets fill with cars, taxis, and motor scooters, blaring their horns as they weave in and out of traffic; the sidewalks become overrun with bleary-eyed office workers rushing off to their desks, but not before stealing into crowded cafés for their first cappuccino of the day. The shops lining the streets open for business by raising their protective metal grilles as loudly as possible, seeming to delight in their contribution to the general din. And before long he many fruit-and-vegetable stands are abuzz with activity, as housewives, maids, widowers, cooks, and others arrive to purchase their day's supply of fresh produce, haggling over price and caviling over quality.

By 10am the tourists are on the street, battling the crowds and traffic as they wend their way from Renaissance palaces and baroque buildings to the famous ruins of antiquity. Indeed, Rome often appears to have two populations: one of Romans and one of visitors. During the summer months especially, Rome seems to become one big host for the countless sightseers who converge upon it, guidebook and camera in hand. To all of them—Americans, Europeans, Japanese—Rome extends a warm and friendly welcome, wining them, dining them, and entertaining them in its inimitable fashion. Of course, if you visit in August, you may see only tourists—not Romans, as the locals flee at that time. Or as one Roman woman once told us, "Even if we're too poor to go on vacation, we close the shutters and pretend we're away so neighbors won't find out we couldn't afford to leave the city."

The traffic, unfortunately, is worse than ever, restoration programs seem to drag on forever, and as the capital, Rome remains at the center of the major political scandals and corruption known as *Tangentopoli* ("bribe city"), which sends hundreds of government bureaucrats to jail each year.

But in spite of all this metropolitan and political horror, Romans still experience the good life. After you've done your "duty" to culture, wandering through the Colosseum, being awed that the

Pantheon's still there, after you've traipsed through St. Peter's Basilica and thrown a coin in the Trevi Fountain, you can pause in the early evening to experience the charm of Rome as evening comes. Find a café at summer twilight and watch the shades of pink turn to gold and copper before the night finally falls. That's when a new Rome comes alive, and when its restaurants and cafés grow more animated and more fun, especially if you've found one on an antique piazza or along a narrow alley deep in Trastevere. After dinner you can stroll by the fountains, or through Piazza Navona, have a gelato (or an espresso in winter), and the night is yours.

In Chapter 6 we'll take you on seemingly endless treks through ancient monuments and basilicas. But monuments are not the total picture. In Rome, you'll find yourself embracing life with intensity. In other words, "When in Rome . . ."

1 Frommer's Favorite Rome Experiences

- **A Walk Through Ancient Rome:** There is a vast, almost unified archeological park cut through the center of Rome—all the way from the Rome of the Caesars to Via Appia Antica. For those who want specific guidance, we have an entire chapter devoted to the most sight-filled of Roman walks. However, it's far more adventuresome to wander at will through the very streets where Julius Caesar's carriage once rolled, or (much later) that of Lucrezia Borgia. A slice of history unfolds at every turn—an ancient fountain, a long-forgotten statue, the ruins of a temple dedicated to some long-faded cult. A narrow street will suddenly open and you'll have a vista of a triumphal arch. The Roman Forum and the Palatine Hill are the most rewarding targets for your archeological probe, but the glory of Rome is hardly confined to these dusty fields. If you wander long enough, you'll eventually emerge onto Piazza della Rotunda—and stare in awe at one of Rome's most glorious sights, the Pantheon (see below).
- **A Picnic on Isola Tiberina:** In Roman times this boat-shaped island stood across from the port of Rome, and from 293 B.C. a temple stood here dedicated to the Aesculapius, god of healing. On the ruins of this ancient temple a church was constructed in the 10th century. You can reach the island from the Jewish Ghetto by a footbridge, Ponte Fabricio, the oldest original bridge over the Tiber, dating from 62 B.C. Romans come here to sunbathe and escape the traffic and the crowds, sitting along the river's embankment. Arrive with the makings of a picnic from literally hundreds of shops scattered throughout the city—and the day is yours.
- **A Sunday Bike Ride in Rome:** Weekdays are too traffic-clogged, but on a clear Sunday morning while Romans are still sleeping off too much *vino* from Saturday night, you can rent a bike and explore at your leisure. Without so much traffic, you'll realize just how scenic Rome is. Start early after dawn while the streets are still cool from the night. The best places to cycle are the parks, including Villa Borghese. Within its 4-mile borders, it's a world unto itself, with museums and galleries, a riding school, an artificial lake, and a grassy amphitheater. Another choice place for Sunday biking is Villa Doria Pamphili, an extensive park lying above the Janiculum. Laid out in the mid-1600s, this is Rome's largest park, with numerous fountains and some summer houses.
- **A Sunset Stroll in the Pincio Gardens:** Above the landmark Piazza del Popolo, this terraced and lushly planted hillside is the most romantic place for a twilight walk. A dusty orange-rose glow often colors the sky, giving an aura to the park's umbrella pines and broad avenues. The ancient Romans turned this hill into gardens, but today's look came from the design of Giuseppe Valadier in the 1800s. Everybody from King Farouk of Egypt to Mussolini found it fashionable to stroll

here—even Richard Strauss or a visitor to Rome like Gandhi. Pause at the main piazza, Napoleone I, for a spectacular view of the city, stretching from the Janiculum to Monte Mario. The Egyptian-style obelisk you see was erected by Hadrian on the tomb of his great love, Antinous, a beautiful male slave who died prematurely.

- **Roma de Notte:** *La dolce vita* is still alive at night in Rome and the ancient monuments such as the Forum are bathed in a theatrical white light. Of course, don't get too carried away with the romance of the Colosseum with the moon rising behind and through its arches. Remember that this is where the Henry James heroine Daisy Miller met her downfall. Begin your nocturnal diversions with a Roman *passeggiata* (early-evening stroll) along Via del Corso or Piazza Navona. There's plenty of action going on inside the clubs too—from Via Veneto to Piazza Navona. Clubbers flock to the colorful narrow streets of Trastevere and the Pantheon areas—even more remote Testaccio, once viewed as "Siberia." The jazz scene is especially good, and big names often pop in. All you need is a young *Roman Holiday* Gregory Peck (or Audrey Hepburn, depending on your tastes) and a motorscooter to show you around Rome by night. Open-air opera, classical music, and jazz concerts load the calendar from late June until the end of September. A little publication, *Info Rome* (in English), will keep you abreast of what's happening.
- **Hanging Out at the Pantheon:** The world's best preserved ancient monument is now a hot spot—especially at night. Find a café table out on the square and take in the action, which needs a young Fellini to record it on tape. The Pantheon has become a symbol of Rome itself, and we owe our thanks to Hadrian for leaving the world this monument. When you tire of people-watching and cappuccino, you can go inside to inspect the tomb of Raphael, who was buried here in 1520. (His mistress, La Fornarina, wasn't allowed to attend the services.) Nothing is more dramatic than to be in the Pantheon during a rainstorm, watching the sheets of water splatter on the colorful marble floor. It enters through an oculus on top, which provides the only light for the interior.
- **Campo de' Fiori at Mid-Morning:** In an incomparable setting of medieval houses, this is the liveliest fruit and vegetable market in Rome. It's best viewed after 9am any day Monday to Saturday. By 1pm the stalls are closing down. Once this was the major site for the medieval inns of Rome, and this square maintains some of the old bohemian atmosphere. Many of these inns were owned by Vannozza Catanei, the 15th-century courtesan and lover of Pope Alexander VI Borgia. We come here every day we're in Rome for a lively view of local life that no other place seems to match. Often you'll spot your favorite trattoria chef bargaining for the best and freshest produce—everything from fresh cherries to the perfect vine-ripened tomato. The stamping ground of everybody from aristocrats to fishmongers, even through Renaissance times, the market stalls still peddle their wares as they've done for centuries.
- **Opening Night at the Rome Opera:** The Milanese claim that the stellar quality of their operas at La Scala diminish the operas presented at Rome. Roman opera buffs, of course, disagree. Decide for yourself at Rome's Teatro dell'Opera, whose season runs between December and June. Programs concentrate on the classics, and that means Bellini, Donizetti, Puccini, and Rossini. A recent opening-night performance of *The Barber of Seville* was better than the same opera performed in Seville. No one seems to touch the Roman's operatic soul more than Giuseppe Verdi (1813–1901), who became a national icon in his support for Italian unification. His *Aïda* used to be performed by this opera house at the Baths of

Caracalla. But nowadays you're more likely to witness his *La Traviata* as it remains a perennial favorite, even though the reviewer for *The Times* of London, upon first hearing it at its debut, found it filled "with foul and hideous horrors."

- **A Tour of the Janiculum:** On the Trastevere side of the river, where Garibaldi in 1849 held off the attacking French troops, the Janiculum Hill was always strategic in Rome's defense. Today a walk in this park at the top of the hill is a much-needed retreat from the traffic-filled and often hot streets of Trastevere. Filled with monuments to Garibaldi and his brave men, the hill is no longer peppered with monasteries as it was in the Middle Ages. Today you can go for long walks, inspecting the monuments and fountains while enjoying panoramic views of Rome. The best view is from Villa Lante, a Renaissance summer residence. If you choose to visit the Janiculum, you're in good company. The poet Torquato Tasso liked to sit in the park contemplating the meaning of life before he died in 1595. The most serene part of the park is the 1883 Botanical Gardens, with their palm trees, orchids, bromeliads, and sequoias—in all, more than 7,000 plant species from all over the world.
- **Strolling Along the Tiber:** Without the Tiber, there may have been no Rome. It's been a key player in the city's history since the founding of Rome, and it used to flood the capital every winter until it was "tamed" in 1870. It is these very massive lungotevere embankments on both sides of the Tiber that form such memorable strolls today. You not only get to walk along the river from which Cleopatra made her grand entrance into Rome, but you'll also view the riverside life of such characteristic neighborhoods as Trastevere and the Jewish Ghetto. At some point you can cross over to visit Isola Tiberina, the island in the middle of the Tiber, taking in panoramas of the river in both directions. You can start at Piazza della Bocca della Verità and go for some 2 or more miles or until you tire. Walks along the river are best in the early evening.
- **Following in the Footsteps of Bernini:** One of the most enjoyable ways to view Rome is to follow the trail of Giovanni Lorenzo Bernini (1598–1680), who left a greater mark on the city than most, even Michelangelo. Under the patronage of three different popes, Bernini "baroqued" Rome. Start at Largo di Santa Susanna, north of the Stazione Termini, at the Church of Santa Maria della Vittoria, housing one of Bernini's most controversial sculptures, the *Ecstasy of St. Teresa* from 1646. Walk from here along Via Barberini to Piazza Barberini, in the center of which stands Bernini's second most dramatic fountain, the Fontana del Tritone. From the piazza go along Via delle Quattro Fontane, bypassing (on your left) the Palazzo Barberini designed by Bernini and others for Pope Urban VIII. At the famous crossroads of Rome, Le Quattro Fontane, take Via del Quirinale to see the facade of Sant'Andrea, one of the artist's greatest churches. Arm yourself with a good map at this point and continue west, bypassing the Pantheon to arrive eventually at Piazza Navona, which Bernini remodeled for Pope Innocent X. Bernini designed the central fountain, the Fontana dei Fiumi, his masterpiece. The figures symbolizing the four rivers were sculpted by others to his plans. For many, this fabulous Bernini fountain, with its rocks, shells, and other natural forms, will complete their Bernini fix for the day.
- **A Day on the Appian Way:** Dating from 312 B.C., the Appian Way (Via Appia) once traversed the whole peninsula of Italy, the road on which Roman legions marched to Brindisi and their conquests in the East. One of its darkest moments was the crucifixion of the rebellious slave army of Spartacus in 71 B.C., whose bodies lined the road from Rome to Capua. Fashionable Romans were buried here, and early Christians dug catacombs to flee their persecutors. Begin at the Tomb

of Cecilia Metella and proceed up Via Appia Antica past a series of tombs and monuments, including everybody from Marcus Servilius and Seneca, the great moralist who committed suicide on the orders of Nero, to Pope St. Urban, who reigned 222–30. The sights along Via Appia Antica are among the most evocative in Rome. You can go all the way to the Church of Domine Quo Vadis.

- **Drinking in Rome:** The grape reigns supreme, although Rome is filled with famous drinking fountains as well, bringing fresh and sweet water from the surrounding hills through a system of pipes and aqueducts (but never drink from a fountain where a sign says ACQUA NON POTABILE). While in Rome, do as the Romans do and enjoy a carafe of dry white wine from the warm climate of Lazio. In restaurants and trattorie you'll find the most popular brand, Frascati, but try some of the other wines from the Castelli Romani too, including Colli Albani, Velletri, and Marino. All these wines come from one grape: Trebbiano. Sometimes a dash of Malvasia is added for greater flavor and an aromatic bouquet. Of course, you don't have to wait until dinnertime to drink wine, but can sample it at any of the hundreds of wine bars throughout the city. At these bars you'll find all the great reds and whites from throughout Italy, especially Tuscany and the Piedmont where the reds come from. Naturally, nothing beats sipping a bitter, herb-flavored apéritif—perhaps Campari or Martini—at one of Rome's legendary cafés.
- **Gelato on a Summer Night:** Sampling Roman ice cream (gelato) at a gelateria is worth waiting through the long winter. Tubs of homemade ice cream—among the best in the world—await you in a dazzling array of flavors: everything from candied orange peels with chocolate to watermelon to rice. *Gelaterie* offer *semifreddi* concoctions (made with cream instead of milk), in such flavors as almond, *marengo* (a type of meringue), and *zabaglione* (eggnog). Naturally, seasonal fresh fruits are made into ice creams of blueberry, cherry, peach, or whatever. Italians often like their ice cream with espresso. *Granite* (crushed ice) flavored with sweet fruit tastes are another cool delight on a sultry night. Tre Scalini at Piazza Navona is the most fabled spot for enjoying the *divino tartufo,* a chocolate concoction made by the gods.
- **A Roman Dinner on a Hidden Plaza:** If you're in Rome with that special someone, take her/him to a typical trattoria that opens onto an almost forgotten square deep in the heart of ancient Rome. If the evening dinner extends for 3 or 4 hours, who's really counting time? This is a special experience, and Rome has dozens of these little restaurants that often don't appear in guidebooks, but are ready and waiting to serve you. The waiters won't rush you out the door when you've obviously overstayed your time at the table. Two come to mind: Archimede, on Piazza dei Caprettari (☎ 06/686-1616), with outdoor tables placed on this tiny square with its architectural gems, including a small Renaissance palace and the Chiesa di Sant'Eustachio. Try fried zucchini flowers stuffed with cheese and anchovies or partake of one of the freshest seafood antipasti around Piazza Navona. Or else sample the wares at Vecchia Roma, Piazza Campitella 18 (☎ 06/686-4604), with a theatrical setting on one of the loveliest squares to be on on a summer evening in Rome. Order spaghetti with double-"horned" clams or traditional pastas and seafood while enjoying an ambience that remains unspoiled in spite of the restaurant's long-lasting popularity with savvy local foodies.
- **Music in the Churches:** Classical music lovers flock to Rome if for no other reason than to hear music in the city's churches. World-famed artists like Plácido Domingo and Luciano Pavarotti have performed in Roman venues ranging from churches to ancient ruins. Music is performed mostly in concerts—not at services. By decree of Pope John Paul II, it must be sacred music—not some dirty boogie.

Roma 2000

In A.D. 1,000, at the dawn of Christendom's second millennium, thousands of devoutly religious Romans gathered on the city's hilltops, anxiously awaiting the return of Christ the Majesty to judge the living and the dead. Despite the fanatical predictions of many mystics and visionaries that the world would end a thousand years after the arrival of Christ, nothing particularly eventful happened. The masses of the Roman faithful, it's reported, rather dejectedly returned to their homes, churches, and workday rituals to continue their lives in the Eternal City.

Rome doesn't plan to let that happen again! Plans, upheaval, and work projects are now underway to make the end of the second millennium much more event-filled than its dawn. Even visitors arriving in 1997 and 1998 before the big event will see the fuss being raised. It might explain why you can't go inside the Colosseum or sit on the Spanish Steps—restoration is to blame. During the life of this edition more special restrictions may be imposed, including new pedestrians-only zones proposed and even the possibility of a new Metro line between the Colosseum and the Vatican.

Every civic planner since the days of Mussolini has agreed that many of the streets of Rome are too narrow, that the city lacks a coherent system of public transport, and that driving through (and parking in) some neighborhoods has contributed to more hypertension and heart failure than anything else in Italy. Only the most powerful of autocrats (Mussolini and some of the Renaissance popes) have ever been able to slice thoroughfares through historic neighborhoods, and the results have never—at least artistically—been completely embraced by historians.

But ironically, the prospect of millions of devoted pilgrims flooding the city from virtually everywhere to celebrate the turn of the millennium has provided the incentive that civic planners have needed to right some of modern Rome's chronic ills. Broad-based powers—and funds—have been placed at their disposal to do so. The tension between designing new facilities within the context of an ancient Christian core is truly Olympian.

Although as you read this the Jubilee year will still be 2 or 3 years away, the city will be affected beginning around 1997 by the initial stages of the eventual

When church concerts are being performed, programs appear not only outside the church but on various announcements posted throughout Rome. The top professionals play at the "big name" churches, but don't overlook those smaller hard-to-find churches on hidden squares. Some of the best music we've ever heard has been by up-and-coming musicians getting their start in these little-known churches. The biggest event is the RAI (national broadcasting company) concert on December 5 at St. Peter's—even the pope attends. Other favorite venues for church music include Sant'Ignazio di Loyola, on Piazza di Sant'Ignazio, and San Paolo Fuori le Mura, at Via Ostiense 186.

- **From Fountain to Fountain:** While Londoners might be on a pub crawl, Romans are out walking on summer nights from fountain to cooling fountain—especially those who live in crowded ghetto apartments without air-conditioning. It's an artistic experience for the visitor as well, as some of Rome's greatest artists worked to create these fountains. Everybody makes at least one trip to Bernini's fountain on Piazza Navona, after stopping off at the Trevi Fountain to toss in a coin and alterations to its architecture and layout. Here's a rundown on changes Rome plans to implement:

Beginning in 1997, a series of cultural programs will focus on the role of Rome as a crucible of civilization, attracting musicians and artists from around the world. In the city's museums, renovations to the exhibition space and to the restaurant and toilet facilities will begin, and an enlargement of the security staff will be implemented. As the millennium approaches, additional gallery space will open, perhaps in unused municipal buildings, for the special exhibitions that will be organized. Throughout the city, vast numbers of information packets, in every conceivable language, will keep printing presses working overtime. In anticipation of a critical shortage of housing, many churches and schools plan to transform some of their public areas into low-cost lodgings for the faithful, sometimes with funds provided by public sources.

Urban renovation will proceed at a frantic rate. Some historic but decrepit neighborhoods will be restored, and—as part of the process—many additional parking spaces, some of them underground, will be added. The intention is to transform some squares, presently suffocated by parked cars, into open spaces where people can meet and socialize. Some parking areas will be planned on the city's outskirts, near the junction of rail lines and *autostrada.* From those far-flung fields of cars, high-speed train and bus connections, departing about every 5 minutes, will carry as many as 120,000 people in and out of the historic core during peak hours. There, direct access by most private cars and tourist buses will be reduced, or—except for deliveries—forbidden altogether. The neighborhoods around the basilicas that anticipate the greatest crush of visitors will ban the entrance of vehicular traffic altogether. An overhaul of the city's railway stations (both the Stazione Termini and the Stazione Tiburtina) and the enlargement of their parking facilities are a part of the renovation plans, although the details of this are among the least clear of any that affect the celebration. As part of the beautification process, scores of new trees will be planted, flowerbeds laid out, and efforts made to improve the appearance of the Eternal City with a 2,000th-anniversary face-lift.

thus ensure their return to Rome—but there are hundreds more. Our favorite is the Fontana delle Tararughe, in tiny Piazza Mattei. It has stood there since 1581—a jewel of Renaissance sculpture showing youths helping tortoises into a basin. In spite of its charm, it's still considered a "secret" fountain of Rome. Back on the main fountain-hopping trail, you'll encounter our favorite Bernini fountain at Piazza Barberini, the Fontana del Tritone, a magnificent work of art from 1642 showing the sea god blowing through a shell. If you think you can still jump into these fountains and paddle around as Anita Ekberg did in *La Dolce Vita,* forget it. That's now against the law.

- **The Campidoglio at Night:** There is no more splendid place to be at night than Piazza del Campidoglio, where Michelangelo designed both the geometric paving and the facades of the buildings. A broad flight of steps, the Cordonata, takes you up to this panoramic site, citadel of ancient Rome from which traitors to the empire were once tossed to their deaths. Home during the day to the Capitoline Museums, it takes on a different aura at night when it's dramatically lit, its measured Renaissance facades glowing like jewel boxes. The views of the brilliantly lit Forum and Palatine at night are worth the long trek up those stairs. There's no more stunning cityscape view at night than from this hill, even if the gilded temple to Jupiter is long gone the way of the empire. Few places in all of Europe are filled with as many memories of ancient glories as the Campidoglio.

- **Flea-Market Shopping:** We have never discovered an original Raphael, much less a Michelangelo, at Rome's Porta Portese flea market, which locals call *mercato delle pulci.* But we've picked up some interesting souvenirs over the years. It all began after World War II when black marketers needed an outlet for their illegal wares. Today the authentic art and antiques you could once buy here are now usually fake—but a lot is for sale, including World War II cameras, caviar from immigrant Russians, luggage (fake Gucci), spare parts, Mussolini busts, whatever. This is the largest flea market in Europe. Near Porta Sublicio in Trastevere, the market has some 4,000 stalls, but it's estimated that only 10% of them have a license. Sunday from 5am to 2pm is the time to visit, and, yes, the pickpockets begin plying their trade early in the day.

2 Rome Today

Some people in Rome may be gearing up for Jubilee Year / Roma 2000 (see box), but others not directly concerned with earning their living from some construction project related to this event are more blasé. As one Roman confided to us, "When it comes, I'll deal with it then."

Even before "the big event," as it's called, the jubilee celebration may affect your visit to Rome—especially when you find more pedestrian zones created (making traffic problems even more unbearable than they already are) or wonder why the Spanish Steps are torn up or why you can't go into the Colosseum. Bear in mind that other special restrictions and more monument restoration may interfere with your sightseeing agenda.

There is little other cause for celebration in Rome today. The city is presiding over a country of contradictions: a Roman Catholic state ruled by the mores and values of a staunchly religious consciousness which nevertheless is the most corrupt country in Western Europe.

The nation's politicians centered at Rome claim to fight corruption, but often get involved in scandal after scandal themselves. Italy is a land whose sons and daughters emigrated to form large populations throughout the world, especially in America, but its citizens today in large numbers remain viciously opposed to and prejudiced against immigrants arriving on their own shore.

"In the course of a century, we've gone from being a land of emigrants to one that takes in immigrants," said Luigi Manconi, a sociologist. "We're just not equipped." Rome, in particular, has become overrun with immigrants, often illegal, straining already-precarious facilities.

Widespread unemployment has enhanced racism and prejudice, primarily directed toward the North African contingent which has descended in search of jobs. These workers are not accepted into the tight-knit Roman communities. Recent violence and retribution have prompted the government to impose limits on immigration.

Although that government might try to limit immigration, any attempt to clean up its own image seems hopeless. *La politica e una cosa sporca* (politics are dirty) is an expression often heard in Rome. The charge is certainly justified. Corruption, scandal, and political chaos are parts of everyday life on the Roman landscape. The

Impressions

In Rome you have to do as the Romans do, or get arrested.
—Geoffrey Harmsworth, *Abyssinian Adventure* (1935)

word *politician* is almost always preceded by the word *corrupt.* It is virtually assumed that anyone entering politics is doing so for personal gain.

Rome presides over a modern political system—55 governments since World War II—that has been compared by many political analysts to the ill-fated First Republic.

Rome's latest and most notorious scandal involving a political figure is the ongoing trial in Palermo of Giulio Andreotti, seven-time Italian prime minister. Andreotti is on trial for alleged Mafia dealings. The trial is expected to last two years and cover thousands of pages of allegations. In addition, Andreotti is on trial for his suspected involvement in the assassination of an investigative journalist in Rome.

These proceedings, along with numerous other cases involving high-ranking officials, create a tremendous lack of faith and trust in the political system. They are at the core of a sweeping aura of discontent that's common among Romans. When the subject of politics is breached, Romans today throw up their hands in frustration. They have also learned to live and work outside the government.

Although Italy ranks sixth among world economics, the instability of the lira in global markets has forced the country to retain its position as a second-class participant in global commerce. Its true economy cannot be measured because of the vast underground economy (*economia sommersa*) controlled by the Mafia. Almost every Roman has some unreported income or expenditure. Other global competitors refrain from investing in Italian ventures because of lack of confidence in the government.

Besides soccer (*calcio*), the family, and affairs of the heart, the national obsession of Italy today is *il sorpasso,* a term that describes Italy's surpassing of its archrivals France and Britain in economic indicators. Economists disagree about whether or not il sorpasso has happened, and statistics (complicated by the presence of Italy's vast underground economy) vary widely from source to source. All levels of Roman society are actively engaged to some degree in withholding funds from the government. Today Rome's underground economy competes on a monumental scale with the official economy, with participation by all sorts of otherwise respectable businesses and individuals. Complicating problems for economists, the police, and politicians is the constant interference of the Mafia, whose methods—despite numerous more or less heartfelt crackdowns—continue today even more ruthlessly than ever.

Before they get thrown out of office, politicians pass laws and more laws, adding to the horde already on the books. Affecting the entire nation, more laws are passed in Rome than in any other nation of Western Europe. Because of these Draconian rules, Romans are forced to live "outside the law" to survive.

Michael Mewshaw, author of *Playing Away,* notes that: "Something as simple as cashing a check or paying a bill can devour half a day. To escape the brambles of red tape, Romans have become marvelous improvisers and corner-cutters. Whenever possible they bypass the sclerotic public sector and negotiate private deals *fra amici*—among friends."

Red tape and politics aside, what most visitors come for is to pay homage to a glorious past. Rome contains a greater number of historic buildings, monuments, and ruins than any other city in the world. Palaces, parks, churches, museums, piazze, statues, and fountains abound. Ancient and massive ruins—mocking the ambitions of humankind for immortality—bask in the sun, and baroque grandeur adorns almost every street corner. The sheer volume of sights has crafted one of the most memorable urban landscapes in the world.

Today, despite the city's status as capital of both modern Italy and as the site of the Vatican center of the Catholic church, Rome seems permeated with the temperament and sensuality of southern Europe. Familiar with power from the time of its earliest inhabitants, the city is famous for its blasé acceptance of the inevitability of death, its *joie de vivre* (known locally as a *gioia di vivere*), and its stoic acceptance of the inevitable rise and fall of personal and political fortunes.

The city is simultaneously strident, romantic, and sensual, and has forever altered the Western world's standards of beauty and excellence in such fields as art, religion, and government. And although today the romantic poets would probably be horrified at the traffic, pollution, overcrowding, crime, political discontent, and barely controlled chaos of modern Rome, the city endures and thrives in a way that has often been described as eternal.

Modern Roman society faces daunting problems, including insufficient housing, a rapid rise in the cost of living, impossible traffic, a bureaucracy that tends to strangle personal initiative, a rising crime rate, and pollution that has caused irreparable damage to many of the city's monuments. However, Rome still manages to live a relatively relaxed way of life. Romans, along with their southern cousins in Naples, are specialists in the *arte di arrangiarsi,* the art of coping and surviving with style, a mode that's pursued with both passion and a sense of tragic resignation. The Romans have humanity if not humor, a 2,000-year-old sense of cynicism, and a strong feeling of belonging to a particular place.The city's attractions seem as old as time itself, and despite the frustrations of the city's daily life, Rome continues to lure new visitors every year to sample its ancient pleasures and temptations anew.

3 A Look at the Past

Many of the key events that shaped the rich and often gory tapestry of Italian history originated in Rome. Although parts of Italy (especially Sardinia and Sicily) were inhabited as early as the Bronze Age, the region around Rome was occupied relatively late. Some historians claim that the presence of active volcanoes in the region during the Bronze Age prevented prehistoric tribes from living there, but regardless of the reason, Rome has unearthed far fewer prehistoric graves and implements than neighboring Umbria and Tuscany have.

THE ETRUSCANS The arrival around 800 B.C. of the Etruscans in Umbria has never fully been understood by sociologists or historians (the many inscriptions they left behind—mostly on graves—are of no help, since the Etruscan language has never been deciphered). While the Etruscans built temples at Tarquinia and Caere (present-day Cerveteri), the few nervous Latin tribes who remained outside their

Dateline

- **Bronze Age** Tribes of Celts, Teutonics, and groups from the eastern Mediterranean inhabit the Italian peninsula.
- **1200–1000 B.C.** The Etruscans migrate from the eastern Mediterranean (probably Mesopotamia) and occupy territory north and south of Rome.
- **800 B.C.** Sicily and southern Italy (especially Naples) flourish under Greek and Phoenician protection; independent of most outside domination, Rome evolves as an insignificant community of shepherds with loyalties

continues

sway gravitated to the strategic position of what was later known as Rome.

From their base at Rome, the Latins remained free of the Etruscans until about 600 B.C., when the Etruscans were able to establish a military stronghold in Rome. Under the combined influences of the Greeks and the Mesopotamian east, Roma grew enormously. A new port was opened at Ostia, near the mouth of the Tiber. Artists from Greece carved statues of Roman gods to resemble Greek divinities. From this enforced (and not always peaceable) mélange of the Latin tribes with the Etruscans grew the roots of what eventually became the Republic of Rome.

THE ROMAN REPUBLIC Gauls from the alpine regions invaded the northern Etruscan territory around 600 B.C., and the Latin tribes revolted in about 510 B.C., toppling the Etruscan-linked rulers from their power bases and establishing the southern boundary of Etruscan influence at the Tiber. Greeks from Sicily ended Etruscan sea power in 474 B.C., during the battle of Cumae off the Italian coastline just north of Naples. By 250 B.C. the Romans and their allies in Campagna had vanquished the Etruscans, wiping out their language and religion.

Tempered in the fires of military adversity, the stern Roman republic was characterized by belief in the gods, the necessity of learning from the past, strength of the family, education through books and public service, and most important, obedience. The all-powerful Senate presided as Rome defeated rival powers one after the other in a steady stream of staggering military successes.

As the population grew, the Romans gave to their Latin allies, and then to conquered peoples, partial or complete Roman citizenship, always with the obligation of military service. Colonies of citizens were established on the borders of the growing empire and were populated with soldiers/farmers and their families. Later, as seen in the history of Britain and the Continent, colonies began to thrive as semiautonomous units on their own, heavily fortified, and linked to Rome by well-maintained military roads and a well-defined hierarchy of military command.

The final obstacle to the unrivaled supremacy of Rome was the defeat, during the 3rd century B.C., of the city-state of Carthage during the two Punic Wars. An ancient Phoenician trading post on the

divided among several Latin tribes.

- **753 B.C.** Rome's traditional founding date.
- **660 B.C.** Etruscans occupy Rome as the capital of their empire; the city grows rapidly and a major seaport (Ostia) opens at the mouth of the Tiber.
- **510–250 B.C.** The Latin tribes, still centered in Rome, maintain a prolonged revolt against the Etruscans; alpine Gauls attack the Etruscans from the north and Greeks living in Sicily destroy the Etruscan navy.
- **250 B.C.** The Romans and their allies finally purge the Etruscans from Italy; Rome flourishes as a republic and begins the accumulation of a vast empire.
- **250–50 B.C.** Rome obliterates its chief rival, Carthage, during two Punic Wars; Carthage's defeat allows unchecked Roman expansion into Spain, North Africa, Sardinia, and Corsica.
- **44 B.C.** Julius Caesar is assassinated; his successor, Augustus, transforms Rome from a city of brick to a city of marble, and solidifies Rome's status as a dictatorship.
- **40 B.C.** Rome and its armies control the entire Mediterranean world.
- **3rd century A.D.** Rome declines under a series of incompetent and corrupt emperors.
- **4th century A.D.** Rome is fragmented politically as administrative capitals are established in such cities as Milan and Trier, Germany.
- **A.D. 395** The empire splits: Constantine establishes a

continues

"New Rome" at Constantinople (Istanbul); Goths invade Rome's provinces in northern Italy.

- **410–455** Rome is sacked by barbarians—Alaric the Goth, Attila the Hun, and Galseric the Vandal.
- **475** Rome falls, leaving only the primate of the Catholic church in control; the pope slowly adopts many of the responsibilities and the prestige once reserved for the Roman emperors.
- **731** Pope Gregory II renounces Rome's spiritual and political link to the authorities in Constantinople.
- **800** Charlemagne is crowned Holy Roman Emperor by Pope Leo III; Italy dissolves into a series of small warring kingdoms.
- **1065** The Holy Land falls to the Muslim Turks; the Crusades are launched.
- **1303–77** Papal schism: A rival pope is established at Avignon.
- **1377** The "antipope" is removed from Avignon, and the Roman popes emerge as sole contenders to the legacy of St. Peter.
- **Mid-1400s** Originating in Florence, the Renaissance blossoms throughout Italy; Italian artists receive multiple commissions from the ecclesiastical communities of Rome.
- **1508** Ordered by the pope, Michelangelo begins work on the ceiling of the Vatican's Sistine Chapel.
- **1527** Rome is attacked and sacked by Charles V, who—to the pope's rage—is elected Holy Roman Emperor the following year.
- **1796–97** Napoléon's military conquests of Italy arouse Italian nationalism.

continues

coast of Tunisia, Carthage had grown into one of the premier naval and agricultural powers of the Mediterranean with strongly fortified positions in Corsica, Sardinia, and Spain. Despite the impressive victories of the Carthaginian general Hannibal, Rome eventually eradicated Carthage in one of the most famous defeats in ancient history. Rome was able to immediately expand its power into North Africa, Sardinia, Corsica, and Iberia.

THE ROMAN EMPIRE By 49 B.C. Italy ruled all of the Mediterranean world either directly or indirectly, with all political, commercial, and cultural pathways leading directly to Rome. The possible wealth and glory to be found in Rome lured many there, but drained other Italian communities of human resources. As Rome transformed itself into an administrative headquarters, imports into the city from other parts of the empire hurt local farmers and landowners. The seeds for civil discord were sown early in the empire's life, although as Rome was embellished with temples, monuments, and the easy availability of slave labor from conquered territories, many of its social problems were overlooked in favor of expansion and glory.

On the eve of the birth of Christ, Rome was a mighty empire whose generals had brought all of the Western world under the influence of Roman law, values, and civilization. Only in the eastern third of the Mediterranean did the existing cultures—especially the Greek—withstand the Roman incursions. Despite its occupation by Rome, Greece, more than any other culture, permeated Rome with new ideas, values, and concepts of art, architecture, religion, and philosophy.

Meanwhile, the ideals of democratic responsibility in the heart of the empire had begun to break down. The populace began to object violently to a government that took little interest in commerce, and seemed interested only in foreign politics. As taxes and levies increased, the poor emigrated in huge and idle numbers to Rome and the rich cities of the Po Valley. Entire generations of war captives, forced into the slave-driven economies of large Italian estates, were steeped in hatred and ignorance.

Christianity, a new and (at the time) revolutionary religion, probably gained a foothold in Rome about 10 years after Christ's crucifixion. Feared far more for its political implications than for its spiritual presuppositions, it was at first brutally suppressed before moving through increasingly tolerant stages of acceptability.

After the death of Julius Caesar, political control became entrenched in the hands of a series of all-powerful emperors, whose sweeping strengths brought Rome to new, almost giddy, heights. Augustus transformed the city from brick to marble in some of the most grandiose building projects in history, but as corruption spread, Rome endured a steady decay in the ideals and traditions upon which the empire had been founded. As the uncorruptible Roman soldier of an earlier era became increasingly rare, the army became filled with barbarian mercenaries. The tax collector became the scourge of the countryside, often killing the incentive for economic development and causing many to abandon their farms altogether in favor of a life of impoverishment in the cities. For every good emperor (Augustus, Trajan, Vespasian, Hadrian, to name a few), there were three or four corrupt, debased, and possibly insane heads of state (Caligula, Nero, Domitian, Caracalla, and many more).

As the decay progressed, the Roman citizen either lived on the increasingly swollen public dole and spent his days at gladiatorial games and imperial baths, or was a disillusioned patrician at the mercy of emperors who might murder him for his property. The 3rd century A.D. saw so many emperors that it was common, as H. V. Morton tells us, to hear in the provinces of the election of an emperor together with a report of his assassination. Despite a well-intentioned series of reforms in the 4th century A.D. by Diocletian, the empire continued to weaken and decay. Although he reinforced imperial power, paradoxically at the same time he weakened Roman dominance and prestige by establishing administrative capitals of the empire at such outposts as Milan, Trier in Germany, and elsewhere.

This practice was followed by Constantine when he moved the administrative capital away from Rome altogether, an act that sounded a death knell for a city already threatened by the menace of barbarian attacks. The sole survivor of six rival emperors, Constantine recognized Christianity as the official religion of the Roman Empire, and built an entirely new, more easily defensible capital on the banks of the Bosporus. Named in his honor (Constantinople, or Byzantium), it was later renamed Istanbul by the Ottoman Turks. When he moved to the new capital, Constantine and his heirs took with him the best of the artisans, politicians, and public figures of Rome. Rome, reduced to little more than a provincial capital controlling the much-threatened western half of the once-mighty empire, continued to founder and decay. As for the Christian church, although the popes of Rome were under the nominal

- **1861** Rome is declared the capital of the newly established Kingdom of Italy; the Papal States (but not the Vatican) are absorbed into the new nation.
- **1929** A concordat between the Vatican and the Italian government delineates the rights and responsibilities of both parties.
- **1935** Italian invasion of Abyssinia (Ethiopia).
- **1941** Italian invasion of Yugoslavia.
- **1943** General Patton lands in Sicily and soon controls the island.
- **1945** Mussolini killed by a mob in Milan.
- **1946** Establishment of Rome as the capital of the newly created Republic of Italy.
- **1960s** Rise of left-wing terrorist groups; flight of capital from Italy; continuing problems of the impoverished south cause an exodus from the countryside into such cities as Rome.
- **1980s** *Il Sorpasso* imbues Rome (and the rest of Italy) with dreams of an economic rebirth.
- **1994** Right-wing forces win in Italian national elections.
- **1996** Dini steps down as prime minister, as the president dissolves both houses of parliament; in general elections, the center-left coalition known as the Olive Tree sweeps both the Senate and the Chamber of Deputies; Romano Prodi becomes prime minister.

Impressions

Vile in its origin, barbarous in its institutions, a casual association of robbers and of outcasts became the destiny of mankind.

—Lady Morgan, *Italy* (1820)

auspices of an exarch from Constantinople, their power increased slowly but steadily as the power of the emperors declined.

THE EMPIRE FALLS The eastern and western sections of the Roman Empire split in A.D. 395, leaving Italy without the support it had formerly received from east of the Adriatic. When the Goths moved toward Rome in the early 5th century, citizens in the provinces, who had grown to hate and fear the cruel bureaucracy set up by Diocletian and sustained by succeeding emperors, often welcomed the invaders. And then the pillage began.

Rome was sacked by Alaric in 410. After less than 40 troubled years, Attila the Hun laid siege. He was followed in 455 by Gaiseric the Vandal, who engaged in a 2-week spree of looting and destruction. The Empire of the West lasted for only another 20 years; finally, the sacking and chaos ended it in A.D. 476, and a burned-out, much humiliated Rome was left to the ministrations of the popes. Without Rome, Italy disintegrated into anarchy, with order maintained by family clans strong enough to hold power within their fortified citadels. Into the vacuum stepped the leaders of the church and a handful of ruling families, whose authority eventually became closely intertwined.

THE HOLY ROMAN EMPIRE After the fall of the Western Empire, the pope took on more and more of the powers of the emperor, despite the lack of any political unity in Italy. Decades of mismanagement by the Roman emperors were followed by the often anarchic rule by barbarian Goths. These were followed by takeovers in different parts of the country by various strong warriors, such as the Lombards. Italy was thus divided into several spheres of control, but always with the permeating influence of the Roman popes.

In 731 Pope Gregory II renounced Rome's spiritual dependence on Constantinople. Papal Rome turned forever toward Europe, and in 800 a king of the barbarian Franks was crowned Holy Roman Emperor by Pope Leo III. The new emperor's name was Charlemagne, and he established a capital at Aachen (known today to the French as Aix-la-Chapelle). This coronation marked a major milestone whereby a Roman pope collaborated with (and later conflicted with) a temporal European power. Although Charlemagne pledged allegiance to the Catholic church, he launched northwestern Europe on a course of what would eventually become bitter political opposition to the meddling of the papacy in temporal affairs.

Meanwhile, the religious powers in Rome looked with dismay at the increasing fragmentation of Italy into war zones between Lombards, Franks, Magyars, Venetians, Saracens, and Normans. As Italy dissolved, the feudal landowners of Rome gained control of the papacy and a series of questionably religious pontiffs endured a diminishment of their powers. Eventually, even the process for determining the election of the popes fell into the hands of the increasingly Germanic Holy Roman Emperor, although this power balance would very soon shift.

Rome during the Middle Ages was a quaint, rural town. Narrow lanes with overhanging buildings filled many of what were originally built as showcases of ancient imperial power, including the Campus Martius. Great basilicas built and embellished with golden-hued mosaics, forums, mercantile exchanges, temples, and expansive theaters of the imperial era slowly disintegrated and collapsed. The decay of ancient Rome was assisted by periodic earthquakes, centuries of neglect, and the growing need for building materials. The seat of the Catholic church, it was a state almost completely controlled by priests, who had an insatiable need for new churches and convents.

By the end of the 11th century the popes shook off the controls of the Roman aristocracy, rid themselves of what they considered the excessive influence of the emperors at Aachen, and began an aggressive expansion of church influence and acquisitions. The deliberate and conscious organization of the church into a format modeled on the hierarchies of the ancient Roman Empire put the church on a collision course with the empire and the other temporal leaders of Europe, resulting in an endless series of power struggles.

THE MIDDLE AGES The papacy soon became essentially a feudal state, and the pope became a medieval (later Renaissance) prince engaged in many of the worldly activities that brought criticism upon the church in later centuries. The fall of the Holy Land to the Turks in 1065 catapulted the papacy into the forefront of world politics, primarily because of the Crusades, most of which were judged to be military and economic disasters, and many of which the popes directly caused or encouraged. During the 12th and 13th centuries the bitter rivalries that rocked the secular and spiritual bastions of Europe took their toll on the stability of the Holy Roman Empire, which grew weaker as city-states buttressed by mercantile and trade-related prosperity grew stronger, and as France emerged as a potent nation in its own right. Each investiture of a new bishop to any influential post became a cause for endless jockeying for power among many political and ecclesiastical factions.

These conflicts achieved their most visible impasse in 1303 with the full-fledged removal of the papacy from Rome to the French city of Avignon. For more than 70 years, until 1377, viciously competing popes (one in Rome, another under the protection of the French kings in Avignon) made simultaneous claims to the legacy of St. Peter, underscoring as never before the degree to which the church was both a victim and a victimizer of European politics.

The seat of the papacy was eventually returned to Rome, where a series of popes were every bit as interesting as the Roman emperors they replaced. The great families—Barberini, Medici, Borgia—enhanced their status and fortunes impressively whenever one of their sons was elected pope.

THE RENAISSANCE Rome's age of siege was not yet over. In 1527 Charles V spearheaded the worst sack in the city's history. To the horror of Pope Clement VII (a Medici), the entire city was brutally pillaged by the man who was to be crowned Holy Roman Emperor the following year.

During the years of the Renaissance, Reformation, and the Counter-Reformation, Rome underwent major physical changes. The old centers of culture reverted to pastures and fields, while great churches and palaces were built with the stones of ancient Rome. This building boom, in fact, did far more damage to the temples of the

Impressions

The Romans would never have had time to conquer the world if they had been obliged to learn Latin first of all.

—Heinrich Heine, *Das Buch Le Grand, In Reisebilder* (1826–31)

Caesars than did any barbarian or Teutonic sack. Rare marbles were stripped from the imperial baths and used as altarpieces or sent to lime kilns. So enthusiastic was the papal destruction of imperial Rome that it's a miracle anything is left.

THE MOVE TOWARD A UNITED ITALY During the 17th, 18th, and 19th centuries the fortunes of Rome rose and fell with the general political and economic situation of the rest of Italy. Since the end of the 13th century Italy had been divided into a series of regional states, each with mercenary soldiers, its own judicial system, and an interlocking series of alliances and enmities that had created a network of intensely competitive city-states. (Some of these families had attained formidable power under such *signori* as the Esse family in Ferrara, the Medici in Florence, and the Sforza families in Milan.) Rome, headquarters of the Papal States, maintained its independence and (usually) the integrity of its borders, although at least some of the city's religious power had been quenched as increasing numbers of Europeans converted to Protestantism.

Napoléon made a bid for power in Italy beginning in 1796, fueling his propaganda machines with what was considered a relatively easy victory. During the 1815 Congress of Vienna, which followed Napoléon's defeat, Italy was once again divided among many different factions: Austria was given Lombardy and Venetia, and the Papal States were returned to the popes. Some duchies were put back into the hands of their hereditary rulers, whereas southern Italy and Sicily went to a newly imported dynasty related to the Bourbons. One historic move, which eventually assisted in the unification of Italy, was the assignment of the former republic of Genoa to Sardinia (which at the time was governed by the House of Savoy).

By now political unrest had become a fact of Italian (and Roman) life. At least some of it was encouraged by the rapid industrialization of the north and the almost total lack of industrialization in the Italian south. Despite these barriers, in 1861 the Kingdom of Italy was proclaimed and Victor Emmanuel of the House of Savoy, king of Sardinia, became head of the new monarchy. In 1861 the designated capital of the newly united country, following a 2,000-year-old precedent, became Rome. In a controversial move that engendered resentment many decades later, the borders of the Papal States were eradicated from the map as Rome was incorporated into the new nation of Italy. The Vatican, however, did not yield its territory to the new order, despite guarantees of nonintervention proferred by the Italian government, and relations between the pope and the political leaders of Italy remained rocky until 1929.

At that time Mussolini defined the divisions that, to the present, have separated the Italian government and the Vatican by signing a concordat that granted political and fiscal autonomy to Vatican City. It also made Roman Catholicism the official state religion of Italy, although this designation was removed through revision of the concordat in 1978. In 1984 Bruno Craxi officially annulled the concordat of 1929.

WORLD WAR II & THE AXIS With Rome now firmly entrenched as the seat of Italian power, the history of the city was now tightly linked to that of Italy as a whole. Mussolini's support of the Fascists during the Spanish civil war helped encourage the formation of the "Axis" between Italy and Nazi Germany.

Despite its outdated military equipment, Italy added to the general horror of the era by invading Abyssinia (Ethiopia) in 1935, supposedly to protect Italian colonial interests there. In 1941 Italy invaded neighboring Yugoslavia, and in 1942 thousands of Italian troops were sent to assist Hitler in his disastrous campaign along the Russian front. In 1943 General Patton, leading American and (with General Montgomery) British troops, controlled all of Sicily within a month of their first attack.

Impressions

It is not impossible to govern Italians. It is merely useless.

—Attributed to Benito Mussolini

Faced with this defeat and humiliation, Mussolini fled from Rome after being overthrown by his own cabinet. The Allies made a separate deal with Italy's king, Vittorio Emanuele III. A politically divided Italy watched as battalions of fanatical German Nazis moved south to resist the Allied march northward up the Italian peninsula. The Nazis released Mussolini from his Italian jail cell to establish the short-lived Republic of Salo, headquartered on the edge of Lake Garda, hoping for a groundswell of popular opinion in favor of Italian fascism. Events quickly proved this nothing more than a futile dream.

In April 1945, with almost half a million Italians rising in a mass demonstration against him and the German war machine, and Rome almost paralyzed by public insurgencies, Mussolini was captured by Italian partisans as he fled into Switzerland. With his mistress, Claretta Petacci, and several others of his intimates, he was shot and strung up upside down from the roof of a gasoline station in Piazzale Loreto, a few blocks east of the central railway station of Milan.

MODERN ROME Rome today serves as the capital of the Republic of Italy, which was formed in 1946 in the aftermath of World War II. In the 1950s Italy became one of the leading industrialized nations of the world, a giant in the manufacture of automobiles and office equipment, and an agricultural breadbasket of international repute.

In the 1960s Rome became the campaign ground for an increasingly powerful Socialist party. Meanwhile, as the city's wealthy grew increasingly alarmed at the growing socialization of their country, Rome and the rest of Italy suffered an unprecedented flight of capital and an increase in bankruptcies, inflation (almost 20% during most of the 1970s), and unemployment.

During the late 1970s and early 1980s Rome was rocked by the rise of terrorism instigated both by right-wing neo-fascists and by left-wing intellectuals from the socialist-controlled universities of the north.

In the 1990s some 6,000 businesspeople and politicians were implicated in a billion-dollar government graft scandal. Such familiar figures as Bettino Craxi, who headed the Socialist party, and Giulio Andreotti, the seven-time prime minister, were accused of corruption.

Hoping for a renewal after all this exposure of greed, Italian voters in March 1994 turned to the right wing to head their government. In overwhelming numbers, voters elected a former cruise-ship singer turned media billionaire, Silvio Berlusconi, its new leader. Berlusconi swept to an unprecedented victory in national elections, emerging as prime minister. His Forza Italia (Go, Italy) party formed an alliance with the neo-fascist National Alliance and the secessionist Northern League to sweep to victory. These elections were termed "the most critical" for Italy in four decades. The new government was beset with an almost hopeless array of new problems, including destabilization caused by the Mafia and its underground economies, and when the Northern League defected from the coalition in December 1994, Berlusconi resigned.

Treasury Minister Lamberto Dini, a nonpolitical international banker, replaced him. Dini signed on merely as a transitional player in Italy's topsy-turvy political game. His austerity measures enacted to balance Italy's budget, including cuts in

The City & Its People

Rome, according to legend, was built on seven hills. These hills are only 44 feet above sea level at the Pantheon, rising to 462 feet above sea level at Monte Mario, present site of the deluxe Cavalieri Hilton hotel.

The seven hills rise from the marshy lowlands of the Campagna and are mostly on the left bank of the Tiber. They include the Quirinale (seat of the modern Italian government), Esquiline, Viminal, Caelian, and Aventine—and all combine to form a crescent-shaped plateau of great historical fame. In its center rises the Palatine Hill, all-powerful seat of the imperial residences of ancient Rome, which looks down upon the ancient Forum and the Colosseum. To the northwest rises the Capitoline Hill. Some historians have suggested that Rome's geography—set above a periphery of marshy and swelteringly hot lowlands—contributed to the fall of the Roman Empire because of its propensity to breed malaria-inducing mosquitoes.

The modern city of Rome is composed of 22 districts, covering an area of nearly 10 square miles. The Tiber makes two distinct bends within Rome, below Ponte Cavour, one of the city's major bridges, and again at the history-rich island of Tiberina.

With bloodlines including virtually every race ever encompassed by the borders of the ancient Roman Empire, the people of Rome long ago grew accustomed to seeing foreign influences come and go. Picking their way through the architectural and cultural jumble of Rome, they are not averse to complaining (loudly) of the city's endless inconveniences, yet they are the first to appreciate the historical and architectural marvel that surrounds them. Cynical but hearty, and filled with humanity, modern Romans seem to propel themselves through the business of life with an enviable sense of style.

The crowds of pilgrims and the vast numbers of churches and convents exist side by side with fleshier and more earthbound distractions, the combination of which imbues many Romans with an overriding interest in pursuing the pleasures and distractions of the moment. This sense of theatricality can be seen in Roman driving habits; in animated conversations and gesticulations in restaurants and cafés; in the lavish displays of flowers, fountains, food, and architecture, the nation's trademark; and in the 27 centuries of building projects dedicated to the power and egos of long-dead potentates.

Despite the crowds, the pollution, the heat, and the virtual impossibility of efficiency, Romans for the most part take life with good cheer and *pazienza.* Translated as "patience," it seems to be the frequently uttered motto of modern Rome, and an appropriate philosophy for a city that has known everything from unparalleled glory to humiliation and despair. Romans know that since Rome wasn't built in a day, its charms should be savored slowly and with an appreciation for the cultures that contributed to this panoply.

pensions and health care, were not popular among the mostly blue-collar Italian workers or the highly influential labor unions. Pending a predicted defeat in a no-confidence vote, Dini also stepped down. His resignation in January 1996 left beleaguered Italians shouting *Basta!* (enough). This latest shuffling in Italy's political deck prompted President Oscar Scalfaro to dissolve both houses of the Italian parliament.

Once again Italians were faced with forming a new government. Elections in April 1996 proved a shocker, not only for the defeated politicians but for the victors as well. The center-left coalition known as the Olive Tree, led by Romano Prodi, swept both the Senate and the Chamber of Deputies. The Olive Tree, whose roots stem from the old Communist party, achieved victory by shifting toward the center and focusing its campaign on a strong platform protecting social benefits and supporting Italy's bid to become a solid member of the European Union.

4 Famous Romans

Antonioni, Michelangelo (b. 1912) One of the best-known film directors in Italian history. His films deal with the boredom, despair, and alienation of the upper-middle classes in Italy. He is best remembered for a trilogy of films: *La Notte* (1960), *L'Avventura* (1960), and *L'Eclisse* (1961).

Apuleius, Lucius (2nd century A.D.) The works of this Roman satirist are the only extant examples of Latin-language prose fiction. His most famous work is *The Golden Ass* (also known as *Metamorphoses*).

Caesar, Augustus (63 B.C.–A.D. 14) Designated as the favorite heir of Julius Caesar, he launched his political career as part of the triumvirate assigned to avenge the murder of his benefactor. After hunting down and destroying the conspirators and defeating the other members of the triumverate at the battle of Actium in 31 B.C., he was elevated to the role of Rome's first emperor. During the long reign that followed, the Empire was relatively peaceful, and it flourished with the literature of such writers as Horace, Ovid, and Virgil.

Caesar, Julius (100–44 B.C.) The most famous and multifaceted figure from the ancient world, he provided fodder for legends that outlived him by 2,000 years, and eventually helped destroy the Republican fabric of the Roman Empire. Originally a candidate for the pagan priesthood, and an acclaimed author in his own right, he subdued all of Gaul in 53 B.C., launched two major campaigns into Britain, and added regions of Iberia, the Alps, and North Africa to Roman domains. During a six-month stopover in the Roman-occupied Nile Delta, he fathered a child with Cleopatra, thereby contributing to some of the events leading to her eventual suicide and the destruction of her dynasty. In 48 B.C. he was elevated to the role of absolute dictator. His murder on the Senate steps by a group of Republican conspirators (a ringleader was his protégé, Brutus) inspired plays by such luminaries as Shakespeare centuries later.

Bernini, Giovanni Lorenzo (1598–1680) This Renaissance sculptor and architect changed forever the architecture of Rome, designing many of its fountains (including those in Piazza Navona). Even more famous are his designs for the piazza in front of St. Peter's, and the canopy whose corkscrew columns cover the landmark's principal altar.

Cellini, Benvenuto (1500–71) The most famous goldsmith in history, and a notable sculptor (*Perseus with the Head of Medusa*) as well, he was the author of a famous *Autobiography,* which, when first published in 1728, established him as one of the greatest rakes of the Renaissance.

Fellini, Federico (1920–93) This neorealist film director was known for his zany, visually striking, and sometimes grotesque interpretations of social and psychological dilemmas. Examples of his work include *La Strada, La Dolce Vita* (a title adopted by an entire generation of fun-loving Italians as their mode of living), *8½, Juliet of the Spirits, Satirycon,* and, of course, *Roma.*

Fermi, Enrico (1901–54) Roman physicist, and U.S. resident after 1939, he postulated the existence of the atomic particle known as the neutrino, and produced element 93, neptunium. He was awarded the Nobel Prize for physics in 1938, and his work contributed heavily to the development of the atomic bomb.

Gregory XIII (1502–85) Roman pope from 1572 until his death, he launched the Counter-Reformation and departed from the policies of earlier popes by maintaining an unassailable (or at least discreet) personal comportment. He also developed the calendar used today throughout the Western world.

Magnani, Anna (1908–73) This fiery Italian actress—who Tennessee Williams once called "my favorite"—was making films in Italy in the 1930s and 1940s, long before she won an Academy Award in 1955 for *The Rose Tattoo,* written by Williams and co-starring Burt Lancaster. Dubbed in countless languages, her films were shown around the world, including the 1960 *The Fugitive Kind* opposite Marlon Brando and the 1968 *The Secret of Santa Vittoria.*

Montessori, Maria (1870–1952) Physician and educational theorist, she developed a method of education for young children that directs the child's energies into becoming the adult he or she wants to be within an environment of pedagogical freedom. In 1894 she became the first woman to receive an M.D. in Italy. Her most widely distributed work is *Pedagogical Anthropology.*

Moravia, Alberto (1907–90) The most famous Italian-language author of modern times, he was born in Rome and christened as Alberto Pincherle. He later adopted his parents' region of emigration—Moravia, in today's Czech Republic—for his pen name. One of the most scathing interpreters of middle-class boredom and apathy since Edward Albee, he has been judged as one of the most perceptive critics of family values and interpersonal psychologies in Europe, and an internationally acclaimed novelist and essayist.

Nero (A.D. 37–68) During the decade that he ruled most of the known world (A.D. 58–68), he murdered both his wife and his mother, and initiated a reign of terror under which hundreds of Romans were tortured, brutalized, or executed. Although it has never been proven, he is believed to have ordered the fires in A.D. 65 that eventually destroyed most of his city. Since his suicide at the age of 31, he has been accepted as a universal symbol of how absolute power corrupts, and condemned as a persecutor of Christians and one of the greatest megalomaniacs in human history.

Sixtus V (Felice Peretti; 1520–90) Ambitious and relentlessly hard-working, this former head of the Franciscans was one of the most influential and repressive Renaissance popes. A tireless inquisitor of heretics and Protestants, he meddled shamelessy in European politics, allying the Vatican with the fanatically religious Philip II of Spain. During his 5-year reign (1585–90) as pope, he radically reorganized church finances to make the papacy solvent after the fiscal excesses of earlier popes, and sent groups of Catholic evangelists to territories in the Philippines and South America. Best known for his lavish building programs in Rome, he altered the geography of the Eternal City by clearing away medieval debris and establishing some of the city's major roads and streets. One of the straightest of these—Via del Corso—was originally conceived as a venue for horseracing.

5 Architecture 101

The mysterious **Etruscans,** whose earliest origins probably lay somewhere in Mesopotamia, brought the first truly impressive architecture to mainland Italy. Little remains of their building, but historical writings by the Romans themselves record their powerful walls, bridges, and aqueducts, which were very similar to the Mycenaean architecture of Crete. As Rome asserted its own identity and overpowered its Etruscan masters, it borrowed heavily from their established themes.

In architecture, **ancient Rome** flourished magnificently, advancing in size and majesty far beyond the examples set by the Greeks. Part of this was because of the development of a primitive form of concrete, but even more important was the fine-tuning of the arch, which was used with a logic, rhythm, and ease never before seen. Monumental buildings were erected, each an embodiment of the strength, power, and careful organization of the empire itself. Examples include forums and baths scattered across the Mediterranean world (the greatest of which were Trajan's Forum and the Baths of Caracalla, both in Rome). Equally magnificent were the Colosseum and a building that later greatly influenced the Palladians during the Renaissance, Hadrian's Pantheon. These immense achievements were made possible by two major resources: almost limitless funds pouring in from all regions of the empire, and an unending supply of slaves captured during military campaigns.

The influence of Roman architecture was to have enormous impact on building throughout most of the world, leading in time to a neoclassic revival centuries later in Britain and America. Although unromantic, it was the use of concrete that was to have such a major influence on buildings to come. Concrete is material that seemingly lasts forever, as evidenced by the giant concrete dome of Rome's Pantheon and Baths of Caracalla. Concrete made vast buildings possible. Even in Roman times this allowed *insulae* (apartment blocks) to climb to seven floors or more, something almost unheard of before. Even though Rome didn't invent the arch or the aqueduct, or even concrete, Romans perfected these building forms.

Following in the footprints of the Romans, **early Christians** copied Roman architectural styles, although they lacked the rich marbles, slave labor, and other materials that made Rome glorious. The earliest basilicas were hastily constructed and poorly designed. Basilicas were entered at the west, with the apse in the east—the direction of Palestine. None of the basilicas remaining from this period is intact, as all were incredibly altered or changed over the centuries.

Because the Christian world was also ruled from the East, **Byzantine** architecture came into play. The roofing device of the Near East—covering a building with a dome—was adapted to the basic rectangular plan of the early Christian basilica.

The art and architecture in the centuries that followed the collapse of Rome became known as early medieval or **Romanesque.** In its many variations, it flourished between A.D. 1000 and 1200.

Roman architecture was so innovative and powerful that it continued to influence builders even beyond the Romanesque and during the **Gothic** period. The best examples of domestic Gothic architecture in Italy, however, are in Florence and Siena, not in Rome. Santa Maria Sopra Minerva (see "Near Piazza Navona & the Pantheon" in Chapter 6) is the only real exception.

The **Renaissance** flowered in Italy almost 2 centuries before it reached such countries as England. In the early Renaissance, architecture in Rome was still heavily influenced by classicism, although using building techniques perfected during the Gothic period. Rome's greatest building achievement of the Renaissance is St. Peter's Basilica, until the last decade the largest church ever constructed. Its sheer massiveness overwhelms (about five times the area of a football field). Urbino-born Donato Bramante (1444–1514) was only the first of a series of architects who would create this monumental design. Regrettably, very little is left of Bramante's original concept—the decorative excess of this present building was not in Bramante's vision.

Even Michelangelo was an architect of St. Peter's (from 1547 to 1564), designing and beginning construction of the massive dome.

In the early 17th century and into the 18th century, the **baroque** (meaning absurd or irregular) movement swept Europe, including Rome. The development of the baroque movement was linked to the much-needed reforms and restructuring of the Catholic church that followed the upheavals of the Protestant Reformation. Many great Italian churches and *palazzi* were constructed during this period.

The great name from this period was Giovanni Lorenzo Bernini (1598–1680), whose chief work is the piazza in front of St. Peter's. Completion of the basilica itself was the greatest architectural accomplishment of the early baroque period. Francesco Borromini (1559–1667) is the second great architect of the age. His Church of Sant'Agnese in Rome reveals his mastery, with curved indentations on its facade.

As is obvious to any visitor to Rome, the 19th and 20th centuries did not see the grand architectural achievements of the Romans or the Renaissance. The later baroque and flamboyant excesses of their more recent past were dismissed as "gay excesses" by 19th-century architects, and a revival of **neoclassicism** swept Europe in the late 1700s. Neoclassic architects of the 19th century were mainly copyists, adding little of their own creativity. In the early 20th century Mussolini was more intent on producing "pompous" neoclassical buildings than in achieving breakthroughs in modern architectural design. Many of the buildings constructed in Rome during his dictatorship have been called "Fascist" and uninspired architecture (visit the EUR district south of the center for an example; see Chapter 6).

If Italy produced any great modern architect in the **20th century,** it was Pier Luigi Nervi, born in 1891 in Milan. He faced the same problems the Romans did: covering a vast enclosure with concrete vaulting. He was innovative, creating new buildings in daring styles and shapes best represented by Rome's Palazzo della Sport designed for the 1960 Olympics. Nervi's buildings are both poetic and practical. For the sports palace he made a bold pattern of concrete thrusts balanced with counterthrusts on the inside. He went on to build a smaller sports arena in Rome, the Palazetto, which is still called "the world's most beautiful sports arena."

6 Art Through the Ages

There's an amazing richness of Italian art—there's so much, in fact, that it's often stuck away in dark corners of unlighted churches in Rome. You'll have to carry a pocketful of small coins to drop in boxes to turn on the lights in some churches. Rome has so much art that some paintings—world masterpieces that would be the focal point of most major museums—are often tucked away in obscure rooms of rarely visited galleries. There's too much of a good thing and not enough room to display such artistic bounty, much less maintain the art and protect it from thieves.

How did it all begin?

As **ancient Rome** continued to develop its empire, its artisans began to turn out an exact, realistic portrait sculpture that became its hallmark. It differed distinctly from the more idealized forms of Greek sculpture. Rome was preoccupied with sculpted images—in fact, sculptors made "bodies" en masse and later fitted a particular head on the sculpture upon the demand of a Roman citizen. Most Roman painting that survives is in the form of murals in the fresco technique, and most of these were uncovered when Pompeii and Herculaneum, on the Bay of Naples, were excavated. Rome's greatest artistic expression was in architecture, not in art such as painting.

The aesthetic concepts of the Roman Empire eventually evolved into early Christian and **Byzantine** art. More concerned with moral and spiritual values than with the physical beauty of the human form or the celebration of political grandeur, early Christian artists turned to the supernatural and spiritual world for their inspiration. Basilicas and churches were lavishly decorated with mosaics and colored marble, whereas painting depicted the earthly suffering (and heavenly rewards) of martyrs and saints. Supported by monasteries or churches, art was almost wholly concerned with ecclesiastical subjects, frequently with the intention of educating the often illiterate worshippers who studied it. Biblical parables were carved in stone or painted into frescoes, often useful teaching aids for a church eager to spread its messages.

Early in the 1300s, Tuscan artists such as Cimabue and Giotto blazed new trails and brought emotional realism into their work in what was later seen as a complete break from Byzantine gloom and rigidity, and an early harbinger of the Renaissance. However, artists in Rome continued to retain reminders of ancient Rome in their work.

The Italian **Renaissance** was born in Florence during the 15th century and almost immediately spread to Rome. Brunelleschi designed a dome for Florence's cathedral that has been hailed ever since as "a miracle of design." Keenly competitive with Florence, ecclesiastical planners in Rome hired Urbino-born Donato Bramante to work on a design for an amplified version of St. Peter's Basilica, the most significant and imposing building of the High Renaissance. Its interior required massive amounts of sculpture and decoration. To fill the void, artists, including Michelangelo, flooded into Rome from throughout Italy.

Perhaps it was in painting, however, that the Renaissance excelled. The artistic giant Raffaello (Raphael) Santi was commissioned to fresco the apartments of Pope Julius II in Rome. Simultaneously, Michelangelo painted the ceiling frescoes of the Sistine Chapel, an assignment that took 4 backbreaking years to complete. Italy—with infinite input from the patrons and artists in Rome—remained Europe's artistic leader for nearly 200 years.

The transitional period between the Renaissance and the baroque came to be called **"mannerism."** Although Venice's Tintoretto remains the most famous artist of this group, out of this period emerged such other (Rome-based) artists as Giulio Romano, Perin del Vaga, Rosso Fiorentino, and Parmigianino. Although little remains of their work (Rome was sacked and many artworks destroyed or carried away in 1527 during the siege of the city by Charles V), their restless and sometimes contorted style soon spread from Rome throughout the rest of Italy.

In the early 17th century and into the 18th century, the **baroque** (meaning absurd or irregular) age altered forever the architectural skyline of Rome (see "Architecture 101," earlier in this chapter). Simultaneously, great artists emerged, such as Bernini, renowned both as a sculptor and painter; Carracci, who decorated the Roman palace of Cardinal Farnese; and Caravaggio, one of the baroque masters of earthy realism and dramatic tension.

Shortly thereafter the even more flamboyant **rococo** grew out of the baroque style. The baroque age also represented the high point of *trompe l'oeil* (illusionistic painting) whereby ceilings and walls were painted with disturbingly realistic landscapes that fool the eye with architecturally sophisticated perspectives and angles. Drop in on the second floor of Trastevere's Villa Farnesina for an excellent example (see Walking Tour 4, "Trastevere," in Chapter 7).

During the 17th, 18th, and 19th centuries the great light had gone out of art in Italy. Rome in particular, capitalizing on the vast ruins that lay scattered within its

Impressions

Neque protinus uno est Condita Roma die. (Rome was not built in a day.)
—Pietro Angelo Manzolli (Palingenius, Pseud.), *Zodiacus Vitae*

boundaries, became a magnet for the **neoclassical** craze sweeping through France, Britain, and Germany. Thousands of foreign and Italian artists descended upon Rome to feed off its 2,000 years of artistic treasures. The era's return to the aesthetic ideals of ancient Greece and Rome helped to fuel the growing sense of pan-Italian nationalism. By the 19th century the beacon of artistic creativity was picked up by France, whose artists ushered in a wide array of different artistic traditions (including impressionism) whose tenets were for the most part ignored in Italy.

The **20th century** witnessed the creative apexes of several major Italian artists whose works once again captured the imagination of the world. De Chirico and Modigliani (the latter's greatest contribution lay in a new concept of portraiture) were only two among many. Today the works of many of Italy's successful futurist and metaphysical painters can be seen in Rome's Galleria Nazionale d'Arte Moderna. Sadly, although many of the works contained therein are world-class art of international stature, they tend to be overlooked in a city whose artworks encompass two millennia of treasures.

7 Literature: The Classics & Beyond

The passion for empire building spilled over into the development of forms of Roman literature that would affect every literary development in the Western world for the next 2,000 years.

The first true Latin poet was Livius Andronicus (c. 284–204 B.C.), a Greek slave who translated Homer's *Odyssey* into Latin, but abandoned the poetic rhythms of ancient Greek in favor of Latin's Saturnian rhythm. Quintus Ennius (239–169 B.C.) was the father of Roman epic literature, his *Annales* permeated with a sense of the divine mission of Rome to civilize the world. Quintus's bitter rival was M. Porcius Cato the Censor (234–149 B.C.), who passionately rejected Rome's dependence on Hellenistic models in favor of a distinctly Latin literary form.

Part of the appeal of Latin literature was the comedies performed in front of vast audiences. The Latin cadences and rhythms of Plautus (254–184 B.C.) were wholly original, and C. Lucilius (c. 180–102 B.C.) is credited as the first satirist, developing a deliberately casual, sometimes lacerating, method of revealing the shortcomings and foibles of individuals and groups of people (statesmen, poets, gourmands, etc.).

Latin prose and oratory reached their perfect form with the cadences of Marcus Tullius Cicero (106–43 B.C.). A successful and popular general and politician, he is credited with the development of the terms and principles of oratory, which are still used by debating societies everywhere. His speeches and letters are triumphs of diplomacy, and his public policies are credited with binding Rome together during some of its most wrenching civil wars.

Poetry also flourished. The works of Catullus (84–54 B.C.), primarily concerned with the immediacy and strength of his own emotions, presented romantic passion in startlingly vivid ways. Banned by some of the English Victorians, Catullus's works continue to shock anyone who bothers to translate them.

One of the Roman republic's most respected historians was Livy, whose saga of early Rome is more or less the accepted version. Julius Caesar himself (perhaps the most pivotal—and biased—eyewitness to the events he recorded) wrote accounts of his military exploits in Gaul and his transformation of the Roman republic into a dictatorship. Military and political genius combine with literary savvy in his *De Bello Gallica* (Gallic Wars) and *De Bello Civili* (Civil War).

Ancient Roman literature reached its most evocative peak during the Golden Age of Augustus (42 B.C.–A.D. 17). Virgil's (70–19 B.C.) *The Aeneid,* a 12-volume Roman creation myth linking Rome to the demolished city of Troy, has been judged equal to the epics of Homer.

Horace (Quintus Horatius Flaccus; 63–8 B.C.) became a master of satire, as well as the epic "Roman Odes," whose grandeur of style competes with Virgil. Frequently used as an educational text for princes and kings during the Renaissance 1,500 years later, Horace's works often reveal the anxiety he felt about the centralization of unlimited power in Rome after the end of the Republic. Many centuries later some of the themes of Horace were embraced during the Enlightenment of 17th-century Europe, and were even used as ideological buttresses for the tenets that led to the French Revolution.

Ovid (43 B.C.–A.D. 17), master of the elegy, had an ability to write prose that reflected the traumas and priorities of his own life and emotional involvements. Avoiding references to politics (the growing power of the emperors was becoming increasingly repressive), the elegy grew into a superb form of lyric verse focused on such tenets as love, wit, beauty, pleasure, and amusement. Important works that are read thousands of years later for their charm and mastery of Latin include *Metamorphoses* and *The Art of Love.*

Between A.D. 17 and 170 Roman literature was stifled by a growing fear of such autocrats as Tiberius, Claudius, Nero, and Caligula. An exception is the work of the great Stoic writer, Lucius Annaeus Seneca (4 B.C.?–A.D. 65), whose work commented directly, and sometimes satirically, on events of his time, advocating self-sufficiency, moderation, and emotional control.

For several hundred years after the collapse of the Roman Empire very little was written of any enduring merit in Rome. The exceptions include Christian Latin-language writings from such apologists and theologians as St. Jerome (A.D. 340–420) and St. Augustine (354–430), whose works helped bridge the gap to the beginning of the Middle Ages.

From this time onward literature in Rome parallels the development of Italian literature in general. Medieval Italian literature was represented by religious poetry, secular lyric poetry, and sonnets. Although associated with Florence, and not Rome, Dante Alighieri (1265–1321) broke the monotony of a thousand-year literary silence with the difficult-to-translate *terza rima* of *The Divine Comedy.* Called the first masterpiece in Italian—to the detriment of Rome, the Tuscan dialect in which he wrote gradually became accepted as the purest form of Italian—it places Dante, rivaled only by medieval Italian-language poets Petrarch and Boccaccio, in firm control as the founder of both the Italian language and Italian literature.

Rome, however, continued to pulsate with its own distinctive dialect and preoccupations. The imbroglios of the city's power politics during the 1400s and 1500s, and the mores of its ruling aristocracy, were recorded in *The Courtier,* by Baldassare Castiglione (1478–1529), still read as a source of insight into customs, habits, and ambitions during the Renaissance.

Between 1600 and around 1850, as the reins of international power and creativity shifted from Italy, literature took a second tier to such other art forms as music, opera, and architecture. The publication of Alessandro Manzoni's (1785-1873)

Impressions

Oh! Rome, tremendous, who, beholding thee,
Shall not forget the bitterest private grief
That e'er made havoc of one single life?

—Fanny Kemble (Mrs. Butler), "A Year Of Consolation" (1847)

romantic epic *I Promessi Sposi* (The Betrothed) in 1827 signaled the birth of the modern Italian novel.

During the 19th century Rome's literary voice found its most provocative spokesperson in Giuseppe Gioacchino Belli (1792–1863), who wrote more than 2,000 satirical sonnets (*I Sonetti Romaneschi,* published 1886–96) in Roman dialect rather than academic Italian. A statue in his honor decorates Piazza Belli in Trastevere.

In modern times, Alberto Moravia has won an international following. Born in Rome of a well-to-do family, Moravia (the pseudonym of Alberto Pincherle) intiated the neorealism movement in the Italian novel, winning fame for *Two Women* and *The Empty Canvas.* His novels describe in painful detail the apparent emptiness of life in an era of mass conformity.

8 The Romans: From Myth to Language

ON STAGE Rome is one of the world's leading cultural centers. It's a city of music, with concerts performed in venues that range from medieval churches and Renaissance palazzi to parks and cloisters to piazze and local auditoriums. Even more popular with Romans is opera, which continues as a growth industry among new legions of the young every year.

In theater, Pirandello and Goldoni remain perennial favorites, although Roman audiences are also quite familiar with the works of Shakespeare, particularly those plays using Italy as a background like *Romeo and Juliet.*

The RAI—Radio Televisione Italiana, the state network—dazzles Roman audiences with a symphony orchestra and chorus rated among the finest on earth. The Rome orchestra most often performs its regular season at the Foro Italico. Annually a special concert is staged for the pope, either at St. Peter's or within the precincts of the Vatican.

There is no national theater; instead, different theater companies perform in repertory in Rome. Of course, you'll need to have a good understanding of the Italian language to appreciate these programs. Outstanding Roman theater companies include Teatro di Roma, Teatro di Genoa, and Centro Teatrale Bresciano.

MYTH Although modern visitors know Rome as the headquarters of Catholicism, the city also developed one of the world's most influential bodies of mythology.

During the days when Rome was little more than a cluster of sheepherder's villages, a body of gods were worshipped whose characters remained basically unchanged throughout the course of Roman history. To this panoply, however, were added and assimilated the deities of other conquered territories (especially Greece) until the roster of Roman gods bristled with imports from around the Mediterranean. In its corrupted (later) version, the list grew impossibly unwieldy as more-or-less demented emperors forced their own deification and worship upon the Roman masses. After the Christianization of Europe, the original and ancient gods retained their astrological significance and provided poetic fodder for endless literary and lyrical comparisons.

A brief understanding of each of the major gods' functions will enhance insights during explorations of the city's museums and excavations.

Apollo was the representative of music, the sun, prophecy, healing, the arts, and philosophy. He was the brother of **Diana** (symbol of chastity and goddess of the hunt, the moon, wild animals, and later, of commerce) and the son of **Jupiter** (king of the gods and god of lightning), by a lesser female deity named **Leto. Cupid** was the god of falling in love.

Juno, the wife of Jupiter, was attributed with vague but awesome powers and a very human sense of outrage and jealousy. Her main job seemed to be wreaking vengeance against the hundreds of nymphs seduced by Jupiter, and punishment of the thousands of children he supposedly fathered.

Mars, the dignified but bloodthirsty god of war, was reputed to be the father of **Romulus,** cofounder of Rome.

Mercury, symbol of such Geminis (twins) as Romulus and Remus, was one of the most diverse and morally ambiguous of the gods. He served as the guide to the dead as they approached the underworld, and as the patron of eloquence, travel, negotiation, diplomacy, good sense, prudence, and (to a very limited extent) thieving.

Neptune, god of the sea, was attributed with almost no moral implications, but represents solely the watery domains of the earth.

Minerva was the goddess of wisdom, arts and crafts, and (occasionally) of war. A goddess whose allure was cerebral and whose discipline was severe, she wears a helmet and breastplate emblazoned with the head of **Medusa** (the snake-haired monster whose gaze could turn men into stone). During the Renaissance she became a symbol much associated, oddly enough, with the wisdom and righteousness of the Christian popes.

Venus, whose mythological power grew as the empire expanded, was the goddess of gardens and every conceivable variety of love. She was reportedly the mother of **Aeneas,** mythical ancestor of the ancient Romans. Both creative and destructive, Venus's appeal and duality are as primeval as the earth itself.

Ceres, goddess of the earth and of the harvest, mourned for half of every year (during winter) when her daughter, **Proserpine,** abandoned her to live in the house of **Pluto,** god of death and the underworld.

Vulcan was the half-lame god of metallurgy, volcanoes, and furnaces, whose activities at his celestial forge crafted superweapons for an array of military heroes beloved by the ancient Romans.

Finally, **Bacchus,** the god of wine, undisciplined revelry, drunkenness, and absence of morality, gained an increasing importance in Rome as the city grew decadent and declined.

RELIGION Rome is the world's greatest ecclesiastical center. Few regions on earth have been as religiously prolific—or had such a profound influence on Christianity—as Italy.

Even before the Christianization of the Roman Empire, the ancient Romans artfully (and sometimes haphazardly) mingled their allegiance to the deities of ancient Greece with whatever religious fad happened to be imported at the moment. After its zenith, ancient Rome resembled a theological hodgepodge of dozens of religious and mystical cults, which found fertile soil amid a crumbling empire. Eastern (especially Egyptian) cults became particularly popular, and dozens of emperors showed no aversion to defining themselves as gods and enforcing worship by their subjects.

In A.D. 313 the emperor Constantine, a Christian convert himself, signed the Edict of Milan, stopping the hitherto merciless persecution of Christians. Since then, Italy has adhered, in the main, to Catholicism.

Today the huge majority (99%) of Italians describe themselves as Roman Catholic, although their form of allegiance to Catholicism varies widely according to individual conscience. Despite the fact that only about one-third of the country attends mass with any regularity, and only about 10% claim to receive the sacrament at Easter, the country is innately—to its very core—favored by the Catholic tradition. That does not always mean that the populace follows the dictates of the Vatican. An example of this is that, despite the pressure by the Holy See against voting in favor of Communist party members (in 1949 the Vatican threatened to excommunicate—*ipso facto*—any Italian who voted for Communist or Communist-inspired candidates), the Communist platform in Italy used to receive up to 33% of the popular vote in certain elections.

Modern Italy's adherence to Catholicism is legally stressed by a law enacted in 1848 by the Kingdom of Sardinia (later reaffirmed by the Lateran Treaty) which states: "The Catholic apostolic and Roman religion is the sole religion of the [Italian] State." The same treaties, however, give freedom of worship to other religions, but identify Rome as "the center of the Catholic world and a place of pilgrimage," and confer onto the State of Italy the responsibility of safeguarding the security of the pope and his emissaries, and respecting church property and church law in the treatment of certain matters, such as requests for divorces or annulments.

Significantly, throughout history Italy has produced more upper-echelon leaders to staff the Vatican than any other country in the world. Only recently, with the election of a Polish-born pope (John Paul II), has a pattern of almost complete domination of the papacy by Italian prelates been altered. Because of the sometimes inconvenient juxtaposition of the Vatican inside the administrative capital of Italy, the Lateran Treaty of February 11, 1929, which was confirmed by Article 7 of the constitution of the Italian republic, recognizes the Vatican City State as an independent and sovereign state and established and defined its relationship to the Italian State. That treaty, originally signed by Mussolini, lasted until 1984.

FOLKLORE The most formal manifestation of folk rituals in all of Rome is the Commedia dell'Arte. Although it greatly influenced theatrical styles of France in the 17th century, it is unique to Italy. The plots almost always develop and resolve an imbroglio where the beautiful wife of an older curmudgeon dallies with a handsome swain, against the advice of her maid and much to the amusement of the husband's valet.

Italy, even before the Christian era, was a richly religious land ripe with legends and myths. Modern Italy blends superstition, ancient myths and fables, and Christian symbolism in richly folkloric ways. Throughout Rome, rites of passage—births, first communions, marriages, and deaths—are linked to endless rounds of family celebrations, feasts, and gatherings. Faithful Romans might genuflect when in front of a church, when entering a church, when viewing an object of religious veneration (a relic of a saint, for example), or when hearing a statement that might tempt the Devil to meddle in someone's personal affairs.

LANGUAGE Italian, of course, is the official language of Rome, but it's spoken with a particular dialect that has always given linguistic delight to anyone born in the city. Although the purest form of Italian is said to be spoken in Tuscany (a legacy of medieval author Dante Alighieri, who composed *The Divine Comedy* in the Tuscan dialect), the Romans have always maintained a fierce pride in the particular stresses, intonations, and vocabulary of their own native speech patterns.

Regardless of the dialect, Italian is more directly derived from Latin than any of the other Romance languages. Many older Italians had at least a rudimentary grasp

Impressions

Rome's just a city like anywhere else. A vastly overrated city, I'd say. It trades on belief just as Stratford trades on Shakespeare.

—Anthony Burgess, *Inside Mr. Enderby* (1963)

of ecclesiastical (church) Latin because of the role of Latin in the Catholic mass. Today, however, as the vernacular Italian has replaced the use of Latin in most church services, the ancient tongue can be read and understood only by a diminishing number of academics and priests.

Linguists consider Italian the most "musical" and mellifluous language in the West, and the Italian language easily lends itself to librettos and operas. The language is a phonetic one; this means that you pronounce a word the way it's written, unlike many other languages, including English. It has been said that if an Italian sentence sounds "off key," it's because the grammar is incorrect.

The Italian alphabet is not as extensive as the English alphabet in that it doesn't normally use such letters as *j, k, w, x,* and *y.*

Even as late as World War II, many Italian soldiers couldn't understand each other, as some men spoke only in their local dialects. But with the coming of television, more and more Italians speak the language with similarity.

9 Rome at the Table

MEALS & DINING CUSTOMS You'll find restaurants of international renown here and an infinite number of *trattorie* and *rosticcerie* that offer good meals at moderate prices. The main meals are from noon to 3pm and 8 to 11pm, but you can get food at other hours at the more informal trattorie and rosticcerie. Many restaurants throughout Rome offer fixed-price meals that include two courses, a dessert, a house wine, and service. For more details, refer to Chapter 5, "Dining."

THE CUISINE Many visitors from North America erroneously think of Italian cuisine as limited. Of course, everybody's heard of minestrone, spaghetti, chicken cacciatore, and spumoni ice cream. But chefs hardly confine themselves to such a limited repertoire.

Throughout your Roman holiday you'll encounter such savory viands as *zuppa di pesce* (a soup or stew of various fish, cooked in white wine and herbs, *cannelloni* (tube-shaped pasta baked with any number of stuffings), *riso col gamberi* (rice with shrimp, peas, and mushrooms, flavored with white wine and garlic), *scampi alla griglia* (grilled prawns, one of the best-tasting, albeit expensive, dishes in the city), *quaglie con risotto e tartufi* (quail with rice and truffles), *lepre alla cacciatore* (hare flavored with tomato sauce and herbs), *zabaglione* (a cream made with sugar, egg yolks, and marsala), *gnocchi alla romana* (potato-flour dumplings with a sauce made with meat and covered with grated cheese), *stracciatella* (chicken broth with eggs and grated cheese), *abbacchio* (baby spring lamb, often roasted over an open fire), *saltimbocca alla romana* (literally "jump-in-your-mouth"—thin slices of veal with cheese, ham, and sage), *fritta alla romana* (a mixed fry that's likely to include everything from brains to artichokes), *carciofi alla romana* (tender artichokes cooked with mint and garlic, and flavored with white wine), *fettuccine all'uovo* (egg noodles served with butter and cheese), *zuppa di cozze o vongole* (a hearty bowl of mussels or clams cooked in broth), *fritta di scampi e calamaretti* (baby squid and prawns fast-fried), *fragoline* (wild strawberries, in this case from the Alban Hills), and *finocchio* (or fennel, a celerylike raw vegetable, the flavor of anisette, often eaten as a dessert and in salads).

Incidentally, except in the south, Italians do not use as much garlic in their food as most foreigners seem to believe. Most northern Italian dishes are butter based. Virgin olive oil is preferred in the south. Spaghetti and meatballs is not an Italian dish, although certain restaurants throughout the country have taken to serving it "for homesick Americans."

Rome also has many specialty restaurants that represent every major region of the country. The dishes they serve carry such designations as *alla genovese* (Genoa), *alla milanese* (Milan), *alla napolitana* (Naples), *alla fiorentina* (Florence), and *alla bolognese* (Bologne).

WINES & OTHER DRINKS Italy is the largest wine-producing country in the world; as far back as 800 B.C. the Etruscans were vintners. It's said that more soil is used in Italy for the cultivation of grapes than for growing food. Many Italian farmers produce wine just for their own consumption or for their relatives in a big city. However, it wasn't until 1965 that laws were enacted to guarantee regular consistency in winemaking. Wines regulated by the government are labeled "DOC" (*Denominazione di Origine Controllata*). If you see "DOCG" on a label (the "G" means *garantita*), that means even better quality control.

Lazio (Rome's region) is a major wine-producing region of Italy. Many of the local wines come from the Castelli Romani, the hill towns around Rome. Horace and Juvenal sang the praises of Latium wines even in imperial times. These wines, experts agree, are best drunk when young, and they are most often white, mellow, and dry (or else demi-sec). There are seven different types, including **Falerno** (yellowish straw in color) and **Cecubo** (often served with roast meat). Try also **Colli Albani** (straw-yellow with amber tints and served with both fish and meat). The golden-yellow wines of **Frascati** are famous, produced both in a demi-sec and a sweet variety, the latter served with dessert.

Romans drink other libations as well. Their most famous drink is **Campari,** bright red in color and herb flavored, with a quinine bitterness to it. It's customary to serve it with ice cubes and soda.

Beer is also made in Italy and, in general, is lighter than German beer. If you order beer in a Roman bar or restaurant, chances are it will be imported unless you specify otherwise, for which you'll be charged accordingly. Some famous names in European beer making now operate plants in Italy, where the brew has been "adjusted" to Italian taste.

High-proof **grappa** is made from the "leftovers" after the grapes have been pressed. Many Romans drink this before or after dinner (some put it into their coffee). To an untrained foreign palate, it often appears rough and harsh; some say it's an acquired taste.

Italy has many **brandies** (according to an agreement with France, it is not supposed to use the word *cognac* in labeling them). A popular one is Vecchia Romagna.

Other popular drinks include several **liqueurs,** to which the Romans are addicted. Try herb-flavored Strega, or perhaps an Amaretto tasting of almonds. One of the best known is Maraschino, taking its name from a type of cherry used in its preparation. Galliano is also herb flavored, and Sambuca (anisette) is made of aniseed and is often served with a "fly" (coffee bean) in it. On a hot day a true Roman orders a vermouth, Cinzano, with a twist of lemon, ice cubes, and a squirt of soda water.

10 Recommended Books, Films & Recordings

BOOKS

GENERAL & HISTORY Luigi Barzini's *The Italians* (Macmillan, 1964) should almost be required reading for anyone contemplating a trip to Rome. Critics have hailed it as the liveliest analysis yet of the Italian character.

Edward Gibbon's 1776 *The History of the Decline and Fall of the Roman Empire* is published in six volumes, but Penguin issues a manageable abridgement. It has been hailed as one of the greatest histories ever written. No one has ever recaptured the saga of the glory that was Rome the way that Gibbon did.

Giuliano Procacci surveys the spectrum in his *History of the Italian People* (Harper & Row, 1973), which provides an encompassing look at how Italy became a nation.

One of the best books on the long history of the papacy—detailing its excesses, triumphs, defeats, and most vivid characters—is Michael Walsh's *An Illustrated History of the Popes: Saint Peter to John Paul II* (St. Martin's Press, 1980).

The roots of modern Italy are explored in Christopher Hibbert's *Garibaldi and His Enemies: The Clash of Arms and Personalities in the Making of Italy* (Penguin, 1989).

In the 20th century the most fascinating period in Italian history was the rise and fall of Fascism, as detailed in countless works. One of the best biographies of Il Duce is Denis M. Smith's *Mussolini: A Biography* (Random House, 1983). Eugen Weber writes of *Varieties of Fascism: Doctrines of Revolution in the Twentieth Century* (Krieger, 1982). Stein Larsen edited *Who Were the Fascists? Social Roots of European Fascism* (Oxford University Press, 1981). With the rise of neofascists within the Italian government, this book is being read with even more interest in the 1990s.

One subject that's always engrossing is the Mafia, which is detailed in Pino Arlacchi's *Mafia Business: The Mafia Ethic and the Spirit of Capitalism* (Routledge, Chapman & Hall, 1987).

William Murray's *The Last Italian: Portrait of a People* (Prentice Hall, 1991) is his second volume of essays on his favorite subject—Italy, its people and civilization. The *New York Times* called it "a lover's keen, observant diary of his affair."

Once Upon a Time in Italy: The Vita Italiana of an American Journalist, by Jack Casserly (Roberts Rinehart, 1995), is the entertaining and affectionate memoir of a former bureau chief in Rome from 1957 to 1964. He captures the spirit of *Italian sparita* (bygone Italy) with such celebrity cameos as those of Maria Callas and the American expatriate singer, Bricktop.

ART & ARCHITECTURE Giorgio Vasari's *The Lives of the Most Eminent Italian Architects, Painters, and Sculptors* was published in 1550 and, in spite of some fanciful inventions, it remains the definitive work on Renaissance artists—by one who knew many of them personally—from Cimabue to Michelangelo. Penguin Classics issues a paperback abridged version, called *Lives of the Artists* (1985).

T. W. Potter provides one of the best accounts of the art and architecture of Rome in *Roman Italy* (University of California Press, 1987), which is also illustrated. Another good book on the same subject is *Roman Art and Architecture,* by Mortimer Wheeler (World of Art Series, Thames & Hudson, 1990).

The Sistine Chapel: A Glorious Restoration, by Michael Hirst et al. (Abrams, 1994), uses nearly 300 color photographs to illustrate the lengthy and painstaking restoration of Michelangelo's 16th-century frescoes in the Vatican.

FICTION & BIOGRAPHY John Hersey's Pulitzer Prize winning *A Bell for Adano* (Knopf, 1944) is now a classic and is frequently reprinted. It's a well-written and disturbing story of the American invasion of Italy.

Benvenuto Cellini's *Autobiography,* also available in Penguin Classics, was first printed in Italy in 1728, although Cellini lived from 1500 to 1571. It's a Renaissance romp, filled with gossip and interesting details, so much so that it has been compared to a novel. It launched the tide of the romantic movement.

Irving Stone's *The Agony and the Ecstasy* (Doubleday, 1961), which was filmed with Charlton Heston playing Michelangelo, is the easiest to read and the most pop version of the life of this great artist.

Dante's *The Divine Comedy* is famed throughout the world. It's a brilliant synthesis of the medieval Christian world view. *The Inferno* in Volume I was issued by Penguin in 1984, *Purgatory* in Volume II was published by Penguin in 1985, and *Paradiso* in Volume III was published by Penguin in 1986.

Giorgio Bassani, born in 1916, provides the bourgeois milieu of a Jewish community under Mussolini in *The Garden of the Finzi-Contini* (Harcourt Brace Jovanovich, 1977).

The novels of Alberto Moravia, born in 1907, are classified as neorealism. Moravia is one of the best-known Italian writers read in English. Notable works include *Roman Tales* (Farrar, Straus, and Cudahy, 1957), *The Woman of Rome* (Penguin, 1957; also available in the Playboy paperback series), and *The Conformist* (Greenwood Press, 1975).

First published in 1959, when it caused a scandal, Pier Paolo Pasolini's *A Violent Life* (Pantheon, 1991) is a novel written by the controversial filmmaker. Once viewed with disdain, it's now a classic of postwar Italian fiction.

For the most recent look at one of the movers and shakers in Italy, you might enjoy Alan Friedman's *Agnelli and the Network of Italian Power* (Harrap, 1989).

TRAVEL H. V. Morton's *A Traveler in Italy* (Methuen, 1964) is a towering work by one of the world's most widely read travel writers who has a rare sense of history.

Many great writers—when faced with the challenge of Italy—decided to become travel writers. These have included Charles Dickens, who wrote *Pictures from Italy* (Ecco Press, 1988), a classic 19th-century account of the Grand Tour, going from Tuscany to Naples via Rome. Wolfgang Goethe's *Italian Journey* (Penguin, 1982) devotes more attention to Roman antiquities, and Henry James's *Italian Hours* (1909) is young James at his best, capturing the special atmosphere of Italy. It's currently issued by Ecco Press.

D. H. Lawrence and Italy (Viking Press, 1972) is three classic Italian travelogues collected in a single volume, including *Sea and Sardinia* and *Twilight in Italy.* It also includes *Etruscan Places,* which was published posthumously. Lawrence writes of a way of life that was disappearing even as he wrote the work.

FILMS

Italian films have never regained the glory they enjoyed in the postwar era. Roberto Rossellini's *Rome, Open City* (1946) influenced Hollywood's films noirs of the late 1940s and Vittorio De Sica's *Bicycle Thief* (1948) achieved world renown.

The late Federico Fellini burst into Italian cinema with his highly individual style, beginning with *La Strada* (1954) and going on to such classics as *Juliet of the Spirits* (1965), *Amarcord* (1974), *Roma* (1972), and *The City of Women* (1980). *La Dolce Vita* (1961) helped to define an era.

Marxist, homosexual, and practicing Catholic, Pier Paolo Pasolini was the most controversial of Roman filmmakers until his mysterious murder in 1975. Explicit sex scenes in *Decameron* (1971) made it a world box-office hit.

Bernardo Bertolucci, once an assistant to Pasolini, achieved fame with such films as *The Conformist* (1970), based on the novel by Moravia. His *1900* is an epic spanning 20th-century Italian history and politics.

Michelangelo Antonioni swept across the screens of the world with his films of psychological anguish, including *La Notte* (1961), *L'Avventura* (1964), and *The Red Desert* (1964).

Mediterraneo, directed by Gabriele Salvatores, was a whimsical comedy that won an Oscar for best foreign-language film in 1991. It tells the story of eight Italian soldiers stranded on a Greek island in World War II.

Giuseppe Tornatore, who achieved such fame with *Cinema Paradiso,* which won the Academy Award for best foreign-language film of 1989, directed one of three vignettes in the 1992 film *Especially on Sunday.* The Taviani brothers, Paolo and Vittorio, both directors, created a stir in 1994 with the release of their film *Fiorile.*

Caro Diario (1994), starring and directed by Nanni Moretti, is a three-part traipse through modern-day Italy. Moretti, a cult figure in Italy, began to make an impression in America with this film. The actor-director is noted for his prickly personality, quirky sense of humor, and deadpan tone.

The Flight of the Innocent (1995) is one of the finest films to come out of Italy in recent times—and one that quickly gained an international audience. The director, Carlo Carlei, takes us inside the world of a 10-year-old boy fleeing for his life. It's one of the best depictions ever of a child alone who must improvise and cope with a world he doesn't understand.

Although directors more than stars have dominated Italian cinema, three actors have emerged to gain worldwide fame, including Marcello Mastroianni, star of such hits as *La Dolce Vita* (1961), and Sophia Loren, whose best film is considered *Two Women* (1961). Mastroianni was Fellini's favorite male actor and he starred him once again in *8½.* Anna Magnani not only starred in Italian films, but made many American films as well, including *The Rose Tattoo* (1955), with Burt Lancaster, and *The Fugitive Kind* (1960), with Marlon Brando.

RECORDINGS

MEDIEVAL & RENAISSANCE MUSIC An excellent collection of the late Renaissance's sonatas, canzonettas, and madrigals, played on original Renaissance instruments, is entitled *Music from the Time of Guido Reni.* (Guido Reni, born 1575 and died 1642, was a Renaissance painter who probably caused more public discord because of his philandering and political intrigues than any other in Italian history. He was eventually exiled from Rome in 1622.) This particular collection of works by this artist's musical contemporaries was recorded by the Aurora Ensemble (Tactus TAC 56012001).

ORCHESTRAL & OPERATIC WORKS The best way for most novices to begin an appreciation of opera is to hear an assemblage of great moments of opera accumulated onto one record. A good example contains works by the most evocative and dramatic singer who ever hit a high "C" on the operatic stage, Maria Callas. *La Voce: Historic Recordings of the Great Diva* (Suite SUI 5002) brings together "La Callas's" spectacular arias from *Lucia di Lammermoor, La Traviata, Norma,* and *The Barber of Seville.*

Recordings of complete and unedited operas are even more rewarding. Excellent examples include the following: Bellini's *Norma,* featuring the divine and legendary Maria Callas, accompanied by the orchestra and the chorus of Milan's La Scala, is one of the world's great operatic events; Tullio Serafin conducts (Angel Records 3517C/ANG 35148-35150). Giuseppe Verdi's genius can be appreciated through *Nabucco,* performed with Plácido Domingo by the Rydl Choir and Orchestra of the Dutch National Opera, conducted by Giuseppe Sinopoli (Deutsche Gramophone DDD 410 512-2-GH2). Also insightful for the vocal techniques of Verdi, his *Complete Songs* is recorded by Renata Scotto (soprano) and Paolo Washington (bass), accompanied by Vincenzo Scalera (piano) (Nuova Era NUO 6855). Rossini's great opera *Il Barbiere di Siviglia* and Puccini's *Tosca,* both recorded in their complete versions by the Turin Opera Orchestra and Chorus, are both conducted by Bruno Campanella (Nuova Era NUO 6760 and Foyer FOY 2023, respectively).

And no compendium of Italian opera would be complete without including the immortal tenor Luciano Pavarotti, whose interpretations of Verdi's idealistic heroes have become almost definitive. His *La Traviata* is particularly memorable and passionate. A classic, this version is available on a two-cassette collection from C.I.M.E. (PTP-5123-4).

Planning a Trip to Rome

2

This chapter is devoted to the where, when, and how of your trip—the advance-planning issues required to get it together and take on the road.

After deciding where to go, most people have two fundamental questions: What will it cost? and How do I get there? This chapter will answer both these questions and also resolve other important issues, such as when to go, what pretrip preparations are needed, where to obtain more information about Rome, and much more.

1 Visitor Information & Entry Requirements

VISITOR INFORMATION

Before you go, you can contact the **Italian National Tourist Office** at 630 Fifth Ave., Suite 1565, New York, NY 10111 (☎ 212/245-4822); 401 N. Michigan Ave., Chicago, IL 60611 (☎ 312/644-0990); or 12400 Wilshire Blvd., Suite 550, Los Angeles, CA 90025 (☎ 310/820-0098). In Canada, contact the Italian National Tourist Office at 1 place Ville-Marie, Suite 1914, Montréal, QB H3B 3M9 (☎ 514/866-7667); and in England at 1 Princes St., London W1R 8AY (☎ 0171/408-1254).

@ROME

Although Yahoo (**http://www.yahoo.com/Recreation/Travel**), Excite (**http://www.excite.com/Subject/Regional**), Lycos (**http://www.lycos.com**), Infoseek (**http://www.infoseek.com**), and the other major Internet indexing sites all have travel subcategories, one of the best hotlists for travel and destination-specific information in general is Excite's "city.net" (**http://www.city.net/countries/italy/rome**).

The best Rome site, no holds barred, is run by Travelocity (**http://www.travelocity.com**). From the homepage, click on the "Destinations & Interests" button, then navigate your way to "Rome and Environs." It has hundreds of listings—full-fledged write-ups in most cases—for everything from sights, hotels, and restaurants to shopping, nightlife, tour companies, and an excellent festivals and events calendar.

Another great site, complete with pictures, is Roma 2000 (**http://www.roma2000.it**). It's very graphics-heavy, and the English translation reads a bit like stereo instructions, but it has a wealth of information on sightseeing, including some walking tours. It also lists dozens of hotels, restaurants, and shops, but mostly gives just the addresses and phone numbers. "In Italy" (**http://www.lainet.com/~initaly**) not only contains well-done information on Italy and Rome presented in a very personal and friendly way, but it also has one of the best set of links to other Italy-related sites on the Net. If you want still more, try the Webfoot Guides (**http://www.webfoot.com**), which has links to information on Italy and the Vatican. And for an unrelentingly religious site with a wonderful armchair photo tour of the Vatican and its art treasures, head to Christus Rex (**http://www.christusrex.org**).

ENTRY REQUIREMENTS

DOCUMENTS U.S., Canadian, Australian, New Zealand, and Irish citizens, and British subjects, with a valid passport do not need a visa to enter Italy if they don't expect to stay more than 90 days and don't expect to work there. Those who, after entering Italy, find that they'd like to stay more than 90 days can apply for a permit for an additional stay of 90 days, which as a rule is granted immediately. Check with your nearest Italian consulate. If you plan to drive while abroad, it may prove helpful (although not strictly necessary) to obtain an International Driver's Permit to accompany your state or territorial driver's license. You can get an application from your local AAA office.

CUSTOMS Most items designed for personal use can be brought to Rome duty-free. This includes clothing (new and used), books, camping and household equipment, fishing tackle, a sporting gun and 200 cartridges, a pair of skis, two tennis racquets, a tape recorder, a baby carriage, two ordinary hand cameras with 10 rolls of film, one video camera with 10 blank tapes, a portable radio set (subject to a small license fee), and 400 cigarettes (two cartons) or a quantity of cigars or pipe tobacco not exceeding 500 grams (1.1 lb.). There are strict limits on importing alcoholic beverages. However, limits are much more liberal for alcohol bought tax-paid in other countries of the European Union.

Upon leaving Italy, citizens and permanent residents of the United States who have been outside the country for 48 hours or more are allowed to bring back home $400 worth of merchandise duty-free—that is, if they have claimed no similar exemption within the past 30 days. If you make purchases in Italy, it's important to keep your receipts; U.S. travelers over 21 may bring back 1 liter of alcohol duty-free.

2 Money

There are no restrictions as to how much foreign currency you can bring into Italy, although visitors should declare the amount brought in; this proves to the Italian Customs Office that the currency came from outside the country and therefore the same amount or less can be taken out. Italian currency taken into or out of Italy may not exceed 200,000 lire in denominations of 50,000 lire or lower.

The basic unit of Italian currency is the **lira** (plural: **lire**), abbreviated in this book as **L.** Because of fluctuations in relative values of world currencies, we suggest that you contact any bank for the latest official exchange rate before going to Italy.

Coins are issued in denominations of 10, 20, 50, 100, 200, and 500 lire; there are two different versions of both the 50- and 100-lire pieces (the new ones are much smaller). Bills come in denominations of 1,000, 5,000, 10,000, 50,000, 100,000, and 500,000 lire.

The Italian Lira, the U.S. Dollar & the U.K. Pound

At this writing, $1 U.S. = approximately 1,565 Italian lire (or 1,000L = 65¢), and this was the rate of exchange used to calculate the dollar values given throughout this book. The rate fluctuates from day to day, depending on a complicated series of economic and political factors, and might not be the same when you travel to Italy.

Likewise, the ratio of the British pound to the lira fluctuates constantly. At press time, £1 = approximately 2,380L (or 1,000L = 40p), an exchange rate reflected in the table below.

Lire	U.S.$	U.K.£	Lire	U.S.$	U.K.£
50	.03	.02	30,000	19.20	12.60
100	.06	.04	40,000	25.60	16.80
250	.16	.13	50,000	32.00	21.00
500	.32	.21	60,000	38.40	25.20
750	.48	.29	70,000	44.80	29.40
1,000	.64	.42	80,000	51.20	33.60
1,500	.96	.63	90,000	57.60	37.80
2,000	1.28	.84	100,000	64.00	42.00
2,500	1.60	1.05	125,000	80.00	52.50
3,000	1.92	1.26	150,000	96.00	63.00
4,000	2.56	1.68	175,000	112.00	73.50
5,000	3.20	2.10	200,000	128.00	84.00
7,500	4.80	3.15	250,000	160.00	105.00
10,000	6.40	4.20	300,000	192.00	126.00
15,000	9.60	6.30	400,000	256.00	168.00
20,000	12.80	8.40	500,000	320.00	210.00
25,000	16.00	10.50	750,000	480.00	315.00

TRAVELER'S CHECKS Before leaving home, purchasing traveler's checks can give you an extra measure of security. In the event of theft, if the traveler's checks are properly documented, their value will be refunded. Most large banks sell traveler's checks, charging fees that average between 1% and 2% of the value of the checks you buy, although some out-of-the-way banks, in rare instances, have charged as much as 7%. If your bank wants more than a 2% commission, it sometimes pays to call the traveler's check issuers directly for the address of outlets where this commission charge will be less.

Issuers sometimes have agreements with groups to sell checks commission-free. For example, the American Automobile Association (AAA) clubs sell their members American Express traveler's checks in several currencies without a commission charge.

American Express (☎ **800/221-7282** in the U.S. and Canada) is one of the largest and most immediately recognized issuers of traveler's checks, and for holders of certain types of American Express charge cards, no commission is charged. For questions or problems that arise outside the U.S. or Canada, contact any of the company's many regional representatives.

What Things Cost in Rome	U.S. $
Taxi from the central rail station to Piazza di Spagna	8.80
Subway or public bus (to any destination)	.95
Local telephone call	.14
Double room at the Hassler (very expensive)	416.00
Double room at the Hotel Columbus (moderate)	172.80
Double room at the Hotel Corot (inexpensive)	96.00
Continental breakfast (cappuccino and croissant at most cafés and bars)	3.00
Lunch for one at Ristorante da Pancrazio (moderate)	19.20
Dinner for one, without wine, at Relais Le Jardin (very expensive)	75.00
Dinner for one, without wine, at L'Eau Vive (inexpensive)	32.00
Dinner for one, without wine, at Otello alla Concordi (inexpensive)	23.00
Pint of beer	3.95
Glass of wine	2.00
Coca-Cola	1.50
Cup of coffee	1.30
Roll of color film, 36 exposures	6.50
Admission to the Vatican museums and Sistine Chapel	9.60
Movie ticket	7.95

There's also **Citicorp** (☎ **800/645-6556** in the U.S. and Canada, or 813/623-1709, collect, from anywhere else) and **Thomas Cook** (☎ **800/223-7373** in the U.S. and Canada, or 609/987-7300, collect, from other parts of the world), which issues MasterCard traveler's checks. **Interpayment Services** (☎ **800/732-1322** in the U.S. and Canada, or 212/858-8500, collect—which will change "soon" to 44-1733/318-949—from other parts of the world) sells Visa checks which are issued by a consortium of member banks and the Thomas Cook organization.

Each of these agencies will refund your money if the checks are lost or stolen, provided you produce sufficient documentation. When purchasing checks, ask about refund hotlines; American Express and Bank of America have the greatest number of offices around the world.

CURRENCY EXCHANGE For the best exchange rate, go to a bank, *not* to hotels or shops. Currency and traveler's checks (for which you'll receive a better rate than cash) can be changed at the airport and some travel agencies, such as American Express and Thomas Cook. Note the rates—it can pay to shop around.

ATM NETWORKS Plus, Visa, and some other automated-teller machine networks operate in Italy (at last check, Cirrus was not one of them). Branches of major Italian banks—Banca Nazionale del Lavoro, Banca Monte dei Pasci de Siena, Banca Populare di Milano, to name a few—have *Bancomats* (ATM machines) throughout Rome. Most of them are open 24 hours and accept American Express, Diners Club, MasterCard, and Visa (Discover cards are accepted only in the United States). Remember that Eurocard is often synonomous for North American versions of either MasterCard or Visa. If your bank card or credit card has been programmed with a PIN (Personal Identification Number), it's likely that you can use your card at ATMs abroad to withdraw money from your account or as a cash advance on your credit card. Also, check to see if your PIN code must be reprogrammed for usage in Italy.

MONEYGRAM If you find yourself out of money, a new wire service provided by American Express can help you tap willing friends and family for emergency funds. Through **MoneyGram,** 6200 S. Quebec St. (P.O. Box 5118), Englewood, CO 80155 (☎ **800/926-9400**), money can be sent around the world in less than 10 minutes. Senders should call AMEX to learn the address of the closest outlet that handles MoneyGrams. Cash, credit card (Visa, MasterCard, or Discover only, *not* the American Express card), or the occasional personal check (with ID) are acceptable forms of payment. AMEX's fee for the service is $20 for the first $200 with a sliding scale for larger sums. The service includes a short telex message and a 3-minute phone call from the sender to the recipient. The claimant must present a photo ID at the outlet where the money is received.

3 When to Go

CLIMATE

The most pleasant times to be in Rome, weatherwise, are spring and fall. In the height of summer it can get quite hot and humid. The temperatures can stay in the 90s for days, but nights are most often comfortably cooler. The high temperatures begin in May and often last until October. Rome experiences its lowest average temperatures in December, 47°F; its highest in July, 82°F.

Rome's Average Daytime Temperature & Rainfall

	Jan	Feb	Mar	Apr	May	June	July	Aug	Sept	Oct	Nov	Dec
Temp (°F)	49	52	57	62	70	77	82	78	73	68	56	47
Rain (in.)	3.6	3.2	2.9	2.2	1.4	0.7	0.2	0.7	3.0	4.0	3.9	2.8

HOLIDAYS

Offices and shops are closed on the following days: January 1 (New Year's Day), Easter Monday, April 25 (Liberation Day), May 1 (Labor Day), August 15 (Assumption of the Virgin), November 1 (All Saints' Day), December 8 (Feast of the Immaculate Conception), December 25 (Christmas), and December 26 (Santo Stefano).

ROME CALENDAR OF EVENTS

For more information about these and other events, contact the Rome tourist office, Ente Provinciale per il Turismo (see "Orientation" in Chapter 3). Dates vary from year to year.

January

- **Carnival,** in Piazza Navona. This marks the last day of the children's market and lasts until dawn of the following day. Usually January 5.
- **Festa di Sant'Agnese,** at Sant'Agnese Fuori le Mura. In this ancient ceremony, two lambs are blessed and shorn. The wool is then used later for palliums. Usually January 17.

March

- **Festa di Santa Francesca Romana,** at Piazzale del Colosseo, near the Church of Santa Francesca Romana in the Roman Forum. It's a blessing of cars. Usually March 9.

- **Festa di San Giuseppe,** in the Trionfale Quarter, north of the Vatican. The heavily decorated statue of the saint is brought out at a fair with food stalls, concerts, and sporting events. Usually March 19.

April

- **Festa della Primavera.** The Spanish Steps are decked out with banks of flowers, and later orchestral and choral concerts are presented in Trinità dei Monti. Dates vary.
- **Holy Week.** The most notable procession is led by the pope, passing the Colosseum and the Roman Forum up to Palatine Hill. A torchlit parade caps the observance. Sometimes at the end of March, but often in April.
- **Easter Sunday,** from the balcony of St. Peter's Basilica. The pope gives his blessing, and it's broadcast around the world.

May

- **International Horse Show,** at Piazza di Siena in the Villa Borghese. May 1–10, but dates vary.

June

- **Son et Lumière.** The Roman Forum and Tivoli are dramatically lit at night. Early June to the end of September.
- **Festa di San Pietro,** in St. Peter's Basilica. The most significant Roman religious festival is observed with solemn rites. Usually around June 29.

July

✪ **La Festa Di Noiantri.** Trastevere, the most colorful quarter of Old Rome, becomes a gigantic outdoor restaurant in mid-July as tons of food and drink are consumed at tables lining the streets. Merrymakers and musicians provide the entertainment. After reaching the quarter, find the first empty table and try to get a waiter. But guard your valuables. Details available from Ente Provinciale per il Turismo, Via Parigi 11, Roma 00185 (☎ **06/4889-9200**). Mid-July.

August

- **Festa della Catene,** in the Church of San Pietro in Vincoli. The relics of St. Peter's captivity go on display. August 1.
- **Ferragosto.** Beginning on August 15, most city residents not directly involved with the tourist trade take a two-week vacation (many restaurants are closed as well). This is a good time *not* to be in Rome.

September

- **Sagra dell'Uva,** in the Basilica of Maxentius in the Roman Forum. During the harvest festival, musicians in ancient costumes entertain, and grapes are sold at reduced prices. Usually early September, but dates vary.

December

- **Papal Blessing "Urbi et Orbi"** (to the city and to the world), from the balcony of St. Peter's Basilica. It's broadcast around the world. December 25 at noon.

4 Health & Insurance

STAYING HEALTHY You'll encounter few health problems while visiting in Rome. The tap water is generally safe to drink, the milk is pasteurized, and health services are good. Occasionally the change in diet may cause some minor diarrhea.

Carry all your vital medication in your carry-on luggage and bring enough prescribed medicines to last you during your stay. Bring along copies of your prescriptions written in the generic—not brand-name—form. If you need a doctor, your hotel can recommend one or you can contact your embassy or consulate. You can also obtain a list of English-speaking doctors before you leave from the **International Association for Medical Assistance to Travelers (IAMAT)** in the United States at 417 Center St., Lewiston, NY 14092 (☎ **716/754-4883**), or in Canada at 40 Regal Rd., Guelph, ON N1K 1B5 (☎ **519/836-0102**).

If you suffer from a chronic illness or special medical condition, talk to your doctor before taking the trip. For conditions such as epilepsy, diabetes, or a heart condition, wear Medic Alert's identification bracelet or necklace, which will immediately alert any doctor to your condition, and provide Medic Alert's 24-hour hotline phone number so that foreign doctors can obtain medical information on you. The initial membership costs $35, then $15 annually. Contact the **Medic Alert Foundation,** 2323 Colorado Ave., Turlock, CA 95381-1009 (☎ **800/432-5378**).

INSURANCE Before purchasing any additional insurance, check your homeowner's, automobile, and medical insurance policies as well as the insurance provided by credit- and charge-card companies and auto and travel clubs. You may have adequate off-premises theft coverage, or your card company may even provide cancellation coverage if the ticket is paid for with its card.

Note that to submit any claim you must always have thorough documentation, including all receipts, police reports, medical records, and such. Medicare only covers U.S. citizens traveling to Mexico and Canada.

If you're prepaying your vacation or are taking a charter or any other flight that has cancellation penalties, look into cancellation insurance.

The following companies will provide further information:

Travel Guard International, 1145 Clark St., Stevens Point, WI 54481 (☎ **800/826-1300**), offers comprehensive policies, including a $44 7-day policy that covers basically everything: emergency assistance, accidental death, trip cancellation and interruption, medical coverage abroad, and lost luggage. This company is the only one to offer "cancel-for-any-reason coverage."

At **Travel Insured International, Inc.,** P.O. Box 280568, East Hartford, CT 06128-0568 (☎ **800/243-3174** in the U.S., or 203/528-7663 outside the U.S.), accident and illness coverage starts at $10; $500 worth of coverage for lost, damaged, or delayed baggage costs $20; and trip cancellation goes for $5.50 for $100 worth of coverage (written approval is necessary for cancellation coverage above $10,000).

Mutual of Omaha (Tele-Trip), Mutual of Omaha Plaza, Omaha, NE 68175 (☎ **800/228-9792**), offers travel insurance packages that feature travel assistance services, trip cancellation, trip interruption, flight and baggage delays, accident medical, sickness, 24-hour accidental death and dismemberment, and medical evacuation coverages. Packages begin at $49 per person; a deluxe package costing $213 per couple doubles the coverage.

HealthCare Abroad (MEDEX), c/o Wallach & Co., 107 W. Federal St. (P.O. Box 480), Middleburg, VA 22117-0480 (☎ **800/237-6615** or 540/687-3166), offers a $3-a-day package, including accident and sickness coverage to the tune of $100,000. Medical evacuation is also included, along with $25,000 accidental death and dismemberment compensation. Trip cancellation can also be written into this policy at a nominal cost.

Access America, 6600 W. Broad St., Richmond, VA 23230-1188 (☎ **800/284-8300**), has a 24-hour emergency hotline for advice and help on medical, legal, and travel problems. The company also offers comprehensive travel insurance packages, including medical expenses, on-the-spot hospital payments, medical transportation, baggage insurance, trip cancellation/interruption insurance, and collision insurance for car rentals.

Insurance for British Travelers Most big travel agents offer their own insurance and will probably try to sell you their package when you book a holiday. Think before you sign. Britain's Consumers' Association recommends that you insist on seeing the policy and reading the fine print before buying travel insurance.

You should also shop around for better deals. You might contact **Columbus Travel Insurance Ltd.** (☎ **0171/375-0011** in London) or, for students, **Campus Travel** (☎ **0171/730-3402** in London). Columbus Travel will sell travel insurance only to people who have been official residents of Britain for at least a year. If you're unsure about who provides what kind of insurance and the best deal, contact the **Association of British Insurers,** 52 Gresham St., London EC2V 7HQ (☎ **0171/600-3333**).

5 Tips for Travelers with Special Needs

FOR PEOPLE WITH DISABILITIES Before you go, there are many agencies that can provide advance-planning information.

You may want to consider joining a tour for visitors with disabilities. Names and addresses of operators of such tours can be obtained by writing to the **Society for the Advancement of Travel for the Handicapped,** 347 Fifth Ave., New York, NY 10016 (☎ **212/447-7284**). Annual membership dues are $45, or $25 for senior citizens and students. Send a stamped, self-addressed envelope.

FEDCAP Rehabilitation Services (formerly known as the Federation of the Handicapped), 154 W. 14th St., New York, NY 10011 (☎ **212/727-4200**), operates summer tours to Europe and elsewhere for its members. Membership costs $4 yearly.

You can also obtain a copy of **"Air Transportation of Handicapped Persons,"** published by the U.S. Department of Transportation. It's free if you write to Free Advisory Circular No. AC12032, Distribution Unit, U.S. Department of Transportation, Publications Division, M-4332, Washington, DC 20590.

For the blind or visually impaired, the best information source is the **American Foundation for the Blind,** 15 W. 16th St., New York, NY 10011 (☎ **800/232-5463** in the U.S., or 212/502-7600). It offers information on travel and various requirements for the transport and border formalities for seeing-eye dogs. It also issues identification cards to those who are legally blind.

Tips for British Travelers with Disabilities The **Royal Association for Disability and Rehabilitation (RADAR),** Unit 12, City Forum, 250 City Rd., London ECIV 8AF (☎ **0171/250-3222**), publishes three holiday "fact packs," which sell for £2 each or £5 for the set of all three. The first one provides general information, including planning and booking a holiday, insurance, finances, and useful organization and holiday providers. The second outlines transport and equipment, transportation available when going abroad, and equipment for rent. The third deals with specialized accommodations.

Another good resource is **Holiday Care Service,** Imperial Building, 2nd Floor, Victoria Road, Horley, Surrey RH6 7PZ (☎ **01293/774-535;** fax 01293/784-647), a national charity that advises on accessible accommodations for elderly and persons with disabilities. Annual membership costs £25. Once a member, one can receive a newsletter and access to a free reservation service offering discounted rates for hotels throughout the world.

FOR GAY MEN & LESBIANS Before you go to Rome, men can order ***Spartacus,*** the international gay guide, for $32.95 from Giovanni's Room, 1145 Pine St., Philadelphia, PA 19107 (☎ **215/923-2960**) and other gay and lesbian bookstores around the country. Both lesbians and gay men also might want to pick up a copy of ***Gay Travel A to Z*** ($16).

Our World, 1104 N. Nova Rd., Suite 251, Daytona Beach, FL 32117 (☎ **904/441-5367**), is a magazine devoted to options and bargains for gay and lesbian travel worldwide. It costs $35 for 10 issues. ***Out and About,*** 8 W. 19th St., Suite 401, New York, NY 10011 (☎ **800/929-2268**), has been hailed for its "straight" reporting about gay travel. It profiles the best gay and gay-friendly hotels, gyms, clubs, and other places, with coverage of destinations throughout the world. Its cost is $49 a year for 10 information-packed issues. It aims for the more upscale gay male traveler, and has been praised by everybody from *Travel & Leisure* to the *New York Times.* Both of these publications are also available at most gay and lesbian bookstores.

FOR SENIORS Many senior discounts are available, but note that some may require membership in a particular association.

For information before you go, write for a free booklet called "101 Tips for the Mature Traveler," available from **Grand Circle Travel,** 347 Congress St., Suite 3A, Boston, MA 02210 (☎ **800/221-2610,** or 617/350-7500).

SAGA International Holidays, 222 Berkeley St., Boston, MA 02116 (☎ **800/343-0273** in the U.S.), runs all-inclusive tours for seniors, preferably for those 50 and over. Insurance is included in the net price of these tours.

In the United States, the best organization to belong to is the **American Association of Retired Persons (AARP),** 601 E St. NW, Washington, DC 20049 (☎ **202/434-AARP**). Members are offered discounts on car rentals, hotels, and airfares.

Information is also available from the **National Council of Senior Citizens,** 1331 F St. NW, Washington, DC 20005-1171 (☎ **202/347-8800**), which charges $12 per person or per couple, for which you receive a monthly newsletter, part of which is devoted to travel tips. Reduced discounts on hotel and auto rentals are available.

Golden Companions, P.O. Box 5249, Reno, NV 89513 (☎ **702/324-2227**), might provide the answer if you're 45 or older and need a travel companion. A research economist, Joanne R. Buteau, founded this helpful service and is quick to point out that it's *not* a dating service. Travelers meet potential companions through a confidential mail network and make their own travel arrangements. Created in 1987, this organization draws members from many walks of life. Members also receive a bimonthly travel newsletter, *The Golden Gateways.* Membership for a full year costs $94 per person. Free brochure and sample newsletter are $2.

Mature Outlook, P.O. Box 104488, Des Moines, IA 50306 (☎ **800/336-6330**), is a membership program for people more than 50 years of age. Members are offered discounts at ITC-member hotels and will receive a bimonthly magazine. The annual membership fee of $14.95 entitles members to free coupons for discounts at Sears & Roebuck Co. Savings are also offered on selected auto rentals and restaurants.

Tips for British Seniors **Wasteels,** Victoria Station, opposite Platform 2, London SW1V 1JZ (☎ **0171/834-6744**), currently provides an over-60s Rail Europe Senior Card. Its price is £5 to any British person with government-issued proof of his or her age. To qualify, British residents must present a valid British Senior Citizen rail card, which you can get for £16, along with proof of age and British residency, at any BritRail office.

FOR SINGLES Unfortunately for the 85 million single Americans, the travel industry is far more geared toward couples, and singles often wind up paying the penalty. It pays to travel with someone, and one company that resolves this problem is **Travel Companion,** which matches single travelers with like-minded companions. It's headed by Jens Jurgen, who charges $99 for a 6-month listing in his well-publicized records. People seeking travel companions fill out forms stating their preferences and needs and receive a minilisting of potential travel partners. A bimonthly newsletter averaging 46 large pages also gives numerous money-saving travel tips of special interest to solo travelers. A sample copy is available for $5. For an application and more information, contact Jens Jurgen, Travel Companion, P.O. Box P-833, Amityville, NY 11701 (☎ **516/454-0880;** fax 516/454-0170).

Another agency to check is **Grand Circle Travel,** 347 Congress St., Suite 3A, Boston, MA 02210 (☎ **800/248-3737** in the U.S., or 617/350-7500), which offers escorted tours and cruises for retired people, including singles.

Since single supplements on tours can be rather hefty, some tour companies will arrange for you to share a room with another single traveler of the same gender. One such company that offers a "guaranteed-share plan" is **Cosmos** (☎ **800/221-0090**). Book through your travel agent or call directly.

Tips for British Singles Single people sometimes feel comfortable traveling with groups composed mostly of other singles. One tour operator whose groups are usually at least 50% unattached persons is **Explore World-wide Ltd.,** 1 Frederick St., Aldershot, Hampshire GU11 1LQ (☎ **01252/344-161**). Groups rarely include more than 20 participants, and children under 14 are not allowed.

FOR FAMILIES ***Family Travel Times*** is published 10 times a year by TWYCH, Travel with Your Children, and includes a weekly call-in service for subscribers. Subscriptions cost $55 a year and can be ordered by writing to TWYCH, 45 W. 18th St., 7th Floor, New York, NY 10011 (☎ **212/477-5524**). You can get a description of TWYCH's publications, including a recent sample issue, by sending $3.50 to the above address.

Families Welcome!, 21 W. Colony Place, Suite 140, Durham, NC 27705 (☎ **800/326-0724** in the U.S., or 919/489-2555), a travel company specializing in worry-free vacations for families, offers "City Kids" packages to Rome, featuring accommodations in family-friendly hotels or apartments. Some hotels include a second room for children free or at a reduced rate during certain time periods. Packages can include car rentals, train and ferry passes, and special air prices, and are individually designed for each family. A welcome kit is distributed, containing "insider's information" for families traveling in Rome—reliable baby-sitters, where to buy diapers, restaurants that are good to visit with children, and similar advice.

Tips for British Families The best deals for families are often package tours put together by some of the giants of the British travel industry. Foremost among these is **Thomsons Tour Operators.** Through its subsidiary, **Skytours** (☎ **0171/387-9321**), it offers dozens of air/land packages to Italy where a designated number of airline seats are reserved for the free use of children under 18 who accompany their parents. To qualify, parents must book airfare and hotel accommodations lasting two weeks or more, and book as far in advance as possible. Savings for families with children can be substantial.

FOR STUDENTS The largest travel service for students is **Council Travel,** a subsidiary of the Council on International Educational Exchange, 205 E. 42nd St., New York, NY 10017 (☎ **800/226-8624** or 212/822-2700), which provides details about budget travel, study abroad, work permits, and insurance. It also sells a number of publications for young people considering traveling abroad. For a copy of *Student Travels* magazine, providing information on all of Council Travel's services and CIEE's programs and publications, send $1 in postage. For $16 the organization issues to bona fide students the International Student Identity Card (ISIC), an internationally recognized proof of student status that will entitle you to savings on flights, sightseeing, food, and accommodation. It also carries most of the basic insurance coverage you'll need. Call 800/GET-AN-ID to find out where the closest office is to you.

The **International Youth Hostel Federation (IYHF)** was designed to provide bare-bone overnight accommodations for serious budget-conscious travelers. For information, contact **Hostelling International / American Youth Hostels (HI-AYH),** 733 15th St. NW, Suite 840, Washington, DC 20005 (☎ **800/444-6111** or 202/783-6161). Membership costs $25 annually; it's $10 for children 17 and under, and $15 for seniors 54 and over.

Tips for British Students The British equivalent of Council Travel is **Campus Travel,** 52 Grosvenor Gardens, London SW1W 0AG (☎ **0171/730-3402**), which provides a wealth of information and offers for the student traveler, ranging from route planning to flight insurance, including railcards. It also sells the International Student Identity Card (ISIC) for £5. See the description under Council Travel, above, for details.

Youth hostels are the place to stay if you're a student. You'll need an **International Youth Hostels Association** card, which you can purchase from the youth hostel store at 14 Southampton St., London WC2 7HY (☎ 0171/836-1036), or from Campus Travel (☎ 0171/823-4739). Take both your passport and some passport-size photos of yourself, plus your membership fee of £9.30. More information on membership is available from the Youth Hostels Association of England and Wales (YHA), 8 St. Stephen's Hill, St. Albans, Hertfordshire AL1 2DY (☎ 01727/855-215).

The Youth Hostel Association puts together *The Hostelling International Budget Guide,* listing every youth hostel in 31 European countries. It costs £6.99 at the Southampton Street store in London (see above). Add 61p postage for delivery within the United Kingdom.

6 Getting There

BY PLANE

"All roads lead to Rome" in ways the emperors never dreamed of. But of all the various ways of reaching Rome, the airplane is the best…and the cheapest.

If you're already in Europe, you'll have an easy time booking a flight to Rome. Alitalia flies to all the major capitals of Europe, while each of the national carriers of the various countries (such as Air France, British Airways, and Lufthansa) flies to Rome and/or Milan. However, for Americans and Canadians, it's sometimes expensive to book these flights once you're in Europe; it's cheaper to have Rome or Milan written into your ticket when you first book your flight to Europe from North America.

THE MAJOR AIRLINES

Specific upheavals that shook the airline industry during the early 1990s have subsided a bit as of this writing. Despite the relative calm, the industry may still undergo some changes during the life of this edition. For last-minute conditions, including a list of the carriers that fly to Rome, check with a travel agent or the individual airlines. Here's a rundown on the current status:

From North America **American Airlines** (☎ **800/624-6262** in the U.S.) was among the first North America–based carriers to fly into Italy. From Chicago's

O'Hare Airport, American flies nonstop every evening to Milan, where there are frequent connections into Rome. Flights from all parts of American's vast network fly regularly into Chicago.

TWA (☎ **800/221-2000** in the U.S.) offers daily nonstop flights from New York's JFK to both Rome and Milan. Because of the frequency of flights, it's often convenient and cost-effective to fly into Rome and depart from Milan, or vice-versa, depending on your travel plans.

Delta (☎ **800/241-4141** in the U.S.) flies from New York's JFK to both Milan and Rome. Flights depart every evening for both destinations, with fine links to the rest of Delta's network of domestic and international destinations. In midwinter, service might be reduced to six flights a week.

For anyone interested in combining a trip to Italy with a stopover in, say, Britain or Germany along the way, there are sometimes attractive deals offered by **British Airways** (☎ **800/AIRWAYS** in the U.S.) and **Lufthansa** (☎ **800/645-3880** in the U.S.).

Canadian Airlines International (☎ **800/426-7000** in Canada) flies daily from Toronto to Rome. Two of the flights are nonstop, whereas others touch down en route in either Montréal or Milan.

One well-known Italian specialist, **Alitalia** (☎ **800/223-5730** in the U.S.), flies nonstop to both Rome and Milan from several American cities, including New York's JFK, Boston, Chicago, Los Angeles, and Miami. The airline also runs joint flights with Malev (the national airline of Hungary) to Italy from Newark, New Jersey. Schedules are designed for easy transfers to such cities as Venice and Palermo. Alitalia, incidentally, participates in the frequent-flyer programs of other airlines, including Continental and USAir.

Be aware that Alitalia's (and most other airlines') cheapest tickets are nonrefundable. Alitalia's sole exception to this rule is in the event of your hospitalization or the death of someone in your immediate family. Fares are higher for weekend (Friday to Sunday) travel.

From Great Britain Both **British Airways** (☎ **0181/897-4000** in London) and **Alitalia** (☎ **0181/745-8200** in London) have frequent flights from London's Heathrow Airport to Rome, Milan, Venice, Pisa (the gateway to Florence), and Naples. Flying time from London to these cities is anywhere from 2 to 3 hours. British Airways also has one direct flight a day from Manchester to Rome.

Regular Fares

Most of the major airlines that fly to Rome charge approximately the same fare, but if a price war should break out over the Atlantic (and these are almost always brewing over the most popular routes), fares could change overnight.

The key to getting a budget ticket is "advance booking." The number of seats allocated to low-cost "advance-purchase" fares is severely limited (sometimes to less than 25% of the capacity of a particular plane), so you have to make your reservations early to book a low-cost seat.

A large number of discounts are also available for passengers who can travel either midweek or midwinter in either direction. High season on most airlines' routes to Rome usually stretches from June 1 until September 15 (this could vary), and it's both the most expensive and most crowded time to travel.

All the major carriers offer an **APEX** (advance-purchase excursion) ticket, which is generally their cheapest transatlantic option. Usually such a ticket must be purchased between 14 and 21 days in advance and a stopover in Italy must last at least 7 days but not more than 30 days. Changing the date of departure from

North America within 21 days of departure will sometimes entail a penalty of around $150 with some APEX tickets, whereas with others no changes of any kind are permitted.

A more flexible (but more expensive) option is the **regular economy fare.** This offers the same seating and the same services as passengers using an excursion ticket, but doesn't require the 7-day minimum stay that the APEX ticket does. One of the most attractive benefits of a regular economy-class ticket is the absolute freedom granted to a passenger (if space is available) regarding last-minute changes in flight dates.

Business class and **first class** are both ideal for long-legged and well-heeled passengers who prefer wide, roomy comfort, free drinks, savory meals served on fine linen and china, and (in first class) extra-wide seats that convert into sleepers.

Other Good-Value Choices

Alitalia clusters the price of tickets to its destinations in Italy into four different zones, each centered around a major city—Milan, Rome, Naples, and Palermo. If you intend to fly from North America to local airports at, say, Genoa, Venice, Rimini, or any of the towns of Sardinia or Sicily, you can add on a connecting flight from the main airport of that region to a secondary airport within the same region without any additional charge. (Alitalia calls these "common-rated" fares, meaning that it costs no more to fly to Venice from New York than it would have cost to fly to Milan from New York). Considering the distance between Milan and Venice, or the distance from Rome to Pisa or Florence, and the extra expense you'd have encountered on the train or highway, it's an attractive offer.

And for students, or anyone aged 12 to 24, special extensions are granted on the length of time they can stay abroad. Alitalia's youth fare permits a stay abroad for up to 1 year. The round-trip high-season fare from New York to Rome is currently $1,008. With the year-long validity of the return half of the ticket, a North American student could, say, complete two full semesters at the University of Bologna and still fly home at a substantial savings over equivalent fares on some other airlines.

CONSOLIDATORS Tickets at consolidators (sometimes called "bucket shops") are frequently—but not always—up to 35% less than the full fare. Terms of payment can vary—anywhere from 45 days prior to departure to last-minute sales offered in a final attempt by an airline to fill an empty aircraft.

Since dealing with unknown consolidators might be a little risky, it's wise to call the Better Business Bureau in your area to see if complaints have been filed against the company from which you plan to purchase a ticket. Consolidators abound from coast to coast, but to get you started, here are a few listings:

In New York, try **TFI Tours International,** 34 W. 32nd St., 12th Floor, New York, NY 10001 (☎ **800/745-8000** in the U.S. outside New York State, or 212/736-1140 in New York State). This tour company offers services to 177 cities worldwide, including Rome.

For the Midwest, explore the possibilities of **Travel Avenue,** 10 S. Riverside Plaza, Suite 1404, Chicago, IL 60606 (☎ **800/333-3335** in the U.S.). Its tickets are often cheaper than at most consolidators, and it charges the customer only a $25 fee on international tickets, rather than taking the usual 10% commission from an airline. Travel Avenue rebates most of that commission back to the customers—hence, the lower fares.

Another possibility is **TMI (Travel Management International),** 3617 Dupont Ave. South, Minneapolis, MN 55409 (☎ **800/245-3672** in the U.S.), which offers a wide variety of discounts, including youth fares, student fares, and access to other kinds of air-related discounts as well. Among others, its destinations include Rome.

One of the biggest U.S. consolidators is **Travac,** 989 Ave. of the Americas, New York, NY 10018 (☎ **800/TRAV-800** in the U.S., or 212/563-3303), which offers discounted seats from the United States to most cities in Europe, including Rome, on airlines that include TWA, United, and Delta. Another branch office is at 2601 E. Jefferson St., Orlando, FL 32803 (☎ 407/896-0014).

UniTravel, 1177 N. Warson Rd., St. Louis, MO 63132 (☎ **800/325-2222** in the U.S.), offers tickets to Rome and elsewhere in Europe at prices that may or may not be lower than the regular fare, but it can provide discounts if you decide (or need) to get to Europe on short notice.

Another option, suitable only for clients with supremely flexible travel plans, is **Airhitch,** 2641 Broadway, 3rd Floor, New York, NY 10025 (☎ **800/326-2009** or 212/864-2000). You provide any 5 consecutive days in which you're available to fly and Airhitch agrees to find you a flight within those 5 days from a particular region in the United States (the Northeast, Southeast, Midwest, West Coast, or Northwest). It will attempt to fly you to and from the city of your choice, but makes no guarantees. One-way fares range from $169 to $269.

One final name for our list is **1-800-FLY-4-LESS,** RFA Building, 5440 Morehouse Dr., San Diego, CA 92121. Even if you're unable to buy tickets 3 weeks in advance, you can still use this service to obtain low discounted fares. 1-800-FLY-4-LESS specializes in finding only the lowest fares.

CHARTER FLIGHTS There's no way to predict whether a proposed flight to Rome will cost less on a charter or less through a bucket shop. You'll have to investigate at the time of your trip.

Some charter companies have proved unreliable in the past. Among the reliable charter-flight operators is **Council Charter,** 205 E. 42nd St., New York, NY 10017 (☎ **800/COUNCIL** in the U.S., or 212/661-1450). This company, run by the Council on International Educational Exchange, can arrange charter seats on regularly scheduled aircraft to most major European cities.

One of the biggest New York charter operators is **Travac,** 989 Ave. of the Americas, New York, NY 10018 (☎ **800/TRAV-800** in the U.S., or 212/563-3303).

TRAVEL CLUBS Another possibility for low-cost air travel is the travel club, which supplies an unsold inventory of tickets, offering discounts in the usual range of 20% to 60%.

After you pay an annual fee, you're given a hotline number to call to find out what discounts are available. Many of these discounts become available several days in advance of actual departure, sometimes as long as a week and sometimes as much as a month. Of course, you're limited to what's available, so you have to be fairly flexible.

Some of the best clubs are:

Moment's Notice, 7301 New Utrecht Ave., New York, NY 11228 (☎ **212/486-0500**), charges $25 per year for membership, which allows spur-of-the-moment participation in dozens of tours. Each is geared to impulse purchases and last-minute getaways, and each offers air and land packages that sometimes represent a substantial savings over what you'd have paid through more conventional channels. Although membership is required for participation in the tours, anyone can call the company's hotline (☎ **212/873-0908**) to learn what options are available. Most of the company's best-valued tours depart from New Jersey's Newark airport.

Sears Discount Travel Club, 3033 S. Parker Rd., Suite 900, Aurora, CO 80014 (☎ **800/433-9383** in the U.S.), offers members, for $50, a catalog (issued four times a year), maps, discounts at select hotels, and a limited guarantee that equivalent packages will not be undersold by any other travel organization. It also offers a 5% rebate on the value of all airline tickets, tours, hotels, and car rentals that are purchased through them. (To collect this rebate, you must fill out some forms and photocopy your receipts and itineraries.)

Encore Travel Club, 4501 Forbes Blvd., Lanham, MD 20706 (☎ **800/638-8976** in the U.S.), charges $49.95 a year for membership in a club which offers 50% discounts at more than 4,000 well-recognized hotels, sometimes during off-peak periods. It also offers substantial discounts on airfares, cruises, and car rentals through its volume-purchase plans. Membership includes a travel package outlining the company's many services and use of a toll-free phone number for advice and information.

A NOTE FOR BRITISH TRAVELERS A regular fare from the U.K. to Rome is extremely high, so savvy Brits usually call a travel agent for a "deal"—either a charter flight or some special air travel promotion. If one is not possible for you, then an APEX ticket might be the way to keep costs trimmed. These tickets must be reserved in advance, however they offer a discount without the usual booking restrictions. You might also ask the airlines about a "Eurobudget ticket," which has restrictions or length-of-stay requirements.

British newspapers are always full of classified advertisements touting "slashed" fares to Rome. One good source is *Time Out* magazine. London's *Evening Standard* has a daily travel section, and the Sunday editions of almost any newspaper will run many ads. Recommended companies include **Trailfinders** (☎ **0171/937-5400**). It offers access to tickets on such carriers as SAS, British Airways, and KLM.

In London, there are many **bucket shops** around Victoria and Earl's Court that offer low fares. Make sure that the company you deal with is a member of the IATA, ABTA, or ATOL. These umbrella organizations will help you out if anything goes wrong.

CEEFAX, a British television information service included on many home and hotel TVs, runs details of package holidays and flights to Europe, including Rome. Just switch to your CEEFAX channel and you'll find a menu of listings that includes travel information.

BY TRAIN

If you plan to travel heavily on the European and/or British railroads, you'll do well to secure the latest copy of the ***Thomas Cook European Timetable of Railroads.*** This comprehensive, 500+-page timetable documents all of Europe's mainline passenger rail services with detail and accuracy. It's available exclusively in North America from **Forsyth Travel Library,** P.O. Box 2975, Shawnee Mission, KS 66201 (☎ **800/FORSYTH**), at a cost of $24.95 plus $4.50 postage (priority airmail in the U.S.; U.S. $4.50 for shipments to Canada).

Train from the U.K. Many different rail passes are available in the U.K. for travel in Europe. Stop in at the **International Rail Centre,** Victoria Station, London SW1V 1JY (☎ **0171/834-2345**), or **Wasteels,** 121 Wilton Rd., London SW1V 1JZ (☎ **0171/834-7066**). They can help you find the best option for the trip you're planning. Some of the most popular passes, including Inter-Rail and EuroYouth, are only for travelers under 26 years of age, entitling them to unlimited second-class travel in 26 European countries.

Eurotrain "Explorer" tickets are another worthwhile option for travelers who can show proof that they're under 26. These allow you to move in a leisurely fashion from London to Rome, with as many stopovers as you want, and a different route southbound (through Belgium, Luxembourg, and Switzerland) from the return route northbound (exclusively through France). All travel must be completed within 2 months of the date of departure. Such a ticket sells for £195 round-trip.

Persons under 26 who want to travel from London to Rome as quickly and directly as possible pay £153 round-trip for a ticket allowing no stopovers. The cost of either of these tickets includes ferryboat transport across the Channel. **Campus Travel,** 52 Grosvenor Gardens, London SW1W OAG (☎ **0171/730-3402**), can give you prices and help you book tickets.

EURAILPASS Many travelers to Europe take advantage of one of its greatest travel bargains, the **Eurailpass,** which permits unlimited first-class rail travel in any country in Western Europe except the British Isles, and also includes Hungary in Eastern Europe. Oddly, it does *not* include travel on the rail lines of Sardinia, which are organized independently of the rail lines of the rest of Italy. Passes are for periods as short as 15 days or as long as 3 months.

Here's how it works: The pass is sold only in North America. Adults can purchase a pass for unlimited first-class travel lasting 15 days for $522, 21 days for $678, 1 month for $838, 2 months for $1,148, or 3 months for $1,468. Children under 4 travel free providing they don't occupy a seat (otherwise, they're charged half fare); children under 12 travel for half fare. If you're under 26, you can purchase a **Eurail Youthpass,** which entitles you to unlimited second-class travel for 15 days for $418, 1 month for $598, or 2 months for $798.

Travel agents in all towns, and railway agents in such major cities as New York, Montréal, and Los Angeles, sell all these tickets. A Eurailpass is available at the North American offices of CIT Travel Service, the French National Railroads, the German Federal Railroads, and the Swiss Federal Railways.

The **Eurail Saverpass** is a money-saving ticket for groups (three or more people traveling together between April and September; two or more people between October and March). The price of a Saverpass, valid all over Europe, good for first class only, is $452 per person for 15 days, $578 per person for 21 days, and $712 per person for 1 month.

The **Eurail Flexipass** allows passengers to visit Europe with more flexibility. For adults, it's valid in first class and provides a number of individual travel days that can be used over a much longer period of time. That makes it possible to stay in one city and yet not lose a single day of travel. There are two passes: 10 days of travel within 2 months for $616, and 15 days of travel within 2 months for $812. For those under age 26, the **Youth Flexipass,** which operates the same way but in second class, offers 10 days within 2 months for $438 and 15 days within 2 months for $588.

BY CAR

If you're already on the Continent, particularly in a neighboring country such as France or Austria, you may want to drive to Rome. However, arrange this in advance with your car-rental company.

It's also possible to drive from London to Rome, a distance of 1,124 miles via Calais/Boulogne/Dunkirk or 1,085 miles via Oostende/Zeebrugge, not counting Channel crossings. You can cross over from England to France using either one of the ferries or the Chunnel. Once you arrive on the northern coast of France by whatever mode of transport you selected, you still face a 24-hour drive to Rome. Most drivers play it safe and budget a leisurely 3 days for the journey.

Impressions

Chi Asino va a Roma, Asino se ne torna. (If an Asse at Rome doe sojourne. As Asse he shall from thence returne.)

—Fynes Moryson, "Of Travelling in General," an itinerary

Most of the roads from Western Europe leading into Italy are toll free, with some notable exceptions. If you use the Swiss superhighway network, you'll have to purchase a special tax sticker at the frontier. You'll also pay to go through the St. Gotthard Tunnel into Italy. Crossings from France are through the Mont Blanc Tunnel, for which you'll pay, or you can leave the French Riviera at Menton (France) and drive directly into Italy along the Italian Riviera heading toward San Remo.

If you don't want to drive such distances, ask a travel agent to book you on a Motorail arrangement where the train carries your car. This service, however, is good only to Milan, as there are no car-and-sleeper expresses running the 390 or so miles south to Rome.

ORGANIZED TOURS

Although a sampling of the best-rated tour companies follows, you should consult a good travel agent for advice.

Perillo Tours, 577 Chestnut Ridge Rd., Woodcliff Lake, NJ 07675-9888 (☎ **800/431-1515** in the U.S., or 201/307-1234), was established in 1945 and has sent more than a million travelers to Italy in comfort. As one of the world's largest Italy tour operators, it uses more first-class hotel rooms in Italy than any other company in America. Known and well respected for the value it offers, Perillo's tours cost much less than the assembled elements of each tour if each component had been arranged separately.

Perillo operates hundreds of departures year round. Between April and October, nine different itineraries, ranging from 8 to 15 days each, cover broadly different regions of the peninsula. Between November and April, the "Off-Season Italy" tour covers three of Italy's premier cities, including Rome. All tours include airfare from North America (usually on TWA), overnight accommodation in first-class hotels, breakfast and (in all but a few cases) dinner daily, and all baggage handling and taxes. Also included are all sightseeing fees, transfers, and tours by deluxe motorcoach (most with their own lavatory). Tours range from around $1,499 per person, for one of the off-season short tours, to around $3,259 for a deluxe tour to Rome, Florence, and Venice in what some visitors consider the ideal season, September. (Dinners are not included on this particular tour.)

Another contender for the package-tour business in Italy is **Italiatour,** a member of the Alitalia Group (☎ **800/845-3365** in the U.S., or 212/765-2183), which offers a widely varied selection of tours through all parts of the peninsula. The company's strongest appeal is to the free-at-heart (that is, clients who don't want any semblance of a tour at all). Catering to the reluctance of many travelers to commit themselves too rigidly to group travel in a bus, the company specializes in tours for independent travelers who ride from one destination to another by train or by rental car. It offers a wide choice of loosely structured itineraries to Italy's best-known cities, including Rome. In most cases the company sells prereserved hotel accommodations that, because of volume purchases, are usually less expensive than what you'd pay if you had reserved yourself. With any of these tours, there's a strong incentive to book air passage from North America at the same time as the hotel nights, but because of the company's close link with Alitalia, the prices quoted for air passage are sometimes among the most reasonable on the retail market. Repeat travelers to Italy sometimes opt for one of the fly-drive programs, where discounted prices on rental cars are combined with airfare from North America.

Italiatour's longest offering is a loosely supervised 8-day jaunt through the major art cities of Italy, with accommodations in luxury hotels. Prices begin at $1,349 per person. Airfare is included, as well as hotel accommodations (double occupancy), breakfasts, transfers between cities, some city tours, and a gondola ride in Venice.

Getting to Know Rome

This chapter will provide what you need to know to settle into Rome, from arriving at the airport and the basic city layout to driving rules and how to use the busses. There's a quick breakdown of neighborhoods to help you figure out where you'll want to base yourself, and that will help organize and orient all the hotels, restaurants, and sights in the following chapters. We'll round it off with a list of "Fast Facts"—everything from embassies and English-speaking doctors to how to tip people and make a phone call.

1 Orientation

ARRIVING

BY PLANE Chances are that you'll arrive in Italy at Rome's **Leonardo da Vinci International Airport** (☎ **06/65951,** or 06/6595-3640 for information), popularly known as Fiumicino, 18½ miles from the center of the capital. (If you're flying by charter, you might arrive at Ciampino Airport; see below.)

After leaving Passport Control, two information desks—one for Rome, one for Italy—come into view. At the Rome desk you can pick up a general (not a detailed) map and some pamphlets Monday to Saturday from 8:30am to 7pm. A *cambio* (currency exchange) operates daily from 7:30am to 11pm. Luggage storage, in the main arrivals building and open daily, costs 5,000L ($3.20) per bag.

To get into the city, follow the signs marked TRENI for the shuttle service directly to the main rail station, Stazione Termini (arriving on Track 22). It runs between 7am and 10pm for 13,000L ($8.30) one-way. A local train, costing 7,000L ($4.50), also runs between the airport and Tiburtina Station, from which you can go the rest of the way to Termini by subway Line B, costing another 1,000L (65¢).

Should you arrive on a charter flight at **Ciampino** (☎ **06/79461**), take a COTRAL bus, departing every 30 minutes or so, which will deliver you to the Anagnina stop of Metropolitana (subway) Line A. Take Linea A to Stazione Termini where your final connections can be made. Trip time is about 45 minutes, and the cost is 2,000L ($1.30).

Taxis from Fiumicino are quite expensive—70,000L ($44.80) and up—and therefore not recommended for the trip from the airport. If you arrive at Ciampino, you're closer to the city, only about a half-hour ride, but the fare still averages 70,000L ($44.80) into the heart of Rome.

BY TRAIN Trains arrive in the center of old Rome at the **Stazione Termini,** Piazza dei Cinquecento (☎ **06/4775**), the train and subway transportation hub for all of Rome, surrounded by many, especially cheaper, hotels.

If you're taking the Metropolitana (Rome's subway network), follow the illuminated red M signs. To catch a bus, go straight through the outer hall of the Termini and enter the sprawling bus lot of Piazza dei Cinquecento. You'll also find taxis here (see "Getting Around," later in this chapter, for details on public transportation).

The Termini is filled with services. At a branch of the Banca Nazionale delle Communicazioni (between Tracks 8–11 and Tracks 12–15) you can exchange money. Informazioni Ferroviarie (in the outer hall) dispenses information on rail travel to other parts of Italy. There's also a tourist information booth here, along with baggage services, barbershops, gift shops, restaurants, and bars. But beware of pickpockets, perhaps quick-fingered young children. The station is also home to the Albergo Diurno (☎ 06/481-9887), a hotel without beds but with baths, showers, and well-kept toilet facilities that's open daily from 7am to 8pm.

BY BUS Arrivals are at the **Stazione Termini** (see "By Train," above). Information on buses is dispensed at a booth operated by ATAC, the city bus company, at Piazza dei Cinquecento, which is open daily from 7:30am to 7:30pm. For information, call 06/469-5444.

BY CAR From the north, the main access route is **A1 (Autostrada del Sole),** cutting through Milan and Florence, or you can take the coastal route, SSI Aurelia, from Genoa. If you're driving north from Naples, you take the southern lap of the **Autostrada del Sole, A2.** All these autostrade join with the **Grande Raccordo Anulare,** a ring road that encircles Rome, channeling traffic into the congested city. Long before you reach this ring road, you should study a map carefully to see what part of Rome you plan to enter and mark your route accordingly. Route markings along the ring road tend to be confusing.

VISITOR INFORMATION

Tourist information is available at the **Ente Provinciale per il Turismo,** Via Parigi 5, 00185 Roma (☎ **06/4889-9200**), open Monday to Saturday from 8:15am to 7pm. The information dispensed here is meager. There's another information bureau at the Stazione Termini (☎ **06/487-1270**), open daily from 8:15am to 7:15pm.

Rome also operates a trio of **Info-Tourism "Boxes,"** kiosks in the historic center set up in trailers where multilingual clerks will provide brochures and tourist maps and, even better, can answer just about any question you have—from sights and attractions to hotels and restaurants—with the aid of an extensive computer database. You can find these boxes on Largo Carlo Goldoni (☎ **06/687-5027**), off Via del Corso, across from Via dei Condotti; on Via Nazionale (☎ **06/474-5929**), near the Palazzo delle Esposizioni; and on Largo Corrado Ricci (☎ **06/678-0992**), near the Colosseum. All three are open Tuesday to Saturday from 10am to 6pm and on Sunday from 10am to 1pm.

CITY LAYOUT

The drive in to the city is rather uneventful until you pass through the remarkably intact **Great Aurelian Wall,** started in A.D. 271 to calm Rome's barbarian jitters. Suddenly, ruins of imperial baths loom on one side and great monuments can be seen in the middle of blocks. Inside the walls you'll find a city designed for a population

Impressions

All roads lead to Rome.

—Traditional

that walked to get where it was going. Parts of Rome actually look and feel more like an oversize village than the former imperial capital of the Western world.

The Termini faces a huge piazza, **Piazza dei Cinquecento,** named after 500 Italians who died heroically in a 19th-century battle in Africa.

The bulk of ancient, Renaissance, and baroque Rome (as well as the train station) is on the east side of the **Tiber River (Fiume Tevere),** which meanders through town between 19th-century stone embankments. However, several important monuments are on the other side: **St. Peter's Basilica** and the **Vatican;** the **Castel Sant'Angelo** (formerly the tomb of the emperor Hadrian), and the colorful **Trastevere** neighborhood.

The various quarters of the city are linked by large boulevards (large at least in some places) that have mostly been laid out since the late 19th century. Starting from the **Victor Emmanuel monument,** a highly controversial pile of snow-white Brescian marble, there's a street running practically due north to **Piazza del Popolo** and the city wall. This is **Via del Corso,** one of the main streets of Rome—noisy, congested, always crowded with buses and shoppers, called simply "Il Corso." To its left (west) lie the Pantheon, Piazza Navona, Campo de' Fiori, and the Tiber River. To its right (east) you'll find the Spanish Steps, Trevi Fountain, Borghese Gardens, and Via Veneto. Back at the the Vittorio Emmanuele monument, the major artery going west (and ultimately across the Tiber to St. Peter's) is **Corso Vittorio Emanuele.** Behind you to your right, heading toward the Colosseum, is **Via dei Fori Imperiali,** laid out in the 1930s by Mussolini to show off the ruins of imperial forums he had excavated that line it on either side. Yet another central conduit is **Via Nazionale,** running from **Piazza Venezia** (just in front of the Vittorio Emmanuele monument) east to **Piazza della Repubblica** (near the Termini). The final lap of Via Nazionale is called Via Quattro Novembre.

FINDING AN ADDRESS Finding an address in Rome can be a problem because of the narrow streets of old Rome and the little, sometimes hidden *piazze* (squares). Numbers usually run consecutively, with odd numbers on one side of the street and even numbers on the other. However, in the old districts the numbers will sometimes run consecutively up one side of the street to the end, then back in the opposite direction on the other side. Therefore, no. 50 could be opposite no. 308.

STREET MAPS Arm yourself with a detailed street map, not the general overview handed out free at tourist offices. You'll need a detailed map even to find such attractions as the Trevi Fountain. The best ones are published by **Falk,** available at most newsstands. The best selections of maps are sold in bookstores (see "Shopping A to Z" in Chapter 8).

TRAFFIC For the 2¹/₂ millennia before the modern wide boulevards were built, the citizens had to make their way through narrow byways and curves that defeated all but the best senses of direction. These streets—among the most charming aspects of the city—still exist in large quantities, mostly unspoiled by the advances of modern construction. However, this tangled street plan has one troublesome element: automobiles. The traffic in Rome is awful! When the claustrophobic street plans of the Dark Ages open unexpectedly onto a vast piazza, every driver accelerates full

Rome Orientation

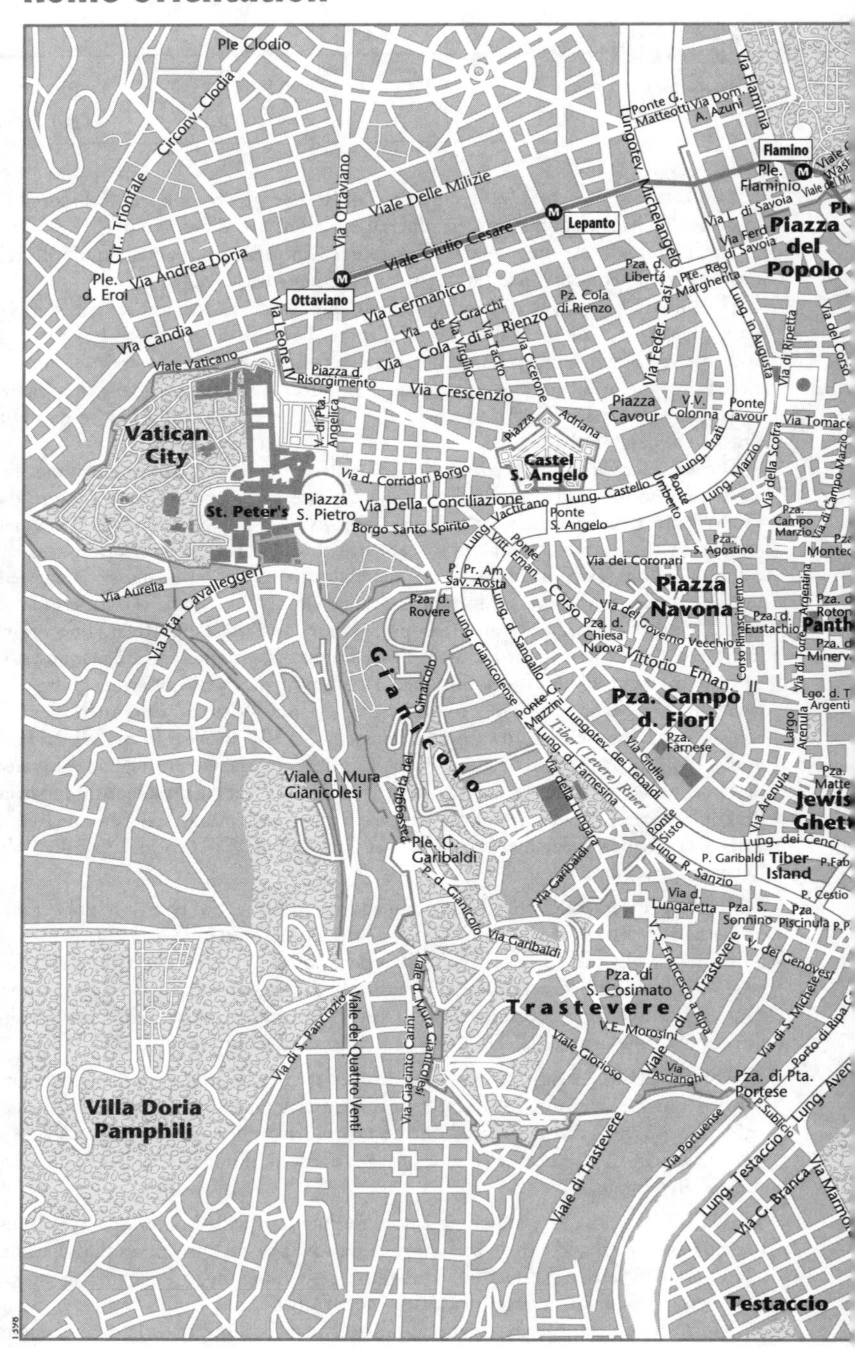

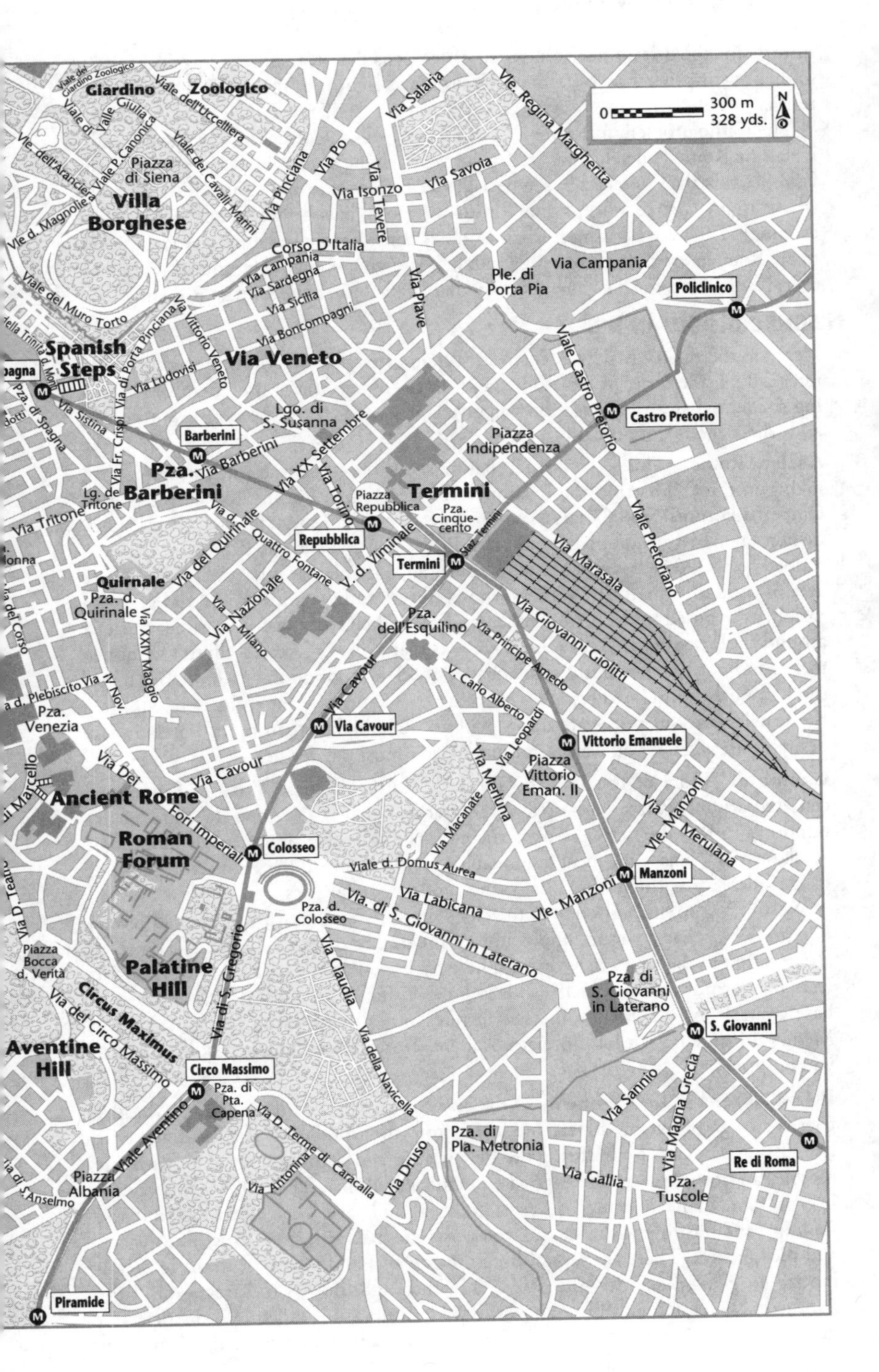

Giardino Zoologico
Villa Borghese
Piazza di Siena
Spanish Steps
Via Veneto
Pza. Barberini
Quirinale
Termini
Ancient Rome
Roman Forum
Palatine Hill
Aventine Hill
Circus Maximus
Barberini
Repubblica
Termini
Castro Pretorio
Policlinico
Via Cavour
Vittorio Emanuele
Colosseo
Manzoni
S. Giovanni
Circo Massimo
Re di Roma
Piramide
300 m
328 yds.
Via Salaria
Vle. Regina Margherita
Via Po
Via Tevere
Via Isonzo
Via Savoia
Via Pinciana
Corso D'Italia
Via Campania
Via Sardegna
Via Sicilia
Via Boncompagni
Via Piave
Ple. di Porta Pia
Viale Castro Pretorio
Viale del Muro Torto
Via Vittorio Veneto
Via Ludovisi
Via Sistina
Via Barberini
Via XX Settembre
Via Torino
Lgo. di S. Susanna
Piazza Repubblica
Piazza Indipendenza
Pza. Cinquecento
Via Marsala
Viale Pretoriano
Via Tritone
Via del Quirinale
Via Nazionale
Via d. Quattro Fontane
V. d. Viminale
Pza. d. Quirinale
Via XXIV Maggio
Pza. dell'Esquilino
Via Giovanni Giolitti
Via Principe Amedeo
V. Carlo Alberto
Via Leopardi
Via Merulana
Piazza Vittorio Eman. II
Via Manzoni
Vle. Manzoni
Pza. Venezia
Via Cavour
Via Dei Fori Imperiali
Viale d. Domus Aurea
Via Labicana
Via. di S. Giovanni in Laterano
Pza. d. Colosseo
Via Claudia
Pza. di S. Giovanni in Laterano
Via di S. Gregorio
Via del Circo Massimo
Piazza Bocca d. Verità
Pza. di Pta. Capena
Via della Navicella
Via D. Terme di Caracalla
Via Antonina
Viale Aventino
Piazza Albania
Via Druso
Pza. di Pla. Metronia
Via Gallia
Via Sannio
Via Magna Grecia
Pza. Tuscole

throttle for the distant horizon, while pedestrians flatten themselves against marble fountains for protection or stride with firm jaws right into the thick of the howling traffic.

The traffic problem in Rome is nothing new. Julius Caesar was so exasperated by it that he banned all vehicular traffic during daylight hours. Sometimes it's actually faster to walk than to take a bus, especially during any of Rome's four daily rush hours (that's right, *four:* to work, home for lunch/riposo, back to work, and home in the evening). The hectic crush of urban Rome is considerably less during August, when many Romans are out of town on holiday. If you visit at any other time of year, however, be prepared for the general frenzy that characterizes the average Roman street.

Neighborhoods in Brief

Here are the main districts of interest, spiraling roughly out from the ancient center, through the heart of old Rome, and on to some of the more interesting outlying residential areas. This section will give you some idea of where you want to stay and where the major attractions are.

Ancient Rome This is the district that most visitors come to Rome to explore first, taking in the Colosseum, the Palatine Hill, the Roman Forum, the Fori Imperiali (Imperial Forums), and Circus Maximus. It forms part of the *centro storico* or historic district (along with Campo de' Fiori and Piazza Navona and the Pantheon, both described below), which with its narrow streets and airy piazzas is the accommodations area of choice for the many visitors who prefer its antique atmosphere and great location, as opposed to the uglier, duller, and more dangerous districts such as the area around the Termini. If you anchor here—as many do—you can walk to the monuments and not hassle with the inadequate public transportation of Rome. But here's the bad news: Hotel owners are well aware that tourists want to be here, and, for the privilege, room prices are often 30% to 50% higher than other hotels in less desirable areas. So if you want atmosphere, you must pay for it.

Campo de' Fiori & the Jewish Ghetto South of Corso Vittorio Emanuele, centered around Piazza Farnese and the market square of Campo de' Fiori, many buildings in this district were constructed in Renaissance times as private homes. Walk on Via Giulia—the most fashionable street in Rome in the 16th century—with its antiques stores, interesting hotels, and modern art galleries.

West of Via Arenula lies one of the city's most intriguing districts, the old Jewish Ghetto, which has far more opportunities for dining than for lodgings. The Jews, about 8,000 at the time, were ordered here by Pope Paul IV in 1556, and the walls were not torn down until 1849. This is another one of the most desirable places to base yourself in Rome, close to many attractions, although we think Ancient and Medieval Rome have a lot more atmosphere. Nevertheless, hoteliers still sock it to you on prices.

Piazza Navona & the Pantheon One of the most alluring areas of Rome, this district is a maze of narrow streets and alleys from the Middle Ages and is filled with churches and palaces built during the Renaissance and baroque eras, often with rare marbles and other materials stripped from ancient Rome. The only way to explore it is on foot. Its nerve center is Piazza Navona, built over the emperor Domitian's stadium, and bustling with sidewalk cafés, *palazzi* (palaces), street artists, musicians, and pickpockets. There are several hotels in the area and plenty of trattorie. Rivaling it—in general activity, the café scene, and nightlife—is the area around the Pantheon, which remains from ancient Roman times surrounded by a district built much later (this "pagan" temple was turned into a church and rescued, whereas the buildings that once surrounded it are long gone). If you'd like to anchor in Medieval Rome, you face the same 30% to 50% increase in hotel prices as you do for Ancient Rome.

Piazza di Spagna & Piazza del Popolo Ever since the 17th century the Spanish Steps—former site of the Spanish ambassador's residence—have been the center of tourist Rome. Keats lived in a house opening onto the steps, and some of Rome's most prestigious shopping streets fan out from it, including Via Condotti. The most elegant address here is the Hassler, one of Rome's grandest hotels. If you want to sleep in the hippest part of town, you must be willing to part with a lot of extra lire. This area of Rome joins with Ancient and Medieval Rome in charging some of the capital's highest prices, not only for hotels, but for restaurants, designer silk suits, and leather loafers. The area extends to the Tiber and Augustus's Mausoleum and up the Corso to Piazza del Popolo, the northern anchor of tourist Rome.

Via Veneto & Piazza Barberini In the 1950s and early 1960s this was the haunt of the *dolce vita* set, as the likes of King Farouk and Swedish actress Anita Ekberg paraded up and down Via Vittorio Veneto to the delight of the *paparazzi*. The street is still there, still the site of luxury hotels and elegant cafés and restaurants, although it no longer has the allure it did in its heyday. Rome city authorities would like to restore this legendary street to some of its former glory. Frank Sinatra and Elizabeth Taylor may never stroll it again, but Rome is trying to spruce up Via Veneto by banning vehicular traffic on the top half of the street. The bottom half empties into Piazza Barberini, a confluence of many major avenues and a metro stop watched over by Bernini's Triton Fountain.

Around Termini The main train station adjoins Piazza della Repubblica, and for many, this will be your introduction to Rome. Much of the area is seedy and filled with gas fumes from all the buses and cars, but there's still much here to see, including the Basilica di Santa Maria Maggiore and the Baths of Diocletian. Although this is one of the least desirable places to stay in Rome—and also one of the most dangerous because of muggings—it's also the cheapest. There are some high-class hotels in the area, including the Grand, but many are long past their heyday. The area directly south of the Termini is traffic-noisy, people-bustling, and seedier than the district to the north. Even though the hotel prices are lower, there's still much overcharging—if innkeepers think they can get away with it. The best *pensioni* and hotels lie north of the Termini, within a 15-minute walk. Many of these hotels are rundown and in dire need of major renovation, although some have recently been improved. There is talk of a "renaissance" for the area.

The Appian Way Via Appia Antica is a 2,300-year-old road that has witnessed much of the history of the ancient world. By 190 B.C. it extended from Rome to Brindisi on the southeastern coast, and its most famous sights today are the catacombs, the graveyards of patrician families (despite what it says in *Quo Vadis?*, they were not used as a place for Christians to hide out while fleeing persecution). This is one of the most history-rich areas of Rome to explore—but don't go there seeking a hotel. There are several restaurants, however.

Testaccio The emperor Nero ordered that Rome's thousands of broken amphoras and terra-cotta roof tiles be stacked in a designated pile to the east of the Tiber, just west of Pyramide and today's Ostiense Railway Station. Over the centuries the mound rose to 200 feet, then compacted to form the centerpiece for one of the city's most unusual neighborhoods. Bordered by the Protestant cemetery, Testaccio is home to restaurants with *very* Roman cuisine (see Chapter 5, "Dining").

Trastevere This is the most authentic district of Rome, lying "across the Tiber," and its people are of mixed ancestry, including Jewish, Roman, and Greek, and speak their own dialect. The area centers around the ancient Churches of Santa Cecilia in Trastevere and Santa Maria in Trastevere. Home to many young expatriates, the district after World War II became a gathering place for hedonists and bohemians. It has been called the last of the capital's old *rioni* (neighborhoods). There are those who speak of it as a "city within a city"—or at least a village within a city. It's said that the language is rougher and the cuisine spicier, and although Trastevere doesn't have the glamorous hotels of central Rome, it does have some of the last remaining and authentic Roman dining. Trastevere used to be a bastion of the budget traveler, but foreigners from virtually anywhere have been buying real estate en masse here, so change is in the air.

Around Vatican City Vatican City is a small city-state, but its influence extends around the world. The Vatican museums and St. Peter's take up most of the land area, and the popes have lived here for six centuries. However, you may not prefer to follow their example. Although the neighborhhod contains some good hotels (and several bad ones), it's somewhat removed from the more happening scene of Ancient or Renaissance Rome, and getting to and from it can be time-consuming. Also, the area is rather dull at night and contains few of Rome's finer restaurants. Vatican City and its surrounding area is best for exploring during the day.

Prati Known only to the connoisseurs of Rome, this district is really a 19th-century middle-class suburb north of the Vatican. It's becoming increasingly patronized by budget travelers because of its low-cost *pensioni* (boarding houses). The Trionfale flower-and-food market itself is worth the trip. The area also abounds in less expensive shopping streets than those found in central Rome. If safety is a main concern for you, Prati is a more tranquil district, usually devoid of the pickpockets and thieves who prey on tourists in Ancient Rome and around the Termini.

Parioli The most elegant residential section of Rome, framed by the green spaces of Villa Borghese to the south and Villa Glori and Villa Ada to the north. It's a setting for some of the city's finest restaurants, hotels, and nightclubs. It's not the most central, however, and staying here can be a hassle if you're dependent on public transportation. Parioli lies adjacent to the Prati but across the Tiber to the east, and, like Prati, is one of the safer districts of Rome.

Monte Mario The northwestern precinct of the city, Monte Mario is the site of the deluxe Cavalieri Hilton, where you can stop in for a drink and the panorama of Rome. If you plan to spend a lot of time shopping and sightseeing in the heart of Rome, it's a difficult and often expensive commute. The area lies north of Prati, away from the hustle and bustle (and in summer, the heat) of central Rome. Take bus no. 913 from the Spanish Steps to the district's heart, Piazzale Maresciallo Giardino.

EUR Originally built under the Fascist regime in hopes of hosting a World's Fair, this cold micro-city of white granite—Mussolini was trying to invoke the look and glory of ancient Rome—was rehabilitated after World War II to become both a government administrative headquarters and a rather deluxe apartment suburb. Today it's of interest mainly as an architectural oddity, and for its Museum of Roman Civilization, which houses a scale model of what ancient Rome looked like at the height of its imperial power.

2 Getting Around

BY PUBLIC TRANSPORTATION

SUBWAY The **Metropolitana,** or **Metro** for short, is the fastest means of transportation in Rome. It has two underground lines: Line A (Linea A) runs between Via Ottaviano, near St. Peter's, and Anagnina, stopping at Piazzale Flaminio (near Piazza del Popolo), Piazza di Spagna, Piazza Vittorio Emanuele, and Piazza San Giovanni in Laterano. Line B (Linea B) connects the Rebibbia district with Via Laurentina, stopping at Via Cavour, Stazione Termini, the Colosseum, Circus Maximus, the Pyramid, St. Paul's Outside the Walls, and EUR. A big red letter M indicates the entrance to the subway.

Tickets are 1,500L (95¢), and are available from vending machines at all stations. These machines accept 50-, 100-, and 200-lire coins, and some of them take 1,000-lire notes. Some stations have managers, but they don't make change. Booklets of tickets (*carnet*) are available at tobacco shops (*tabacchi*) and in some terminals.

Building an underground system for Rome has not been easy, since every time workers start digging, they discover an old temple or other archeological treasure and heavy earth-moving has to cease for a while.

BUS/TRAM Roman buses are operated by **Azienda Tramvie e Autobus del Commune di Roma (ATAC),** Via Volturno 65 (☎ **06/4695-4444** for information).

For only 1,500L (95¢) you can ride to most parts of Rome on quite good bus service. The ticket is valid for 1 hour and 15 minutes, and you can get on many buses during that time period using the same ticket. At the Stazione Termini you can purchase a special **tourist bus pass,** costing 6,000L ($3.85) for 1 day or 24,000L ($15.35) for a week. This allows you to ride on the ATAC network without bothering to purchase individual tickets. The tourist pass is also valid on the subway—but never ride the trains when the Romans are going to or from work or you'll be mashed flatter than fettuccine. On the first bus you board, you place your ticket in a small machine that prints the day and hour you boarded. And you do the same on the last bus you take during the validity period of the ticket.

Buses and trams stop at areas marked FERMATA. At most of these, a yellow sign will display the bus numbers that stop there, and then lists of all the stops along each bus's route in order, so you can easily search out your destination. In general they're in service from 6am to midnight daily. After that and until dawn, you can ride on special night buses (they have an "N" in front of their bus number), which only run on main routes. It's best to take a taxi in the wee hours—if you can find one.

At the bus information booth at Piazza dei Cinquecento, in front of the Stazione Termini, you can purchase a directory complete with maps summarizing the particular routes. Ask there about where to purchase bus tickets, or buy them in a *tabacchi* or at a bus terminal. You must have your ticket before boarding the bus, as there are no ticket-issuing machines on the vehicles.

Take extreme caution riding the overcrowded buses of Rome pick-pockets abound! This is particularly true on bus no. 64, a favorite of tourists because of its route through Rome's historic districts, and thus also a favorite of Rome's vast pickpocketing community. Bus no. 64 has earned various nicknames: "The Pickpocket Express" or "The Wallet Eater." Take heed—planned modification of the city bus lines may create a bit of pandemonium throughout 1997 and 1998.

BY TAXI

If you're accustomed to hopping a cab in New York or London, then do so in Rome. If not, take less expensive means of transport. Avoid paying your fare with large bills—invariably, taxi drivers claim they don't have change, hoping for a bigger tip (only give about 15%). Don't count on hailing a taxi on the street or even getting one at a stand. If you're going out, have your hotel call one. At a restaurant, ask the waiter or cashier to dial for you. If you want to phone for yourself, try one of these numbers: 6645, 3570, or 4994.

The meter begins at 6,400L ($4.10) for the first 3 kilometers, then adds 300L (20¢) per kilometer. Every suitcase is 500L (30¢) extra, and on Sunday a 5,000-lire ($3.20) supplement is assessed, plus another 2,000-lire ($1.30) supplement from 10pm to 7am.

BY CAR

RENTING A CAR Renting a car is easy. All drivers in Rome must have nerves of steel, a sense of humor, a valid driver's license, and a valid passport, and in most cases they must be between the ages of 21 and 70. In all cases, payment and paperwork are simple if you present valid credit or charge cards with your completed rental contract. If that isn't possible, a substantial cash deposit will probably be required in advance. Insurance on all vehicles is compulsory in Italy. A *carta verde* ("green card") is valid for 15, 30, or 45 days and should be issued to cover your car before your trip to Italy. Beyond 45 days you must have a regular Italian insurance policy.

You'll find a bewildering assortment of car-rental kiosks at the airports and railway stations of Rome, and agencies are also located downtown. **Hertz** has its main office near the parking lot of the Villa Borghese, Via Vittorio Veneto 156 (☎ **06/321-6831**). The **Budget** headquarters are at Via Ludovisi 60 (☎ **06/482-0966**). ☎ **Maggiore,** an Italian company, has an office at Via di Tor Cervara (☎ **06/229351**).

DRIVING & PARKING All roads may lead to Rome if you're driving, but don't count on much driving once you get there. Since reception desks of most Roman hotels have at least one English-speaking person, it's wise to call ahead to find out the best route into Rome from wherever you're starting out.

Find out if the hotel has a garage. If not, you're usually allowed to park your car in front of the hotel long enough to unload your luggage. Someone at the hotel—a doorman, if there is one—will direct you to the nearest garage or place to park.

To the neophyte, Roman driving will appear like the chariot race in *Ben Hur.* When the light turns green, go forth with caution. Many Roman drivers are still going through the light even though it has turned red. Roman drivers in traffic gridlock move bravely on, fighting for every inch of the road until they can free themselves from the tangled mess. To complicate matters, many zones, such as that around Piazza di Spagna, are traffic-free, and other traffic-free zones are being tried out in various parts of the city.

It's virtually impossible—an act of sheer madness, really—to drive around in Rome. But if you plan to take many excursions from the city—for example, into the hill towns—you'll find a car a most reliable and convenient means of transport.

In other words, try to get your car into Rome as safely as possible, park it, and proceed on foot or by public transportation from then on.

BY BICYCLE, MOTORSCOOTER & MOTORCYCLE

St. Peter Moto Renting & Selling, Via di Porto Castello 43 (☎ **06/6880-4608**), open Monday to Saturday from 9am to 7pm, rents mopeds. Rates range upward from

Impressions

At Florence, you think; at Rome, you pray; at Venice, you love; at Naples, you look.

—Italian proverb, quoted By Maurice Baring in *Round the World in Any Number of Days* (1913)

40,000L ($25.60) per day. Take the Metro to Ottaviano. Another agency that provides mopeds is **Happy Rent,** conveniently located at Piazza Esquilino 8H (☎ **06/481-8185**), 300 yards from the Stazione Termini. Most mopeds cost 40,000L ($25.60) per hour or 60,000L ($38.40) for the entire day. Mopeds are delivered to your hotel free. Happy Rent also offers several guided moped tours of Rome and the surrounding area. It's open Monday to Saturday from 9am to 7pm.

Bicycles are rented at many places throughout Rome. Ask at your hotel for the nearest rental location, or go to **I Bike Rome,** Via Vittorio Veneto 156 (☎ **06/322-5240**), which rents bicycles from the underground parking garage at the Villa Borghese. Most bikes cost 5,000L ($3.20) per hour or 13,000L ($8.30) per day. Mountain bikes rent for 7,000L ($4.50) per hour or 18,000L ($11.50) per day. It's open daily from 9am to 7pm.

ON FOOT

Much of the inner core of Rome is traffic-free—so you'll need to walk whether you like it or not. Walking is the perfect way to see the ancient narrow cobbled streets of Old Rome. However, in many parts of the city it's hazardous and uncomfortable because of overcrowded streets, heavy traffic, and very narrow sidewalks. Sometimes sidewalks don't exist at all, and it becomes a sort of free-for-all with pedestrians competing for space against vehicular traffic (the traffic always seems to win). For such a large city, Rome can be covered on foot because so much of what will interest a visitor lies in various clusters.

FAST FACTS: Rome

American Express The offices of American Express are at Piazza di Spagna 38 (☎ 06/67641). The travel service and tour desk are open Monday to Friday from 9am to 5:30pm and on Saturday from 9am to 12:30pm (May to October the tour desk is also open on Saturday afternoon from 2 to 2:30pm). The financial and mail services are open Monday to Friday from 9am to 5pm and on Saturday from 9am to noon.

Area Code The telephone area code for Rome and its environs is 06 (drop the "0" when calling Rome from outside Italy).

Bookstores See "Shopping A to Z" in Chapter 8.

Business Hours In general, **banks** are open Monday to Friday from 8:30am to 1:30pm and 3 to 4pm. Two U.S. banks in Rome are Chase Manhattan Bank, Via Michele Mercati 39 (☎ 06/809761), and Citibank, Via Bruxelles 61 (☎ 06/478171). **Shopping** hours are governed by the *riposo* (siesta). Most stores are open year round Monday to Saturday from 9am to 1pm and then from 3:30 or 4pm to 7:30 or 8pm. Most shops are closed Sunday.

Car Rentals See "Getting Around," earlier in this chapter.

Climate See "When to Go" in Chapter 2.

Crime See "Safety," below.

Currency Exchange This is possible at all major rail and airline terminals in Rome, including the Stazione Termini, where the *cambio* (exchange booth) beside the rail information booth is open daily from 8am to 8pm. At some cambi you'll have to pay commissions, often 1.5%. Banks, likewise, often charge commissions. Many so-called moneychangers will approach you on the street, but often they're pushing counterfeit lire—however, they offer very good rates for their fake money!

Dentist To secure a dentist who speaks English, call the U.S. Embassy in Rome (☎ 06/46741). You may have to call around in order to get an appointment. There's also the 24-hour G. Eastman Dental Hospital, Viale Regina Elena 287 (☎ 06/445-3228).

Doctor Call the U.S. Embassy (see "Dentist," above), which will provide a list of doctors who speak English. All big hospitals in Rome have a 24-hour first-aid service (go to the emergency room). You'll find English-speaking doctors at the privately run Salvator Mundi International Hospital, Viale delle Mura Gianicolense (☎ 06/588961). For medical assistance, the International Medical Center is on 24-hour duty at Via Giovanni Amendola 7 (☎ 06/488-2371). You could also contact the Rome American Hospital, Via Emilio Longoni 69 (☎ 06/22551), with English-speaking doctors on duty 24 hours a day.

Drugstores A reliable pharmacy is the Farmacia Internazionale, Piazza Barberini 49 (☎ 06/679-4680), open day and night. Most pharmacies are open from 8:30am to 1pm and 4 to 7:30pm. In general, pharmacies follow a rotation system so that several are always open on Sunday (the rotation schedule is posted outside each).

Electricity It's generally 220 volts, 50 Hz A.C., but you might find 125-volt outlets, with different plugs and sockets for each. Pick up a transformer either before leaving home or in any appliance shop in Rome if you plan to use electrical appliances. Check the exact local current at your hotel. You'll also need an adapter plug.

Embassies/Consulates The Embassy of the **United States** is at Via Vittorio Veneto 121 (☎ 06/46741), open Monday to Friday from 8:30am to 12:30pm and 2 to 4:30pm. The consular and passport services are also located at Via Vittorio Veneto 121 (same phone); for **Canada,** it's at Via Zara 30 (☎ 06/445-981), open Monday to Friday from 10am to 12:30pm. For the **United Kingdom,** consular offices are at via XX Settembre 80A (☎ 06/482-5441), open Monday to Friday from 9:15am to 1:30pm. For **Australia,** the embassy is at Via Alessadria 215 (☎ 06/852721), open Monday to Thursday from 8:30am to noon and 2 to 4pm, and on Friday from 8:30am to noon. The Australia Consulate is around the corner in the same building at Corso Trieste 25 (☎ 06/852-2721). For **New Zealand,** the consular office is at Via Zara 28 (☎ 06/440-2928), and it's open Monday to Friday from 8:30am to 12:45pm and 1:45 to 5pm. In case of emergency, embassies have a 24-hour referral service.

Emergencies The police "hotline" number is **21-21-21.** Usually, however, dial **112** for the police, to report a fire, or summon an ambulance. For the state police with an English interpreter, dial **113.** If your car breaks down, dial **116;** the Automobile Club of Italy (ACI) will come to your aid.

Eyeglasses Try Vasari, Piazza della Repubblica 61 (☎ 06/488-2240), adjacent to the Grand Hotel, a very large shop with lots of choices.

Hospitals See "Doctors," above.

Hotlines Dial **113,** which is a general SOS, to report any kind of danger, such as rape. You can also dial **112,** the police emergency number. For an ambulance call **5100;** for personal crises, call Samaritans, Via San Giovanni in Laterano 250 (☎ 06/7045-4444), daily from to 1 to 10pm.

Information See "Visitor Information," earlier in this chapter.

Legal Aid The consulate of your country is the place to turn. Although consular officials cannot interfere in the Italian legal process, they can inform you of your rights and provide a list of attorneys. You'll have to pay for the attorney out of your pocket—there's no free legal assistance. If you're arrested for a drug offense, about all the consulate will do is notify a lawyer and perhaps inform your family.

Liquor Laws Wine with meals has been a normal part of Italian family life for hundreds of years. There is no legal drinking age for buying or ordering alcohol, and alcohol is sold day and night throughout the year.

Lost Property Usually lost property is gone forever. But you might try checking at Ogetti Rinvenuti, Via Nicolò Bettoni 1 (☎ 06/581-6040), open Monday to Friday from 8:30am to 4pm and on Saturday from 8:30 to 11:30am. A branch at the Stazione Termini off Track 1 (☎ 06/47301) is open daily from 8am to noon and 2 to 8pm.

Luggage Storage/Lockers These are available at the Stazione Termini along Tracks 1 and 22 daily from 5am to 1am. The charge is 1,500L (95¢) daily per piece of luggage.

Mail Mailboxes in Italy are red and are attached to walls. The left slot is only for letters intended for the city; the right slot is for all other destinations.

The main post office of Rome is at Piazza San Silvestro 19, 00186 Roma (☎ 06/6771), between Via del Corso and Piazza di Spagna. It's open Monday to Friday from 8:25am to 7:40pm and on Saturday from 8:20 to 11:50pm. To claim mail addressed to you in care of this central office, with *fermo posta* written after the name and address of the post office, simply present your passport as identification. Stamps (*francobolli*) can be purchased at *tabacchi* (tobacconists).

Vatican City mailboxes are blue, and you can buy Vatican stamps at the Vatican City Post Office, adjacent to the information office in St. Peter's Square. It's open Monday to Friday from 8:30am to 7pm and on Saturday from 8:30am to 6pm. Letters mailed at Vatican City reach North America far more quickly than does mail sent from within Rome for the same cost. With both the Vatican and the Italian mail, letters and postcards to the U.S. cost about 1300L (85¢).

Newspapers/Magazines You can get the *International Herald Tribune* and *USA Today* at most newsstands, and the *New York Times* at many, as well as *Time* and *Newsweek* magazines. The expatriate magazine (in English) *Wanted in Rome* comes out monthly and lists current events and shows. If you want to try your hand at reading Italian, the Thursday edition of the newspaper *La Repubblica* contains *TrovaRoma*, a magazine supplement full of cultural and entertainment listings.

Police The all-purpose number for police emergency assistance in Italy is **113.**

Radio/TV Major radio and television broadcasts are on RAI, the Italian state radio and TV network. Occasionally during the tourist season it will broadcast special programs in English; look in the radio and TV guide sections of local newspapers. Vatican Radio also carries foreign-language religious news programs, often in English. Shortwave transistor radios pick up broadcasts from the BBC (Britain), Voice of America (United States), and CBC (Canada). More expensive hotels often have TVs in the bedrooms with the CNN news network.

Rest Rooms There are facilities near many of the major sights, often with attendants, and at bars, nightclubs, restaurants, cafés, and hotels, plus at the airports and the railway station. You're expected to leave 200L to 500L (10¢ to 30¢) for the attendant.

Safety Pickpocketing is the most common problem. Men should keep their wallets in their front pockets or inside jacket pockets. Purse-snatching is also commonplace, with young men on Vespas who will ride past you and grab your purse. To avoid trouble, women should stay away from the curb, and keep their purse on the wall side of their body and the strap over both shoulders across their chest. In general, don't lay anything valuable on tables or chairs where it can be grabbed up easily. Gypsy children are a particular menace. You'll often virtually have to fight them off, if they completely surround you. They'll often approach you with pieces of cardboard hiding their stealing hands.

Taxes As a member of the European Union, Italy imposes a tax on most goods and services. It's a "value-added tax," called IVA in Italy. The tax affecting most visitors is at hotels, ranging from 9% in first- and second-class hotels and pensions to 13% in deluxe hotels. The value-added tax is not the same for all items—for example, it's 12% on clothing but 19% on most luxury goods. Tax rebates may be given on large purchases (see "The Shopping Scene" in Chapter 8).

Telephone/Fax/Telegrams If your hotel doesn't have a **fax,** try a *tabacchi* (tobacconist) or photocopy shop. You can send **telegrams** from all post offices during the day and from the telegraph office at the central post office in San Silvestro, off Via della Mercede, at night. Through ITALCABLE, you can dictate both internal and foreign telegrams over the phone (dial 186).

A **public telephone** is always near at hand in Italy, especially if you're near a bar. Local calls cost 200L. You can use 100-, 200-, or 500-lira coins. Most phones, especially in the cities, accept a multiple-use phone card called a *carta telefonica,* which can be purchased at all *tabacchi* and bars in increments of 5,000L or 10,000L. Break off the corner, insert the card into the slot, and then dial. A digital display will keep track of how many lire you use up during your call. The card is good until it runs out of lire, so don't forget to take it with you when you hang up.

Thanks to ITALCABLE, **international calls** to the United States and Canada can be dialed directly. Dial 00 (the international access code from Italy), then the country code (1 for the United States and Canada), the area code, and the number. Calls dialed directly are billed on the basis of the call's duration only. A reduced rate is applied from 11pm to 8am Monday to Saturday and all day Sunday.

If you wish to make a **collect call** from a pay phone, simply deposit 200L (don't worry—you'll get it back when you're done) and dial 170 for an English-speaking ITALCABLE operator. For **calling-card calls,** drop in the refundable 200L, then dial the number for your card's company to be connected with an operator in the States: 172-1011 for AT&T, 172-1022 for MCI, and 172-1877 for Sprint.

If you make a long-distance call from a public telephone, there is no surcharge. *However, hotels have been known to double or triple the cost of the call, so be duly warned.*

Time Rome is 6 hours ahead of eastern time in the United States. Daylight saving time goes into effect in Italy each year from May 22 to September 24.

Tipping This custom is practiced with a flair in Italy—many people depend on tips for their livelihoods. In hotels, the service charge of 15% or 18% is already added to a bill. In addition, it's customary to tip the chambermaid 2,000L ($1.30) per day; the doorman (for calling a cab), 1,000L (65¢); and the bellhop or porter,

2,000L ($1.30) per bag. A concierge expects 3,000L ($1.90) per day, as well as tips for extra services performed, which could include help with long-distance calls, newspapers, or stamps.

In restaurants, 15% is added to your bill to cover most charges. An additional tip for good service is almost always expected. It's customary in certain fashionable restaurants to leave an additional 10%, which, combined with the assessed service charge, is a very large tip indeed. The sommelier expects 10% of the cost of the wine. Checkroom attendants now expect 1,500L (95¢). Romans still hand washroom attendants 200L to 300L (10¢ to 20¢), more in deluxe and first-class establishments. Restaurants are required by law to give receipts.

In cafés and bars, tip 15% of the bill, and give a theater usher 1,500L (95¢). Taxi drivers expect at least 15% of the fare.

Transit Information Call the following numbers: 06/65951 for Leonardo da Vinci International Airport, 06/794941 for Ciampino Airport, 06/4695-4444 for bus information, and 06/4775 for rail information.

Water Rome is famed for its drinking water, which is generally safe, even from its outdoor fountains. If it isn't, there's a sign reading ACQUA NON POTABILE. Romans traditionally order bottled mineral water in restaurants to accompany the wine with their meals.

4 Accommodations

After a long and careful process of elimination, we offer this list of recommended hotels. Although they come in several different price categories, they all share something in common—style. We've looked for places with architectural grace and a relaxed ambience, establishments where the management is alert and understanding, where the facilities provide all necessary comforts. But more specifically we've sought out those hotels with personality, hotels that treat you like a guest instead of a walking traveler's check.

Our selections are divided into four major categories: "Very Expensive," "Expensive," "Moderate," and "Inexpensive." Rome's poshest hotels, while no bargain, are among the most luxurious in Europe. The bulk of this chapter, however, concerns moderately priced hotels, where you'll find rooms with private bath. The final group is "Inexpensive" hotels, and a charming group they are; each one has been judged clean and cheerful and offers surprisingly more in services and facilities than you'd expect from the prices charged. In the less expensive categories, you'll find a few pensions, the Rome equivalent of a boarding house.

HOTELS Italy controls the prices of its hotels, designating a minimum and a maximum rate. The difference between the two may depend on the season, the location of the room, or even its size. Hotels are classified by stars indicating their category of comfort: five stars for deluxe, four for first class, three for second class, two for third class, and one for fourth class. Most former *pensioni* are now rated as one- or two-star hotels. The distinction between a pension hotel (where some degree of board was once required along with the room) and a regular hotel is no longer officially made, although many smaller, family-run establishments still call themselves *pensioni.* Government ratings don't depend on sensitivity of decoration or frescoed ceilings, but rather on facilities, such as elevators and the like. Many of the finest hostelries in Rome have a lower rating because they serve only breakfast (a blessing really, for those seeking to escape the board requirements).

Hotels in Rome today are divided on the question of whether breakfast is included in the room price. Usually the more expensive establishments charge extra for this meal, which most often consists of cappuccino (coffee with milk) and *cornetti* (croissants), with fresh butter and jam. First-class and deluxe establishments serve what is known as either an English breakfast or an American breakfast—meaning ham and eggs—but this must nearly always be ordered from the à la carte menu. Many smaller hotels and pensions serve only continental breakfast. If you're really watching your lire, always determine exactly what's included and what's extra.

The concierge of your hotel, incidentally, is usually a reliable dispenser of information.

BED & BREAKFASTS In Rome, these establishments are commonplace, and they offer the best accommodation value. Finding a suitable one, however, may be tricky. Often B&B places are family homes or apartments, so don't count on hotel services, or even private baths. Sometimes, however, B&Bs are in beautiful private homes, lovely guesthouses, or restored mansions. Prices range from $30 to $60 or more per person nightly, including breakfast. Sometimes you can arrange to order an evening meal. Tourist offices generally keep a list of this type of accommodation.

PARKING It's rare for hotels to have private garages; many were constructed before the advent of the automobile. Others built after the automobile didn't find enough room in overcongested Rome for garage space. Hotel reception desks will advise you about nearby garages. Fees range from 5,000L to 60,000L ($3.20 to $38.40) per night. Of course, the higher price would be for garage space in the heart of Rome where your car would be under a roof, guarded and protected by a nightwatchman. The lower price would be for an open-air unguarded place somewhere on the outskirts of Rome.

RESERVATIONS It's always a good idea to make reservations before you go, and this can be done through a travel agent or by writing or faxing directly to the hotel (some establishments require deposits, and this takes a great deal of time, especially considering how slow the Italian mails are). Some of the more expensive hotels have toll-free 800 numbers in North America. It's invariably easy to obtain an expensive room at any time of the year, but low-cost accommodations are generally heavily booked.

In case you haven't made reservations, however, you're bound to find some place that can put you up for the *first night.* Our advice, in that event, is to time your arrival for shortly before 9am and head straight for your first choice of hotel. If there's any space to be had, you'll be assured of getting first chance at it.

TAXES All Italian hotels impose an IVA (Imposta sul Valore Aggiunto), or value-added tax. This tax is in effect throughout the European Union countries. It replaces some 20 other taxes and is an effort to streamline the tax structure.

What that means for you is an increase in the price you'll pay for a hotel room. Deluxe hotels will slap you with a whopping tax of 13%, whereas first-class, second-class, and other hotels will impose 9%. Most hotels will quote you a rate inclusive of this tax. However, other establishments prefer to add it on when you go to pay the bill. To avoid unpleasant surprises, ask to be quoted an all-inclusive rate—that is, with service, even a continental breakfast (which is often obligatory)—when you check in.

THE PRICE CATEGORIES In hotels rated **"Very Expensive,"** you can spend 450,000L ($288) and up for a double room. Hotels judged **"Expensive"** charge 300,000L to 450,000L ($192 to $288) for a double room; those in the **"Moderate"** category ask 240,000L to 300,000L ($153.60 to $192) for a double. Anything from 80,000L ($51.20) all the way up to 240,000L ($153.60) is judged **"Inexpensive,"** at least by the inflated Roman standards of hotel pricing.

Unless otherwise specified, breakfast is of the continental variety.

1 Best Bets

- **Best Historic Hotel:** The truly grand **Le Grand Hotel** (☎ **800/221-2340** in the U.S.) was inaugurated by its creator, César Ritz, in 1894, with the great chef, Escoffier, presiding over a lavish banquet. Its roster of guests has included some of the greatest names in European history, including royalty, naturally, but also such New World moguls as Henry Ford and J. P. Morgan. The diarist, Anaïs Nin, met her old friend (then nemesis) Gore Vidal here, trying to win his permission to print passages in her diary that virtually libeled him. He granted it!
- **Best for Business Travelers:** On the west side of the Tiber about 6 short blocks northeast of the Vatican, the **Hotel Atlante Star** (☎ **06/687-3233**) operates in conjunction with its sibling, the Atlante Garden, a block away. Together they share a conference room and a well-run business center. Many young executives check into either hotel (depending on their expense account) and find a willing, helpful staff composed mainly of multilingual European interns eager to help visitors with their problems in the Eternal City. All the latest business equipment is available, and the reception desk is excellent at receiving messages.
- **Best for a Romantic Getaway:** A private villa in the exclusive Parioli residential area, the **Hotel Lord Byron** (☎ **06/322-0404**) is an elite retreat and one of the most fashionable ones in Rome. It still maintains its clublike ambience, and everybody is oh, so very discreet here—regardless of the party you check in with! You get personal attention in a subdued opulence, and the staff definitely respects that DO NOT DISTURB sign on the door. You don't even have to leave the romantic premises for dinner, as the Relais Le Jardin is among the finest—some say the very best—restaurant in Rome.
- **Best Trendy Hotel:** Hemingway and Ingrid Bergman don't hang out here anymore, but the **Hotel Eden** (☎ **800/225-5843** in the U.S.) remains glamorous. After a $20-million renovation by Forte, it has come back better than ever before. Fellini, a former guest, isn't around to record the scene today, but the rich and famous (and often infamous) of the world parade through its *fin-de-siècle* grandeur. Everything looks as though it's waiting for photographers from *Architectural Digest* to arrive.
- **Best Lobby for Pretending You're Rich:** In the "Hollywood on the Tiber" heyday of the 1950s, you might've encountered Elizabeth Taylor in the lobby, accompanied by her husband of the moment—usually Richard Burton or Eddie Fisher. They're gone now, but the grandeur of the lobby in the **Excelsior** (☎ **800/221-2340** in the U.S.) lingers on with all its memories. The city's most opulent hotel is just the place to meet someone you're trying to impress (even if you're not a guest). Its sprawling lounges are formal, with all those elegant touches such as glittering chandeliers, lots of marble, and high ceilings.
- **Best for Families:** Near the Stazione Termini (in one of the safer areas), the **Hotel Venezia** (☎ **06/445-7101**) is graced with rooms often large enough to accommodate families. Some have balconies for surveying the action on the street below. The housekeeping is superb, and the management really seems to care. Extra beds can be brought into the room for children.
- **Best Moderately Priced Hotel:** Just half a block from the Spanish Steps, the **Hotel Internazionale** (☎ **06/6994-1823**) has been luring savvy travelers for years. It's not just the location that counts here, but the hotel itself has the atmosphere of a small inn. The traditionally furnished rooms and cozy public areas create a warm, inviting ambience. It can quickly become "your home in Rome."

- **Best Budget Hotel:** Everybody's favorite budget hideaway seems to be the **Albergo Campo de' Fiori** (☎ **06/6880-6865**). Lying in the historic center of Rome in a market area that has existed since the 1500s, this cozy, narrow, six-story hotel offers rustic rooms—many quite tiny and sparcely adorned, but others with a lot of character. The best (restored) rooms are on the first floor, but the most lavish is the honeymoon retreat on the sixth floor with a canopied king-size bed.
- **Best Friendly Pensione:** You can't get much simpler than the **Pensione Papà Germano** (☎ **06/486919**). It's a favorite budget choice, but it's warm and welcoming. A high-turnover clientele of European and American students check in here—often with backpacks—as the address is passed around from campus to campus. The energetic family owners may not speak the Queen's English, but somehow are receptive to your needs and are willing to share their home.
- **Best Service:** Both management and staff at the **Hotel de la Ville Inter-Continental Roma** (☎ **800/327-0200** in the U.S. and Canada) prove highly professional and exceedingly hospitable. From the moment a smartly uniformed doorman ushers you inside, you know you're in good company. The reception staff has your reservation and the maids have prepared your room, waiting to cure you of jet lag. Room service is available 24 hours daily.
- **Best Location:** Right at the top of the Spanish Steps, directly across the small piazza from the deluxe Hassler, is the **Scalinata di Spagna** (☎ **06/679-3006**). Could there be any more desirable location in all of Rome? The interior is like an old inn—the public rooms are small with bright print slipcovers, old clocks, and low ceilings. You can soak up the atmosphere inside or head for the roof garden with its sweeping view of the dome of St. Peter's across the Tiber. When you step out your door, the heart of Rome is at your feet, including the best shopping streets, at the bottom of the Spanish Steps.
- **Best Views:** From its perch on top of Monte Mario, set on 15 acres of landscaped grounds, the deluxe **Cavalieri Hilton** (☎ **800/445-8667** in the U.S. and Canada) opens onto panoramic views of the Eternal City that are almost unequaled in the capital. The skyline of Rome is especially evocative at either dawn or sunset. Of course, panoramic views are possible from all the bedrooms, but many guests, even Romans themselves, drive up here for a drink at night just to take in the lights of the city. It's memorable, and you'll want to linger.
- **Best View from Your Window:** You can't beat the view at the **Albergo del Sole al Pantheon** (☎ **06/678-0441**). From your bedroom window one of the architectural gems of the ancient world, the Pantheon, stares back at you. The present-day albergo is one of the oldest hotels in the world—the first records of it as a hostelry appeared in 1467. One can see why the original builders chose it as a site, considering that view. Taking in the scene over the centuries has been everybody from Frederick III of the Habsburg dynasty to Simone de Beauvoir and her lover, Jean-Paul Sartre. A lot of other lovers as well have found the view the most evocative in Rome.
- **Best Elegant Hotel:** Of course, it's not as elegant or as grand as the Excelsior, Eden, or Hassler, but in its own way the **Hotel d'Inghilterra** (☎ **06/69981**) has a subdued opulence. Two blocks west of the Spanish Steps, it offers public rooms with black and white marble floors like a checkerboard. Upholstered lounges filled with antiques add the traditional touch. The fifth floor has some of the loveliest terraces in Rome, and the romantic restaurant down below has *trompe l'oeil* clouds giving it the aura of a courtyard terrace with cumulus clouds floating across.
- **Best in a Roman Neighborhood:** You couldn't get more Roman than by booking in at the **Teatro di Pompeo** (☎ **06/6830-0170**). The hotel is actually built

on top of the ruins of the Theater of Pompey, dating from 55 B.C. The little charmer lies near the spot where Julius Caesar met his fate. It's on a quiet piazzetta near the Palazzo Farnese and Campo de' Fiori, which is, in our view at least, the most character-filled neighborhood of Rome with its open-air market. This is one of the most fascinating parts of Renaissance Rome for shopping and nightlife. Restaurants and pizzerie keep the area lively late into the night.

- **Best Value:** A three-star establishment, the **Hotel delle Muse** (☎ **06/808-8333**) lies half a mile north of the Villa Borghese. It's run by the efficient, English-speaking Giorgio Lazar. The furnishings are modern and come in a wide range of splashy colors. In summer Mr. Lazar operates a restaurant in the garden serving a reasonably priced fixed-price menu, and he keeps his bar open 24 hours a day, in case you get thirsty at 5 o'clock in the morning. It's one of the real bargains of Rome, and you should consider checking in before he wises up and raises his rates.

2 Near Ancient Rome

EXPENSIVE

Hotel Forum. Via di Tor de Conti 25–30, 00184 Roma. ☎ **06/679-2446.** Fax 06/678-6479. 80 rms, 6 suites. A/C TV TEL. 350,000L–450,000L ($224–$288) double; 490,000L ($313.60) triple; 500,000L–630,000L ($320–$403.20) suite. Rates include breakfast. AE, DC, MC, V. Parking 40,000L ($25.60). Bus: 27, 81, 85, 87, or 186.

The Hotel Forum, built around a medieval bell tower off the Fori Imperiali, offers an elegance that savors the drama of Old Rome, as well as tasteful, sometimes opulent accommodations. At the peak of the *dolce vita* in the 1950s, this former convent was converted into a hotel. The bedrooms, which look out on the sights of the ancient city, are well appointed with antiques, mirrors, marquetry, and Oriental rugs. The hotel's lounges are conservatively conceived as a country estate, with paneled walls and furnishings that combine Italian and French provincial styles. Dining is an event in the roof-garden restaurant. Reserve well in advance.

INEXPENSIVE

Colosseum Hotel. Via Sforza 10, 00184 Roma. ☎ **06/482-7228.** Fax 06/482-7285. 50 rms. TEL TV. 220,000L ($140.80) double. Rates include breakfast. AE, DC, MC, V. Parking 30,000L ($19.20). Metro: Cavour. Bus: 11, 27, or 81.

Not far from the Basilica di Santa Maria Maggiore, the Colosseum Hotel offers baronial living on a miniature scale. The bedrooms are furnished with well-conceived antique reproductions (beds of heavy carved wood, dark-paneled wardrobes, leatherwood chairs)—and all with monklike white walls. Air-conditioning is available on request for 20,000 lire ($12.80) per day extra. The drawing room, with its long refectory table, white walls, red tiles, and provincial armchairs, invites lingering.

Hotel Duca d'Alba. Via Leonina 14, 00184 Roma. ☎ **06/484471.** Fax 06/488-4840. 27 rms, 11 with shower only, 16 with bath. MINIBAR TV TEL. 180,000L ($115.20) double with shower only, 240,000L ($153.60) double with bath. Rates include breakfast. AE, DC, MC, V. Parking 30,000L ($19.20). Metro: Cavour.

A bargain close to the Roman Forum and the Colosseum, this hotel lies in the Suburra *quartier* where the "plebs" of ancient Rome resided. This area of Rome is being gentrified—it had become seedy—and this hotel is part of that renaissance. Although completely restored, it still retains some of the aura of the 19th century when it was first built. The bedrooms are tasteful, even a bit decorated, with soothing colors and light-wood pieces. The most desirable rooms are the four with private balconies.

3 Near Campo de' Fiori

MODERATE

$ Teatro di Pompeo. Largo del Pallaro 8, 00186 Roma. ☎ **06/6830-0170.** Fax 06/6880-5531. 12 rms. A/C TV TEL. 250,000L ($160) double. Rates include breakfast. AE, DC, MC, V. Bus: 46, 62, or 64.

Built on the top of the ruins of the Theater of Pompey, which dates from about 55 B.C., this small charmer lies near the spot where Julius Caesar met his end. Intimate and refined, it's on a quiet piazzetta near the Palazzo Farnese and Campo de' Fiori. The bedrooms, all doubles, are decorated in an old-fashioned Italian style with hand-painted tiles. The beamed ceilings date from the days of Michelangelo. There's no restaurant, but breakfast is served. Since this is such a historic gem with such a small capacity, book as early as possible.

INEXPENSIVE

$ Albergo Campo de' Fiori. Via del Biscione 6, 00186 Roma. ☎ **06/6880-6865.** Fax 06/687-6003. 27 rms, 9 with bath; 1 honeymoon suite. 120,000L ($76.80) double without bath, 140,000L ($89.60) double with shower, 190,000L ($121.60) double with bath; 155,000L ($99.20) triple without bath, 180,000L ($115.20) triple with shower, 240,000L ($153.60) triple with bath. Rates include breakfast. MC, V. Bus: 46, 62, or 64 from the Termini to Museo di Roma; then arm yourself with a good map for the walk.

Everybody's favorite budget hideaway in the historic center of Rome, this cozy, narrow six-story hotel offers rustic rooms, many quite tiny and sparsely adorned, others with a lot of character. The best, on the first floor, have been restored. Yours might have a ceiling of clouds and blue skies along with mirrored walls. The best accommodation is the honeymoon retreat on the sixth floor, with a canopied king-size bed. Honeymooners beware: There's no elevator. Guests can enjoy the panorama from the terrace overlooking the vegetable market below (which has been around since the 1500s), and, in the distance, St. Peter's. There's no restaurant or bar.

4 Near Piazza Navona & the Pantheon

EXPENSIVE

✪ Albergo del Sole al Pantheon. Piazza della Rotonda 63, 00186 Roma. ☎ **06/678-0441.** Fax 06/6994-0689. 26 rms, 4 suites. A/C MINIBAR TV TEL. 450,000L ($288) double; 600,000L ($384) suite. Rates include breakfast. AE, DC, MC, V. Parking 35,000L ($22.40). Bus: 62, 64, 70, 87, or 119.

The Albergo del Sole al Pantheon, overlooking the Pantheon, is an absolute gem. The present-day *albergo* is one of the oldest hotels in the world; the first records of it as a hostelry appear in 1467. Long known as a retreat for emperors and sorcerers, the hotel has hosted such guests as Frederick III of the Habsburg family. Mascagni celebrated the première of *Cavalleria Rusticana* here. Later it drew such distinguished company as Jean-Paul Sartre and his companion, Simone de Beauvoir. Today the rooms are exquisitely furnished and decorated with period pieces and stylized reproductions.

Albergo Nazionale. Piazza Montecitorio 131, 00186 Roma. ☎ **06/695001.** Fax 06/678-6677. 87 rms, 15 suites. TV TEL. 380,000L ($243.20) double; 800,000L ($512) suite. Rates include breakfast. AE, DC, MC, V. Bus: 52, 53, 58, 85, or 95.

The Albergo Nazionale faces one of Rome's most historic squares, Piazza Colonna, with its Column of Marcus Aurelius, the Palazzo di Montecitorio, and the Palazzo Chigi. Because it's next to the parliament buildings, the *albergo* is frequently used by

Family-Friendly Hotels

Cavalieri Hilton *(see p. 91)* This hotel is like a resort at Monte Mario, with a swimming pool, gardens, and plenty of grounds for children to run and play, yet it's only 15 minutes from the center of Rome, reached by the hotel shuttle bus.

Hotel Massimo d'Azeglio *(see p. 84)* This hotel near the Stazione Termini has long been a family favorite. The rooms are large, well kept, and comfortable, and the well-trained staff is solicitous of children.

San Giorgio *(see p. 85)* Near the train station, this family-owned hotel is ideal for parents traveling with children. Many of its corner rooms can be converted into larger quarters by opening doors.

Hotel Venezia *(see p. 86)* At this good, moderately priced family hotel near the Stazione Termini, the rooms have been renovated and most are large enough for extra beds for children.

government officials and diplomatic staff. Although it maintains the atmosphere of a gentlemen's club, women are welcome, too. There are many nooks conducive to conversation in the public lounges. The lobbies are wood-paneled, and there are many antiques throughout the hotel. Rooms are usually spacious and decorated in a traditional style, either carpeted or floored with marble.

Hotel Raphael. Largo Febo 2, 00186 Roma. ☎ **06/682831.** Fax 06/687-8993. 53 rms, 20 suites. A/C MINIBAR TV TEL. 460,000L–600,000L ($194.40–$384) double; 580,000L–1,000,000L ($371.20–$640) suite. AE, DC, MC, V. Parking nearby. Bus: 64, 70, 87, 90, or 492.

In the heart of ancient Rome adjacent to Piazza Navona, this hidden retreat lies within easy distance of many of Rome's attractions. Its rooftop garden terrace boasts a panorama of the ancient city. The charming ivy-covered facade invites one to enter the lobby decorated with antiques that might rival local museums. Some of the suites have private terraces, and all the well-appointed bedrooms have direct-dial phones and satellite TV. Some of the rooms are quite small, however. The elegant restaurant and bar, Café Picasso, serves an international cuisine, and among the services provided are room service, baby-sitting, laundry, and currency exchange. They also have a fitness room.

INEXPENSIVE

Albergo Cesàri. Via di Pietra 89A, 00186 Roma. ☎ **06/679-2386.** Fax 06/679-0882. 50 rms, 40 with bath. A/C TV TEL. 130,000L ($83.20) double without bath, 180,000L–256,000L ($115.20–$163.85) double with bath; 245,000L–310,000L ($156.80–$198.40) triple with bath; 285,000L–355,000L ($182.40–$227.20) quad with bath. AE, DC, MC, V. Parking 45,000L ($28.15). Bus: 492 from the Termini.

The Albergo Cesàri, on an ancient street in the old quarter of Rome, has occupied its desirable location between the Trevi Fountain and the Pantheon since 1787. Its guests have included Garibaldi and Stendhal, and its well-preserved exterior harmonizes with the Temple of Neptune and many little antiques shops nearby. The bedrooms have mostly functional modern pieces, but there are a few traditional trappings as well to maintain character. In 1996, 16 bedrooms were completely renovated. Breakfast is the only meal served.

Pensione Navona. Via dei Sediari 8, 00186 Roma. ☎ **06/686-4203.** Fax 06/6880-3802. 22 rms, 17 with bath (shower). 115,000L ($73.60) double without bath, 125,000L ($80) double with bath. Rates include breakfast. AE. Bus: 64, 70, 75, 87, or 492.

Accommodations Near Campo de' Fiori & Piazza Navona

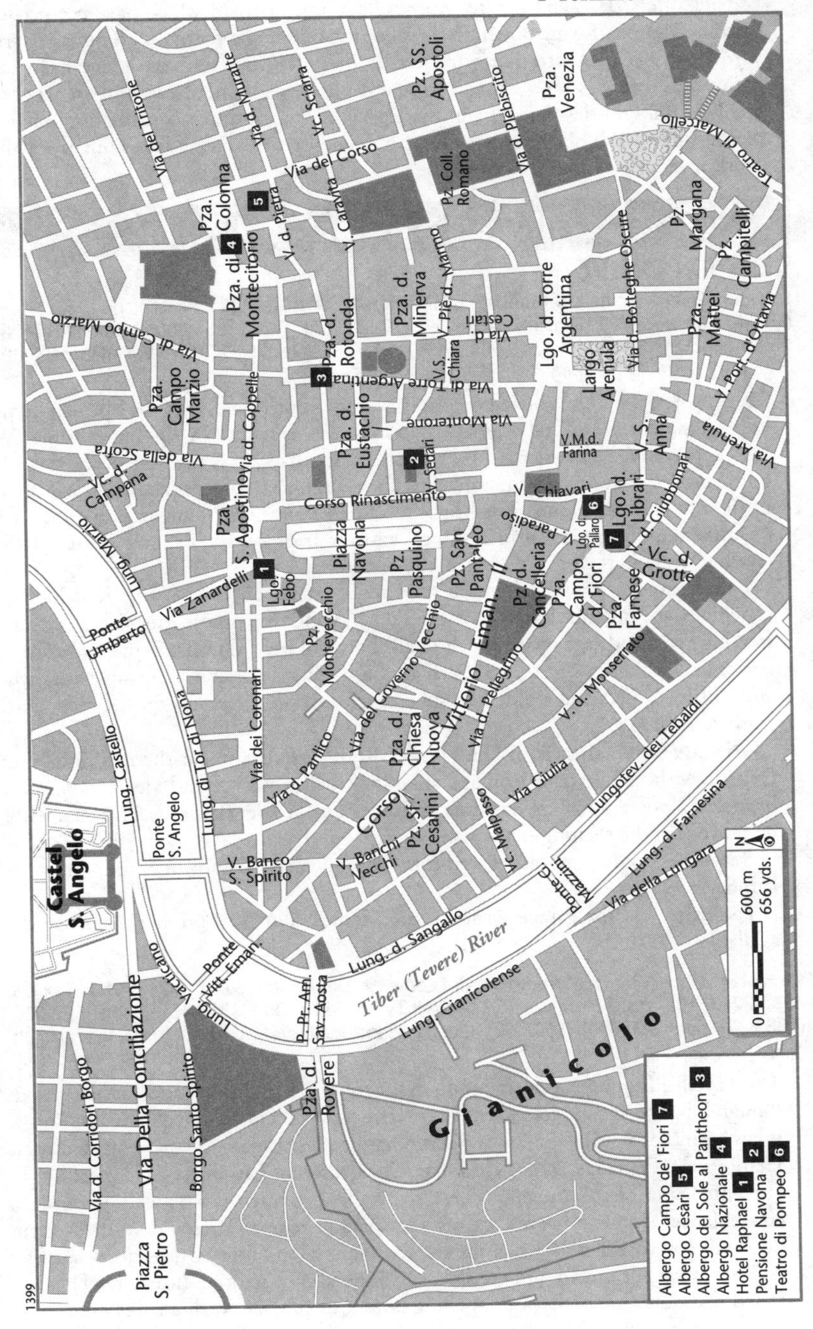

Although the rooms are not as glamorous as the exterior of this palace, the Pensione Navona offers clean and decent accommodations, many of which have been renovated and some of which open to views of the building's central (and quiet) courtyard. Run by an Australian-born family of Italian descent, the place has tiled bathrooms, ceilings high enough to relieve the midsummer heat, and an array of architectural oddities that remain the legacy of the continual construction on this palace since 1360. The *pensione* lies on a small street that radiates out from the southeastern tip of Piazza Navona.

5 Near Piazza di Spagna & Piazza del Popolo

VERY EXPENSIVE

Hassler. Piazza Trinità dei Monti 6, 00187 Roma. ☎ **800/223-6800** in the U.S., or 06/699340. Fax 06/6789991. 85 rms, 15 suites. A/C MINIBAR TV TEL. 650,000L–950,000L ($416–$608) double; 1,550,000L–2,950,000L ($992–$1,888) suite. AE, DC, MC, V. Parking 40,000L ($25.60). Metro: Pz. di Spagna.

The Hassler, the only deluxe hotel in this old part of Rome, uses the Spanish Steps as its grand entrance. The original 1885 Hassler was rebuilt in 1944, and while the crown worn by the Hassler is a bit tarnished these days, as is the tiara of the Grand, both hostelries have such a mystique that they continue to prosper and endure in spite of their overpriced rooms. The brightly colored rooms, the lounges with a mixture of modern and traditional furnishings, and the bedrooms with their "Italian Park Avenue" trappings all strike a faded 1930s note.

The bedrooms, some of which tend to be small, have a personalized look—Oriental rugs, tasteful draperies at the French windows, brocade furnishings, comfortable beds, and (the nicest touch of all) bowls of fresh flowers. Some rooms have balconies with views of the city. Each accommodation contains a private bath, usually with two sinks and a bidet. In spite of all this, the Excelsior, for the most part, has better rooms.

Dining/Entertainment: The Hassler Roof Restaurant, on the top floor, is a favorite with visitors and Romans alike for its fine cuisine and view. Its Sunday brunch is a popular rendezvous time in Rome. The Hassler Bar is ideal for an apéritif or a drink; in the evening it has piano music.

Services: Room service, telex and fax, limousine, in-room massages, in-house laundry.

Facilities: Nearby garage, fitness center, tennis court (in summer), free bicycles available.

✪ **Hotel d'Inghilterra.** Via Bocca di Leone 14, 00187 Roma. ☎ **06/69981.** Fax 06/6992-2243. 102 rms, 12 suites. A/C MINIBAR TV TEL. 496,000L ($317.45) double; 599,000L ($383.35) triple; 840,000L ($537.60) suite. Rates include breakfast. AE, DC, MC, V. Metro: Pz. di Spagna.

The Hotel d'Inghilterra nostalgically holds onto its traditions and heritage, even though it has been completely renovated. The most fashionable small hotel in Rome, it has been the favorite of many a discriminating personage—Anatole France, Ernest Hemingway, Franz Liszt, Alec Guinness. The bedrooms have mostly old pieces—gilt and much marble, mahogany chests, and glittery mirrors—as well as modern conveniences. Some, however, are just too small. The hotel's restaurant, the Roman Garden, serves excellent Roman dishes. The main salon of the hotel is dominated by an impressive gilt mirror and console, surrounded by Victorian furniture. The preferred bedrooms are higher up, opening onto a tile terrace, with a balustrade and a railing covered with flowering vines and plants. The English-style bar is a favorite

Accommodations Near the Spanish Steps & Ancient Rome

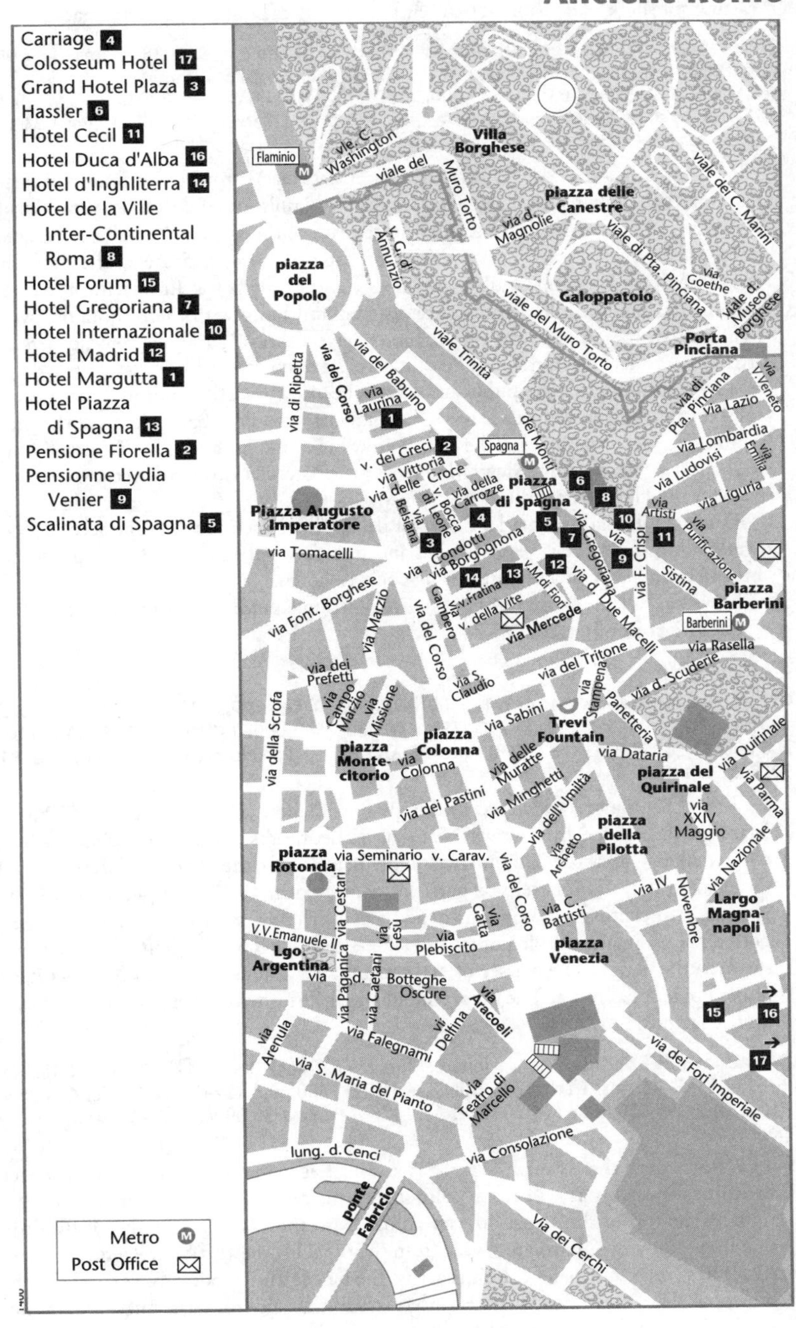

gathering spot in the evening, with its paneled walls, tip-top tables, and old lamps casting soft light. The Roman Garden Lounge offers light lunches and snacks.

✪ **Hotel de la Ville Inter-Continental Roma.** Via Sistina 67–69, 00187 Roma. ☎ **800/327-0200** in the U.S. and Canada, or 06/67331. Fax 06/678-4213. 192 rms, 23 suites. A/C MINIBAR TV TEL. 510,000L–645,000L ($326.40–$412.80) double; 800,000L–1,525,000L ($512–$976) suite. Rates include breakfast. AE, DC, MC, V. Parking 35,000L ($22.40). Metro: Pz. di Spagna or Pz. Barberini.

This hotel looks deluxe (it's officially rated first class) from the minute you walk through the revolving door attended by a smartly uniformed doorman. Once inside this palace, built in the 19th century on the site of the ancient Lucullus's Gardens, you'll find Oriental rugs, marble tables, brocade-covered furniture, and a staff who speak English. There are endless corridors leading to what at first seems a maze of ornamental lounges, all elegantly upholstered and hung with their quota of crystal lighting fixtures. Some of the public rooms have a sort of 1930s elegance, others are strictly baroque, and in the middle of it all is an open courtyard.

The bedrooms and the public areas have been completely renovated in a beautifully classic and yet up-to-date way. The higher rooms with balconies have the most panoramic views of Rome to be found anywhere, and all guests are free to use the roof terrace with the same view. Many savvy guests prefer this hotel to the overpriced glory of the Hassler next door.

Dining/Entertainment: La Piazzetta de la Ville Restaurant, on the second floor overlooking the garden, serves Italian and international cuisine. The hotel also has an American bar with a pianist during cocktail hours.

Services: Room service (24 hours), baby-sitting, laundry and valet service.

Facilities: Roof terrace.

EXPENSIVE

Grand Hotel Plaza. Via del Corso 126, 00186 Roma. ☎ **06/6992-1111.** Fax 06/6994-1575. 194 rms, 10 suites. A/C MINIBAR TV TEL. 390,000L–540,000L ($249.60–$345.60) double; 700,000L–1,200,000L ($448–$768) suite. AE, DC, MC, V. Parking 30,000L ($19.20). Bus: 81, 90, 90b, or 119.

Empress Carlotta of Mexico received Pope Pius IX here in 1866, and in 1933 Pietro Mascagni composed his *Nerone* in one of its bedrooms. Vincent Price stayed here while making "all those bad movies," and when you see the very grand decor, you'll understand why. The hotel was partially renovated in 1993. The public rooms are vintage 19th century and contain stained-glass skylights, massive crystal chandeliers, potted palms, inlaid marble floors, and a life-size stone lion guarding the entrance to the ornate stairway. The bar seems an interminable distance across the parquet floor of the opulent ballroom. The hotel contains well-furnished modern bedrooms, many quite spacious.

✪ **Scalinata di Spagna.** Piazza Trinità dei Monti 17, 00187 Roma. ☎ **06/679-3006.** Fax 06/6994-0598. 15 rms, 1 suite. A/C MINIBAR TV TEL. 380,000L ($243.20) double; 480,000L ($307.20) triple; 650,000L ($416) suite. AE, MC, V. Parking 35,000L ($22.40). Metro: Pz. di Spagna.

This hotel near the Spanish Steps has always been one of the most sought-after in Rome—possibly it will reach four-star status and increase its prices soon. It's right at the top of the steps, directly across from the Hassler, in a delightful little building—only two floors are visible from the outside—nestled between much larger structures, with four relief columns across the facade and window boxes with bright blossoms. The recently redecorated interior is like an old inn—the public rooms are small with bright print slipcovers, old clocks, and low ceilings.

The decorations vary radically from one room to the next; some have low, beamed ceilings and ancient-looking wood furniture, whereas others have loftier ceilings and more average appointments. Everything is spotless and most pleasing to the eye. In season, breakfast is served on the roof-garden terrace with its sweeping view of the dome of St. Peter's across the Tiber. Reserve well in advance.

MODERATE

Carriage. Via della Carrozze 36, 00187 Roma. ☎ **06/699-0124.** Fax 06/678-8279. 24 rms, 2 suites. A/C MINIBAR TV TEL. 295,000L ($188.80) double; 380,000L ($243.20) triple; 380,000L–536,000L ($243.20–$343.05) suite. Rates include breakfast. AE, DC, MC, V. Metro: Pz. di Spagna.

The aptly named Carriage caters to the "carriage trade," which in today's sense means staff members of the British and French embassies, plus an occasional movie star or film director. The 18th-century facade covers some charming, although small, accommodations (ask for one of the two rooftop bedrooms). Antiques have been used tastefully, creating a personal aura, even in the bedrooms with their matching bedcovers and draperies. Each bedroom has a radio and other amenities. To meet your fellow guests, head for the Renaissance-style salon that's called an American bar or the roof garden. There's no dining room.

Hotel Cecil. Via Francesco Crispi 55A, 00187 Roma. ☎ **06/679-7998.** Fax 06/679-7996. 41 rms. TV TEL. 270,000L–290,000L ($172.80–$185.60) double. Rates include breakfast. AE, MC, V. Parking 25,000L–30,000L ($16–$19.20). Metro: Pz. Barberini. Bus: 60, 61, 62, or 492.

This hotel in a 17th-century building lies in the heart of Rome near such monuments as Piazza di Spagna and the Fontana di Trevi. It has entertained everybody from Casanova to Henrik Ibsen, who wrote *Brandt* and conceived *Peer Gynt* here. Today it's attractively streamlined, with comfortable bedrooms, each with private bath, satellite TV, and radio. Since this is an extremely noisy part of Rome, double windows have been installed in accommodations facing the busy street. There's a roof garden with bar service and a panoramic terrace for viewing "monumental Rome."

Hotel Gregoriana. Via Gregoriana 18, 00187 Roma. ☎ **06/679-4269.** Fax 06/678-4258. 19 rms. A/C TV TEL. 300,000L ($192) double. Rates include breakfast. No credit cards. Parking 25,000L ($16). Metro: Pz. di Spagna.

Although surrounded by much chicer and better neighbors like the Hassler, the small Gregoriana is elite with fans of its own—mainly members of the Italian fashion industry. The ruling matriarch of an aristocratic family left the building to an order of nuns in the 19th century, but they eventually retreated to other quarters. Today there might be a slightly more elevated spirituality in Room C than in the rest of the hotel, as it used to be a chapel. Throughout the establishment the smallish rooms provide comfort and Italian design. The elevator cage is a black-and-gold art deco fantasy, and the door to each room has a reproduction of an Erté print whose fanciful characters indicate the letter designating that room. You'll pay the bill in the tiny, rattan-covered lobby.

$ **Hotel Internazionale.** Via Sistina 79, 00187 Roma. ☎ **06/6994-1823.** Fax 06/678-4764. 42 rms, 2 suites. A/C MINIBAR TV TEL. 295,000L ($188.80) double; from 600,000L ($384) suite. Rates include breakfast. AE, MC, V. Parking 35,000L ($22.40). Bus: 60, 61, 62, or 492 from the Termini.

Although this *albergo* sits on the ruins of a series of buildings known as Horti Lucullani from the 1st century B.C., the present structure is rooted in a series of buildings dating from the 1500s. Since 1870 the present hotel has operated, just half a block from the top of the Spanish Steps, on one of the most fashionable shopping streets of Rome. Although lacking the style and grace of the d'Inghilterra, it has antique charm of its own, in spite of the modern intrusions. Accommodations facing narrow Via Sistina have double windows to cut down the noise. Some antique wingback chairs and coffered ceilings charm the bedrooms, contrasting with contemporary built-in pieces.

Hotel Madrid. Via Mario de' Fiori 94–95, 00187 Roma. ☎ **06/699-1511.** Fax 06/679-1653. 26 rms, 7 suites. A/C MINIBAR TV TEL. 260,000L ($166.40) double; 360,000L ($230.40) suite for four. Rates include breakfast. AE, DC, MC, V. Parking 32,000L–34,000L ($20.50–$21.75). Metro: Pz. di Spagna.

The Hotel Madrid evokes *fin-de-siècle* Roma on its interior in spite of the modern intrusions in its well-maintained and comfortable, if rather minimalist, bedrooms. The hotel appeals to the individual traveler who wants a good standard of service. Guests often take their breakfast amid ivy and blossoming plants on the roof terrace with a panoramic view of rooftops and the distant dome of St. Peter's. Some of the doubles are large, equipped with small scatter rugs, veneer armoires, and shuttered windows. Others are quite small, so make sure you know what you're getting before you check in. The hotel is an ocher building with a shuttered facade on a narrow street practically in the heart of the boutique area centering around Via Frattina, near the Spanish Steps.

Hotel Piazza di Spagna. Via Mario de' Fiori 61, 00187 Roma. ☎ **06/679-6412.** Fax 06/679-0654. 16 rms. A/C MINIBAR TV TEL. 250,000L ($160) double. Rates include breakfast. AE, MC, V. Metro: Pz. di Spagna. Bus: 61, 71, 81, or 85.

Set about a block from the downhill side of the Spanish Steps, this hotel was once just an unknown, rundown *pensione* until new owners in the 1990s took it over and substantially upgraded it, as befits its choice location. Originally built in the early 1800s, it has always occupied prime real estate. It's small but classic, with a warm, inviting atmosphere. Some rooms even have a Jacuzzi. The decor of the rooms is functionally streamlined, although hardly inspired. The neighborhood is filled with lots of options for drinking and dining.

INEXPENSIVE

Hotel Margutta. Via Laurina 34, 00187 Roma. ☎ **06/322-3674.** Fax 06/320-0395. 21 rms. 147,000L ($94.10) double; 190,000L ($121.60) triple. Rates include breakfast. AE, DC, MC, V. Metro: Flaminio. Bus: 95, 119, 490, or 495.

The Hotel Margutta, on a cobblestone street near Piazza del Popolo, offers attractively decorated rooms and a helpful staff. The hotel is housed in a two-century-old building that was transformed into a small hotel in 1961. Located off the paneled, black stone-floored lobby is a simple breakfast room with framed lithographs. The best rooms are on the top floor, each with a view. Two of these three rooms (nos. 50 and 51) share a terrace, and the larger bedroom has a private terrace. Management always reserves the right to charge a 20% to 35% supplement for these accommodations. Be alert to the fact that the hotel is not air-conditioned, nor does it have room phones.

Pensione Fiorella. Via del Babuino 196, 00187 Roma. ☎ **06/361-0597.** 7 rms, none with bath. 82,000L ($52.50) double. Rates include breakfast. No credit cards. Metro: Flaminio.

A few steps from Piazza del Popolo is this utterly basic, unstylish, but comfortable *pensione*. Antonio Albano and his family are one of the best reasons to stay—they speak little English, but their humor and warm welcome make renting one of their well-scrubbed bedrooms a lot like visiting a lighthearted Italian relative. The bedrooms open onto a high-ceilinged hallway. The doors of the Fiorella shut at 1am. Reservations can only be made a day before you check in.

Pensione Lydia Venier. Via Sistina 42, 00187 Roma. ☎ **06/679-1744.** Fax 06/679-7263. 30 rms, 10 with shower only, 10 with bath. 150,000L ($96) double without bath, 180,000L ($115.20) double with shower only, 200,000L ($128) double with bath. Rates include breakfast. AE, DC, MC, V. Metro: Pz. Barberini or Pz. di Spagna.

This respectable but cost-conscious *pensione* is set on one of the upper floors of a gracefully proportioned apartment building on a street that radiates out from the top of the Spanish Steps. The bedrooms are utterly simple with understated furnishings, a dignified combination of slightly battered modern and antique, and an occasional reminder (such as a ceiling fresco) of an earlier era.

6 Near Via Veneto & Piazza Barberini

VERY EXPENSIVE

✪ **Excelsior.** Via Vittorio Veneto 125, 00187 Roma. ☎ **800/325-3589** in the U.S. and in Canada, or 06/4708. Fax 06/482-6205. 327 rms, 45 suites. A/C MINIBAR TV TEL. 530,000L–590,000L ($339.20–$377.60) double; 1,000,000L–1,600,000L ($640–$1,024) suite. AE, DC, MC, V. Metro: Pz. Barberini.

This hotel is far livelier and better than its sibling, the Grand. It's also got a lot more *joie de vivre,* even though Elizabeth Taylor checked out a long time ago. She has been replaced by Arab princesses and international financiers. The Excelsior (pronounced Ess-*shell*-see-or) is a limestone palace whose baroque corner tower, which looks right over the U.S. Embassy, is a landmark in Rome. Guests enter a string of cavernous reception rooms with thick rugs, marble floors, gilded garlands and pilasters decorating the walls, and Empire furniture (supported by winged lions and the like). Everything looks just a little bit tarnished today, and competition has drained much of its former patronage, but the Excelsior endures, seemingly as eternal as Rome itself. In no small part that's because of the exceedingly hospitable staff.

The rooms come in two basic varieties: new (the result of a major renovation) and traditional. Doubles are spacious and elegantly furnished, often with antiques and silk curtains. The furnishings in singles are also of high quality. Most of the bedrooms are different, many with a sumptuous Hollywood-style bath—marble-walled with separate bath and shower, sinks, bidet, and a mountain of fresh towels.

Dining/Entertainment: The Excelsior Bar, open daily from 10:30am to 1am, is the most famous on Via Vittorio Veneto, and La Cupola is known for its national and regional cuisine, with dietetic and kosher food prepared on request.

Services: Room service, baby-sitting, laundry and valet service.

Facilities: Beauty salon, barbershop.

✪ **Hotel Eden.** Via Ludovisi 49, 00187 Roma. ☎ **800/225-5843** in the U.S., or 06/478121. Fax 06/482-1584. 101 rms, 11 suites. A/C MINIBAR TV TEL. 600,000L–700,000L ($384–$448) double; 1,300,000L–2,000,000L ($832–$1,280) suite. AE, DC, MC, V. Parking 40,000L ($25.60).

For several generations after its inauguration in 1889, this richly ornate five-story hotel reigned over one of the most stylish shopping neighborhoods in the world. Hemingway, Maria Callas, Ingrid Bergman, Fellini—all the big names checked in here during its heyday. In 1994, after its purchase in 1989 by Trusthouse Forte, it reopened after 2 years (and $20 million) of radical renovations that enhanced its *fin-de-siècle* grandeur and added the modern amenities its five-star status calls for. Near the top of the Spanish Steps, its hilltop position guarantees a panoramic view over the city from most bedrooms, which guests consider worth the rather high expense. The rooms contain marble-sheathed bathrooms, draperies worthy of the pages of *Architectual Digest,* and a plushly configured allegiance to the decor of the late 19th century. Understated elegance is the rule. There's a gym and health club on the premises, a piano bar, and a glamorous restaurant, La Terrazza, that's recommended separately (see Chapter 5).

EXPENSIVE

Victoria Roma. Via Campania 41, 00187 Roma. ☎ **06/473931.** Fax 06/487-1890. 108 rms. A/C MINIBAR TV TEL. 350,000L ($224) double. Rates include breakfast. AE, DC, MC, V. Parking 30,000L–40,000L ($19.20–$25.60). Metro: Pz. Barberini. Bus: 52, 53, 490, 495, or 910.

Its chic *la dolce vita* glory days have passed, but this hotel still keeps abreast of changing times. Its location remains one of its most desirable assets, and you can sit on wrought-iron chairs on its roof garden, drinking your *aperativo* in a forest of palms and potted plants, overlooking the Borghese Gardens with the illusion that you're in a country villa. The lounges and living rooms retain that country-house decor, with soft touches that include high-backed chairs, large oil paintings, bowls of freshly cut flowers, provincial tables, and Oriental rugs. The Swiss owner, Alberto H. Wirth, has set unusual requirements of innkeeping (no groups), and has attracted a fine clientele over the years—diplomats, executives, artists. The recently refurbished bedrooms are well furnished and maintained. Meals can be taken à la carte in the elegant grill room, which serves the best of Italian and French cuisine.

MODERATE

Alexandra. Via Vittorio Veneto 18, 00187 Roma. ☎ **06/488-1943.** Fax 06/487-1804. 39 rms, 6 suites. A/C MINIBAR TV TEL. 260,000L ($166.40) double; 360,000L ($230.40) suite. Rates include breakfast. AE, DC, MC, V. Parking 35,000L ($22.40). Metro: Pz. Barberini. Bus: 52, 53, 56, 58, 95, or 586.

Although guidebooks ignore it, here's one of your few chances to stay on Via Veneto without going broke. Set behind the dignified stone facade of what was originally a 19th-century private mansion, this hotel offers clean, comfortable rooms filled with antique furniture and modern conveniences. Rooms facing the front are exposed to the roaring traffic and animated street life of Via Veneto; those in back are quieter but have less of a view. No meals are served other than breakfast, although the hall porter or a member of the staff can carry drinks to clients in the reception area. The breakfast room is especially appealing: Inspired by an Italian garden, it was designed by the noted architect Paolo Portoghesi.

Hotel Oxford. Via Boncompagni 89, 00187 Roma. ☎ **06/4282-8952.** Fax 06/4281-5349. 57 rms, 2 suites. A/C MINIBAR TV TEL. 240,000L ($153.60) double; 290,000L ($185.60) triple; 350,000L ($224) suite. Rates include breakfast. AE, DC, MC, V. 15% reductions Jan–Mar 15. Parking 30,000L–50,000L ($19.20–$32). Bus: 3, 4, 38, 56, 58, or 62.

The centrally located Hotel Oxford is a decent, although not spectacular, choice adjacent to the Borghese Gardens. Recently renovated, the rooms are now centrally heated with simple modern furnishings and full carpeting. The rooms are a bit sterile and functional in decor, but well maintained. There's a pleasant lounge and a cozy bar (which serves snacks), plus a dining room offering a good Italian cuisine.

La Residenza. Via Emilia 22–24, 00187 Roma. ☎ **06/488-0789.** Fax 06/485721. 27 rms, 6 suites. A/C MINIBAR TV TEL. 248,000L ($158.70) double; 280,000L ($179.20) suite. Rates include buffet breakfast. AE, MC, V. Parking (limited) 5,000L ($3.20). Metro: Pz. Barberini. Bus: 52, 53, 56, 58, 95, or 586.

La Residenza successfully combines the intimacy of a generously sized town house with the elegant appointments of a well-decorated hotel. It's a bit old-fashioned and homelike, and doesn't in any way try to pursue chicdom, but is still a favorite among international travelers. The location is superb but noisy. The converted villa has an ivy-covered courtyard and a labyrinthine series of upholstered public rooms with

Accommodations Near Via Veneto & Termini

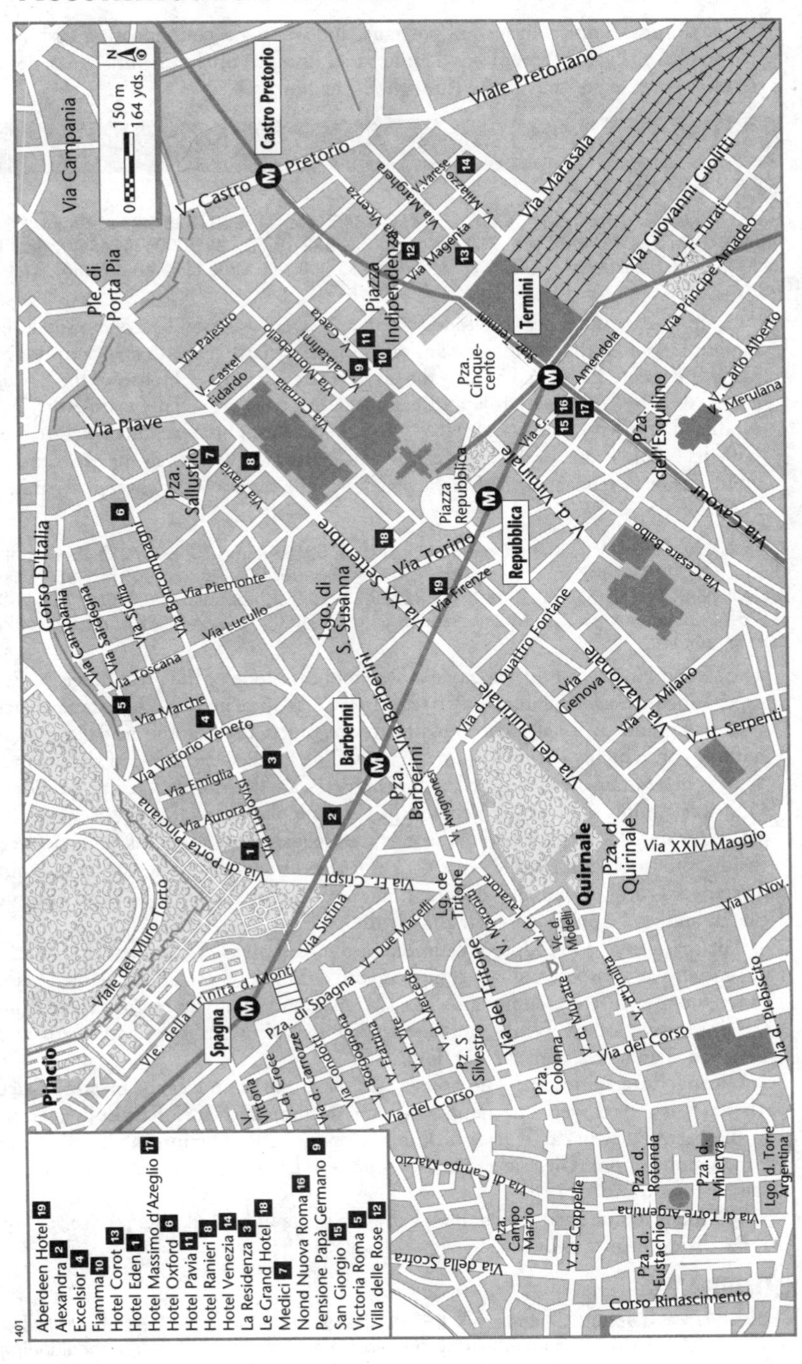

Oriental rugs, Empire divans, oil portraits, and warmly accommodating cushioned rattan chairs. Each bedroom has a radio in addition to other amenities. A series of terraces is scattered strategically throughout the hotel.

7 Near the Termini

VERY EXPENSIVE

Hotel Massimo d'Azeglio. Via Cavour 18, 00184 Roma. ☎ **800/223-9832** in the U.S., or 06/487-0270. Fax 06/482-7386. 210 rms. A/C MINIBAR TV TEL. 385,000L ($246.40) double. Rates include breakfast. AE, DC, MC, V. Parking 35,000L–40,000L ($22.40–$25.60). Metro: Termini.

This up-to-date hotel near the train station and opera was established as a small restaurant by one of the founders of an Italian hotel dynasty more than a century ago. Today this centrally located hotel is the Casa Madre, or Mother House, of the Bettoja chain. Run by Angelo Bettoja and his charming wife, who hails from America's southland, it offers clean, comfortable accommodations, plus a bar and a well-trained staff. Its facade is one of the most elegant neoclassical structures in the area, and its lobby has been renovated, with light paneling. The restaurant is covered separately in Chapter 5.

✪ **Le Grand Hotel.** Via Vittorio Emanuele Orlando 3, 00185 Roma. ☎ **800/221-2340** in the U.S., or 800/955-2442 in Canada, or 06/4709. Fax 06/474-7307. 134 rms, 36 suites. A/C MINIBAR TV TEL. 530,000L–580,000L ($339.20–$371.20) double; 900,000L–1,600,000L ($576–$1,024) suite. AE, DC, MC, V. Parking 35,000L–40,000L ($22.40–$25.60). Metro: Pz. della Repubblica.

The Grand Hotel, just off Piazza della Repubblica, is one of the great hotels in Europe. When it was inaugurated by its creator, César Ritz, in 1894, Le Grand struck a note of grandeur it has tried to maintain ever since. Its location near the railway station—once highly desirable—no longer is. The Hassler at the top of the Spanish Steps is more dramatically located, and many VIPs are flocking to the restored Eden. Only a few minutes from Via Veneto, the Grand looks like a large late-Renaissance palace, its five-floor facade covered with carved loggias, lintels, quoins, and cornices. Inside, the floors are marble with Oriental rugs, the walls are a riot of baroque plasterwork, and crystal chandeliers, Louis XVI furniture, potted palms, antique clocks, and wall sconces complete the picture.

The spacious and soundproof bedrooms are conservatively decorated with matching curtains and carpets, and are equipped with a dressing room and fully tiled bath. Every room is different, although some are less grand than you might expect from the impressive lobby. While most are traditional, with antique headboards and Venetian chandeliers, some are modern.

Dining/Entertainment: The hotel's Le Grand Bar is an elegant meeting place where tea is served every afternoon in winter, accompanied by a harpist or pianist. At the Salad Bar you can enjoy quick meals, or try Le Restaurant, the hotel's more formal dining room. Dietetic and kosher foods can be arranged with advance notice. Service is first-rate.

Services: Room service (24 hours), baby-sitting, laundry and valet service.

Facilities: Beauty salon.

MODERATE

Medici. Via Flavia 96, 00187 Roma. ☎ **06/482-7319.** Fax 06/474-0767. 68 rms. MINIBAR TV TEL. 200,000L ($128) double. Rates include breakfast. AE, DC, MC, V. Air-conditioning 20,000L ($12.80) extra. Parking 28,000L–35,000L ($17.90–$22.40). Metro: Pz. della Repubblica.

Quite a comedown from the Grand, the Medici, built in 1906, is still a substantial hotel with easy access to the shops along Via XX Settembre and the train station. Many of its better rooms overlook an inner patio garden, with Roman columns holding up greenery and climbing ivy. The lounge, with its white-coved ceiling, has many nooks connected by wide white arches. The furnishings, in the public areas and the generous-sized rooms, are traditional, with lots of antiques. Only a few rooms are air-conditioned.

Nord Nuova Roma. Via Giovanni Amendola 3, 00185 Roma. ☎ **800/223-9832** in the U.S., or 06/488-5441. Fax 06/481-7163. 159 rms. A/C MINIBAR TV TEL. 250,000L ($160) double. Rates include breakfast. AE, DC, MC, V. Parking 35,000L–45,000L ($22.40–$28.80). Metro: Termini.

This is the best bargain in the family-run Bettoja chain, although a rather plain hotel. It has garage parking for 100 cars and a small, intimate bar. It's well-maintained and most rooms are standard and modernized, making the hotel a good family choice. You can arrange a savory lunch or dinner at the nearby Massimo d'Azeglio Restaurant.

San Giorgio. Via Giovanni Amendola 61, 00185 Roma. ☎ **800/223-9832** in the U.S., or 06/482-7341. Fax 06/488-3191. 186 rms, 5 suites. A/C MINIBAR TV TEL. 340,000L ($217.60) double; from 465,000L ($297.60) suite. Rates include breakfast. AE, DC, MC, V. Parking 35,000L–45,000L ($22.40–$28.80). Metro: Termini.

A four-star hotel built in 1940, the San Giorgio is constantly being improved by its founders, the Bettoja family (it was the first air-conditioned hotel in Rome, and is now also soundproof). It's a more inspired choice than the Nord Nuova Roma (above), and is connected to the Massimo d'Azeglio so guests can patronize its fine restaurant. The hotel is ideal for families, as many of its corner rooms can be converted into larger quarters. Each bedroom has a radio, along with other amenities that often lie behind wood-veneer doors. Breakfast is served in a light and airy room, and the staff is most helpful.

INEXPENSIVE

Aberdeen Hotel. Via Firenze 48, 00184 Roma. ☎ **06/482-3920.** Fax 06/482-1092. 26 rms. A/C MINIBAR TV TEL. 230,000L ($147.20) double. Rates include breakfast. AE, DC, MC, V. Parking 25,000L ($16). Metro: Termini.

This is a completely renovated hotel near the Rome Opera House, central to both landmarks and the train station. It's in a quiet and fairly safe area of Rome—in front of the Ministry of Defense. The rooms are furnished in an uninspired modern style, with such amenities as hair dryers and radios. Only a breakfast buffet is served, but many inexpensive *trattorie* are nearby.

Fiamma. Via Gaeta 61, 00185 Roma. ☎ **06/481-8436.** Fax 06/488-3511. 79 rms. TV TEL. 180,000L–230,000L ($115.20–$147.20) double. Rates include breakfast. AE, DC, MC, V. Parking 10,000L ($6.40). Metro: Termini.

The Fiamma, on the far side of the Baths of Diocletian, is a renovated old building, with five floors of shuttered windows and a ground floor faced with marble and plate-glass windows. It's an enduring favorite, although critics say that it's long past its heyday. The lobby is long and bright, filled to the brim with a varied collection of furnishings, including overstuffed chairs, blue enamel railings, and indirect lighting. On the same floor is a monklike breakfast room made of marble. Some of the comfortably furnished bedrooms are air-conditioned.

Hotel Corot. Via Marghera 15–17, 00185 Roma. ☎ **06/4470-0900.** Fax 06/4470-0905. 20 rms. A/C MINIBAR TV TEL. 150,000L–190,000L ($96–$121.60) double; 170,000L–205,000L

($108.80–$131.20) triple; 190,000L–220,000L ($121.60–$140.80) quad. Rates include breakfast. AE, DC, MC, V. 15% weekend discounts for multiple-night weekend stays. Parking 25,000L–28,000L ($16–$17.90). Metro: Termini.

Modernized and comfortable, this hotel occupies the second and third floors of a turn-of-the-century building that contains a handful of private apartments and another, somewhat less accessorized hotel. The Corot is a safe but lackluster bet north of the Termini, and far better than some of the horrors south of the station. Guests register in a small, paneled area on the building's street level, then take an elevator to their respective floors. The bedrooms are airy, high-ceilinged, and filled with simple but traditional furniture and soothing colors. The bathrooms are modern and contain hair dryers. There's a residents' bar near the sun-flooded windows in one of the public rooms.

Hotel Pavia. Via Gaeta 83, 00185 Roma. ☎ **06/483801.** Fax 06/481-9090. 50 rms. A/C MINIBAR TV TEL. 130,000L–190,000L ($83.20–$121.60) double. Rates include breakfast. AE, DC, MC, V. Parking 12,000L–20,000L ($7.70–$12.80). Metro: Termini.

The Hotel Pavia is a popular choice on this quiet street near the gardens of the Baths of Diocletian. Established in the 1980s, it occupies a much-renovated century-old private villa. You'll pass through a wisteria-covered passageway that leads to the recently modernized reception area and the public rooms, tastefully covered in light-grained paneling with white lacquer accents and carpeting. The staff is attentive. Front rooms tend to be noisy, but that's the curse of all Termini hotels. Nevertheless, the rooms are comfortable and fairly attractive, with simple, modern wood furnishings and soothing colors. All in all, it's a safe haven in an unsafe area.

Hotel Ranieri. Via XX Settembre 43, 00187 Roma. ☎ **06/481-4467.** Fax 06/481-8834. 40 rms. A/C MINIBAR TV TEL. 180,000L–250,000L ($115.20–$160) double. Rates include breakfast. AE, MC, V. Weekend discounts (except in Oct). Parking 20,000L–30,000L ($12.80–$19.20). Metro: Pz. della Repubblica.

The Ranieri is a winning three-star hotel in a very old, freshly restored building. The guest rooms received substantial renovation in 1995, complete with new furniture, carpets, wall coverings, and even new bathrooms. The location is good; from the hotel you can stroll to the Rome Opera, Piazza della Repubblica, and Via Veneto. The public rooms, the lounge, and the dining room are attractively decorated, in part with contemporary art. You can arrange for a home-cooked meal in the dining room.

$ **Hotel Venezia.** Via Varese 18, 00185 Roma. ☎ **06/445-7101.** Fax 06/495-7687. 61 rms. A/C MINIBAR TV TEL. 235,000L ($150.40) double; 320,000L ($204.80) triple. Rates include breakfast. AE, DC, MC, V. Parking 30,000L ($19.20). Metro: Termini.

The location of the Hotel Venezia is good, near the corner of Via Marghera—3 blocks from the railroad station, in a part-business, part-residential area dotted with a few old villas and palm trees. The Venezia had a total renovation in 1991, transforming it into a good-looking and cheerful hostelry with a charming collection of public rooms. The floors are brown marble. The bedrooms are furnished in some cases with furniture in the 17th-century style, although some are beginning to look shop-worn. All units have Murano chandeliers, and some have a balcony for surveying the action on the street below. The housekeeping is superb—the management really cares.

$ **Pensione Papà Germano.** Via Calatafimi 14A, 00185 Roma. ☎ **06/486919.** 13 rms, 2 with bath. TEL. 60,000L ($38.40) double without bath, 69,000L ($44.15) double with bath;

90,000L ($57.60) triple without bath, 85,000L ($53.15) triple with bath. AE, MC, V. 10% discounts Nov–Feb. Metro: Termini.

It's about as basic and simple as anything in this book. This 1892 belle époque building has undertaken some recent renovations, yet retains its simple, modest ambience. Chances are that your fellow residents will arrive, backpack in tow, directly from the train station 4 blocks to the south. Located on a block-long street immediately east of the Baths of Diocletian, this *pensione* has simple but clean accommodations with plain furniture, well-maintained showers, and a high-turnover clientele of European and North American students. The energetic, English-speaking owner, Gino Germano, offers advice on sightseeing to anyone who asks. No breakfast is served, but there are dozens of cafés nearby.

Villa delle Rose. Via Vicenza 5, 00185 Roma. ☎ **06/445-1788.** Fax 06/445-1639. 38 rms. A/C TV TEL. 240,000L–260,000L ($153.60–$166.40) double. Rates include breakfast. AE, DC, MC, V. Free parking. Metro: Termini or Castro Pretorio.

Set less than 2 blocks north of the railway station, behind a dignified cut-stone facade inspired by the Renaissance, this hotel was originally built as a private home in the late 1800s. Despite many renovations, you can still see the ornate trappings of the wealthy family who built the place, including a set of Corinthian-capped marble columns in the lobby and a flagstone-covered terrace that fills part of a verdant garden in back. Much of the interior has been redecorated with traditional wall coverings and new carpets. Morning breakfasts in the garden, where the hotel's namesake rows of pink and red roses bloom, do a lot to add country flavor to an otherwise very urban and noisy location. The English-speaking staff is helpful and tactful.

Staying in J. Paul Getty's Former Villa

La Posta Vecchia, in Palo Laziale, just south of Ladispoli (☎ **06/994-9501;** fax 06/994-9507), lies 22 miles northwest of Rome and about 14 miles up the coast from Leonardo da Vinci airport. Set on foundations of villas possibly built by Tiberius, this palatial villa was owned between 1960 and 1976 by one of the world's richest men, J. Paul Getty. In 1654 it was a guesthouse for the nearby Castello Oldescalchi. Set behind iron gates, the stucco-sided building stands amid formal gardens in an 8-acre park.

The villa retains many antiques collected by Getty, as well as many carefully disguised steel doors, escape routes, and security devices installed to protect him from intruders. Following the tragic kidnapping of his son in the early 1970s, Getty declared that the building's access to the sea was an unacceptable security risk. The house was sold and became a private home until 1990, when it was transformed into an exceptionally elegant hotel. Guests stay in 14 sumptuously decorated suites, which range in price from 640,000L to 2,140,000L ($409.60 to $1,369.60) a night. With discretion and politeness, staff members serve an international cuisine during lunch and dinner in a richly formal dining room. The villa is closed from January 15 to March 30.

Extensive renovations initiated during Getty's ownership revealed hundreds of ancient Roman artifacts, many of which are on display in a mini-museum. There's an indoor pool, plus a staff (some of whom used to work for Getty) adept at maintaining the illusion that clients have arrived as friends of the long-departed billionaire.

8 Near Vatican City

VERY EXPENSIVE

✪ Hotel Atlante Star. Via Vitelleschi 34, 00193 Roma. ☎ **06/687-3233.** Fax 06/687-2300. 80 rms, 10 suites. A/C MINIBAR TV TEL. 490,000L ($313.60) double; 580,000L ($371.20) suite. Rates include breakfast. AE, DC, MC, V. Parking 40,000L ($25.60). Metro: Ottaviano. Bus: 23, 64, 81, or 492. Tram: 19 or 30.

The Atlante Star is a first-class hotel a short distance from the Vatican, with the most striking views of St. Peter's of any hotel in Rome. The tastefully renovated lobby is covered with dark marble, chrome trim, and lots of exposed wood, whereas the upper floors give the impression of being inside a luxuriously appointed ocean liner. This stems partly from the lavish use of curved and lacquered surfaces, walls upholstered in freshly colored printed fabrics, modern bathrooms, and wall-to-wall carpeting. Even the door handles are art deco–inspired. The rooms are small but posh, outfitted with all the modern comforts. There's also a royal suite with a Jacuzzi. If there's no room at this inn, the owner will try to get you a room at his less desirable Atlante Garden nearby.

Dining/Entertainment: The restaurant, Les Etoiles, is an elegant roof-garden choice at night, with a 360° panoramic view of Rome and an illuminated St. Peter's in the background. The flavorful cuisine is inspired in part by Venice.

Services: Room service (24 hours), laundry/valet, baby-sitting, express checkout.

Facilities: Roof garden, foreign-currency exchange, business center (with secretarial services in English and translation services).

MODERATE

Hotel Atlante Garden. Via Crescenzio 78, 00193 Roma. ☎ **06/687-2361.** Fax 06/687-2315. 43 rms. A/C MINIBAR TV TEL. 350,000L ($224) double. Rates include breakfast. AE, DC, MC, V. Parking 40,000L ($25.60). Metro: Ottaviano. Bus: 23, 32, 49, 51, or 492. Tram: 19 or 30.

The Atlante Garden stands on a tree-lined street near the Vatican. Although not as attractive or well appointed as its sibling, the Atlante Star (above), it's much cheaper. The entrance takes you through a garden tunnel lined with potted palms, which eventually leads into a series of handsomely decorated public rooms. More classical in its decor than the Atlante Star, the Garden offers freshly papered and painted 19th-century–style bedrooms that contain tastefully conservative furniture and all the modern accessories. The renovated baths are tiled, and each is equipped with a Jacuzzi.

Hotel Columbus. Via della Conciliazione 33, 00193 Roma. ☎ **06/686-5435.** Fax 06/686-5435. 105 rms, 4 suites. A/C MINIBAR TV TEL. 270,000L ($172.80) double; 380,000L ($243.20) suite. Rates include breakfast. AE, DC, MC, V. Free parking. Bus: 64.

An impressive 15th-century palace built some 12 years before its namesake set off for America, the Hotel Columbus was once the private home of the wealthy cardinal who later became Pope Julius II and tormented Michelangelo into painting the Sistine Chapel. The building looks much as it must have centuries ago—a severe, time-stained facade, small windows, and heavy wooden doors leading from the street to the colonnades and arches of the inner courtyard. The cobbled entranceway leads to a reception hall with castlelike furniture, then on to a series of baronial public rooms. Note especially the main salon with its walk-in fireplace, oil portraits, battle scenes, and Oriental rugs.

The bedrooms are considerably simpler than the tiled and tapestried salons, done in soft beiges and furnished with comfortable and serviceable modern pieces. All

Accommodations in the Vatican Area

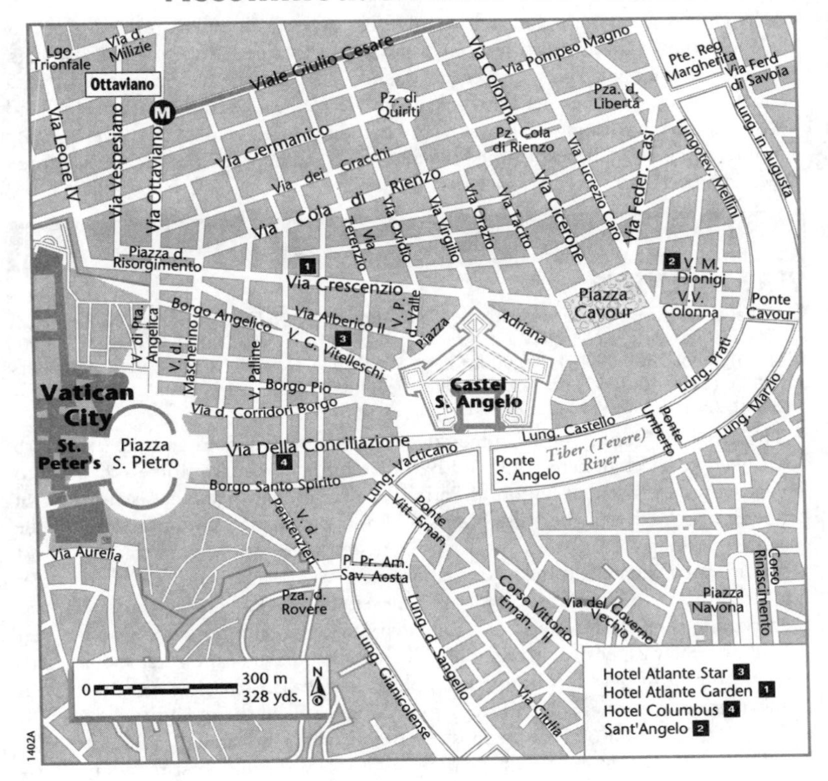

accommodations are spacious, but a few are enormous and still have such original details as decorated wood ceilings and frescoed walls. The hotel restaurant serves lunch and dinner.

INEXPENSIVE

Sant'Angelo. Via Mariana Dionigi 16, 00193 Roma. ☎ **06/322-0758.** Fax 06/320-4451. 24 rms. TV TEL. 140,000L ($89.60) double. AE, DC, MC, V. Parking 25,000L ($16). Bus: 49, 70, 87, 492, or 813.

Right off Piazza Cavour (northeast of the Castel Sant'Angelo), this hotel stands in a relatively untouristy area. Maintained and operated by several members of the Torre family, the hotel occupies the second and third floors of an imposing 200-year-old building whose other floors are devoted to offices and private apartments. The bedrooms are simple, modern, clean, and uncomplicated, with wooden furniture and views either of the street or of a rather bleak but quiet courtyard in back. Only breakfast is served, but the neighborhood offers many acceptable dining choices.

9 In Prati

Giulio Cesare. Via degli Scipioni 287, 00192 Roma. ☎ **06/321-0751.** Fax 06/321-1736. 86 rms. A/C MINIBAR TV TEL. 400,000L ($256) double. Rates include breakfast. AE, DC, MC, V. Free parking. Bus: 280.

The tasteful Giulio Cesare, an elegant villa that was the former house of Countess Paterno Solari, lies in a sedate part of Rome across the Tiber from Piazza del Popolo.

The guest salon, where the countess once entertained diplomats from all over the globe, is mostly furnished with antiques and Oriental carpets. Tapestries, Persian rugs, mirrors, ornate gilt pieces, and crystal chandeliers grace the public rooms. In yet a smaller salon, guests gather for drinks in an atmosphere of fruitwood paneling and 18th-century furnishings. The carpeted bedrooms look like part of a lovely private home; some contain needlepoint-covered chairs. Other facilities include a garden where breakfast is served, a snack bar, and a piano bar.

10 In Parioli

VERY EXPENSIVE

✪ **Hotel Lord Byron.** Via G. de Notaris 5, 00197 Roma. ☎ **06/322-0404.** Fax 06/322-0405. 28 rms, 9 suites. A/C MINIBAR TV TEL. Apr–July and Sept–Oct, 430,000L–540,000L ($275.20–$345.60) double; 800,000L–1,200,000L ($512–$768) suite. Nov–Mar and July–Aug, 360,000L–550,000L ($230.40–$352) double; 550,000L–1,000,000L ($352–$640) suite. Rates include breakfast. AE, DC, MC, V. Metro: Flaminio. Bus: 26 or 52.

The savvy set, fleeing those landmarks of yesterday (the Grand and the Excelsior), are likely to check in here. The Lord Byron exemplifies modern Rome—an art deco villa set on a residential hilltop in Parioli, an area of embassies and exclusive town houses at the edge of the Villa Borghese. From the curving entrance steps off the staffed parking lot in front, you'll notice design accessories that attract the most sophisticated clientele in Italy. An oval Renaissance urn in chiseled marble occupies a niche in the reception area. Flowers are everywhere, the lighting is discreet, and everything is on a cultivated small scale that makes it seem more like a well-staffed (and extremely expensive) private home than a hotel. Each of the guest rooms is different, but most have lots of mirrors, upholstered walls, a spacious bathroom with gray marble accessories, a big dressing room/closet, and all the amenities. Check into Rooms 503, 602, or 603 for the most panoramic views of Rome.

Dining/Entertainment: On the premises is one of Rome's best restaurants, recommended separately in Chapter 5.

Services: Concierge desk, room service (24 hours), laundry and valet service.

MODERATE

Hotel degli Aranci. Via Barnaba Oriani 9–11, 00197 Roma. ☎ **06/808-5250.** Fax 06/808-5250. 54 rms, 3 suites. A/C MINIBAR TV TEL. 260,000L ($166.40) double; 350,000L ($224) suite. Rates include breakfast. AE, DC, MC, V. Free parking. Bus: 3 or 53 from the Termini.

The degli Aranci is a long way down the ladder from its Parioli neighbor, the Lord Byron, in style, grace, and amenities, but is still worthy of serious consideration—and it doesn't charge the rarified prices of the Lord Byron. It's a former private villa on a tree-lined residential street in Parioli, surrounded by similar villas now used, in part, as consulates and ambassadorial town houses. Most of the accommodations have tall windows opening onto city views, and are filled with provincial furnishings or English-style reproductions. The public rooms have memorabilia of ancient Rome scattered about, including bisque-colored medallions of soldiers in profile, old engravings of ruins, and classical vases highlighted against the light grained paneling. A marble-top bar in an alcove off the sitting room adds a relaxed touch. From the glass-walled breakfast room, at the rear of the house, you can see the tops of orange trees.

INEXPENSIVE

$ **Hotel delle Muse.** Via Tommaso Salvini 18, 00197 Roma. ☎ **06/808-8333.** Fax 06/808-5749. 61 rms. TV TEL. 160,000L–180,000L ($102.40–$115.20) double; 220,000L ($140.80) triple. Rates include buffet breakfast. AE, DC, MC, V. Bus: 4. Tram: 19.

The Hotel delle Muse, a three-star establishment half a mile north of the Villa Borghese, is a winning but unheralded choice. It's run by the efficient, English-speaking Giorgio Lazar. A majority of the rooms have been renewed, but remain rather spartan and minimalist. In the summer Lazar operates a restaurant in the garden. A bar is open 24 hours a day in case you get thirsty at 5am. There's also a TV room, plus a writing room and a dining room.

11 In Monte Mario

✪ **Cavalieri Hilton.** Via Cadiolo 101, 00136 Roma. ☎ **800/445-8667** in the U.S. and Canada, or 06/35091. Fax 06/3509-2241. 376 rms, 17 suites. A/C MINIBAR TV TEL. 450,000L–515,000L ($288–$329.60) double; from 1,000,000L ($640) suite. AE, DC, MC, V. Parking 5,000L–30,000L ($3.20–$19.20). Free shuttle bus to/from the city center.

The Cavalieri Hilton combines all the advantages of a resort hotel with the convenience of being a 15-minute drive from the center of Rome. Overlooking the city and the Alban Hills from its perch on top of Monte Mario, it's set in 15 acres of trees, flowering shrubs, and stonework. Its facilities are so complete that many visitors—who have seen the city before—never leave the hotel grounds.

The guest rooms and suites, many with panoramic views, are designed to fit contemporary standards of comfort, quality, and style. Soft furnishings in pastel colors are paired with Italian furniture in warm-tone woods. Each unit has a keyless electronic lock, independent heating and air-conditioning, color TV with in-house movies, radio, and bedside controls for all electric apparatus in the room, as well as a spacious balcony. The bathrooms, sheathed in Italian marble, are equipped with large mirrors, a hair dryer, international electrical sockets, a vanity mirror, piped-in music, and a phone.

Dining/Entertainment: The hotel's stellar restaurant, La Pergola, has among the best dining views in Rome. In summer, a garden restaurant, Il Giardino dell'Uliveto, with a pool veranda, is an ideal choice.

Services: Concierge (24 hours), room service, laundry/valet, bus to/from the city center.

Facilities: Tennis courts, jogging paths, fitness center, spa, indoor arcade of shops, indoor and outdoor swimming pool, facilities for the disabled.

5 Dining

Rome is one of the world's greatest capitals for dining. From elegant, deluxe spots with lavish trappings to little trattorie opening onto hidden piazzas deep in the heart of Old Rome, the city abounds in good restaurants in all price ranges.

The better-known restaurants have menus printed in English. Even some of the lesser-known establishments have at least one person on the staff who speaks English a bit to help you get through the menu.

Most Italian restaurants are either called a **trattoria** or a **ristorante.** Supposedly there's a difference, but we've yet to discern one. Trattorie presumably are smaller and less formal, but sometimes in a kind of reverse snobbism the management will call an elegant place a trattoria. A ristorante is supposed to be more substantial, but often the opposite is true.

Roman meals customarily include at least three separate courses: pasta, a main course (usually a meat dish with vegetables or salad), and dessert. Meats, while tasty, are definitely secondary to the pasta dishes, which are much more generous and filling. The wine is so excellent (especially the white Frascati wine from the nearby Castelli Romani) and moderate in price that you may want to do as the Romans do and have it with both lunch and dinner.

Meal hours are rather confining in Italy. If you don't take continental breakfast at your hotel, you can have coffee and a pastry at any **bar** (really a café, although there will be liquor bottles behind the counter) or a **tavola calda** ("hot table"). These are stand-up snack bar–type arrangements, open all day long and found all over the city. Restaurants generally serve lunch between 1 and 3pm and dinner between about 8 and 10:30pm; at all other times, restaurants are closed. Dinner, by the way, is taken late in Rome, so while the restaurant may open at 7:30, even if you get there at 8pm, you'll often be the only one in the place. Romans think in terms of "dinner" in the afternoon *(pranzo)* and "supper" in the evening *(cena).*

Further, we'd recommend that you leave a few hours free for dinner and go to a restaurant in a different part of town each night. It's a great way to see Rome.

PRICES For our purposes, restaurants rated **"Very Expensive"** usually charge more than 120,000L ($76.80) for a three-course meal for one; **"Expensive,"** 70,000L to 120,000L ($44.80 to $76.80); and **"Moderate,"** 40,000L to 70,000L ($25.60 to $44.80). Any restaurant charging less than 40,000L ($25.60) is rated **"Inexpensive,"** at least in Rome. These prices are computed on the basis of a three-course meal (not the most expensive items on the menu), including a carafe of the house wine, service, and taxes.

A FINAL CAVEAT Most Roman restaurants are closed at least one day a week—usually Sunday or Monday, but that varies. Also, beware of the month of August, when most Romans go on holiday. Scores of restaurants close down, displaying only a lonely CHIUSO PER FERIE (closed for vacation) sign. It's always best to call a restaurant before you head there.

1 Best Bets

- **Best Romantic Dinner:** If you're getting ready to propose to someone, invite her/him to the **Relais Le Jardin** (☎ **06/361-3041**), a stunner of a place which also just happens to serve the best Italian cuisine in town. The decor is as romantic as the mood and atmosphere—aggressively lighthearted with white lattice and bold Italian colors along with artistically arranged masses of flowers. The setting is in the Relais & Châteaux–member hostelry the Lord Byron, an art deco villa set on a residential hilltop in Parioli, an area of embassies and exclusive town houses at the edge of the Villa Borghese.
- **Best Business Lunch:** The location of **George's** (☎ **06/4208-4575**) on Via Marche, right off Via Veneto, is most central (not far from the heartbeat Piazza Barberini), and the setting and clublike atmosphere are just perfect for doing business—and also for dining well. Here, one of the most professional and best-trained staffs in Rome will serve you in elegantly decorated dining rooms, being discreet when needed, allowing you time to make the deal, especially when the meal is fueled by one of Rome's finest wine cellars. If the weather is fair, you may want to request a table in the lovely garden where you're certain to be awarded the contract.
- **Best for a Celebration:** Romans have been flocking to **Checchino dal 1887** (☎ **06/574-3816**) since the early 19th century for fun and hearty food. With a bountiful array of wine and foodstuff, every night seems like a party. The location is Monte Testaccio, which was once a pile of broken amphoras and terra-cotta roof tiles collected back in Nero's day. The tables are packed nightly, and the place is a local legend. You'll have fun while still enjoying some of the best cuisine in town.
- **Best Decor:** Chic Romans along with savvy foreign visitors show up at **El Toulà** (☎ **06/687-3498**) at night to patronize "The Hayloft," an elegant establishment set near the fabled Caffè Greco and some of the most fashionable boutiques in Rome. It's no bargain, but once you see the sumptuous setting and, more important, enjoy the cuisine, you'll think it's worth the price. Haute cuisine is served in a subdued, tasteful setting of antiques, paintings, ever-so-discreet lighting, and oh-to-die-for flower arrangements.
- **Best View:** The stars really do come out at night at **Les Etoiles** (The Stars) (☎ **06/689-3434**), which has been labeled "the most beautiful rooftop in Italy." This restaurant is a virtual garden in the sky, with a 360° view of Roman landmarks, including the floodlit dome of St. Peter's. Try for a table alfresco in summer, but even in winter the same incredible view can be seen through picture windows. Fortunately, the food is the best in the area around the Vatican, a delicately prepared Mediterranean cuisine using the freshest of ingredients deftly handled by a professional and well-trained kitchen staff.
- **Best Wine List:** The food is only secondary at the **Trimani Wine Bar** (☎ **06/446-9630**), but the wine list is fabulous, a deluxe tour through the vineyards of

Italy. One of the best "tasting centers" in Rome for both French and Italian vintages, this elegant wine bar offers a dazzling array of wines at reasonable prices. The Trimani family has had a prestigious name in the wine business since 1821. By drinking and eating at their wine bar you'll be taken on a tour showing off the oenological bounty of their land. All you'll have to do to take this tour is sit down at one of their tables or stools and let the wine pourers begin.

- **Best Value:** For less than $20, at the **Ristorante del Pallaro** (☎ **06/6880-1488**) you'll be served one of the finest fixed-price menus in Rome, each dish lovingly prepared by the chef-owner, Paola Fazi, who urges her diners to *Mangia! Mangia!* The moment you're seated at the table the dishes start to flow, beginning with a selection of antipasti and going on to the homemade and rather succulent pastas of the day, followed by such meat courses as tender roast veal. Everything's included—even a carafe of the house wine.
- **Best for Kids:** After their tour of the Vatican or St. Peter's, many savvy Roman families head for the **Ristorante Il Matriciano** (☎ **06/321-2327**), a long-established and widely respected family dining room. It's not fancy, but the price is right and in summer you can opt for a sidewalk table. Let your kids feast on good and reasonably priced homemade fare, including ricotta-stuffed ravioli, a kid's favorite if there ever was one. At the next table you're likely to see some priests from the Vatican dining. It's a safe, wholesome environment, and the food is really tasty.
- **Best Continental Cuisine:** The city's finest restaurant is now **La Terrazza** (☎ **06/478121**), edging out a position long held by Sans Souci. In the restored Hotel Eden, former stamping ground of Hemingway, Ingrid Bergman, and Fellini, you can dine on continental cuisine that has both flair and innovation. The menu changes with the season and it's the most polished and urbane cuisine in Rome, as reflected by such dishes as a "symphony" of seafood or else some of the town's best and most succulent pasta dishes.
- **Best Italian Cuisine:** Italian food as you've almost never had it before is served at the **Relais Le Jardin** (☎ **06/361-3041**), a refined citadel of haute cuisine. In a luxurious setting, with a surprisingly long menu, you can feast on some of the best and most traditional fare of such regions as Lazio and Abruzzi. Everything is given an innovative and light touch. The most demanding Roman palates are wined and dined here, enjoying the freshest of produce in any season, beginning with the bright zucchini blossoms of spring.
- **Best Nuova Cucina:** A short walk north of Ponte Cavour is **Il Canto del Riso** (☎ **06/324-0128**), a barge and passenger ship permanently moored at a quay of the Tiber. In warm weather the management expands its premises by setting up tables on the riverside quay. Although the setting is memorable, it's the lighthearted cuisine—*nuova cucina,* or nouvelle cuisine—that draws the demanding clients. Dishes are light with many imaginative and innovative touches, as reflected in the marvelous array of risottos made with fresh-from-the-market ingredients, most often vegetables such as asparagus or artichokes. The menu is changed frequently so that it will always reflect the finest of local produce available on any given day at the market.
- **Best Emilia Romagna Cuisine:** The area around Bologna has long been celebrated for serving the finest cuisine in Italy, and the little trattoria **Colline Emiliane** (☎ **06/481-7538**) does much to maintain that stellar reputation among Romans. The pastas here are among the best in Rome, especially the handmade tortellini alla panna (cream sauce) with truffles. You can order less expensive pastas as well, all of them good. You're also served prosciutto from a small town near Parma which is reputedly the best in the world.

- **Best Neapolitan Cuisine:** It's so cornball "O Sole Mio" that you'll think you've been sent to a tourist trap. But the food that emerges from the Neapolitan kitchen at **Scoglio di Frisio** (☎ **06/487-2765**) is the best of its kind in the city. You get not only the crunchy, oozy, and excellent Neapolitan pizzas here, but an array of foodstuff ranging from chicken cacciatore to veal scaloppine that's perfectly prepared. Near the Stazione Termini, the trattoria has been a longtime favorite of visitors to Rome in spite of its somewhat sleazy location.
- **Best Roman Cuisine:** The tempting selection of antipasti is enough of a treat to lure you to **Al Ceppo** ("The Log") (☎ **06/841-9696**). Try such appetizers as stuffed yellow or red peppers or finely minced cold spinach blended with ricotta. Only 2 blocks from the Villa Borghese, this is a dining address jealously guarded by Romans, who often take their friends from out of town here. They feast on the most perfectly done lamb chops—charcoal-grilled to perfection—even quail, liver, or bacon from the grill. Roman dishes and Roman flavors have proven a powerful culinary allure over the years.
- **Best Tuscan Cuisine:** For the most delicious and tender bistecca alla fiorentina (beefsteak Florentine style) in Rome, head for **Girarrosto Toscano,** off Via Veneto (☎ **06/482-3835**). The chefs grill the meats to perfection, seasoning it only with virgin olive oil, salt, and pepper. You get an array of other dishes as well, including one of the best selections of antipasti in town, everything from vine-ripened melon with prosciutto to a delectable Tuscan salami. Oysters and fresh fish from the Adriatic are also served.
- **Best Fruits of the Sea:** For not only the best but the most beautiful seafood restaurant in Rome, go to **Alberto Ciarla** (☎ **06/581-8668**). This place was among the first to create new and innovative preparations of seafood, which Romans traditionally have either fried or put into soups. Overcooked seafood is definitely not on the agenda here. Some Romans even tried raw fish for the first time at this place. Although this restaurant doesn't enjoy the fame it did when it opened, it's just as good as it ever was. Fish dishes are perfectly seasoned but designed to bring out the natural flavor of the sea—and not "drown" the "sea fruits."
- **Best Pizzeria:** Deep in the heart of Trastevere, when a Neapolitan, Vittorio, immodestly admits he makes the best pizzas in Rome, you're inclined to agree with him—especially after you taste one of his pies at **Da Vittorio** (☎ **06/580-0353**). The pizza Vittorio is our favorite—made with fresh basil, fresh tomato, parmesan, and mozzarella. This is a popular and fun place, with outdoor tables in fair weather. The youthful crowd of diners bursts with exuberance.
- **Best Pizza Rustica:** One place, **Pizzeria Est! Est! Est!,** has been serving pizzas since the turn of the century, making it the oldest pizzeria in Rome. Opinions are divided over whether it's the best, but the kitchen has had a long time to perfect its pie technique. The setting is rustic as pizza fanciers eat at wood tables astride antique woodwork, filling up on pizzas with various toppings and calzoni ripieni. The same starched, elderly waiters have seemingly been here forever.
- **Best Wild Game:** The best selection of game specialties in Rome is served at **Da Mario** (☎ **06/678-3818**), although you can order other excellently prepared dishes as well if your dining partner isn't into game. Begin with pappardelle, which comes with a game sauce known as caccia. You'd have to go to Lombardy (Milan) to find better roast quail with polenta. Something that's different and delectable from field and stream is always showing up on the menu. The best wild game dishes are served in autumn.
- **Best Restaurant for Desserts:** It's a bit of an exaggeration to say that people fly to Rome just to sample the dessert specialty—a tartufo—at **Tre Scalini**

(☎ **06/687-9148**), but that would be reason enough to buy an airplane ticket. The dessert is fabled, consisting of a grated bitter chocolate–covered chocolate ice cream ball swathed in whipped cream. It's named for its resemblance to the knobby truffle. There are other desserts as well, and on almost any night you'll find cone seekers (those not dining upstairs) often 3 feet deep at the ice-cream counter outside. If you can take your mind off the tartufo, you'll have a ringside seat at Rome's most beautiful square, Piazza Navona, facing Bernini's Fontana dei Fiumi.

- **Best Restaurant for a 4-Hour Lunch:** On the historic Appian Way, only a short walk from the catacombs of St. Sebastian, the family-run **Hostaria l'Archeologia** (☎ **06/788-0494**), which looks like an 18th-century village tavern, is a place for lingering. If the day is sunny, you can sit late into the afternoon enjoying the wines of Lazio after a robust, hearty, and satisfying Roman-style meal. Opt for the garden out back and find a table shaded from the sun by the spreading wisteria, and you may never want to leave until the waiters start closing down the joint. The wines emerge from a cellar that used to be a Roman tomb. Who knows what might happen after a long meal here? We once took travel guru and founder of this travel series, Arthur Frommer, here for lunch, and before it was over he'd proposed that we write a guide to Italy.
- **Best Late-Night Pastry Shop:** Right on Piazza del Popolo, where young men and women drive up in their Maseratis and Porsches, the **Café Rosati** (☎ **06/322-5859**) gets active as the night wears on. Although you can order whisky, many come here for the delectable Italian pastries. It's also an ideal spot for an ice cream dish while sitting at one of the sidewalk tables.
- **Best Outdoor Restaurant:** In Trastevere, Piazza Santa Maria comes alive at night. It's almost a scene straight from Fellini's *Roma.* If you reserve a sidewalk table at **Sabatini** (☎ **06/581-2026**), you'll have a view of all the action, including the floodlit golden mosaics of the church on the piazza, Santa Maria in Trastevere. At the next table you're likely to see—well, just about anybody (on our most recent visit, Roman Polanski). In addition to the view, you get some of the best grilled fish and Florentine steaks here.
- **Best Restaurant for People-Watching:** Join the fashionable young actors, models, and artists from nearby Via Margutta who descend on Piazza del Popolo at night, which is said to be haunted by the memories of Nero. The square still retains its fashion whereas Via Veneto long ago faded with the memories of *la dolce vita.* Often arriving in sports cars, young men with their silk shirts unbuttoned—hopefully showing off what they view as their Davidesque chests—are definitely on the prowl at night for the female beauties of Rome. At **Dal Bolognese** (☎ **06/361-1426**), you can not only take in this fascinating nighttime scene but you can also enjoy some of the finest dishes from the Bolognese table, which has the most delectable specialties in Italy. Sometimes, however, the scene is so lively it's hard to concentrate on the food.
- **Best Café for People-Watching:** In the 1950s during the heyday of *la dolce vita,* the **Caffè de Paris** (☎ **06/488-5284**) was a gathering place for the *bella gente* (beautiful people) of that era, many appearing in night-owl sunglasses. The night-owl sunglasses are still here, but the big names like Fellini have long gone. However, this remains the best café in Rome if you'd like to see a passing parade from the mainstream of world tourism. You can inspect the people passing by if you opt for a sidewalk table. All fashions, all persuasions, and all types—from the beauties to the beasts—stroll by, inspecting you as you inspect them.
- **Best for a Cappuccino with a View:** Surely the most desirable café in Rome is **Di Rienzo** (☎ **06/686-9097**), but only because of its location. It stands directly

on Piazza della Rotonda fronting the Pantheon, one of the greatest of all monuments to come down from ancient Rome. It was reconstructed by the emperor Hadrian in the first part of the 2nd century A.D. On a summer night there's no better place to be in all of Rome, as you sit and slowly sip your cappuccino. The square in front of you has been called "the living room" of Rome.

- **Best Tavola Calda:** One of the best *tavola caldas* ("hot tables") in Rome is **Cottini** (☎ **06/474-0768**), convenient for those staying in hotels around the Stazione Termini. The food is artfully displayed, and the selection is bountiful—not only freshly made salads but also hot pastas and main courses just prepared. Portions are very generous, and you can fill up fast on the cornucopia of all the bounty of agrarian Latium. Tempting desserts such as a melt-in-your-mouth chocolate cake are prepared at the in-house bakery.
- **Best Tramezzini:** Romans are adept at making *tramezzini,* sandwiches made of sliced white bread in all sorts of tasty concoctions. No one does them better than the staff at **La Casa del Tramezzino** (no phone). The term *tramezzino* dates back to the Mussolini era when the dictator banned the use of foreign words such as "sandwich." Tramezzini are usually less expensive than panini, which are filled rolls. Romans often ask for them to be *riscaldati,* or heated on a griddle. Once that's done a tramezzino becomes *un toast.* The assortment—some 64 in all—is the widest in Rome, everything from the classics such as mozzarella and fresh tomato to something more exotic such as arugula and Gorgonzola.
- **Best Open-Air Food Market:** Between Corso Vittorio Emanuele II and the Tiber, is **Campo de' Fiori,** seemingly everybody's favorite market in Rome—and that's been true for centuries. Romans are extremely picky about their food: You'll see some housewives or housemen going over each cherry, berry by berry. The luscious produce of Lazio is on display here right in the heart of the old city. In spite of its name "field of flowers" (the English translation), this is not a flower market. The name is derived from Flora, lover of Pompey, the great Roman general. If you wish, you can purchase vegetables already chopped and ready to be dropped into the minestrone pot.
- **Best Picnic Fare:** When the weather is cool and the day is sunny, the countyside of Lazio beckons. It's time for a picnic. There is no better place for the ingredients for a *luxe* picnic than the **Campo de' Fiori** open-air market, with stall after stall selling everything from open baskets of ready-stipped broccoli to legumes. There are several excellent delicatessan shops on the square selling virtually anything you'd need for a grand picnic. Visit one of the bread shops for some freshly baked Roman bread, pick up a bottle of wine and a companion—and the day is yours.
- **Best Ristorante:** With one dining room decorated in the style of an 18th-century tavern and another occupying Pompey's ancient theater, the **Ristorante da Pancrazio** (☎ **06/686-1246**) is not only architecurally amusing, but serves good Roman food. It's a national monument, in fact. Here you sample one of the widest selections of Roman dishes, including the kitchen's fabled mixed fish fry. There's also a savory risotto made with a medley of "fruits of the sea."
- **Best Trattoria:** In the heart of the old Jewish Ghetto, a short walk from Michelangelo's Campodoglio, is **Vecchia Roma** (☎ **06/686-4604**), a landmark trattoria that's been feeding savvy Roman foodies for years. Even movie stars have been slipped this address as a place where they can enjoy good food and the "paparazzi will never find you." The antipasto selection is prepared fresh daily and is one of the finest in the area. The pasta and risotto dishes are succulent, and the meats—especially the lamb roasted in Roman ovens to crispy perfection—are from excellent cuts.

- **Best Osteria:** Near Campo de' Fiori, the **Hostaria Grappolo d'Oro** (☎ **06/686-4118**) was put on the tourist map by a *New Yorker* article praising the cuisine here. The owner admitted that he never read the article, although the international world started to show up at this previously unheralded place. One reviewer wrote that this neighborhood trattoria, often frequented by Romans who live nearby, is pure "gastronomic ecstasy." We wouldn't go that far, but it's certainly good, everything washed down with the house white wine.
- **Best Restaurant to See a Movie Star:** Although Elizabeth Taylor is long gone and no one talks about "Hollywood on the Tiber" anymore, glitz and glamour—whatever's left of it—still reign at **Sans Souci** (☎ **06/482-1814**), Rome's most fashionable and flashiest dining room. You'll rarely find a Roman here, but those on the see-and-be-seen international circuit show up. If you had to invite Madonna to dinner during a visit to Rome, this is where you'd take her.
- **Best Gelateria:** Once we spotted Ingrid Bergman entering a gelateria for some ice cream, and we followed her, ordering what she did because we figured this savvy Swede knew what and where to go for a good *coppa*. She did indeed, and we've been patronizing **Giolitti** (☎ **06/699-1243**), near Piazza Colonna, ever since. We think this gelateria serves the best ice cream in Rome, and it comes in all those delectable Italian flavors like melon and cappuccino.

2 Restaurants by Cuisine

Abruzzese

Abruzzi (Near Ancient Rome, *I*)
Majella, La (Near Campo de' Fiori & the Jewish Ghetto, *I*)
Piccolo Abruzzo (Near Via Veneto & Piazza Barberini, *I*)

Bolognese

Dal Bolognese (Near Piazza di Spagna & Piazza del Popolo, *M*)

Calabrese

Maschere, Le (Near Campo de' Fiori & the Jewish Ghetto, *I*)

Continental

Trimani Wine Bar (Near the Termini, *I*)

Emilia-Romagnola

Césarina (Near Via Veneto & Piazza Barberini, *I*)
Colline Emiliane (Near Via Veneto & Piazza Barberini, *I*)

English

Babington's Tea Rooms (Near Piazza di Spagna & Piazza del Popolo, *I*)

Florentine

Da Mario (Near Piazza di Spagna & Piazza del Popolo, *I*)

French

L'Eau Vive (Near Piazza Navona & the Pantheon, *I*)
Sans Souci (Near Via Veneto & Piazza Barberini, *VE*)

International

Alfredo alla Scrofa (Near Piazza Navona & the Pantheon, *M*)
George's (Near Via Veneto & Piazza Barberini, *VE*)
L'Eau Vive (Near Piazza Navona & the Pantheon, *I*)
Ristorante Ranieri (Near Piazza di Spagna & Piazza del Popolo, *I*)
Taverna Flavia di Mimmo (Near the Termini, *M*)
Terrazza, La (Near Via Veneto & Piazza Barberini, *VE*)

Italian

Alvaro al Circo Massimo (Near Ancient Rome, *M*)

Key to Abbreviations: *VE* = Very Expensive; *E* = Expensive; *M* = Moderate; *I* = Inexpensive.

Aurora 10 da Pino il Sommelier (Near Via Veneto & Piazza Barberini, *M*)
Canto del Riso, Il (Near Vatican City, *M*)
Cottini (Near the Termini, *I*)
Hostaria l'Archeologia (On the Appian Way, *I*)
Majella, La (Near Campo de' Fiori & the Jewish Ghetto, *I*)
Montevecchio (Near Piazza Navona & the Pantheon, *M*)
Paella Due / Paella Due Bis (In Trastevere, *I*)
Passetto (Near Piazza Navona & the Pantheon, *M*)
Relais Le Jardin (In Parioli, *VE*)
Ristorante Giardinaccio (Near Vatican City, *I*)
Ristorante Ranieri (Near Piazza di Spagna & Piazza del Popolo, *I*)
Terrazza, La (Near Via Veneto & Piazza Barberini, *VE*)
Vecchia Roma (Near Campo de' Fiori & the Jewish Ghetto, *M*)

Mediterranean

Babington's Tea Rooms (Near Piazza di Spagna & Piazza del Popolo, *I*)
Les Etoiles (Near Vatican City, *E*)

Molisan

Ristorante Giardinaccio (Near Vatican City, *I*)

Neapolitan

Scoglio di Frisio (Near the Termini, *M*)

Pasta

Da Vittorio (In Trastevere, *I*)

Pizza

Da Vittorio (In Trastevere, *I*)

Roman

Al Ceppo (In Parioli, *M*)
Alfredo alla Scrofa (Near Piazza Navona & the Pantheon, *M*)
Angelino a Tormargana (Near Campo de' Fiori & the Jewish Ghetto, *E*)
Carbonara, La (Near Campo de' Fiori & the Jewish Ghetto, *M*)
Césarina (Near Via Veneto & Piazza Barberini, *I*)
Checchino dal 1887 (In Testaccio, *M*)
Cisterna, La (In Trastevere, *M*)
Da Giggetto (Near Campo de'Fiori & the Jewish Ghetto, *I*)
Da Mario (Near Piazza di Spagna & Piazza del Popolo, *I*)
El Toulà (Near Piazza di Spagna & Piazza del Popolo, *E*)
Hostaria dei Bastioni (Near Vatican City, *I*)
Hostaria Grappolo d'Oro (Near Campo de' Fiori & the Jewish Ghetto, *I*)
Hostaria l'Archeologia (On the Appian Way, *I*)
Massimo d'Azeglio (Near the Termini, *M*)
Miraggio, Il (Near Piazza Navona & the Pantheon, *I*)
Monte Arci (Near the Termini, *I*)
Montevecchio (Near Piazza Navona & the Pantheon, *M*)
Osteria dell'Angelo (Near Vatican City, *I*)
Otello alla Concordia (Near Piazza di Spagna & Piazza del Popolo, *I*)
Passetto (Near Piazza Navona & the Pantheon, *M*)
Quirino (Near Piazza Navona & the Pantheon, *I*)
Ristorante da Pancrazio (Near Campo de' Fiori & the Jewish Ghetto, *M*)
Ristorante del Pallaro (Near Campo de' Fiori & the Jewish Ghetto, *I*)
Ristorante Il Matriciano (Near Vatican City, *M*)
Ristorante Pierdonati (Near Vatican City, *M*)
Ristorante 34, Il (Near Piazza di Spagna & Piazza del Popolo, *I*)
Sabatini (In Trastevere, *M*)
Taverna Flavia di Mimmo (Near the Termini, *M*)
Tre Scalini (Near Piazza Navona & the Pantheon, *M*)

Sandwiches

Casa del Tramezzino, La (In Trastevere, *I*)

Sardinian

Drappo, Il (Near Campo de' Fiori & the Jewish Ghetto, *E*)
Hostaria er Belli (In Trastevere, *I*)
Miraggio, Il (Near Piazza Navona & the Pantheon, *I*)
Monte Arci (Near the Termini, *I*)

Seafood

Alberto Ciarla (In Trastevere, *E*)
Sabatini (In Trastevere, *M*)

Sicilian

Quirino (Near Piazza Navona & the Pantheon, *I*)

Spanish

Paella Due / Paella Due Bis (In Trastevere, *I*)

Tuscan

Girarrosto Toscano (Near Via Veneto & Piazza Barberini, *M*)
Ristorante Nino (Near Piazza di Spagna & Piazza del Popolo, *I*)

Vegetarian

Margutta Vegetariano (Near Piazza di Spagna & Piazza del Popolo, *I*)

Venetian

El Toulà (Near Piazza di Spagna & Piazza del Popolo, *E*)

3 Near Ancient Rome

MODERATE

Alvaro al Circo Massimo. Via dei Cerchi 53. ☎ **06/678-6112.** Reservations required. Main courses 12,000L–20,000L ($7.70–$12.80). AE, MC, V. Tues–Sat 1–3pm and 7–11pm, Sun 1–3pm. Closed Aug. Metro: Circo Massimo. Bus: 15, 90, 90b, or 166. ITALIAN.

Alvaro al Circo Massimo, at the edge of the Circus Maximus, is the closest thing in Rome to a genuine provincial inn. Here is all the decor associated with Italian taverns, including corn on the cob hanging from the ceiling and rolls of fat sausages. Their antipasti and pasta dishes are fine and the meat courses well prepared, and there's an array of fresh fish—never overcooked. Other specialties include tagliolini with mushrooms and truffles, and roasted turbot with potatoes. They're especially well stocked with exotic seasonal mushrooms, including black truffles so good you'd have to go directly to Spoleto to find better. A basket of fresh fruit rounds out the repast. Try to linger longer and make an evening of it—the atmosphere is mellow.

INEXPENSIVE

$ **Abruzzi.** Via Vaccaro 1. ☎ **06/679-3897.** Reservations recommended. Main courses 12,000L–23,000L ($7.70–$14.70). DC, MC, V. Sun–Fri 12:30–3pm and 7:30–10:30pm. Closed 2 weeks in Aug (dates vary). Bus: 17, 57, 64, or 70. ABRUZZESE.

Abruzzi takes its name from a little-explored region east of Rome known for its haunting beauty and curious superstitions. The restaurant is located at one side of Piazza SS. Apostoli, just a short walk from Piazza Venezia. The good food here at reasonable prices makes it enduringly popular among students. The chef is justly praised for his satisfying assortment of cold antipasti. With your starter, we suggest a liter of garnet-red wine; we once had one whose bouquet was suggestive of the wildflowers of Abruzzi. If you'd like a soup as well, you'll find a good stracciatella (an egg-and-cheese soup). A typical main dish is saltimbocca (literally "jump-in-the-mouth," a veal and prosciutto dish flavored with marsala).

4 Near Campo de' Fiori & the Jewish Ghetto

EXPENSIVE

Angelino a Tormargana. Piazza Margana 37. ☎ **06/678-3328.** Reservations not necessary. Main courses 50,000L–75,000L ($32–$48). MC, V. Mon–Sat noon–3:30pm and 7:30–11pm. Bus: 64, 90, 90b, 95, or 710. ROMAN.

Goethe once frequented this tavern 3 blocks from Piazza Venezia, as did Anna Magnani, Jean-Paul Sartre, and even Richard Nixon. Back in fashion after a number of years, the tavern has subsequently elevated its prices. Everything else—from the atmosphere to the food—has remained unchanged, and that's why Romans like it so. You can dine alfresco in a setting of old palazzi and cobblestone squares. The food is very much in the typical Roman trattoria style—not exceptionally imaginative, but good. We'd recommend the cold seafood risotto or the penne all'arrabbiata (with a tomato and hot pepper sauce). For a main course, you might select kidneys with mushrooms or veal scaloppine flavored with lemon juice. Other main-dish selections are pollo alla diavola and that staple of Roman cuisine, tripe.

Il Drappo. Vicolo del Malpasso 9. ☎ **06/687-7365.** Reservations required. Main courses 20,000L–25,000L ($12.80–$16); fixed-price menu (including Sardinian wine) 60,000L ($38.40). AE, MC, V. Mon–Sat 8pm–midnight. Closed 2 weeks in Aug. Bus: 46, 62, or 64. SARDINIAN.

Il Drappo, on a narrow street near the Tiber, is operated by a woman known to her habitués only as "Valentina." You'll have your choice of two tastefully decorated dining rooms festooned with yards of patterned cotton draped from supports on the ceiling. Flowers and candles are everywhere. Fixed-price dinners may include a wafer-thin appetizer called carte di musica (sheet-music paper), which is topped with tomatoes, green peppers, parsley, and olive oil, followed by fresh spring lamb (in season), a fish stew made with tuna caviar, or a changing selection of strongly flavored regional specialties that are otherwise difficult to find in Rome. Service is first-rate.

MODERATE

La Carbonara. Piazza Campo de' Fiori 23. ☎ **06/686-4783.** Reservations recommended. Main courses 14,000L–22,000L ($8.95–$14.10). AE, MC, V. Wed–Mon noon–2:30pm and 6:30–10:30pm. Closed 3 weeks Aug. Bus: 64. ROMAN.

In an antique *palazzetto* at the edge of the market square, this amicable trattoria claims to be the home of the original spaghetti carbonara. According to much-disputed legend, the forebears of the present owners devised the recipe in the final days of World War II, when American G.I.s donated their K-rations of powdered eggs and salted bacon to the chef. The result was the egg yolk, cheese, and bacon-enriched pasta dish that's famous throughout the world. The dining room features succulent antipasti, grilled meats, fresh and intelligently prepared seasonal vegetables, and—in addition to the carbonara—several other kinds of pasta, including tagliolini with porcini mushrooms. Another specialty is bucatini al'Amatriciana, with a sauce of tomato, bacon, and hot peppers.

Ristorante da Pancrazio. Piazza del Biscione 92. ☎ **06/686-1246.** Reservations recommended. Main courses 15,000L–30,000L ($9.60–$19.20); fixed-price menu 45,000L ($28.80). AE, DC, MC, V. Thurs–Tues noon–3pm and 7:30–11:15pm. Closed 2 weeks in Aug (dates vary). Bus: 46 or 62. ROMAN.

The Ristorante da Pancrazio is popular as much for its archeological interest as for its culinary allure. One of its two dining rooms is gracefully decorated in the style of an 18th-century tavern; the other occupies the premises of Pompey's ancient theater, and as such is lined with marble columns, carved capitals, and bas-reliefs that would be the envy of many museums. Classified a national monument, it's probably the only such establishment that feeds your body as well as your sense of history. They serve the full range of traditional Roman dishes, such as risotto alla pescatora (with seafood), several kinds of scampi, saltimbocca, and abbacchio al forno (roast lamb with potatoes). You might also order ravioli stuffed with artichoke hearts. No one gets innovative around here—these dishes are prepared according to time-tested recipes. If it was good enough for Caesar, it's good enough for the patrons of da Pancrazio.

Vecchia Roma. Via della Tribuna di Campitelli 18. ☎ **06/686-4604.** Reservations recommended. Main courses 22,000L–25,000L ($14.10–$16). AE, DC. Thurs–Tues 1–3:30pm and 8–11:30pm. Closed 10 days in Aug. Bus: 64, 90, 90b, 97, or 774. ITALIAN.

Vecchia Roma is a charming, moderately priced trattoria in the heart of the ghetto. Movie stars have frequented the place, sitting at the crowded tables in one of the four small dining rooms (the back room is the most popular). The owners are known for their "fruits of the sea," a selection of fresh seafood. The minestrone of the day is made with fresh vegetables, and an interesting selection of antipasti, including salmon or vegetables, is always available. The pastas and risottos are excellent, including linguine alla marinara with scampi. A "green" risotto with porcini mushrooms is invariably good. The chef prepares excellent cuts of meat, including his specialty, lamb.

INEXPENSIVE

Da Giggetto. Via del Portico d'Ottavia 21–22. ☎ **06/686-1105.** Reservations recommended. Main courses 18,000L–24,000L ($11.50–$15.35). AE, DC, MC, V. Tues–Sun 12:30–3pm and 7:30–11pm. Closed Aug 1–15. Bus: 62, 64, 75, 90, or 170. ROMAN.

Da Giggetto, in the old ghetto, is right next to the Theater of Marcellus, and old Roman columns extend practically to its doorway. Romans flock to this bustling trattoria for their special traditional dishes. None is more typical than *carciofi alla giudia,* baby-tender fried artichokes—a true delicacy. The cheese concoction, mozzarella in carrozza, is another delight, as are the zucchini flowers stuffed with mozzarella and anchovies. You could also sample fettuccine al'amatriciana, shrimp sautéed in garlic and olive oil, a bold tripe dish, or saltimbocca (the eternal favorite).

$ Hostaria Grappolo d'Oro. Piazza della Cancelleria 80–81. ☎ **06/686-4118.** Reservations recommended Fri–Sat nights. Main courses 10,000L–16,000L ($6.40–$10.25). AE, MC, V. Mon–Sat noon–3pm and 7:15pm–1am. Closed 2 weeks in Aug. Bus: 62 or 64. ROMAN.

This early 18th-century building near Corso Vittorio Emanuele II and Campo de' Fiori welcomes a mainly local clientele. The setting is pleasant, unpretentious, and polite despite some hysteria that develops whenever the place gets really busy. Menu items read like a lexicon of traditional Roman cuisine, each example of which is prepared in generous, although not particularly innovative ways. Examples include saltimbocca, penne al'amatriciana, roast lamb with potatoes, Roman-style tripe, and a flavorful array of antipasti. It's the type of fresh and well-prepared food Romans love, and chances are you will too.

$ La Majella. Piazza del Teatro di Pompeo 18. ☎ **06/686-4174.** Reservations recommended for dinner. Main courses 15,000L–20,000L ($9.60–$12.80); fixed-price menu 28,000L ($17.90). AE, MC, V. Mon–Sat 12:30–3pm and 8pm–midnight. Closed 2 weeks in Aug. Bus: 62 or 64. ABRUZZESE/ITALIAN.

In 1993, because of the encroachment of a nearby museum, La Majella moved out of the small palazzo where it had served well-prepared food to the likes of Polish Cardinal Karol Wojtyla (before his elevation to the papal throne). It didn't move very far, and is now a trio of old-fashioned dining rooms in an old building a block northeast of Campo de' Fiori. The cuisine, fortunately, has changed hardly at all, and includes such Abruzzi mountain food as partridge and venison with polenta, an array of savory pastas (including pappardelle with rabbit), and roast lamb aromatically flavored with herbs. Fish includes grilled or fried versions of sea bass, flounder, lobster, and shrimp. We especially recommend the risotto with zucchini flowers and wild mushrooms—a *primavera* delight—and the oven-baked pork served with roast potatoes.

Le Maschere. Via Monte della Farina 29. ☎ **06/687-9444.** Reservations recommended. Main courses 18,000L–30,000L ($11.50–$19.20). AE, DC, MC, V. Tues–Sun 7:30pm–midnight. Bus: 26, 44, 60, 65, or 75. CALABRESE.

Le Maschere, near Largo Argentina, specializes in the fragrant, often fiery cookery of Calabria's Costa Viola—lots of fresh garlic and wake-up-your-mouth red peppers. Deep in the heart of Rome, in a cellar from the 1600s decorated with regional artifacts of Calabria, they have recently enlarged the kitchen and added three more dining rooms festooned with fantastic medieval- and Renaissance-inspired murals. Begin with a selection of antipasti calabresi. For *primo,* you can try one of their many different preparations of eggplant or a pasta—perhaps with broccoli or with devilish red peppers, garlic, breadcrumbs, and more than a touch of anchovy. The chef also grills meats and fresh swordfish caught off the Calabrian coast. For dessert, finish with a Calabrian sheep cheese or a fresh fruit salad. If you don't want a full meal, you can visit just for pizza and beer, and in summer you can dine at a small table outside overlooking a tiny piazza.

$ Ristorante del Pallaro. Largo del Pallaro 15. ☎ **06/6880-1488.** Reservations recommended for dinner Sat–Sun. Fixed-price menu 30,000L ($19.20). No credit cards. Tues–Sun 1–3pm and 7:30pm–12:30am. Bus: 46, 62, 64, or 70. ROMAN.

The cheerful and kind-hearted woman in white who emerges with clouds of steam from this establishment's bustling kitchen is the owner, Paola Fazi. She maintains a simple duet of very clean dining rooms where price-conscious Romans go for good food at bargain prices, and she claims—though others dispute it—that Julius

Family-Friendly Restaurants

Ristorante Il Matriciano *(see p. 119)* This is a safe, clean, and reasonably priced family restaurant near St. Peter's. It's good country fare—nothing fancy.

Césarina *(see p. 112)* A long-time family favorite, this restaurant with a cuisine from the Emiliana-Romagna region serves the most kid-pleasing pastas in town, each handmade and presented with a different sauce. You can request a selection of three kinds of pasta on one plate for a little taste of each.

Otello alla Concordia *(see p. 108)* This place is as good as any to introduce your child to the hearty Roman cuisine. If your child doesn't like the spaghetti with clams, then maybe the eggplant parmigiana will tempt. Families can dine in an arbor-covered courtyard.

Tre Scalini *(see p. 106)* All families visit Piazza Navona at some point, and this is the best choice if you'd like a dining table overlooking the square. The cookery is Roman, and the menu is wide enough to accommodate most palates—including children's. Even if your child doesn't like the main course, the tartufi (ice cream with a coating of bittersweet chocolate, cherries, and whipped cream) at the end of the meal is a classic bound to please.

Caesar was assassinated on this very site. No à la carte meals are served, but the fixed-price menu has made the place famous. As you sit down, your antipasto, the first of eight courses, will appear. Then comes the pasta of the day, followed by roast veal, white meatballs, or (only on Friday) dried cod, along with potatoes and eggplant. For your final courses, you're served mozzarella, cake with custard, and fruit in season. The meal also includes bread, mineral water, and half a liter of the house wine. This is the type of food you might be served if you were invited to the home of a prosperous Roman family.

5 Near Piazza Navona & the Pantheon

MODERATE

Alfredo alla Scrofa. Via della Scrofa 104. ☎ **06/6880-6163.** Reservations recommended. Main courses 18,000L–26,000L ($11.50–$16.65); fixed-price menu 45,000L ($28.80). AE, DC, MC, V. Wed–Mon 12:30–3pm and 7:30–11:30pm. Metro: Pz. di Spagna. ROMAN/INTERNATIONAL.

Established in 1925, this restaurant maintains a visitors' autograph book that reads like a retrospective of 20th-century history—Mussolini, Ava Gardner, even Arthur Miller (who arrived with Marilyn Monroe in 1960). The restaurant aggressively trades on its fame of yesterday—it was once virtually mandatory to dine here on a visit to Rome. That's no longer true, but you can still come for the memories. Many first-time visitors order the maestose fettuccine al triplo burro, where waiters make choreography out of whipping butter and cheese on rolling carts at tableside. Main-course specialties include *filetto di tacchino dorato* (sautéed breast of turkey covered with thin slices of Piedmontese white truffles), filet mignon Casanova (prepared with red wine, pepper, and foie gras), roast lamb with potatoes in the Roman style, and saltimbocca.

Montevecchio. Piazza di Montevecchio 22. ☎ **06/686-1319.** Reservations required. Main courses 24,000L–30,000L ($15.35–$19.20). AE, MC, V. Tues–Sun 1–3pm and 8–11:30pm. Closed Aug 10–25 and Dec 26–Jan 9. Bus: 70, 81, 90, 90b, or 492. ROMAN/ITALIAN.

To visit, you must negotiate the winding streets of one of Rome's most confusing neighborhoods, near Piazza Navona. The heavily curtained restaurant on this Renaissance piazza is where both Raphael and Bramante had studios and where Lucrezia Borgia spun many of her intrigues. The entrance opens onto a high-ceilinged room filled with rural mementos and bottles of wine. Your meal might begin with a strudel of porcini mushrooms followed by the invariably good pasta of the day, perhaps a bombolotti stuffed with prosciutto and spinach. Then select roebuck with polenta, roast Sardinian goat, or one of several veal dishes (on one occasion, served with salmon mousse). Many of these recipes, such as the mushroom strudel and the Sardinian goat, are virtually impossible to find on Roman menus anymore.

Passetto. Via Zanardelli 14. ☎ **06/6880-6569.** Reservations recommended. Main courses 24,000L–40,000L ($15.35–$25.60). AE, DC, MC, V. Daily noon–3pm and 7pm–midnight. Bus: 70, 87, or 90. ROMAN/ITALIAN.

Passetto, dramatically positioned at the north end of Piazza Navona, has drawn patrons with its 142-year reputation for excellent Italian food. Regrettably, its success has spoiled it somewhat and service is now among the rudest in town. The interior is stylish—three rooms, one containing frosted-glass cylinder chandeliers. In summer, however, sit outside looking out on Piazza Sant'Apollinare. The pastas are exceptional, including penne alla Norma. One recommended main dish is orata (sea bass) al cartoccio (baked in a paper bag, with tomatoes, mushrooms, capers, and white wine). Another house specialty is rombo passetto (a fish similar to sole) cooked in cognac

Dining near Campo de' Fiori & Piazza Navona

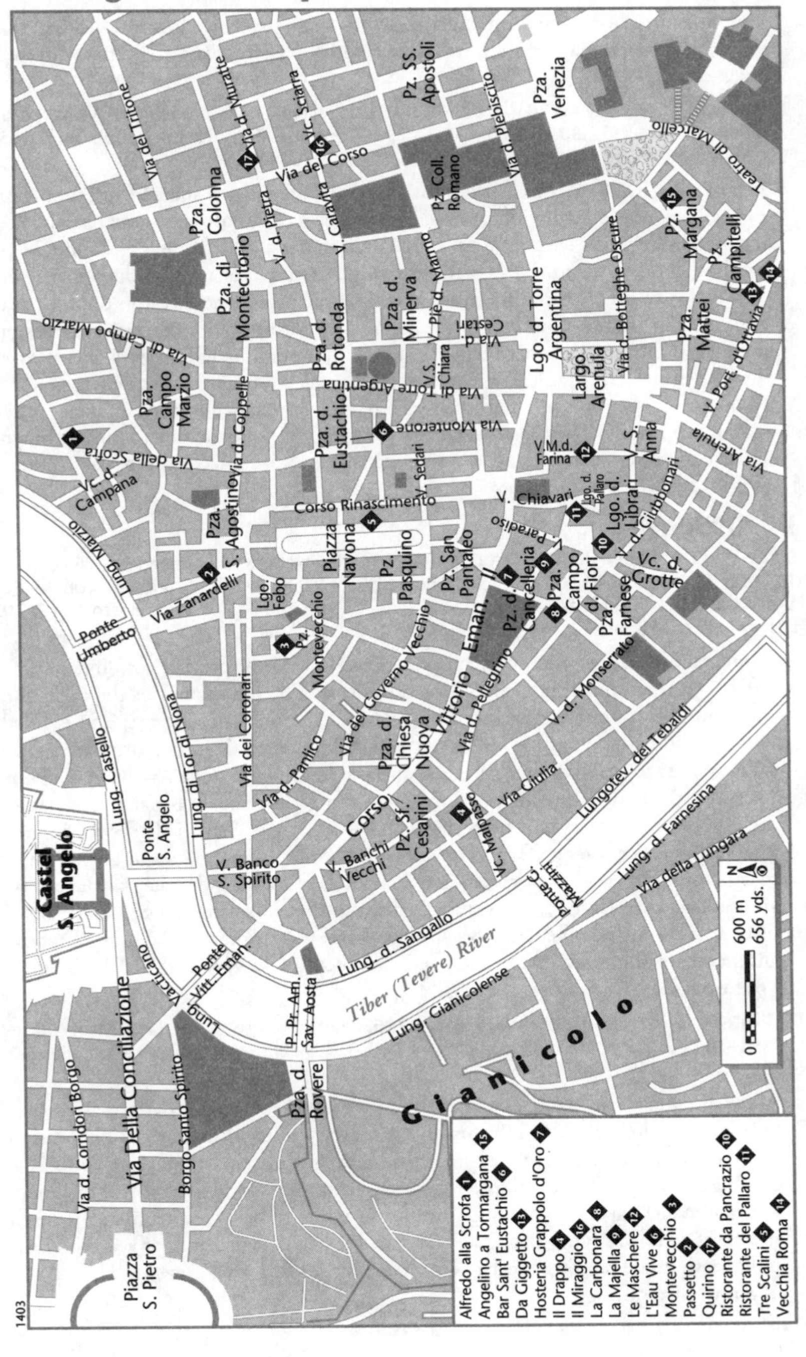

and pine nuts. Fresh fish is often priced by its weight, so tabs can soar quickly. Fresh vegetables are abundant in summer, and a favorite dessert is seasonal berries with fresh thick cream.

Tre Scalini. Piazza Navona 30. ☎ **06/687-9148.** Reservations recommended. Main courses 20,000L–30,000L ($12.80–$19.20). AE, DC, MC, V. Thurs–Tues 12:15–3:30pm and 7:15–11:15pm. Closed Dec–Feb. Bus: 46, 62, 70, 87, or 492. ROMAN.

Established in 1882, this is the most famous and most respected restaurant on Piazza Navona—a landmark for ice cream as well as for more substantial meals. Yes, it's literally crawling with tourists, but its waiters are a lot friendlier and more helpful than those at the nearby Passetto. Although there's a cozy bar on the upper floor, outfitted with simple furniture with a view over the piazza, most visitors opt for a seat either in the ground-floor café or restaurant, or, during warm weather, at tables on the piazza. House specialties include risotto con porcini, spaghetti with clams, roast duck with prosciutto, a carpaccio of sea bass, saltimbocca, and roast lamb in the Roman style. No one will object if you order just a pasta and salad, unlike at other restaurants nearby. Their famous tartufi (ice cream disguised with a coating of bittersweet chocolate, cherries, and whipped cream) and other ice creams cost 10,000L ($6.40) each.

INEXPENSIVE

L'Eau Vive. Via Monterone 85. ☎ **06/6880-1095.** Reservations recommended. Main courses 10,000L–28,000L ($6.40–$17.90); fixed-price menus 15,000L, 22,000L, and 28,000L ($9.60, $14.10, and $17.90). AE, MC, V. Mon–Sat 12:30–2:30pm and 8–10:30pm. Closed Aug 1–20. Bus: 46, 62, 64, 78, or 492. FRENCH/INTERNATIONAL.

Dining at L'Eau Vive, run by lay missionaries who wear the dress or costumes of their native countries, qualifies as an offbeat adventure. The restaurant fills the cellar and the ground floor of the 17th-century Palazzo Lantante della Rovere, and is filled with monumental paintings under vaulted ceilings. In this formal atmosphere, at 10 o'clock each evening, the waitresses sing religious hymns and "Ave Marias." Pope John Paul II used to dine here when he was still archbishop of Krakow. Specialties include hors d'oeuvres and frogs' legs, and the cellar is well stocked with French wines. Main dishes range from guinea hen with onions and grapes in a wine sauce to couscous. Other selections include several kinds of homemade pâté, salade niçoise, and beefsteaks in wine sauce. A smooth finish is the chocolate mousse. The tasteful place settings include fresh flowers and good glassware. Some of the most flamboyant members of international society have adopted L'Eau Vive as their favorite spot. Your tip will be turned over for religious purposes.

Il Miraggio. Vicolo Sciarra 59. ☎ **06/678-0226.** Reservations recommended. Main courses 12,000L–18,000L ($7.70–$11.50). AE, V. Mon–Sat 12:30–3:30pm and 7:30–10:30pm. Bus: 60, 61, 62, or 85. ROMAN/SARDINIAN.

While shopping near Piazza Colonna, you may want to escape the roar of traffic along the Corso by dining at this informal, hidden-away "mirage" in a charming location on a crooked street. It's a cozy neighborhood setting with good simple Roman food—nothing more. The decor includes a wine keg set in the wall. A specialty of the house is tortellini alla papalina. You might want to try filet of beef with truffles, rosetta di vitello modo nostro (veal "our style"), or spiedino alla siciliana (rolls of veal with ham and cheese inside, onions and bay leaves outside, grilled on a skewer). There's also an array of fresh fish.

Quirino. Via delle Muratte 84. ☎ **06/679-4108.** Reservations not necessary. Main courses 15,000L–32,000L ($9.60–$20.50). AE, MC, V. Mon–Sat 12:30–3:30pm and 7–11pm. Closed 3 weeks in Aug. Metro: Pz. Barberini. ROMAN/SICILIAN.

Quirino is a good place to dine right after you've tossed your coin into the Trevi Fountain. The atmosphere inside is typical Italian, with hanging chianti bottles, a beamed ceiling, and muraled walls. The food is strictly in the "home-cooking" style of Roman trattorie. We're fond of a mixed fry of tiny shrimp and squid rings that resemble onion rings. For an opening course, we recommend risotto Milanese style, spaghetti with clams, or the classic Sicilian pasta dish, pasta alla Norma (with tomatoes, eggplant, and salted ricotta). You can also order involtini alla messinese, a roulade of either fish or meat, filled with cheese, grilled, and served with salad greens in the Sicilian style. For dessert, a basket of fresh fruit will be placed on your table.

6 Near Piazza di Spagna & Piazza del Popolo

EXPENSIVE

✪ **El Toulà.** Via della Lupa 29B. ☎ **06/687-3498.** Reservations required for dinner. Main courses 50,000L ($32); fixed-price menu 100,000L ($64). AE, DC, MC, V. Mon 8–11pm, Tues–Sat 1–3pm and 8–11pm. Closed Aug. Bus: 81, 90, 90b, 628, or 913. ROMAN/VENETIAN.

El Toulà ("The Hayloft" in the alpine dialect of Cortina d'Ampezzo) offers the quintessence of Roman haute cuisine with a creative flair, and is the glamorous flagship of an upscale, now international chain. The elegant setting of vaulted ceilings and large archways attracts the international set. Guests stop in the charming bar to order a drink while perusing the impressive, always-changing menu (one section devoted to Venetian specialties, in honor of the restaurant's origins). Items include fegato (liver) alla veneziana, calamari stuffed with vegetables, baccala (codfish mousse served with polenta), and another Venetian classic, broetto, a fish soup made with monkfish and clams. The selection of sherbets changes seasonally—the cantaloupe and fresh strawberry are celestial concoctions—and you can request a mixed plate if you'd like to sample several of them. El Toulà usually isn't crowded at lunchtime.

MODERATE

Dal Bolognese. Piazza del Popolo 1–2. ☎ **06/361-1426.** Reservations required. Main courses 20,000L–26,000L ($12.80–$16.65); fixed-price menu 60,000L ($38.40). AE, MC, V. Tues–Sun 12:30–3pm and 8:15pm–1am. Closed 20 days in Aug. Metro: Flaminio. BOLOGNESE.

This is one of those rare dining spots that's not only chic, with patrons in the latest Fendi drag, but noted for its food as well. Young actors, shapely models, artists from nearby Via Margutta, even industrialists on an off-the-record evening on the town show up here, quickly booking the limited sidewalk tables. To begin your repast, we suggest a misto de pasta—four pastas, each with a different sauce, arranged on the same plate. A worthy substitute would be thin, savory slices of Parma ham or perhaps the prosciutto and melon (try a little freshly ground pepper on the latter). For your main course, specialties include lasagne verde, tagliatelle alla bolognese, and a most recommendable cotolette alla bolognese. You may want to cap your evening by calling on the Café Rosati next door (or its competitor, the Canova, across the street), to enjoy one of the tempting pastries.

INEXPENSIVE

Babington's Tea Rooms. Piazza di Spagna 23. ☎ **06/678-6027.** Main courses 19,000L–37,000L ($12.15–$23.70); brunch 45,000L ($28.80). AE, MC, DC, V. Wed–Mon 9am–11:30pm. Metro: Pz. di Spagna. ENGLISH/MEDITERRANEAN.

When Victoria was on the English throne in 1893, an Englishwoman named Anne Mary Babington arrived in Rome and couldn't find a place for "a good cuppa." With stubborn determination, she opened her own tea rooms near the foot of the

Spanish Steps, and the rooms are still going strong, although because of its heartbeat location prices are too high. You can order everything from Scottish scones and Ceylon tea to a club sandwich and American coffee. Brunch is served at all hours. Pastries cost 4,000L to 13,000L ($2.55 to $8.30), while a pot of tea (dozens of varieties available) goes for 12,000L ($7.70).

Da Mario. Via della Vite 55–56. ☎ **06/678-3818.** Reservations recommended. Main courses 14,000L–20,000L ($8.95–$12.80); fixed-price menu 38,000L–43,000L ($24.30–$27.50). AE, DC, MC, V. Mon–Sat 12:30–3pm and 7:30–11pm. Closed Aug. Metro: Pz. di Spagna. ROMAN/FLORENTINE.

Da Mario is noted for its moderately priced game specialties. Da Mario also does excellent Florentine dishes, although the typical steak is too costly these days for most budgets. You can dine in air-conditioned comfort on the street level or descend to the cellars. A good beginning is the wide-noodle pappardelle, best when served with a game sauce (caccia) or with chunks of rabbit (lepre), available only in winter. Capretto (kid) and beefsteaks are served in the Florentine fashion, although you may prefer roast quail with polenta. We heartily recommend the gelato misto, a selection of mixed ice cream.

Margutta Vegetariano. Via Margutta 119. ☎ **06/3600-1805.** Reservations recommended. Main courses 10,000L–16,000L ($6.40–$10.25). AE, DC, MC, V. Mon–Sat 1–3pm and 7:30–10:30pm. Closed 2 weeks in Aug. Metro: Pz. di Spagna. VEGETARIAN.

Established in 1980 by Claudio Vannini, an enthusiast of new-wave thinking and Indian philosophy, this place functioned for many years as one of Rome's only vegetarian restaurants. Partly because of the patronage of his friend and neighbor, the late Frederico Fellini, and partly because of its excellent cuisine, the restaurant quickly became a stylish favorite of Italian film stars and TV personalities. Its hundreds of clients ignore the traditional riches of Italian cuisine in favor of the high-fiber specials served in this 18th-century building. You can order from a sophisticated list of risottos and pastas, herb-enriched soups, mixed salads, a mélange of fried vegetables, meatless goulash, soyburgers, and a selection of soufflés made with potatoes, spinach, or wild mushrooms. Eggplant parmigiana is a perennial favorite. There's also a large selection of wines and ciders.

Otello alla Concordia. Via della Croce 81. ☎ **06/679-1178.** Main courses 13,000L–36,000L ($8.30–$23.05); fixed-price menu 36,000L ($23.05). AE, DC, MC, V. Mon–Sat 12:30–3pm and 7:30–11pm. Closed 2 weeks in Feb. Metro: Pz. di Spagna. ROMAN.

Set on a side street amid the glamorous boutiques near the northern edge of the Spanish Steps, this is one of the most popular and consistently reliable restaurants in Rome. A stone corridor from the street leads into a dignified building, the Palazzo Povero. Choose a table (space permitting) in either the arbor-covered courtyard or the cramped but convivial series of inner dining rooms. Displays of Italian bounty decorate an interior well known to many of the shopkeepers from the surrounding fashion district. The spaghetti alle vongole veraci (spaghetti with clams) is excellent, as are Roman-style saltimbocca, abbacchio arrosto (roasted baby lamb), eggplant parmigiana, a selection of grilled or sautéed fish dishes (including swordfish), and several different preparations of veal.

Ristorante Nino. Via Borgognona 11. ☎ **06/679-5676.** Reservations recommended. Main courses 20,000L–30,000L ($12.80–$19.20). AE, DC, MC, V. Mon–Sat 12:30–3pm and 7:30–11pm. Closed Aug. Metro: Pz. di Spagna. TUSCAN.

Ristorante Nino, off Via Condotti, a short walk from the Spanish Steps, is a tavern mecca for writers, artists, and an occasional model from one of the nearby high-fashion houses. Nino's enjoys deserved acclaim for its Tuscan cooking—hearty

Dining Near the Spanish Steps & Ancient Rome

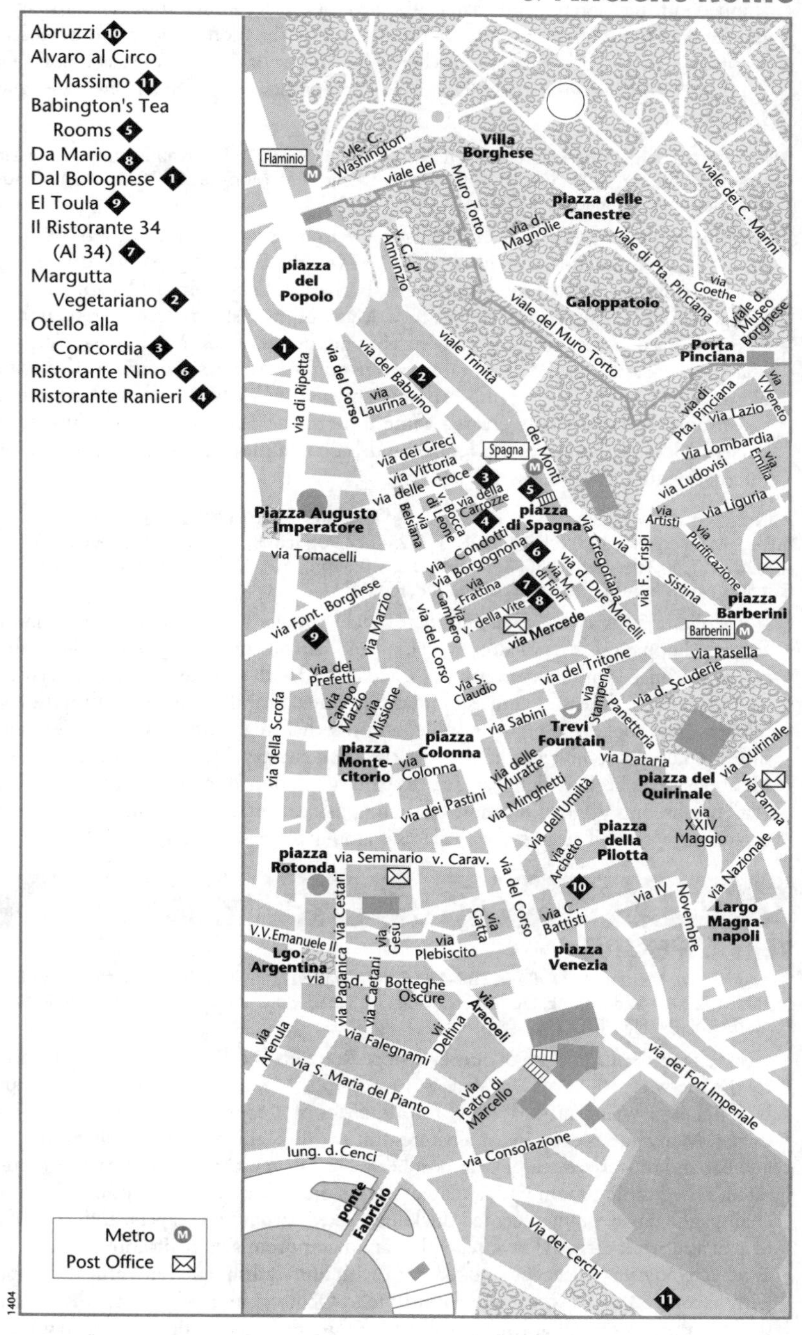

and completely unpretentious. The restaurant is particularly known for its steaks shipped in from Florence and charcoal-broiled, priced according to weight. However, they're not as succulent or tender as those served at the more famous and expensive Girarrosto Toscano. A plate of cannelloni Nino is one of the chef's specialties. Other good dishes include grilled veal liver, fagioli cotti al fiasco, codfish alla livornese, and zucchini pie.

Ristorante Ranieri. Via Mario de' Fiori 26. ☎ **06/679-1592.** Reservations required. Main courses 22,000L–32,000L ($14.10–$20.50). AE, DC, MC, V. Mon–Sat 12:30–3pm and 7:30–11pm. Metro: Pz. di Spagna. INTERNATIONAL/ITALIAN.

Ristorante Ranieri, off Via Condotti, is well into its second century (it was founded in 1843). Neapolitan-born Giuseppe Ranieri was the chef to Queen Victoria. Long a favorite dining place of the cognoscenti, Ranieri still maintains its Victorian trappings. Nothing ever seems to change here. Many of the dishes reflect the restaurant's ties with royalty; veal cutlet à l'Impériale, mignonettes of veal à la Regina Victoria, and tournedos Enrico IV. A suitable starter might be crêpes Ranieri, stuffed with eight kinds of cheese. The imperial veal cutlet dish—served with asparagus and mushrooms—was actually created some time in the 19th century for the queen herself. Most of the dishes are French and Italian, although overall the cookery is international.

Il Ristorante 34 (also Al 34). Via Mario de' Fiori 34. ☎ **06/679-5091.** Reservations required. Main courses 16,000L–28,000L ($10.25–$17.90); fixed-price menu 55,000L ($35.20). AE, DC, MC, V. Tues–Sat 12:30–3pm and 7:30–10:30pm, Sun 12:30–3pm. Closed 1 week at Easter, 3 weeks in Aug. Metro: Pz. di Spagna. ROMAN.

Il Ristorante 34 is a very good and increasingly popular restaurant close to the most famous shopping district of Rome. Its long and narrow interior is sheathed in scarlet wallpaper, ringed with modern paintings, and capped with a vaulted ceiling. In the rear, stop to admire a display of antipasti proudly exhibited near the entrance to the bustling kitchen. The cookery is highly reliable, and the chef might whip caviar and salmon into the noodles to enliven the dish, or else cook chunks of lobster into the risotto. He also believes in rib-sticking fare such as pasta-lentil soup, or meatballs in a sauce with "fat" mushrooms. One of his most interesting pastas comes with a pumpkin-flavored cream sauce, and his spaghetti with clams is among the best in Rome.

7 Near Via Veneto & Piazza Barberini

VERY EXPENSIVE

George's. Via Marche 7. ☎ **06/4208-4575.** Reservations required. Main courses 35,000L–45,000L ($22.40–$28.80). AE, DC, MC, V. Mon–Sat 12:30–3pm and 7:30pm–midnight. Metro: Pz. Barberini. INTERNATIONAL.

George's has been a favorite of ours ever since Romulus and Remus were being tended by the she-wolf. Right off Via Veneto, in a dignified 18th-century building, it's run by Michele Pavia, maître d' hôtel for a quarter of a century before becoming its owner. Many guests drop in for a before-dinner drink, enjoying the music in the piano bar and the relaxed, clublike atmosphere. They then proceed to an elegantly decorated, raised dining room with a tented ceiling. Specialties include filets of sole with champagne sauce, orange-scented duckling, baked turbot with capers, and all kinds of veal and steak dishes. The kitchen has an uncompromising dedication to quality, as reflected by such dishes as smoked trout with horseradish sauce and grilled scampi with bacon and sliced tomatoes. From June to October, in good weather the action shifts to the garden, suitably undisturbed because it's in the garden of a papal villa.

✪ **Sans Souci.** Via Sicilia 20. ☎ **06/482-1814.** Reservations required. Main courses 36,000L–58,000L ($23.05–$37.10). AE, DC, MC, V. Tues–Sun 8pm–1am. Closed Aug 10–30. Metro: Pz. Barberini. Bus: 52, 53, 95, 490, or 495. FRENCH.

Sans Souci may no longer be the best restaurant in Rome—at least Michelin no longer awards it stars—but for glitz and glamour, and nostalgia for *la dolce vita,* nothing quite matches the overly decorated Sans Souci. The cuisine is better at Relais Le Jardin or La Terrazza, but San Souci does serve good food to those on the see-and-be-seen circuit, and might be your best bet for spotting a movie star, albeit a faded one. You enter a dimly lit small lounge to the right at the bottom of the steps. Here, amid tapestries and glittering mirrors, the maître d' will present you with the menu, which you can peruse while sipping a drink. The menu is ever-changing, as "new creations" are devised. You might begin with a terrine of goose liver with truffles, a special creation of the chef. The fish soup is, according to one Rome restaurant critic, "a legend to experience." Soufflés are also popular, including artichoke, asparagus, or spinach, and risottos are prepared for two. One of the most popular pasta dishes is large fettuccine with wild mushrooms and black truffles. Dessert soufflés, also prepared for two, are another specialty, including chocolate or Grand Marnier.

✪ **La Terrazza.** In the Hotel Eden, Via Ludovisi 49. ☎ **06/4781-2552.** Jacket required. Reservations recommended. Main courses 42,000L–68,000L ($26.90–$43.50); fixed-price menu 120,000L ($76.80). AE, DC, MC, V. Daily 12:30–2:30pm and 7:30–10:30pm. Metro: Pz. Barberini. ITALIAN/INTERNATIONAL.

This restaurant serves the finest cuisine in the city (a title shared with the Relais Le Jardin) with a sweeping view over St. Peter's from the fifth floor of the Eden Hotel. Service manages to be formal and flawless, yet not at all intimidating. Chef Enrico Derfligher, the commercial and culinary catalyst behind about a dozen top-notch Italian restaurants throughout Europe, prepares a menu that varies with the season and is among the most urbane and polished in Rome. Examples include a warm salad of grilled vegetables lightly toasted with greens in balsamic vinegar, red tortelli (whose pink coloring comes from a tomato mousse) stuffed with mascarpone cheese and drizzled with lemon, grilled tagliata of beef with eggplant and tomatoes, and a superb "symphony" of seafood. Artfully arranged onto a platter, and prepared only for two or more diners, it includes perfectly seasoned Mediterranean sea bass, turbot, gilthead, and prawns.

MODERATE

Aurora 10 da Pino il Sommelier. Via Aurora 10. ☎ **06/474-2779.** Reservations recommended. Main courses 20,000L–30,000L ($12.80–$19.20). AE, DC, MC, V. Tues–Sun noon–3pm and 7–11:15pm. Metro: Pz. Barberini. ITALIAN.

Established in 1981 a few paces from the top of Via Veneto, this restaurant is in the vaulted interior of what was originally a Maronite convent. The high-energy direction of its Sicilian manager, Pino Salvatore, and his staff have attracted some of the capital's most influential diplomats and a sprinkling of film stars. The place is noted for its awesome array of more than 250 wines, representing every province of Italy. Unusual for Rome, the restaurant features a large soup menu, along with a tempting array of fresh antipasti. Dishes include linguine with lobster, a Sicilian-style fish fry, swordfish in herb sauce, filet of beef with porcini mushrooms, risotto with asparagus, and beef stew flambé. The cookery is savory and first-rate, using top-quality ingredients.

Girarrosto Toscano. Via Campania 29. ☎ **06/482-3835.** Reservations required. Main courses 20,000L–50,000L ($12.80–$32). AE, DC, MC, V. Thurs–Tues 12:30–3pm and 7:30–11:30pm. Bus: 90B, 95, 490, or 495. TUSCAN.

Girarrosto Toscano, facing the walls of the Borghese Gardens, draws a coterie of guests from Via Veneto haunts—which means that you may have to wait. It serves some of the finest Tuscan specialties in Rome under the vaulted ceilings of a cellar. Begin by enjoying an enormous selection of antipasti, from succulent little meatballs and melon with prosciutto to fritatte (omelets) and an especially delicious Tuscan salami. You're then given a choice of pasta, such as fettuccine in a cream sauce. Although expensive, bistecca alla fiorentina—grilled and seasoned with oil, salt, and pepper—is the best item to order. It also serves oysters and fresh fish from the Adriatic every day. Order with care if you're on a budget—both meat and fish are all priced according to weight, and can run considerably more than the prices quoted above. For dessert, we'd recommend the assortment of ice cream called gelato misto.

INEXPENSIVE

Césarina. Via Piemonte 109. ☎ **06/488-0828.** Reservations recommended. Main courses 16,000L–25,000L ($10.25–$16). AE, DC, MC, V. Mon–Sat 12:30–3pm and 7:30–11pm. Bus: 52, 53, 56, 58, or 95. EMILIA-ROMAGNOLA/ROMAN.

Specializing in the cuisines of Rome and the region around Bologna, this former hole-in-the-wall has grown since matriarch Césarina Masi established it around 1960 (many Rome veterans fondly remember Ms. Masi's strict supervision of her kitchen, and how she would lecture regulars who didn't finish their tagliatelle). Although Césarina died in the mid-1980s, the restaurant perpetuates her culinary traditions today in three dining rooms. The tactful and polite staff roll an excellent bollito misto (an array of well-seasoned boiled meats) from table to table on a trolley, and often follow with a misto Césarina—three kinds of handmade pasta, each served with a different sauce. Equally appealing is the saltimbocca and the cotoletta alla bolognese, a veal cutlet baked with ham and cheese. A dessert specialty is semifreddo Césarina served with hot chocolate. The food is excellent, and the selection of fresh antipasti is very appealing.

Colline Emiliane. Via Avignonesi 22. ☎ **06/481-7538.** Reservations required. Main courses 16,000L–25,000L ($10.25–$16). MC, V. Sat–Thurs 12:45–2:45pm and 7:45–10:45pm. Closed Aug. Metro: Pz. Barberini. EMILIA-ROMAGNOLA.

Colline Emiliane, established in 1936, is a small restaurant right off Piazza Barberini, serving the *classica cucina bolognese.* It's a family-run place—the owner is the cook, and his wife makes the pasta (which, incidentally, is about the best you'll encounter in Rome). The house specialty is an inspired tortellini alla panna (with cream sauce) with truffles, but the less expensive pastas are all excellent as well—maccheroncini al funghetto and tagliatelle alla bolognese. As an opener for your meal, we suggest culatello di Zibello, a delicacy from a small town near Parma known for having the finest prosciutto in the world. Main courses include *braciola di maiale,* boneless rolled pork cutlets that have been stuffed with ham and cheese, breaded, and sautéed. *Ciambonnetto* (roast veal Emilian style with roasted potatoes) is another specialty. To finish your meal, we recommend *budino al cioccolato,* a chocolate pudding that's baked like flan.

Piccolo Abruzzo. Via Sicilia 237. ☎ **06/482-0176.** Reservations recommended. Main courses 15,000L–20,000L ($9.60–$12.80). AE, DC, MC, V. Mon–Sat 12:30–3pm and 7pm–midnight. Bus: 95, 490, and 495. Closed 1 week in August. ABRUZZESE.

An imaginative array of antipasti and copious portions make Piccolo Abruzzo one of the most popular restaurants in its neighborhood. Many habitués plan a meal either early or late to avoid the jam, as the place is small and popular. Full meals are priced according to what you take from the antipasto buffet groaning with at least

20 offerings. You can follow with a pasta course, which might be samples of three different versions, followed by a meat course, then cheese and dessert. A meat specialty is agnello d'Abruzzi, roast lamb full of flavor and herbally scented. All this lively scene takes place in a brick- and stucco-sheathed room perfumed with hanging cloves of garlic, salt-cured hams, and beribboned bunches of Mediterranean herbs.

8 Near the Termini

MODERATE

Massimo d'Azeglio. Via Cavour 18. ☎ **06/481-4101.** Reservations recommended. Main courses 22,000L–32,000L ($14.10–$20.50); fixed-price menu 35,000L–45,000L ($22.40–$28.80). AE, DC, MC, V. Mon–Sat 12:30–3pm and 7–11pm. Metro: Termini. ROMAN.

Massimo d'Azeglio, in a hotel but with a separate entrance, has dispensed Roman cuisine since 1875. Built near the Stazione Termini—a fashionable address in the 19th century—it was named after a famous Savoy-born statesman who helped Garibaldi unify Italy. The premises have not changed since: Wood covers the walls and floors, and paintings of heroes of the Risorgimento hang on the walls. The cuisine is classic Italian with some innovation. The bollito (boiled meats and vegetables served with a fruity mustard sauce) has reigned supreme since the restaurant opened. You can begin with Parma ham or melon, but many prefer a succulent pasta dish or risotto with mushrooms and salad. Try the grilled squid with turnip tops (more delectable than it sounds), the mixed grill of Tyrrhenian fish, or the lamb chops aromatically flavored with herbs. The wine cellar has a wide selection, some bottles dating back to the 1800s.

$ **Scoglio di Frisio.** Via Merulana 256. ☎ **06/487-2765.** Reservations recommended. Main courses 16,000L–30,000L ($10.25–$19.20); fixed-price menu 24,000L ($15.35) at lunch, 62,000L–90,000L ($39.70–$57.60) at dinner. AE, DC, MC, V. Mon–Fri 12:30–3pm and 7:30–11pm, Sat–Sun 7:30–11pm. Bus: 714 from the Termini. NEAPOLITAN.

Scoglio di Frisio is the choice *suprême* to introduce yourself to the Neapolitan kitchen. While here, you should get reacquainted with a genuine, plate-sized Neapolitan pizza (crunchy, oozy, and excellent) with clams and mussels. After a medley of stuffed vegetables and antipasti, you may then settle for chicken cacciatore or veal scaloppine. Scoglio di Frisio also makes for an inexpensive night on the town as all the fun, cornball "O Sole Mio" and Neapolitan *bel canto* elements spring forth from a guitar, mandolin, and strolling tenor (who's like Mario Lanza reincarnate). The nautical decor—in honor of the top-notch fish dishes—is complete with a high-ceilinged grotto with craggy walls, fisher's nets, crustaceans, and a miniature three-masted schooner hanging overhead.

Taverna Flavia di Mimmo. Via Flavia 9. ☎ **06/474-5214.** Reservations recommended. Main courses 16,000L–30,000L ($10.25–$19.20). AE, DC, MC, V. Mon–Fri 12:30–3pm and 7:30–11pm, Sat 7:30–11pm. Metro: Pz. della Repubblica. ROMAN/INTERNATIONAL.

The Taverna Flavia di Mimmo, just a block from Via XX Settembre, is a robustly Roman restaurant where during the heyday of *la dolce vita* movie people used to meet over tasty dishes. The restaurant still serves the same food that once delighted Frank Sinatra and the "Hollywood on the Tiber" crowd. As a chic rendezvous, however, its day is long past. Specialties include a risotto with scampi and spaghetti al whisky. A different regional dish is featured daily, which might be Roman-style tripe prepared in such a savory manner that it tastes far better than it sounds. Exceptional dishes include osso buco with peas, a seafood salad, and fondue with truffles.

Dining Near Via Veneto & Termini

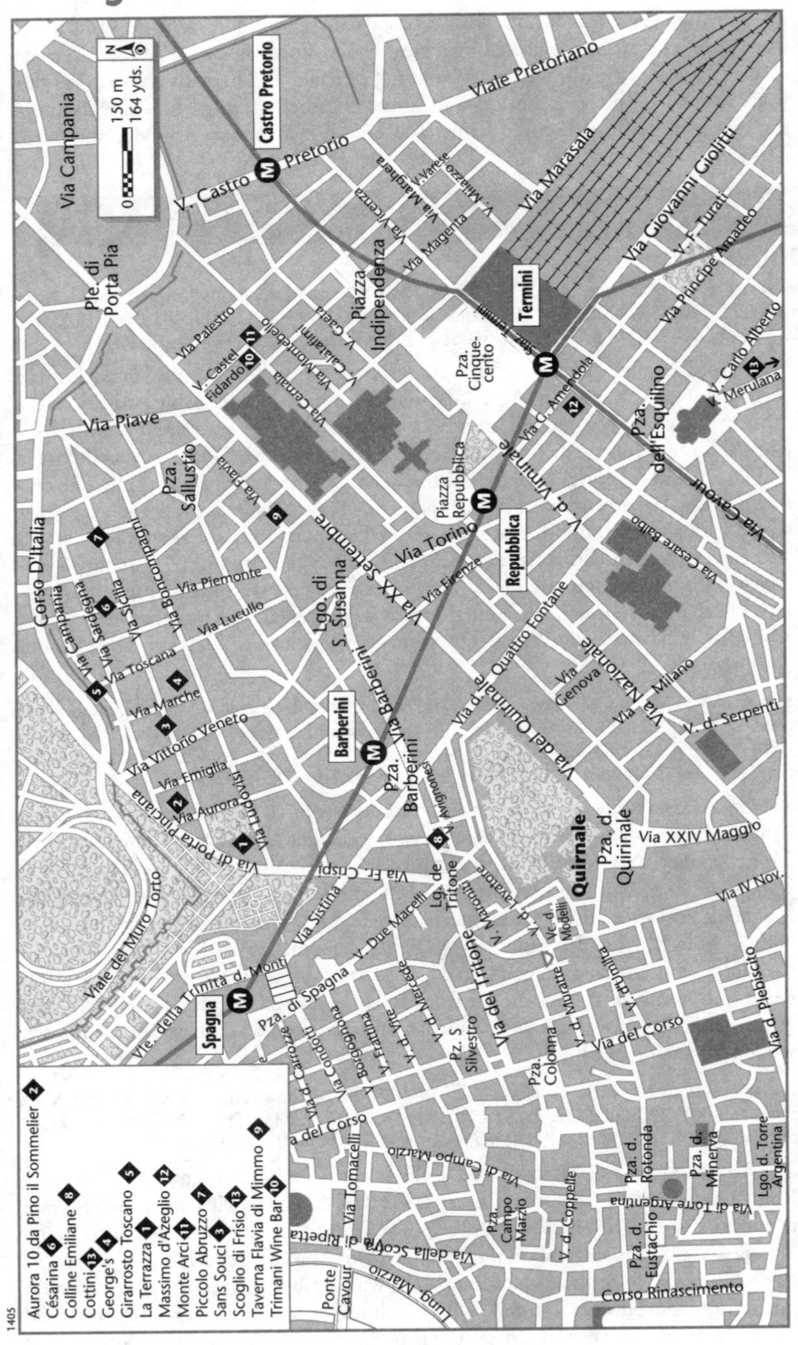

INEXPENSIVE

Cottini. Via Merulana 286–287. ☎ **06/474-0768.** Reservations not accepted. Main courses 4,000L–7,500L ($2.55–$4.80). AE, V. Daily 7am–9pm. Metro: Termini. ITALIAN.

Large, bustling, and confident of its role as one of the most popular *tavola caldas* in this congested neighborhood, this establishment feeds hundreds of hungry office workers and shopkeepers. The venue is self-service, not unlike an American cafeteria, with the noteworthy difference that the food is artfully arranged to include a cornucopia of all the bounty of agrarian Italy. Separate areas are devoted to hot pastas—most priced at 4,500L ($2.90) per heaping portion—meats, and to a lesser extent, fish. High turnover ensures a relatively fresh, if not particularly stylish, array of mass-produced, pan-Italian cuisine.

Monte Arci. Via Castelfidardo 33. ☎ **06/494-1220.** Reservations recommended. Main courses 13,000L–20,000L ($8.30–$12.80). AE, V. Mon–Fri 12:30–3pm and 7–11:30pm, Sat 7–11:30pm. Bus: 36, 75, 310, or 492. ROMAN/SARDINIAN.

Monte Arci, on a cobblestone street near Piazza Indipendenza not far from the Termini, is set behind a sienna-colored facade. The restaurant features low-cost Roman and Sardinian specialties (you'll spend even less for pizza). Typical dishes include nialoreddus (a regional form of gnocchetti); pasta with clams or lobster or those delectable porcini mushrooms; green and white spaghetti with bacon, spinach, cream, and cheese; saltimbocca; and lamb sausage flavored with herbs and pecorino cheese. Much of this food is just like mamma would make, with all the strengths and weaknesses that that implies.

Trimani Wine Bar. Via Cernaia 37b. ☎ **06/446-9630.** Fixed-price lunch 26,000L ($16.65); salads and platters of light food 12,000L–19,000L ($7.70–$12.15); glasses of wine 4,000L–12,000L ($2.55-$7.70), depending on the vintage. AE, DC, MC, V. Mon–Sat 11:30am–3pm and 5:30pm–midnight. Closed several weeks in Aug. Metro: Pz. della Repubblica or Castro Pretorio. CONTINENTAL.

Conceived as a tasting center for French and Italian wines, spumantis, and liqueurs, this elegant wine bar lies at the edge of a historic district. Amid an award-winning postmodern interior decor inspired by classical Rome, you'll find comfortable seating, occasional live music, and a staff devoted to pressurizing half-full bottles of wine between pours. The menu items are inspired by the stylish bistros of Paris, and might include vegetarian pastas (in summertime only), salades niçoises, herb-laden bean soups (fagiole), slices of quiche, Hungarian goulash, and platters of French and Italian cheeses and pâtés. Trimani, a family of wine brokers whose company was established in 1821, maintains a well-stocked shop about 40 yards from its wine bar, at Via Goito 20 (☎ 06/446-9661), where an astonishing array of the oenological bounty of Italy is for sale.

9 On the Appian Way

Hostaria l'Archeologia. Via Appia Antica 139. ☎ **06/788-0494.** Reservations recommended, especially on weekends. Main courses 12,000L–24,000L ($7.70–$15.35); fixed-price menu 25,000L ($16). AE, DC, MC, V. Fri–Wed 12:30–3:30pm and 8–10:30pm. Bus: 660 from San Giovanni. ROMAN/ITALIAN.

The Hostaria l'Archeologia is only a short walk from the Catacombs of St. Sebastian. The family-run restaurant is like an 18th-century village tavern, with lots of atmosphere, strings of garlic and corn, oddments of copper hanging from the ceiling, earth-brown beams, and sienna-washed walls. In summer guests dine in the garden out back under the wisteria. The Roman victuals are first-rate; you can glimpse the kitchen from behind a partition in the exterior garden parking lot. Many Roman families visit on the weekend, sometimes as many as 30 diners in a group. Of special interest is the wine cellar, excavated in an ancient Roman tomb, with bottles dating back to 1800. You go through an iron gate, down some stairs, and into the underground cavern. Along the way, you can still see the holes once occupied by funeral urns.

10 In Testaccio

Checchino dal 1887. Via di Monte Testaccio 30. ☎ **06/574-3816.** Reservations recommended. Main courses 13,000L–28,000L ($8.30–$17.90). AE, DC, MC, V. Tues–Sat 12:30–3pm and 8–11pm, Sun 12:30–3pm. Closed Aug, 1 week around Christmas, and Sun for lunch June–Sept. Bus: 27. ROMAN.

During the 1800s a local wine shop flourished by selling drinks to the butchers working in the neighborhood's many slaughterhouses. In 1887 the ancestors of the present owners obtained a license to sell food, thus giving birth to the restaurant you'll find here today. Slaughterhouse workers in those days were paid part of their meager salaries with the *quinto quarto* (fifth quarter) of each day's slaughter (that is, the tail, the feet, the intestines, and the offal), which otherwise had no commercial value. Following many centuries of Roman traditions, Ferminia, the wine shop's cook, somehow transformed these products into the tripe and oxtail dishes that form an integral part of the menu.

Many Italian diners come here to relish these dishes, which might not be to every foreign visitor's taste. They include rigatone con pajata (pasta with small intestines), coda alla vaccinara (oxtail stew), fagiole e cotiche (beans with intestinal fat), and other examples of *la cocina povera* (food of the poor). Less adventurous, and possibly more appealing, are the restaurant's array of well-prepared salads, soups, pastas, steaks, cutlets, grills, and ice creams, which the kitchens produce in abundance. The English-speaking staff is helpful and kind, tactfully proposing well-flavored alternatives to a cuisine which, at least in Rome, is a well-established legend.

11 In Trastevere

EXPENSIVE

Alberto Ciarla. Piazza San Cosimato 40. ☎ **06/581-8668.** Reservations required, especially on weekends. Main courses 24,000L–45,000L ($15.35–$28.80); fixed-price menu 80,000L–90,000L ($51.20–$57.60). AE, DC, MC, V. Mon–Sat 8:30pm–12:30am. Closed 1 week in Jan and 1 week in Aug. Bus: 44, 75, 170, 280, or 718. SEAFOOD.

Alberto Ciarla is the best and most expensive restaurant in Trastevere. Some critics still consider it one of the finest restaurants in all of Rome, although it's not as chic as it was when discovered by fickle fashion in the late 1980s. In an 1890 building in an obscure corner of an enormous square, it serves some of the most elegant fish dishes in the city. A dramatically modern decor plays shades of brilliant light against patches of shadow for a Renaissance chiaroscuro effect. Specialties include a handful of ancient recipes subtly improved by Signor Ciarla (such as the soup of pasta and beans with seafood). Original dishes include a delectable salmon Marcel Trompier with lobster sauce, a well-flavored sushi, spaghetti with clams, and a full array of shellfish. The filet of sea bass is prepared in at least three different ways, including an award-winning version with almonds.

MODERATE

La Cisterna. Via della Cisterna 13. ☎ **06/581-2543.** Reservations recommended. Main courses 16,000L–30,000L ($10.25–$19.20). AE, DC, MC, V. Mon–Sat 7pm–midnight. Bus: 44, 75, 170, 280, or 710. ROMAN.

Dining in Trastevere

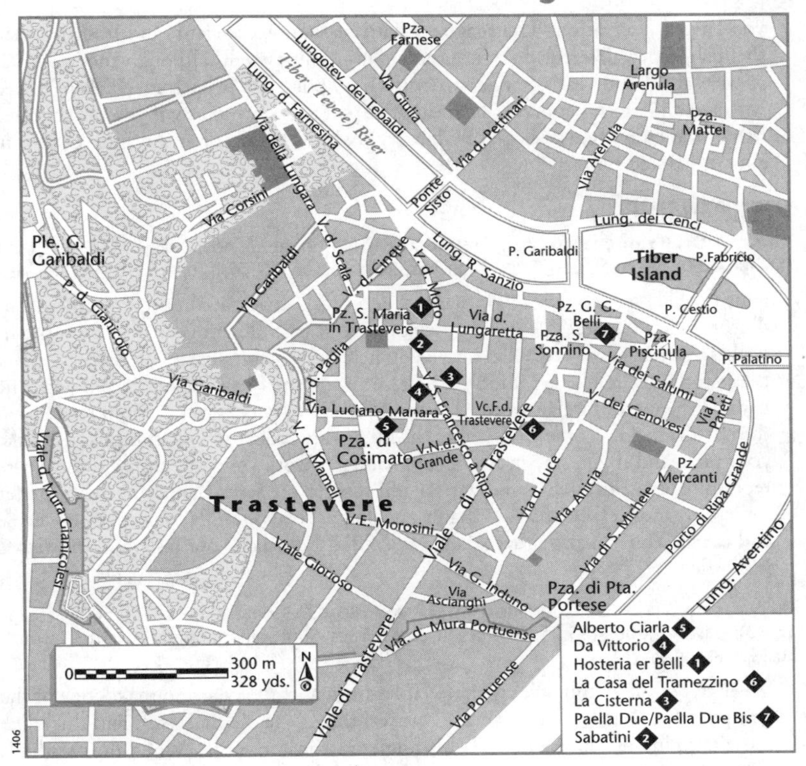

La Cisterna, named for an ancient well from Imperial times discovered in the cellar, lies deep in the heart of Trastevere. For more than half a century it has been run by the Simmi family, who are genuinely interested in serving only the best, as well as providing a good time for all guests. In good weather you can dine outside at sidewalk tables. If it's rainy or cold you'll be in rooms decorated with murals, including *The Rape of the Sabine Women*. Food critics have never awarded any stars to this place—and probably never will—but if you like traditional cookery based on the best of regional produce, then come here. In summer you can inspect the antipasti right out on the street before going in. Specialties of the house include Roman-style suckling lamb (abbacchio), rigatoni a l'amatriciana, pappallini Romana (wide noodles flavored with prosciutto, cheese, and eggs), shrimp, and fresh fish—especially sea bass baked with herbs.

Sabatini. Piazza Santa Maria in Trastevere 13. ☎ **06/581-2026.** Reservations recommended. Main courses 20,000L–40,000L ($12.80–$25.60). AE, DC, MC, V. Daily noon–3pm and 8pm–midnight. Closed 2 weeks in Aug (dates vary). Bus: 44, 75, or 170. ROMAN/SEAFOOD.

This is one of the most popular dining spots in Rome, although the glitz and glitter crowd have moved on to more fashionable oases. At night, Piazza Santa Maria—one of the settings used in Fellini's *Roma*—is the center of the liveliest action in Trastevere. In summer, tables are placed out on the piazza and you can look across at the floodlit golden frescoes of the church. If you can't get a table outside, you may be assigned to a room under beamed ceilings, with stenciled walls, lots of paneling, and framed oil paintings. So popular is this place that you may have to wait even if you have a reservation. The spaghetti with seafood is excellent, and fresh fish and shellfish, especially grilled scampi, may tempt you as well (although they aren't as good as at Alberto Ciarla). For a savory treat, try pollo con pepperoni, chicken cooked with red and green peppers. The meal price will rise exorbitantly if you order grilled fish or the Florentine steaks. For wine, try a white Frascati or an Antinori chianti in a hand-painted pitcher.

INEXPENSIVE

La Casa del Tramezzino. Viale Trastevere 81. No phone. Sandwiches 10,000L–15,000L ($6.40–$9.60). No credit cards. Wed–Mon 7am–2am. Bus: 56, 60, 75, 170, or 710. SANDWICHES.

This is called a *snack bar all'Americana,* good for a snack at almost any time of the day or night. The staff will gladly prepare at least 64 different types of panini (sandwiches). Actually, they're called tramezzini here (large, white-bread sandwiches, rather than stuffed rolls like a panino). The term originated in Mussolini's era when he banned the use of foreign words like *sandwich.* The tramezzini or panini selection is the most varied in Rome. Sometimes the fillings are ordinary, sometimes exotic. Take your pick, and if you stay in Rome long enough, work your way through the entire repertoire. Classics such as mozzarella and tomato are served, but you might prefer something more exotic such as arugula and gorgonzola, certainly the medley of cheese and caviar. You can also order salads and cold dishes when your taste for sandwiches is satisfied.

Da Vittorio. Via di San Cosimato 14A. ☎ **06/580-0353.** Pizzas 9,000L–10,500L ($5.75–$6.70); pastas 9,000L ($5.75). No credit cards. Tues–Sun 6pm–midnight. Metro: Termini. Bus: 75. PIZZA/PASTA.

We'll go out on a limb and say that Naples-born Vittorio Martino makes one of the best pizzas in Rome, what he terms "the real thing"—a pie that's soft and thick like those popping out of the oven in his hometown in the south. When the weather's fair, diners—most often a young crowd—opt for a table outside deep in the heart of Trastevere. Inside it's rather cramped, with a thrown-together decor of hanging utensils, wine bottles on the shelf, and Neapolitan pin-ups on the walls. All the classic pizzas emerge from the oven here, including napoletana (made with fresh tomatoes and anchovies) and Margherita (with tomato and mozzarella). Capricciosa comes with ham, eggs, artichokes, and olives. Vittorio also names one after himself: with fresh basil, fresh tomato, freshly grated parmesan, and lots of mozzarella. Other than a limited selection of antipasti and salads, the choice here is almost exclusively pizzas and pastas.

Hostaria er Belli. Piazza Sant'Appollonia. ☎ **06/580-3782.** Reservations recommended Sat–Sun. Main courses 15,000L–21,000L ($9.60–$13.45). AE, DC, MC, V. Tues–Sun 12:30–2:30pm and 7:30pm–1:30am. Closed 2 weeks in Jan. Bus: 56 or 60. SARDINIAN.

A sometimes boisterous neighborhood local that's intricately tied up in the vivid subculture of Trastevere, this restaurant contains three unpretentious dining rooms that were built in the 1400s, and a location that's only a few steps from the district's most famous square, Piazza Santa Maria in Trastevere. Menu items focus on the strong flavors and earthy cuisine of Sardinia, and include such specialties as spaghetti with seafood or with clams, gnochhetti, ravioli, escalopes of veal prepared at least three different ways, and pepper steak.

Paella Due / Paella Due Bis. Via della Lungarette 173. ☎ **06/588-2876.** Pizzas 7,000L–11,000L ($4.50–$7.05); main courses 15,000L–30,000L ($9.60–$19.20); fixed-price meals (paella) 35,000L–70,000L ($22.40–$44.80) for two people. No credit cards. Tues–Sun noon–midnight. Bus: 23. ITALIAN/SPANISH.

This is one of the best relatively inexpensive restaurants in Trastevere, with references to Spain that derive from a decade the owner/chef spent cooking in a restaurant there. No one will mind if you stop in during midafternoon for just a cup of coffee, or during lunch or dinner for the array of pizzas and pastas. The antipasto buffet contains focaccia, grilled vegetables, sliced mozzarella, and many of the fruits of the Italian harvest—a mini-meal in itself beginning at 10,000L ($6.40). You'll find a trio of dining rooms, paintings of the nearby Tiber, and a sense of old Trastevere. The cost of a heaping paella platter for two varies widely according to what you want it to contain. Least expensive is the vegetarian version; the most is the authentic paella valenciana with seafood and meat. Most clients are served in Paella Due, although if it's full, the overflow heads next door to additional seating in Paella Due Bis.

12 Near Vatican City

EXPENSIVE

✪ **Les Etoiles.** In the Hotel Atlante Star, Via Vitelleschi 34. ☎ **06/689-3434.** Reservations required. Main courses 85,000L–125,000L ($54.40–$80). AE, DC, MC, V. Daily 12:30–2:30pm and 7:30–11pm. Metro: Ottaviano. Bus: 23, 49, 64, 81, or 492. MEDITERRANEAN.

Les Etoiles, "The Stars," deserves all the stars it receives. The restaurant in this previously recommended hotel has been called "the most beautiful rooftop in Italy." At this garden in the sky you'll have an open window over the rooftops of Rome—a 360° view of landmarks, especially the floodlit dome of St. Peter's. A flower terrace contains a trio of little towers, named Michelangelo, Campidoglio, and Ottavo Colle. In summer everyone wants a table outside, but in winter almost the same view is available from tables near the picture windows. The colorful and fragrant refined Mediterranean cuisine, with perfectly balanced flavors, includes quail cooked either with radicchio or in a casserole with mushrooms and herbs, artichokes stuffed with ricotta and pecorino cheese, Venetian-style risotto with squid ink, and roast suckling lamb with mint. The creative chef is rightly proud of his many regional dishes, and the service is deluxe, with a wine list some Roman food critics have labeled "exciting."

MODERATE

Il Canto del Riso. Moored in the Tiber, in front of Lungotevere dei Mellini 7. ☎ **06/324-0128.** Reservations required. Main courses 15,000L–28,000L ($9.60–$17.90). No credit cards. Daily noon–4pm and 8pm–2am. Closed Sun night and Mon in winter. Metro: Pz. Cavour. Bus: 49, 70, 87, or 492. ITALIAN.

This barge and passenger ship is permanently moored beside one of the quays of the Tiber, a short walk north of Ponte Cavour. The barge was originally designed as a floating swimming pool in the 1960s, but has functioned since 1990 as a floating restaurant. Below decks you'll find a cozy dining room outfitted with nautical accessories. Many diners prefer to eat here during warm weather, when management expands its premises by setting up tables on the riverside quay. Then, strings of colored lights and potted plants add a festive note, despite the nearby traffic that races along. The menu is based on the classics, but also manages to include many regional favorites. The food is mild, flavorful, and faultlessly prepared. Menu items include veal, lamb, beef, and lots of fish and seafood, especially shrimp, mussels, and clams in tomato-garlic sauce, served as dressings for pastas or as main courses. Also featured are many kinds of vegetarian risotto.

Ristorante Il Matriciano. Via dei Gracchi 55. ☎ **06/321-2327.** Reservations required, especially for dinner. Main courses 14,000L–24,000L ($8.95–$15.35). AE, DC, MC, V. May–Oct, Sun–Fri 12:30–3pm and 8–11:30pm; Nov–Apr, Thurs–Tues 12:30–3pm and 8–11:30pm. Closed Aug 5–25. Metro: Lepanto or Ottaviano. ROMAN.

Il Matriciano is a family restaurant with a devoted following. Its location near St. Peter's makes it all the more distinguished. The food is good, but it's mostly country fare—nothing fancy. The decor, likewise, is kept to a minimum. In summer, try to get one of the sidewalk tables behind a green hedge and under a shady canopy. For openers, you might enjoy a zuppa di verdura or ravioli di ricotta. From many dishes, we recommend scaloppa alla valdostana, abbacchio (baby lamb) al forno, and trippa (tripe) alla romana. The most obvious specialty of the house, bucatini matriciana, is derived from what some experts say is the favorite sauce in the Roman repertoire: amatriciana. Here it's prepared with bucatini pasta, and richly flavored with bacon, tomatoes, and basil. Dining at the homelike convivial tables, you're likely to see an array of Romans, from prelates and cardinals escaping the confines of the nearby Vatican for a while to stars of the Italian cinema.

Ristorante Pierdonati. Via della Conciliazione 39. ☎ **06/6880-3557.** Reservations not necessary. Main courses 12,000L–28,000L ($7.70–$17.90); fixed-price menu 28,000L ($17.90). AE, MC, V. Fri–Wed noon–3:30pm and 7–10:30pm. Closed Aug. Bus: 23 or 64 from the Termini. ROMAN.

The Ristorante Pierdonati has been serving wayfarers to the Vatican since 1868. In the same building as the previously recommended Hotel Columbus, this restaurant was the former home of Cardinal della Rovere. Today it's the headquarters of the Knights of the Holy Sepulchre of Jerusalem, and the best restaurant in the gastronomic wasteland of the Vatican area. Its severely classical facade is relieved inside by a gargoyle fountain spewing water into a basin. You'll dine beneath a vaulted ceiling. Try the calves' liver Venetian style, the stewed veal with tomato sauce, or ravioli bolognese. To get really Roman, order the tripe. The cuisine is not refined or pretentious, but robust and heavy. It can get rather crowded here on days that see thousands upon thousands flocking to St. Peter's.

INEXPENSIVE

Hostaria dei Bastioni. Via Leone IV 29. ☎ **06/3972-3034.** Reservations recommended Fri–Sat. Main courses 12,000L–19,000L ($7.70–$12.15). AE, MC, V. Mon–Sat noon–3pm and 7–11:30pm. Closed July 15–Aug 1. Metro: Ottaviano. Bus: 23 or 49. ROMAN.

This simple but well-managed restaurant is about a minute's walk from the entrance to the Vatican Museums, and has catered to the appetites of everyone in the neighborhood since the 1960s. Although a warm-weather terrace doubles the establishment's size during the summer, many diners prefer the inside room as an escape from the roaring traffic on the street outside. In a dining room suitable for only 50 people, you can order from the staples of Rome's culinary repertoire, including such dishes as a fisher's risotto, a vegetarian fettuccine alla bastione with orange-flavored creamy tomato sauce (a succulent house special), an array of grilled fresh fish, and saltimbocca.

Osteria dell'Angelo. Via Giovanni Bettolo 24. ☎ **06/372-9470.** Reservations recommended. Main courses at lunch 9,000L–15,000L ($5.75–$9.60); fixed-price dinner 30,000L ($19.20). No credit cards. Mon–Sat 12:30–3:30pm and 8pm–1:30am. Metro: Ottaviano. Bus 32, 62, or 64. ROMAN.

In an angular *moderno* building erected in the Fascist style in 1922 (even its owners cheerfully refer to the architecture as a good example of "Mussoliniana"), this unpretentious trattoria has flourished almost since the building was inaugurated. Inside you'll find two dining rooms that specialize in a robust Roman cuisine and strong, well-conceived flavors. Menu items include saltimbocca, roast lamb with potatoes, fettuccine à la matriciana and à l'arabbiatta, Roman-style tripe, and a medley of veal dishes. The setting is cheerfully old-fashioned, not at all formal, workaday, and brisk.

Dining in the Vatican Area

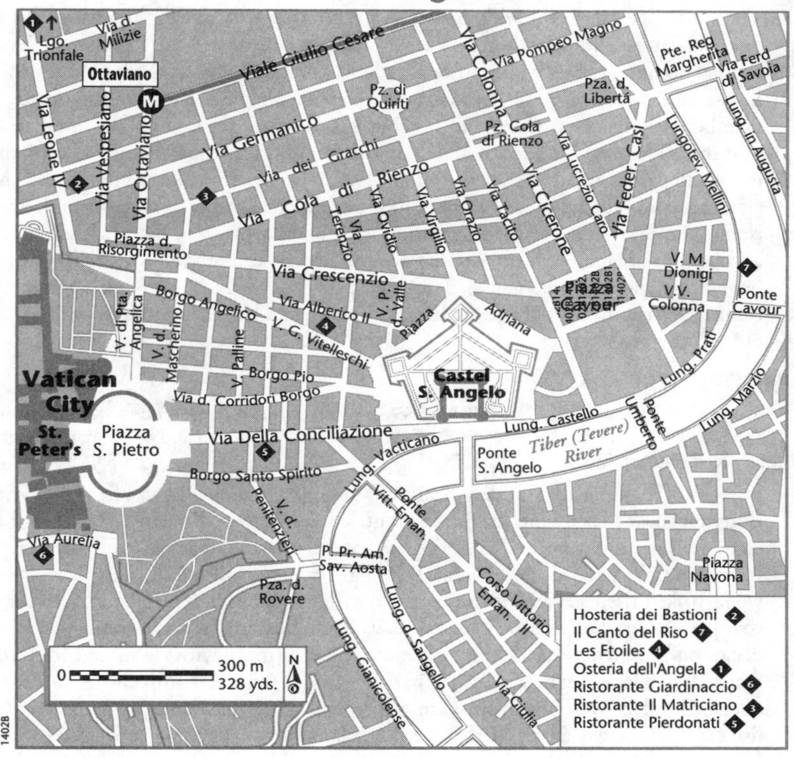

Ristorante Giardinaccio. Via Aurelia 53. ☎ **06/631367.** Reservations recommended, especially Sat–Sun. Main courses 10,000L–15,000L ($6.40–$9.60). AE, DC, MC, V. Wed–Mon 12:15–3:30pm and 7:15–11pm. Bus: 46, 62, or 98. ITALIAN/MOLISIAN.

This popular restaurant, operated by Nicolino Mancini, is only 200 yards from St. Peter's. Unusual for Rome, it offers Molisian specialties from southeastern Italy. It's rustically decorated in the country-tavern style with dark wood and exposed stone. Flaming grills provide succulent versions of perfectly done quail, goat, and other dishes, but perhaps the mutton goulash would be more adventurous. You can order many versions of pasta, including taconelle, a homemade pasta with lamb sauce. Vegetarians and others will like the large self-service selection of antipasti. Some snooty diners might dismiss this food as too regional—or "too peasant" if they're being catty—but it's a perfect introduction to the hearty cuisine of an area rarely visited by Americans.

13 In Parioli

VERY EXPENSIVE

✪ **Relais Le Jardin.** In the Hotel Lord Byron, Via G. de Notaris 5. ☎ **06/361-3041.** Reservations required. Main courses 45,000L–53,000L ($28.80–$33.90). AE, DC, MC, V. Mon–Sat 1–3pm and 8–10:30pm. Closed Aug. Bus: 26 or 52. ITALIAN.

The Relais Le Jardin is one of the best places to go in Rome for both traditional and creative cuisine, and a chi-chi crowd with demanding palates patronize it nightly.

There are places in Rome with greater views, but not such an elegant setting. Inside one of the most elite small hotels of the capital (see Chapter 4), the aggressively light-hearted decor combines white lattice with bold colors and flowers. Many of the cooks and service personnel were trained at embassies or diplomatic residences abroad. A member of Relais Gourmands, the establishment serves a seasonally changing array of dishes. The pasta and soups are among the finest in town, as exemplified by the tonnarelli pasta with asparagus and smoked ham served with concassé tomatoes. The chef can take a dish once served only to the plebes in Roman days, bean soup with clams, and make it elegantly refined. For your main course you face such selections as roast loin of lamb with *carciofi alla romana* (artichokes) or grilled beef sirloin with hot chicory and sautéed potatoes. The single best risotto served in Rome, in our view, is the chef's risotto with pheasant sauce, asparagus, and black truffle flakes with a hint of fresh thyme.

MODERATE

Al Ceppo. Via Panama 2. ☎ **06/841-9696.** Reservations recommended. Main courses 18,000L–25,000L ($11.50–$16). AE, DC, MC, V. Tues–Sun 12:30–3pm and 8–11pm. Closed the last 3 weeks of Aug. Bus: 4, 52, or 53. ROMAN.

Because of its somewhat hidden location (although it's only 2 blocks from the Villa Borghese, near Piazza Ungheria), the clientele is likely to be Roman rather than foreign. This is a longtime and enduring favorite that fashion has passed by, although the cuisine is as good as it ever was. "The Log" (its name in English) features an open wood-stoked fireplace on which the chef does lamb chops, liver, and bacon to charcoal perfection. The beefsteak, which hails from Tuscany, is also succulent. Other dishes on the menu include linguine monteconero (made with clams and fresh tomatoes); a savory spaghetti with peppers, fresh basil, and pecorino cheese; a filet of swordfish filled with grapefruit, parmesan cheese, pine nuts, and dry grapes; and a fish carpaccio (raw sea bass) with a green salad, onions, and green pepper. Save room for dessert, especially the apple cobbler, the pear and almond tart, or the chocolate meringue hazelnut cake.

6

What to See & Do in Rome

Where else but in Rome could you admire a 17th-century colonnade designed by Bernini, while resting against an Egyptian obelisk carried off from Heliopolis while Christ was still alive? Or stand amid the splendor of Renaissance frescoes in a papal palace built on top of the tomb of a Roman emperor? Where else, for that matter, are there vestal virgins buried adjacent to the Ministry of Finance?

Tourists have been sightseeing in Rome for 2,000 years. There is, in fact, almost too much to see, at least for visitors on a typical 20th-century timetable. Would that we could travel as our 19th-century forebears did, in a coach with tons of luggage, stopping a month here and a month there. Instead, we swoop down from the sky, or roar up at the train station, and try to see everything in a few days. Travelers with this approach have met their match in Rome. An absolute minimum of time to see the city with any sort of perspective is 5 days, and that's heavy sightseeing. Seven days would be better. A lifetime, perhaps, adequate.

In addition to the top attractions in the city itself, there are several places in the environs of Rome worth visiting before leaving this part of the country. It would be a shame to strike out for Venice or Florence without having at least visited Hadrian's Villa and the Villa d'Este, not to mention Palestrina and Ostia Antica (see Chapter 10, "Side Trips from Rome").

SUGGESTED ITINERARIES

These itineraries obviously are designed for the first-time visitor; the more seasoned traveler will want to seek out other treasures. However, such sights as the Vatican Museum can be visited over and over, because each time something new and artistically different will be waiting.

If You Have 1 Day

Far too brief—after all, Rome wasn't built in a day and you aren't likely to see it in a day either, but make the most of your limited time. You'll basically have to decide on the legacy of Imperial Rome—mainly the Roman Forum, the Imperial Forum, and the Colosseum, or else St. Peter's and the Vatican. Walk along the Spanish Steps at sunset. At night go to Piazza del Campidoglio for a fantastic view of the Forum below. Have a nightcap on Via Veneto

Major & Outlying Attractions

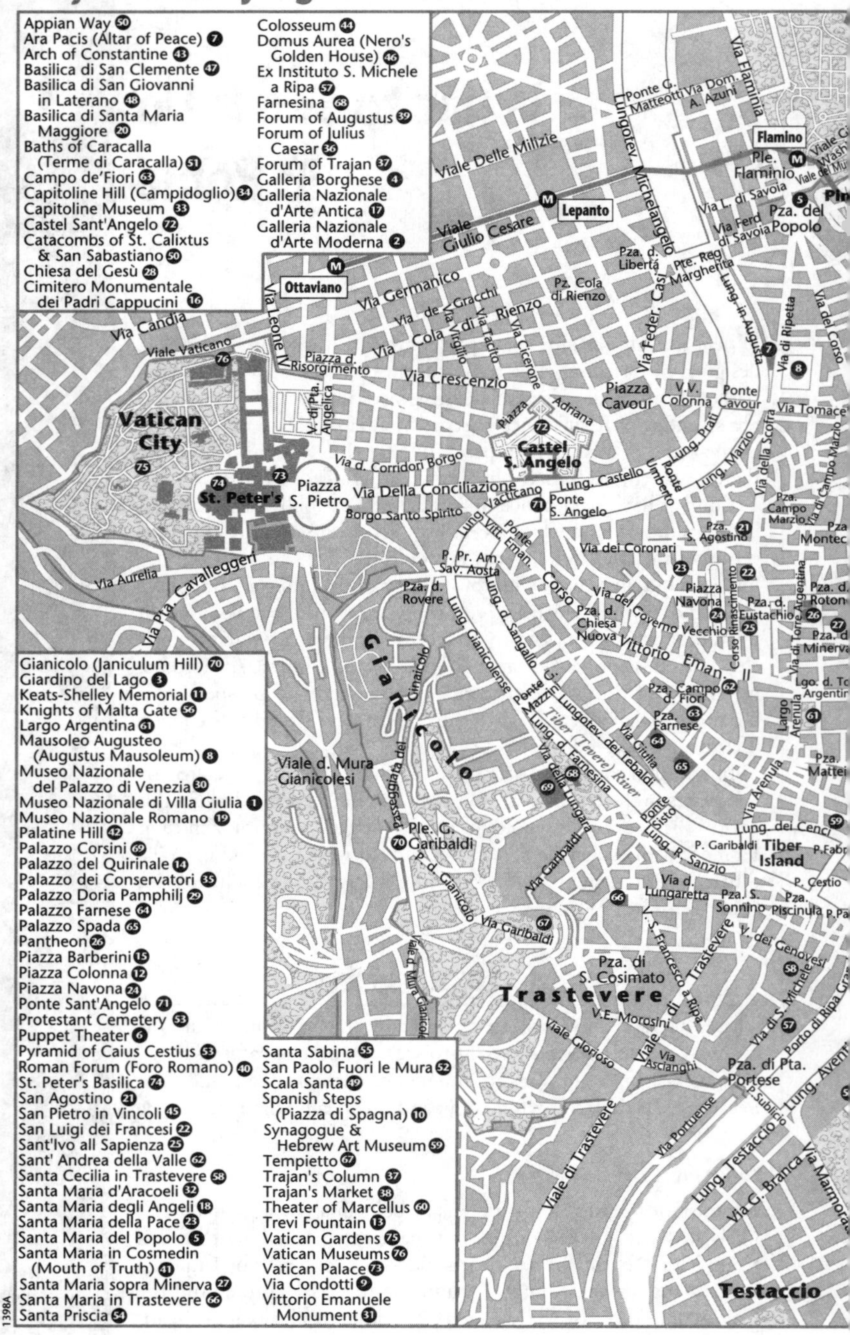

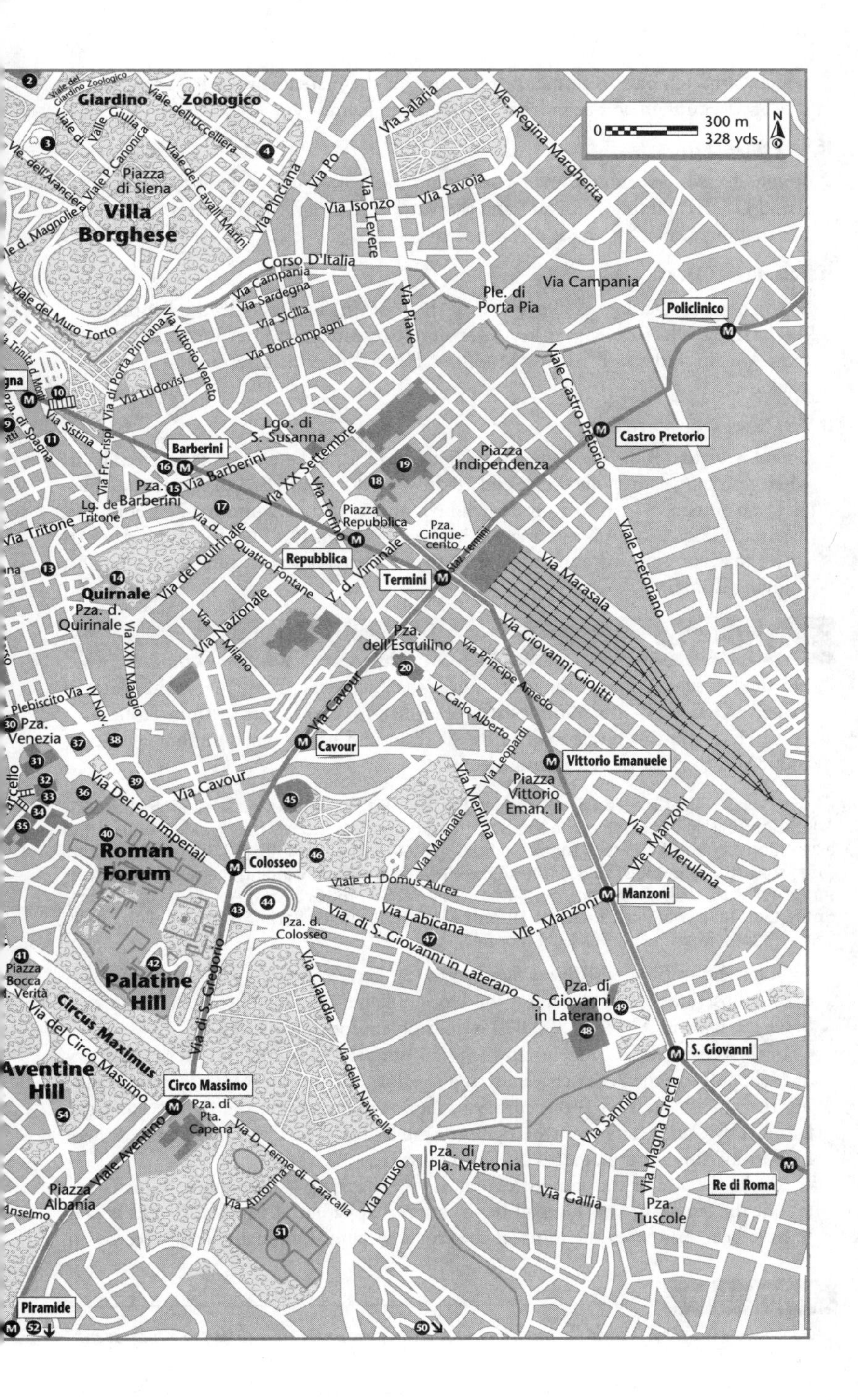

Giardino Zoologico
Villa Borghese
Piazza di Siena
Viale del Giardino Zoologico
Viale dell'Uccelliera
Viale di Valle Giulia
Viale P. Canonica
Vle. dell'Aranciera
Viale d. Magnolie
Viale dei Cavalli Marini
Via Pinciana
Via Po
Via Salaria
Vle. Regina Margherita
Via Isonzo
Via Tevere
Via Savoia
Corso D'Italia
Via Campania
Via Sardegna
Via Sicilia
Via Boncompagni
Via Piave
Ple. di Porta Pia
Policlinico
Viale del Muro Torto
Via di Porta Pinciana
Via Vittorio Veneto
Via Ludovisi
Via Sistina
Via Fr. Crispi
Lgo. di S. Susanna
Via XX Settembre
Barberini
Via Barberini
Pza. Barberini
Lg. de Tritone
Via Tritone
Via Torino
Piazza Repubblica
Pza. Cinquecento
Staz. Termini
Termini
Repubblica
Piazza Indipendenza
Viale Castro Pretorio
Castro Pretorio
Viale Pretoriano
Via Marsala
Via d. Quattro Fontane
Via del Quirinale
V. d. Viminale
Quirinale
Pza. d. Quirinale
Via XXIV Maggio
Via Nazionale
Via Milano
Pza. dell'Esquilino
Via Principe Amedeo
Via Giovanni Giolitti
V. Carlo Alberto
Via Cavour
Cavour
Plebiscito
Via IV Nov.
Pza. Venezia
Via Dei Fori Imperiali
Via Merulana
Via Leopardi
Vittorio Emanuele
Piazza Vittorio Eman. II
Via Manzoni
Vle. Manzoni
Roman Forum
Colosseo
Viale d. Domus Aurea
Via Macanate
Pza. d. Colosseo
Via Labicana
Via. di S. Giovanni in Laterano
Manzoni
Palatine Hill
Piazza Bocca d. Verità
Circus Maximus
Via del Circo Massimo
Via di S. Gregorio
Via Claudia
Pza. di S. Giovanni in Laterano
S. Giovanni
Via della Navicella
Aventine Hill
Circo Massimo
Pza. di Pta. Capena
Via D. Terme di Caracalla
Via Antonina
Via Druso
Pza. di Pla. Metronia
Via Sannio
Via Magna Grecia
Via Gallia
Pza. Tuscole
Re di Roma
Viale Aventino
Piazza Albania
Anselmo
Piramide
0
300 m
328 yds.
N

which, although past its prime, is still a lure for the first-time visitor. Toss a coin in the Trevi Fountain and promise a return visit to Rome.

If You Have 2 Days

If you elected to see the Roman Forum and the Colosseum on your first day, then spend Day 2 exploring St. Peter's and the Vatican Museum (or vice versa). Have dinner that night in a restaurant in Trastevere.

If You Have 3 Days

Spend your first 2 days as above. Go in the morning of Day 3 to the Pantheon in the heart of Old Rome, then try to explore two museums after lunch: the Castel Sant'Angelo and the Etruscan Museum. Have dinner at a restaurant on Piazza Navona.

If You Have 4 or More Days

Spend your first 3 days as above. On Day 4 head for the environs, either to Tivoli, where you can see the Villa d'Este and Hadrian's Villa, or to Ostia to explore the ruins of Ostia Antica, return to Rome for lunch, and visit the Capitoline Museum and Basilica di San Giovanni in Laterano in the afternoon. On Day 5, do the day trip above that you skipped on Day 4, then spend the rest of your time exploring and enjoying Rome.

1 The Vatican & St. Peter's

On the left side of Piazza San Pietro, near the Arco delle Campane, is the **Vatican Tourist Office** (☎ **06/6988-4466**), open Monday to Saturday from 8:30am to 7pm. Here you can buy a map of the Vatican and have your questions answered about St. Peter's or the Vatican museums.

✪ **St. Peter's Basilica (Basilica di San Pietro).** Piazza San Pietro. ☎ **06/6988-4466.** Admission: Basilica (including the sacristy, treasury, and grottoes), free; guided tour of the excavations around St. Peter's tomb, 10,000L ($6.40); dome, 5,000L ($3.20) adults, 1,000L (65¢) students, or 6,000L ($3.85) to take the elevator. Basilica (including the sacristy and treasury), Apr–Aug, daily 7am–7pm; Sept–Mar, daily 7am–6pm. Grottoes, Apr–Sept, daily 7am–6pm; Oct–Mar, daily 7am–5pm. Dome, Mar–Sept, daily 8am–6pm; Oct–Feb, daily 8am–4:30pm. Bus: 23, 30, 32, 49, 51, or 64.

As you stand in Bernini's **Piazza San Pietro** (St. Peter's Square), you'll be in the arms of an ellipse; like a loving parent, the Doric-pillared colonnade reaches out to embrace the faithful. Holding 300,000 is no problem for this square.

In the center of the square is an Egyptian **obelisk,** brought from the ancient city of Heliopolis on the Nile delta, and used to adorn the nearby Nero's Circus. Flanking the obelisk are two 17th-century fountains—the one on the right (facing the basilica) by Carlo Maderno, who designed the facade of St. Peter's, was placed there by Bernini himself; the other is by Carlo Fontana.

Inside, the size of this famous church is awe-inspiring—although its dimensions (about the length of two football fields) are not apparent at first. St. Peter's is said to have been built over the tomb of the crucified saint. Originally it was erected on

Impressions

As a whole St. Peter's is fit for nothing but a ballroom, and it is a little too gaudy even for that.

—John Ruskin, letter to the Rev. Thomas Dale, December 1840

Vatican City

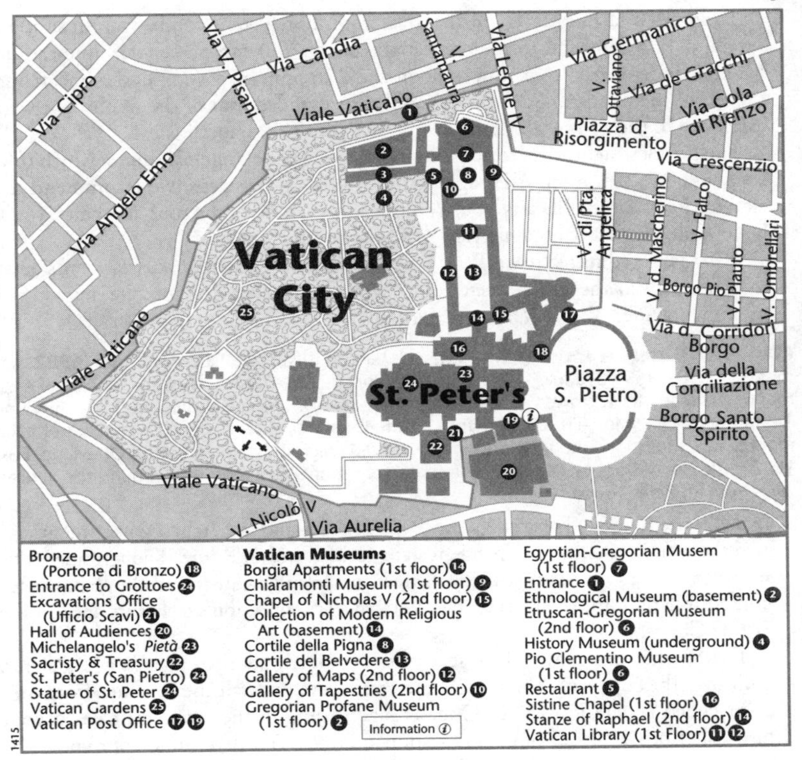

the order of Constantine, but the present structure is essentially Renaissance and baroque; it showcases the talents of some of Italy's greatest artists: Bramante, Raphael, Michelangelo, and Maderno.

In a church of such grandeur—overwhelming in its detail of gilt, marble, and mosaic—don't expect subtlety. But the basilica is rich in art. In the nave on the right (the first chapel) is the best-known piece of sculpture, the ***Pietà*** that Michelangelo sculpted while still in his early 20s. In one of the worst acts of vandalism on record, a madman screaming "I am Jesus Christ" attacked the *Pietà* in the 1970s, battering the Madonna's stone arm, the folded veil, her left eyelid, and her nose. Now restored, the *Pietà* is protected by a wall of reinforced glass.

Much farther on, in the right wing of the transept near the Chapel of St. Michael, rests Canova's neoclassic sculptural tribute to **Pope Clement XIII**. The truly devout are prone to kiss the feet of the 13th-century bronze of **St. Peter**, attributed to Arnolfo di Cambio (at the far reaches of the nave, against a corner pillar on the right). Under Michelangelo's dome is the celebrated ***baldacchino*** by Bernini, resting over the papal altar. The canopy was created in the 17th century—in part, so it is said, from bronze stripped from the Pantheon. However, analysis of the bronze seems to contradict that.

In addition, you can visit the **sacristy and treasury,** filled with jewel-studded chalices, reliquaries, and copes. One robe worn by Pius XII strikes a simple note in these halls of elegance. Later you can make a visit underground to the **Vatican grottoes,** with their tombs, both ancient and modern (Pope John XXIII gets the most adulation).

To go even farther down, to the area around St. Peter's tomb, you must apply several days beforehand to the excavations office. You can make your applications Monday to Saturday from 9am to noon and 2 to 5pm by passing under the arch to the left of the facade of St. Peter's. You'll take a guided tour of the tombs that were excavated in the 1940s, 23 feet beneath the floor of the church.

The grandest sight is yet to come: the climb to **Michelangelo's dome,** which towers about 375 feet high. Although you can walk up the steps, we recommend the elevator for as far as it'll carry you. You can also walk along the roof, for which you'll be rewarded with a panoramic view of Rome and the Vatican.

Note: To be admitted to St. Peter's, women must wear longer skirts or pants (anything that covers the knees); men cannot wear shorts. Sleeveless tops are not allowed for either gender. You *will* be turned away.

✪ **Vatican Museums & the Sistine Chapel.** Vatican City, Viale Vaticano. ☎ **06/6982.** Admission 15,000L ($9.60) adults, 10,000L ($6.40) children, free for everyone the last Sun of each month (be ready for a crowd). June 15–Aug and Nov–Mar, Mon–Sat 8:45am–1pm; Apr–June 14 and Sept–Oct, Mon–Fri 8:45am–4pm, Sat 8:45am–1pm; also open the last Sun of each month. Last admission 1 hour before closing. Closed religious holidays. Metro: Ottaviano. Bus: 19, 23, 32, 34, 49, 51, or 64. *Note:* The museum entrance is a long walk around the Vatican walls from St. Peter's Square.

In 1929 the Lateran Treaty between Pope Pius XI and the Italian government created the world's smallest independent state, located within Rome. Though small, this state contains a gigantic repository of treasures from antiquity and the Renaissance housed in labyrinthine galleries. The Vatican's art collection reaches its apex in the Sistine Chapel.

The Vatican museums comprise a series of lavishly adorned palaces and galleries built over the centuries. You can choose your route through the museum from four color-coded itineraries—A, B, C, or D—according to the time you have at your disposal (from 1½ to 5 hours) and your interests. You determine your choice by consulting large-size panels placed at the entrance, and following the letter/color of your choice.

Obviously, 1, 2, or even 20 trips will not be enough to see the wealth of the Vatican, much less digest it. With that in mind, we've previewed only a representative sampling of masterpieces.

Pinacoteca (Picture Gallery): After climbing the spiral stairway, keep to the right to the Pinacoteca, which houses paintings and tapestries from the 11th to the 19th century. For the break with the Byzantine, see one of the Vatican's finest artworks—the *Stefaneschi Triptych* (six panels) by Giotto and his assistants. You'll also see the works of Fra Angelico, the 15th-century Dominican monk who distinguished himself as a miniaturist (his *Virgin with Child* is justly praised—look for the microscopic eyes of the Madonna).

In the Raphael salon you'll find three paintings by that giant of the Renaissance—including the *Coronation of the Virgin,* the *Virgin of Foligno,* and his massive *Transfiguration* (completed by Raphael shortly before his death). There are also eight tapestries made by Flemish weavers from cartoons by Raphael. Seek out Leonardo da Vinci's masterful—but uncompleted—*St. Jerome with the Lion,* as well as Giovanni Bellini's *Pietà* and one of Titian's greatest works, the *Virgin of Frari.* Finally, feast your eyes on one of the masterpieces of the baroque period, Caravaggio's *Deposition from the Cross.*

Egyptian-Gregorian Museum: Review the grandeur of the Pharaohs by studying sarcophagi, mummies, statues of goddesses, vases, jewelry, sculptured pink-granite statues, and hieroglyphics.

Estruscan-Gregorian Museum: With sarcophagi, a chariot, bronzes, urns, jewelry, and terra-cotta vases, this gallery affords remarkable insights into an ancient civilization. One of the most acclaimed exhibits is the Regolini-Galassi tomb, unearthed at Cerveteri (see Chapter 10, "Side Trips from Rome") in the 19th century. It shares top honors with the *Mars of Todi,* a bronze sculpture that probably dates from the 5th century B.C.

Pio Clementino Museum: Here you'll find Greek and Roman sculptures, many of which are immediately recognizable masterpieces. The rippling muscles of the *Belvedere Torso,* a partially preserved Greek statue (1st century B.C.) that was much admired by the artists of the Renaissance, especially Michelangelo, reveal an intricate knowledge of the human body. In the rotunda is a large gilded bronze of Hercules that dates from the late 2nd century A.D. Other major works of sculpture are under porticoes that open onto the Belvedere courtyard. Dating from the 1st century B.C., one sculpture shows Laocoön and his two sons locked in an eternal struggle with the serpents. The incomparable *Apollo of Belvedere* (a late Roman reproduction of an authentic Greek work from the 4th century B.C.) has become the symbol of classic male beauty.

Chiaramonti Museum: You'll find a dazzling array of Roman sculpture and copies of Greek originals in these galleries. In the following section, called Braccio Nuovo, you can admire *The Nile,* a magnificent reproduction of a long-lost Hellenistic original, and one of the most remarkable pieces of sculpture from antiquity. The imposing statue of Augustus of Prima Porta presents him as a regal commander.

Vatican Library: The Library is richly decorated and frescoed, representing the work of a team of mannerist painters commissioned by Sixtus V.

Stanze di Raphael: While still a young man, Raphael was given one of the greatest assignments of his short life: the decoration of a series of rooms in the apartments of Pope Julius II. The decoration was carried out by Raphael and his workshop between 1508 and 1524. In these works, Raphael achieves the Renaissance aim of blending classic beauty with realism. In the first chamber, the Stanza dell' Incendio, you'll see much of the work of Raphael's pupils but little of the master—except in the fresco across from the window. The figure of the partially draped Aeneas rescuing his father (to the left of the fresco) is sometimes attributed to Raphael, as is the surpised woman with a jug balanced on her head to the right.

Raphael reigns supreme in the next and most important salon, the Stanza della Segnatura, the first room decorated by the artist, where you'll find the majestic *School of Athens,* one of the artist's best-known works, which depicts such philosophers from the ages as Aristotle, Plato, and Socrates. Many of these figures are actually portraits of some of the greatest artists of the Renaissance, including Bramante (on the right as Euclid, bent over and balding as he draws on a chalkboard), Leonardo da Vinci (as Plato, the bearded man in the center pointing heavenward), even Raphael himself (looking out at you from the lower right corner). While he was painting this masterpiece, Raphael stopped work to walk down the hall for the unveiling of Michelangelo's newly finished Sistine Chapel ceiling. He was so impressed that he returned to his *School of Athens* and added to his design a sulking Michelangelo sitting on the steps. Another well-known masterpiece in this room is the *Disputà del Sacramento.*

The Stanza d'Eliodoro, also by the master, manages to flatter Raphael's papal patrons (Julius II and Leo X) without compromising his art (although one rather fanciful fresco depicts the pope driving Attila from Rome). Finally, there's the Sala di Constantino, which was completed by his students after Raphael's death.

Collection of Modern Religious Art: This museum, opened in 1973, represents the American artists' first invasion of the Vatican (the church had limited itself to European art created before the 18th century). But Pope Paul VI's hobby changed all that. Of the 55 rooms in the new museum, at least 12 are devoted to American artists. All the works chosen for the museum were judged on the basis of their "spiritual and religious values." Among the American works is Leonard Baskin's 5-foot bronze sculpture of Isaac. Modern Italian artists such as de Chirico and Manzù are also displayed, and there's a special room for the paintings of the French artist Georges Rouault.

Borgia Apartments: These apartments, frescoed with biblical scenes by Pinturicchio of Umbria and his assistants, were designed for Pope Alexander VI (the infamous Borgia pope). The rooms, although badly lit, have great splendor and style. At the end of the Stanze di Raphael is the Chapel of Nicholas V, an intimate room frescoed by the Dominican monk Fra Angelico, probably the most saintly of all Italian painters.

Sistine Chapel: Michelangelo considered himself a sculptor, not a painter. While in his 30s, he was commanded by Julius II to stop work on the pope's own tomb and to devote his considerable talents to painting ceiling frescoes—an art form of which the Florentine master was contemptuous.

Michelangelo labored for 4 years (1508–12) over this epic project, which was so physically taxing that it permanently damaged his eyesight. All during the task he had to contend with the pope's incessant urgings to hurry up; at one point Julius threatened to topple Michelangelo from the scaffolding—or so Vasari relates.

It's ironic that a project undertaken against the artist's wishes would form his most enduring legend. Glorifying the human body as only a sculptor could, Michelangelo painted nine panels, taken from the pages Genesis, and surrounded them with prophets and sibyls. The most notable panels detail the expulsion of Adam and Eve from the Garden of Eden, and the creation of man—where God's outstretched hand imbues Adam with spirit.

The Florentine master was in his 60s when he began to paint the masterly *Last Judgment* on the altar wall. Again working against his wishes, Michelangelo presents a more jaundiced view of people and their fate; God sits in judgment, and sinners are plunged into the mouth of hell.

A master of ceremonies under Paul III, Monsignor Biagio da Cesena, protested to the pope against the "shameless nudes" painted by Michelangelo. Michelangelo showed he wasn't above petty revenge by painting the prude with the ears of a jackass in hell. When Biagio complained to the pope, Paul III maintained that he had no jurisdiction in hell. However, Daniele de Volterra was summoned to drape clothing over some of the bare figures—thus earning for himself a dubious distinction as a haberdasher.

On the side walls are frescoes by other Renaissance masters such as Botticelli, Perugino, Luca Signorelli, Pinturicchio, Cosimo Roselli, and Ghirlandaio. We'd guess that if these paintings had been displayed by themselves in other chapels, they would be the object of special pilgrimages. But since they have to compete unfairly with the artistry of Michelangelo, they're virtually ignored by most visitors.

The restoration of the Sistine Chapel in the 1990s touched off a worldwide debate among art historians. The Sistine Chapel was on the verge of collapse, from both its age and the weather, and restoration took years, as restorers used advanced computer analyses in their painstaking and controversial work. They reattached the fresco and repaired the ceiling. No longer dark and shadowy, Michelangelo's frescoes are now bright and pastel. Critics claim that in addition to removing centuries of dirt and grime—and several of the added "modesty" drapes—a vital second layer of paint was removed as well. Purists argue that many of the restored figures seem flat compared to the original which had more shadow and detail. Others in the media have hailed the project for having saved Michelangelo's masterpiece for future generations to appreciate.

History Museum: This museum, founded by Pope Paul VI, was established to tell the history of the Vatican. It exhibits arms, uniforms, and armor, some of which dates back to the early days of the Renaissance. The carriages on display are those used by the popes and cardinals in religious processions. Among the showcases of dress uniforms are the colorful outfits worn by the Pontifical Army Corps, which was discontinued by Pope Paul VI.

Ethnological Museum: The Ethnological Museum is an assemblage of works of art and objects of cultural significance from all over the world. The principal route is a half-mile walk through 25 geographical sections, which display thousands of objects covering 3,000 years of world history. The section devoted to China is especially interesting and worthwhile.

THE VATICAN GARDENS

Separating the Vatican from the secular world on the north and west are 58 acres of lush, carefully tended gardens filled with winding paths, brilliantly colored flowers, groves of massive oaks, and ancient fountains and pools. In the midst of this pastoral setting is a small summer house, the Villa Pia, built for Pope Pius IV in 1560 by Pirro Ligorio. You can visit them only by guided tour, which must be arranged in advance and is limited to 33 people, so reserve as far in advance as possible during the busy summer period (*note:* you cannot get tickets by phone). Tours run Monday, Tuesday, and Thursday to Saturday (except holidays) from 10am to noon. Tickets are 16,000L ($10.25) per person, and are available at the Vatican Tourist Office (see above).

PAPAL AUDIENCES

The pope gives public audiences each Wednesday morning except when he is absent from Rome. The audience begins at 11am, but sometimes at 10am in the hot summer. It takes place in the Paul VI Hall of Audiences, although the Basilica di San Pietro and Piazza San Pietro are sometimes used to accommodate very large attendances. Anyone is welcome, but you must obtain a free ticket first from the office of the Prefecture of the Papal Household, accessible from St. Peter's Square by the bronze door where the right-hand colonnade (as you face the basilica) begins. The office is open Monday to Saturday from 9am to 1pm. On Monday and Tuesday, tickets are readily available, but sometimes you won't be able to get into the office on Wednesday morning. Occasionally, if there's enough room, you can attend without a ticket.

You can also write ahead of time to the **Prefecture of the Papal Household,** 00120 Città del Vaticano (☎ **06/6982**), indicating your language, the dates of your visit, the number of people in your party, and, if possible, the hotel in Rome to which the cards should be sent the afternoon before the audience. American Catholics, armed with a letter of introduction from their parish priest, should apply to the **North American College,** Via dell'Umiltà 30, 00187 Rome (☎ **06/678-9184**).

At noon on Sunday the pope speaks briefly from his study window and gives his blessing to the visitors and pilgrims gathered in St. Peter's Square. From about mid-July to mid-September the Angelus and blessing take place at the summer residence at Castelgandolfo, some 16 miles out of Rome and accessible by Metro and bus.

2 The Forum, the Colosseum & the Heart of Ancient Rome

✪ **Roman Forum (Foro Romano).** Via dei Fori Imperiali. ☎ **06/699-0110.** Admission 12,000L ($7.70) adults, free for children 17 and under and for seniors 60 and over. Mon and Wed–Sat 9am to 1 hour before sunset, Sun and Tues 9am–2pm. Last admission 1 hour before closing. Closed Jan 16–Feb 15. Metro: Colosseo. Bus: 27, 81, 85, 87, or 186.

When it came to cremating Caesar, raping Sabine women, purchasing a harlot for the night, or sacrificing a naked victim, the **Roman Forum** was where the action was hot. Traversed by Via Sacra (the Sacred Way), it was built in the marshy land between the Palatine and the Capitoline hills. It flourished as the center of Roman life in the days of the Republic, before it gradually lost prestige to the Imperial Forums.

Be warned: Expect only fragmented monuments, an arch or two, and lots of overturned boulders. That any semblance of the Forum remains today is miraculous, as it was used for years, like the Colosseum, as a quarry. Eventually it reverted to what the Italians call *campo vaccino* (cow pasture). But excavations in the 19th century began to bring to light one of the world's most historic spots.

By day, the columns of now-vanished temples and the stones from which long-forgotten orators spoke are mere shells. Bits of grass and weed grow where a triumphant Caesar was once lionized. But at night, when the Forum is silent in the moonlight, it isn't difficult to imagine that Vestal Virgins still guard the sacred temple fire. (Historical footnote: The function of the maidens was to keep the temple's sacred fire burning—but their own flame under control. Failure to do the latter sent them to an early grave . . . alive!)

You can spend at least a morning wandering alone through the ruins of the Forum. If you're content with just looking at the ruins, you can do so at your leisure. But if you want the stones to have some meaning, you'll have to purchase a detailed map at the gate, as the temples are hard to locate otherwise. The first half of our Walking Tour 1, "Rome of the Caesars," in Chapter 7 will take you around what remains of the ancient buildings and temples, as well as up the Palatine Hill.

A long walk up from the Roman Forum leads to the **Palatine Hill** (you can visit on the same ticket, and at the same hours, as the Forum), one of the seven hills of Rome. The Palatine, tradition tells us, was the spot on which the first settlers built their huts, under the direction of Romulus. In later years the hill became a patrican residential district that attracted such citizens as Cicero. In time, however, the area was gobbled up by imperial palaces, and it drew a famous and infamous roster of tenants, such as Caligula (who was murdered here), Nero, Tiberius, and Domitian.

Only the ruins of its former grandeur remain today, and you really need to be an archeologist to make sense of them, as they're more difficult to understand than the ruins in the Forum. But even if you're not interested in the past, it's worth the climb for the panoramic, sweeping view of both the Roman and Imperial forums, as well as the Capitoline Hill and the Colosseum. To explore, again, see our Walking Tour 1, "Rome of the Caesars," in Chapter 7.

✪ **Colosseum (Colosseo).** Piazzale del Colosseo, Via dei Fori Imperiali. ☎ **06/700-4261.** Admission: Street level, free; upper levels, 8,000L ($5.10). Mon–Tues and Thurs–Sat 9am to 1 hour before sunset, Wed and holidays 9am–2pm. Metro: Colosseo.

In spite of the fact that it's a mere shell, the Colosseum remains the greatest architectural inheritance from ancient Rome. Vespasian ordered the construction of the elliptically shaped bowl, called the Amphitheatrum Flavium, in A.D. 72; it was inaugurated by Titus in A.D. 80 with a many-weeks-long bloody combat between

Ancient Rome & Attractions Nearby

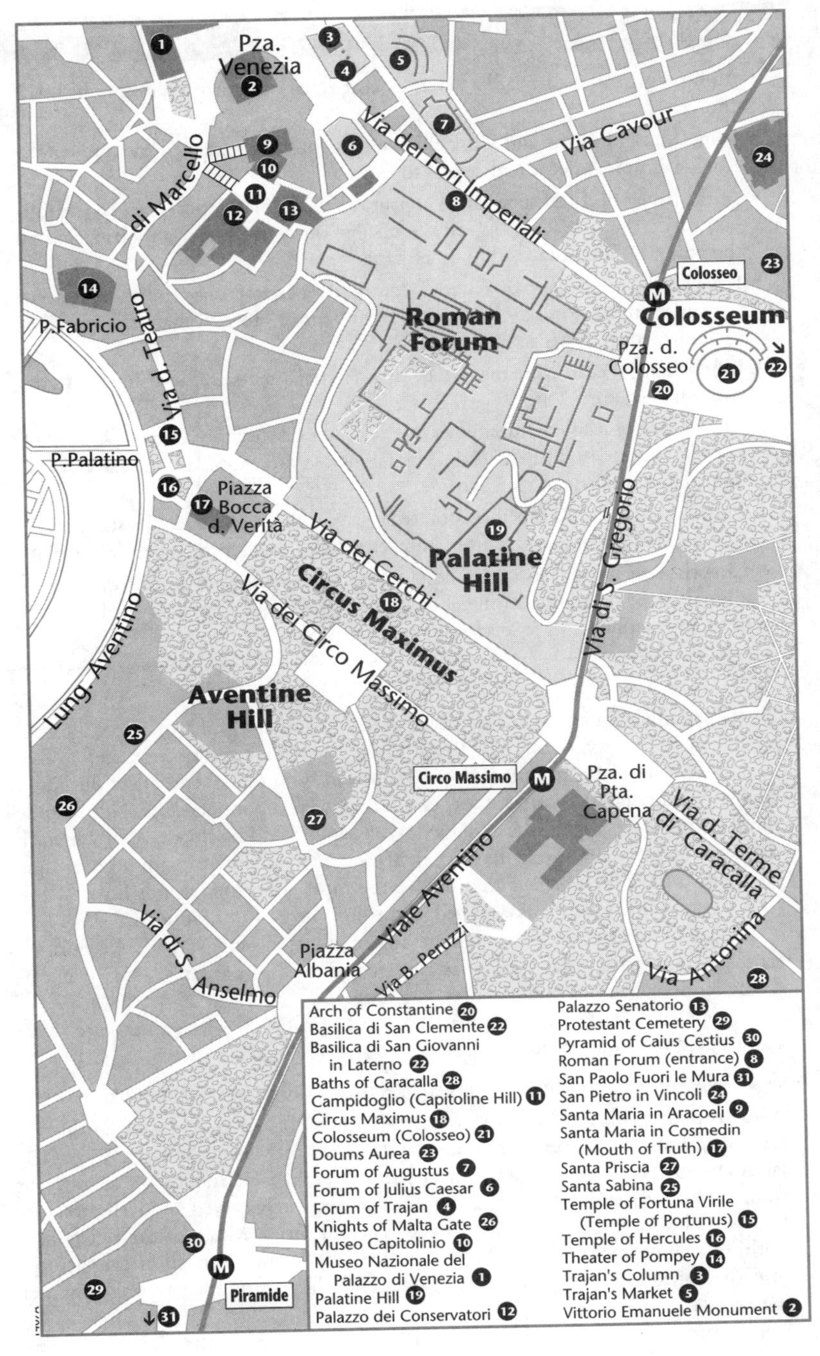

Pza.
Venezia
Via dei Fori Imperiali
Via Cavour
di Marcello
Colosseo
Colosseum
Roman
Forum
Pza. d.
Colosseo
P.Fabricio
Via d. Teatro
P.Palatino
Piazza
Bocca
d. Verità
Via dei Cerchi
Circus Maximus
Palatine
Hill
Via di S. Gregorio
Via dei Circo Massimo
Lung. Aventino
Aventine
Hill
Circo Massimo
Pza. di
Pta.
Capena
Via d. Terme
di Caracalla
Viale Aventino
Via B. Peruzzi
Via di S. Anselmo
Piazza
Albania
Via Antonina
Piramide
Arch of Constantine 20
Basilica di San Clemente 22
Basilica di San Giovanni in Laterno 22
Baths of Caracalla 28
Campidoglio (Capitoline Hill) 11
Circus Maximus 18
Colosseum (Colosseo) 21
Doums Aurea 23
Forum of Augustus 7
Forum of Julius Caesar 6
Forum of Trajan 4
Knights of Malta Gate 26
Museo Capitolinio 10
Museo Nazionale del Palazzo di Venezia 1
Palatine Hill 19
Palazzo dei Conservatori 12
Palazzo Senatorio 13
Protestant Cemetery 29
Pyramid of Caius Cestius 30
Roman Forum (entrance) 8
San Paolo Fuori le Mura 31
San Pietro in Vincoli 24
Santa Maria in Aracoeli 9
Santa Maria in Cosmedin (Mouth of Truth) 17
Santa Priscia 27
Santa Sabina 25
Temple of Fortuna Virile (Temple of Portunus) 15
Temple of Hercules 16
Theater of Pompey 14
Trajan's Column 3
Trajan's Market 5
Vittorio Emanuele Monument 2

Did You Know?

- Along with miles of headless statues and acres of paintings, Rome has 913 churches.
- Some Mongol khans and Turkish chieftains pushed westward to conquer the Roman Empire after it had ceased to exist.
- At the time of Julius Caesar and Augustus, Rome's population reached the million mark, the largest city in the Western world. Some historians claim that by the year A.D. 500 only 10,000 inhabitants were left.
- Pope Leo III sneaked up on Charlemagne and set an imperial crown on his head, a surprise coronation that launched a precedent of Holy Roman Emperors being crowned by popes in Rome.
- More than 90% of Romans live in private apartments, some rising 10 floors without elevators.
- The bronze of Marcus Aurelius in the Capitoline Museums, one of the world's greatest equestrian statues, escaped being melted down because the early Christians thought it was of Constantine.
- The Theater of Marcellus incorporated a gory realism in some of its stage plays: Condemned prisoners were often butchered before audiences as part of the plot.
- Christians were not fed to the lions at the Colosseum, but in one day 5,000 animals were slaughtered (one about every 10 seconds). North Africa's native lions and elephants were rendered extinct.

gladiators and wild beasts. At its peak, under the cruel Domitian, the Colosseum could seat 50,000 spectators. The Vestal Virgins from the temple screamed for blood, as more and more exotic animals were shipped in from the far corners of the empire to satisfy jaded tastes (lion vs. bear, two humans vs. hippopotamus). Not-so-mock naval battles were staged (the canopied Colosseum could be flooded), in which the defeated combatants might have their lives spared if they put up a good fight. Many historians now believe that one of the most enduring legends linked to the Colosseum—that Christians were fed to the lions here—is unfounded.

Long after it ceased to be an arena to amuse sadistic Romans, the Colosseum was struck by an earthquake. Centuries later it was used as a quarry, its rich marble facing stripped away to build palaces and churches.

On one side, part of the original four tiers remains; the first three levels were constructed in Doric, Ionic, and Corinthian styles to lend it variety.

Arch of Constantine. Next to the Colosseum, Piazzale del Colosseo. Metro: Colosseo.

A highly photogenic memorial (next to the Colosseum), the Arch of Constantine was erected in honor of Constantine's defeat of the pagan Maxentius (A.D. 306). It's a landmark in every way. Physically, it's beautiful, perhaps marred by the aggravating traffic that zooms around it at all hours, but so intricately carved and well preserved that you almost forget the racket of the cars and buses. Many of the reliefs have nothing whatsoever to do with Constantine or his works, but tell of the victories of earlier Antonine rulers—they were apparently lifted from other, long-forgotten memorials.

Historically, the arch marks a period of great change in the history of Rome and therefore the history of the world. Converted to Christianity by a vision on the battlefield, Constantine officially ended the centuries-long persecution of the Christians during which many devout followers of the new religion had been put to death, oftentimes horribly. While Constantine did not ban paganism (which survived officially until the closing of the temples more than half a century later), he espoused Christianity himself and began the inevitable development that culminated in the conquest of Rome by the Christian religion. The arch is a tribute to the emperor erected by the Senate in A.D. 315.

Domus Aurea. Via Labicana, on the Esquiline Hill. Metro: Colosseo.

After visiting the Colosseum, it's also convenient to look at the site of the Domus Aurea, or the Golden House of Nero; it faces the Colosseum and is adjacent to the Forum. The Domus Aurea was one of the most sumptuous palaces of all time, constructed by Nero after the disastrous fire that swept over Rome in A.D. 64. Not much remains of its former glory, but once the floors were made of mother-of-pearl and the furniture of gold. The area that is the Colosseum today was an ornamental lake, which reflected the grandeur and glitter of the Golden House. The hollow ruins—long ago stripped of their lavish decorations—lie near the entrance of the Oppius Park.

During the Renaissance, painters such as Raphael chopped holes in the long-buried ceilings of the Domus Aurea to gain admittance. Once there, they were inspired by the frescoes and the small "grotesques" of cornucopia and cherubs. The word *grotto* came from this palace, as it was believed to have been built underground. Remnants of these original, almost-2,000-year-old frescoes and fragments of mosaics remain. All interiors have been closed for years.

3 Near Ancient Rome

The Campidoglio (Capitoline Hill). Bus: 46, 89, 92, 94, 716.

Of the Seven Hills of Rome, the Campidoglio, Piazza del Campidoglio, is the most sacred—its origins stretch way back into antiquity (an Etruscan temple to Jupiter once stood on this spot). The approach to the Capitoline Hill is dramatic—climbing the long, sloping steps designed by Michelangelo. At the top is a perfectly proportioned square, Piazza del Campidoglio, also laid out by the Florentine artist. Michelangelo also positioned the ancient bronze equestrian statue of Marcus Aurelius in the center, but it has now been moved inside to be protected from pollution and you'll only occasionally find a replacement copy out on the pedestal.

One side of the piazza is open; the others are bounded by the **Senatorium** (Town Council), the statuary-filled **Palazza dei Conservatori,** and the **Capitoline Museum** (Museo Capitolino; see below). The Campidoglio is dramatic at night (walk around to the back for a regal view of the floodlit Roman Forum). On your return, head down the small steps on your right. The other steps adjoining Michelangelo's approach will take you to the **Church of Santa Maria d'Aracoeli** (see below).

✪ **Museo Capitolino and Palazzo dei Conservatori.** Piazza del Campidoglio. ☎ **06/6710-2071.** Admission 10,000L ($6.40) for both. Apr–Sept, Tues 9am–1:45pm and 5–8pm, Wed–Fri and Sun 9am–1:30pm, Sat 9am–1:30pm and 8–11pm; Oct–Mar, Tues and Sat 9am–1:45pm and 5–8pm, Wed–Fri and Sun 9am–1:30pm. Bus: 46, 89, 92, 94, or 716.

These museums house some of the greatest pieces of classical sculpture in the world. The **Capitoline Museum** was built in the 17th century, based on an architectural sketch by Michelangelo. In the first room is *The Dying Gaul,* a work of majestic skill. It's a copy of a Greek original that dates from the 3rd century B.C. In a special gallery all her own is *The Capitoline Venus,* who demurely covers herself. This statue (also a Roman copy of a 3rd century B.C. Greek original) was the symbol of feminine beauty and charm down through the centuries. *Amore* (Cupid) and *Psyche* are up to their old tricks near the window.

The famous equestrian statue of Marcus Aurelius, whose years in the middle of the piazza made it a victim of pollution, has recently been restored and is now kept in the museum for protection. This is the only bronze equestrian statue to have survived from ancient Rome, mainly because for centuries it was thought to be a statue of Constantine the Great and Papal Rome respected the memory of the first Christian emperor. It's a beautiful statue even though the perspective is rather odd—it was designed to sit on top of a tall column, hence the foreshortened effect. The statue is housed in a glassed-in room on the street level called the Cortile di Marforio; it's a kind of Renaissance greenhouse, surrounded by windows.

The **Palace of the Conservatori,** across the way, was also based on an architectural plan by Michelangelo, and is rich in classical sculpture and paintings. One of the most notable bronzes—a work of incomparable beauty—is *Lo Spinario* (a little boy picking a thorn from his foot), a Greek classic that dates from the 1st century B.C. In addition, you'll find *Lupa Capitolina* (the Capitoline Wolf), a rare Etruscan bronze that may go back to the 5th century B.C. (Romulus and Remus, the legendary twins that the wolf suckled, were added at a later date). The palace also contains a "Pinacoteca"—mostly paintings from the 16th and 17th centuries. Notable canvases include Caravaggio's *Fortune-Teller* and his curious *John the Baptist, The Holy Family* by Dosso Dossi, *Romulus and Remus* by Rubens, and Titian's *Baptism of Christ.* The entrance courtyard is lined with the remains—head, hands, foot, and a kneecap—of an ancient colossal statue of Constantine the Great.

Santa Maria d'Aracoeli. Piazza d'Aracoeli. ☎ **06/679-8155.** Free admission. Daily 7am–noon and 3:30–5:30pm. Bus: 46, 89, 92, 94, or 95.

Sharing a spot on Capitoline Hill, this landmark church was built for the Franciscans in the 13th century. According to legend, Augustus once ordered a temple erected on this spot, where a sibyl, with her gift of prophecy, forecast the coming of Christ. In the interior of the present building you'll find a coffered Renaissance ceiling and a mosaic of the Virgin over the altar in the Byzantine style. If you're sleuth enough, you'll also find a tombstone carved by the great Renaissance sculptor Donatello.

The church is known for its Bufalini Chapel, a masterpiece of Pinturicchio, who frescoed it with scenes illustrating the life and death of St. Bernardino of Siena. He also depicted St. Francis receiving the stigmata. These frescoes are a high point in early Renaissance Roman painting. The church was also once home to a sacred baby Jesus that's believed to have been carved from an olive tree from the Garden of Gethsemane, the recipient of many letters and prayers from around the world. The statue was stolen in 1994. You have to climb a long flight of steep steps to reach the church, unless you're already on the neighboring Piazza del Campidoglio, in which case you can cross the piazza and climb the steps on the far side of the Museo Capitolino.

Museo Nazionale del Palazzo di Venezia. Via del Plebiscito 118. ☎ **06/679-8865.** Admission 12,000L ($7.70) adults, 8,000L ($5.10) children 11 and under. Tues–Sat 9am–2pm, Sun 9am–1pm. Bus: 64, 75, 85, 170, or 492.

The Museum of the Palazzo Venezia, in the geographic heart of Rome, is the building that served until the end of World War I as the seat of the Embassy of Austria. During the Fascist regime (1928–43) it was the seat of the Italian government. The balcony from which Mussolini used to speak to the Italian people was built in the 15th century. You can now visit the rooms and halls containing oil paintings, porcelains, tapestries, ivories, and ceramics. No one particular exhibit stands out—it's the sum

Impressions

Of Rome, in short, this is my opinion, or rather indeed my most assured knowledge, that her delights on earth are sweet, and her judgments in heaven heavy.

—Sir Henry Wotton, letter to Lord Zouche, May (1592)

total that adds up to a major attraction. The State Rooms are currently only open occasionally to host temporary exhibitions.

Standing outside the museum, you cannot help but notice the 20th-century **monument to Victor Emmanuel II**, king of Italy, built on part of the Capitoline Hill and overlooking the piazza, a lush work that has often been compared to a wedding cake. Here you'll find the Tomb of the Unknown Soldier that was created in World War I.

Santa Maria in Cosmedin. Piazza della Bocca della Verità 18. ☎ **06/678-1419.** Free admission. Daily 9am–1pm and 2:30–6pm. Bus: 15, 23, 57, 95, or 716.

This little church was founded in the 6th century, but subsequently rebuilt—and a campanile was added in the 12th century in the Romanesque style. The church is ever-popular with pilgrims drawn not by its great art treasures but by its "Mouth of Truth," a large disk under the portico. As Gregory Peck demonstrated to Audrey Hepburn in *Roman Holiday,* the mouth is supposed to chomp down on the hand of liars who insert their paws. According to local legend, a former priest used to keep a scorpion in back to bite the fingers of anyone he felt was lying. On one of our visits to the church, a little woman, her head draped in black, sat begging a few feet from the medallion. A scene typical enough—except that this woman's right hand was covered with bandages.

Baths of Caracalla (Terme di Caracalla). Via delle Terme di Caracalla 52. ☎ **06/575-8626.** Admission 8,000L ($5.10) adults, free for children 11 and under. Apr–Sept, Tues–Sat 9am–6pm, Sun–Mon 9am–1pm; Oct–Mar, Tues–Sat 9am–3pm, Sun–Mon 9am–1pm. Bus: 90 or 118.

Named for the emperor Caracalla, the Terme di Caracalla were completed in the early part of the 3rd century. The richness of decoration has faded and the lushness can only be judged from the shell of brick ruins that remain.

San Pietro in Vincoli (Saint Peter in Chains). Piazza di San Pietro in Vincoli 4A, off Via degli Annibaldi. ☎ **06/488-2865.** Free admission. Mon–Sat 7am–12:30pm and 3:30–6pm, Sun 7–11:45am and 3–7pm. Metro: Via Cavour. Bus: 11, 27, or 81.

From the Colosseum, head up the "spoke" street Via degli Annibaldi to this church, founded in the 5th century A.D. to house the chains that bound St. Peter in Palestine. The chains are preserved under glass. But the drawing card is the tomb of Julius II, with one of the world's most famous pieces of sculpture, *Moses* by Michelangelo. As readers of Irving Stone's *The Agony and the Ecstasy* know, Michelangelo was to have carved 44 magnificent figures for Julius's tomb. That didn't happen, of course, but the pope was given one of the greatest consolation prizes—a figure intended to be "minor" that is now numbered among Michelangelo's masterpieces. Of the stern father symbol of Michelangelo's *Moses,* Vasari, in his *Lives of the Artists,* wrote: "No modern work will ever equal it in beauty, no, nor ancient either."

Basilica di San Clemente. Piazza di San Clemente, Via Labicana 95. ☎ **06/7045-1018.** Admission: Basilica, free; grottoes, 2,000L ($1.30). Mon–Sat 9:30am–12:30pm and 3:30–6pm, Sun 10am–noon and 3:30–6pm. Metro: Colosseo. Bus: 81, 85, 87, or 186. Tram: 13 or 30.

From the Colosseum, head up Via di San Giovanni in Laterano to the Basilica of Saint Clement. This isn't just another Roman church—far from it! In this

913 Churches, One Synagogue—Jews in the Capital of Christendom

Nestled midway between the Isola Tiberina and the monument to Vittorio Emanuele II, Rome's Jewish ghetto was designated during the administration of Pope Paul IV between 1555 and 1559. At the time it enclosed several thousand people into a cramped, 2$^1/_2$-acre tract of walled-in, overcrowded real estate that did much to contribute to the oppression of the Jews during the Italian Renaissance.

Jews had played an important part in the life of Rome prior to that time. They migrated to the political center of the known world during the 1st century B.C., and within 200 years their community had grown to a highly noticeable minority. Most of it was based in Trastevere, a neighborhood that for many years was referred to as Contrada Iudaeorum (Jewish Quarter). By 1309 ordinances were passed that forced Jews to illustrate their religious and cultural backgrounds with special garments, and their ability to worship as they wished depended on the indulgence of the pope.

In 1363 additional ordinances were passed that limited Jewish cemeteries to an area adjacent to the Tiber, near the present-day Church of San Francesco a Ripa. During the 1400s the Jewish population regrouped onto the opposite side of the Tiber, in an area around the square that's known today as Piazza Mattei.

In 1492 Queen Isabella and King Ferdinand of Spain killed, tortured, forcibly converted, or forced the emigration of thousands of Jews from Spain. Many came to Rome, swelling the ranks of the city. Pope Alexander VI (1492–1503), whose political sympathies lay firmly with the Spanish monarchs, grudgingly admitted the refugees into his city, on condition that each pay a hefty fee, in gold. His papal bull, *Cum nimis absurdium,* defined the borders of the Jewish ghetto within the boundaries of the Sant'Angelo district, and later enlarged them to include the muddy, frequently flooded banks of the Tiber. Water levels often reached the third floors of the houses of the poorest families, who were forced, by law and by economics, to settle here. Adding humilation upon humiliation, the residents of the

church-upon-a-church, centuries of history peel away. In the 4th century a church was built over a secular house of the 1st century A.D., beside which stood a pagan temple dedicated to Mithras (god of the sun). Down in the eerie grottoes (which you can explore on your own—unlike the catacombs on the Appian Way), you'll discover well-preserved frescoes from the 9th through the 11th century A.D. After the Normans destroyed the lower church, a new one was built in the 12th century. Its chief attraction is the bronze-orange mosaic (from that period) that adorns the apse, as well as a chapel honoring St. Catherine of Alexandria with frescoes by Masolino.

Basilica di San Giovanni in Laterano. Piazza di San Giovanni in Laterano 4. ☎ **06/6988-6433.** Basilica, free; cloisters, 2,000L ($1.30). Daily 7am–6pm. Metro: San Giovanni.

This basilica—not St. Peter's—is the cathedral of the diocese of Rome. Originally built in A.D. 314 by Constantine, the cathedral has suffered the vicissitudes of Rome, and was badly sacked and forced to rebuild many times. Only fragmented parts of the baptistery remain from the original structure.

The present building is characterized by its 18th-century facade by Alessandro Galilei; statues of Christ and the Apostles ring the top. (A terrorist bomb in 1993 caused severe damage, especially to the facade.) Borromini gets the credit (some say nearly uninhabitable riverbanks were forced to pay for the construction of the embankments that prevented the neighborhood from flooding. For centuries no one could enter or leave the ghetto between sundown and sunrise.

In 1848 the walls that had defined and confined the ghetto were demolished under the auspices of the relatively lenient Pope Leo XII. In 1883, during the surge of nationalism that preceeded the unification of Italy, the ghetto was abolished altogether.

Tragically, on October 16, 1943, the segregation of Rome's Jews was reconfirmed once again when German Nazi soldiers rounded up most of the Jews from throughout Rome into a reincarnation of the medieval ghetto and imposed a flabbergastingly high ransom on them. Amazingly, this fee—more than 100 pounds of gold per resident—was eventually collected. Despite having made the payment, the Jews were rounded up and deported to the death camps anyway, as part of one of the most horrible episodes of Italy's participation in the war years.

Today the neighborhood, centered around Piazza Mattei and its elegant Renaissance fountain, lacks any coherent architectural unity, but is instead viewed as a colorful hodgepodge of narrow, twisting streets, sometimes derelict buildings, and the site of some of the most evocative memories in Rome. One of the most unusual streets is Via del Portico d'Ottavia, where medieval houses and pavements adjoin kosher food stores and simple trattorie that almost invariably feature carciofi alla Giudeai—deep-fried artichokes.

Although it bears the scars and honors of centuries of occupation by Jews, today this is a Jewish neighborhood mostly in name only. Its centerpiece is the Synagogue on Via Catalana. Built of travertine marble in 1904 in the Assyrian-Babylonian style, it's capped with a silvery dome crafted entirely of aluminum. Tours of the district are conducted on an as-needed basis from the **Service International de Documentation Judeo-Chrétienne (SIDIG),** Via Plebiscito 112 (☎ **06/679-5307**).

blame) for the interior, built for Innocent X. It's said that in the misguided attempt to redecorate, frescoes by Giotto were destroyed (remains believed to have been painted by Giotto were discovered in 1952 and are now on display against a column near the church entrance on the right inner pier). In addition, look for the unusual ceiling and the sumptuous transept, and explore the 13th-century cloisters with their twisted double columns.

The popes used to live next door at the **Lateran Palace** before the move to Avignon in the 14th century. But the most unusual sight is across the street at the "Palace of the Holy Steps," called the **Santuario della Scala Sancta,** Piazza San Giovanni in Laterano (☎ **06/7049-4619**). It's alleged that these were the actual steps that Christ climbed when he was brought before Pilate. These steps are supposed to be climbed only on your knees, which you're likely to see the faithful doing throughout the day.

4 Around Campo de' Fiori & the Jewish Ghetto

Much of this area, along with the Piazza Navona & the Pantheon neighborhood, is covered on Walking Tour 3, "Renaissance Rome" (see Chapter 7, "Strolling Through Rome").

Campo de' Fiori. Bus: 64 from the Termini to Museo di Roma; then walk.

During the 1500s this site was the geographic and cultural center of secular Rome, site of dozens of inns that would almost certainly have been reviewed by this guidebook had it existed at the time. From its center rises a statue of a severe-looking monk (Giordano Bruno), whose presence is a reminder of the occasional burnings at the stake in this piazza of religious heretics. Today, ringed by venerable and antique houses, the campo is the site of an open-air food market held Monday to Saturday from early in the morning until around noon, or whenever the food runs out.

Palazzo Farnese. Piazza Farnese. Bus: 46, 62, 70, 71, 87, 90, or 186.

Built between 1514 and 1589, this palace designed by Sangallo, Michelangelo, and others was astronomically expensive at the time. Its famous residents have included a 16th-century member of the Farnese family, Pope Paul III, Cardinal Richelieu, and the former Queen Christina of Sweden, who moved to Rome after abdicating her throne. During the 1630s, when the building's heirs could no longer afford to maintain it, the palace became the site of the French embassy, a function it has served ever since. It's closed to the public. The best view of the palazzo is from Piazza Farnese.

Palazzo Spada. Piazza Capo di Ferro 3. ☎ **06/686-1158.** Admission 4,000L ($2.55) adults, free for children 17 and under and for seniors 60 and over. Tues–Sat 9am–7pm, Sun 9am–12:30pm. Bus: 46, 62, 70, 71, 87, 90, or 186.

Built around 1550 for Cardinal Gerolamo Capo di Ferro, and later inhabited by the descendants of several other cardinals, it was sold to the Italian government in the 1920s. Its richly ornate facade, covered as it is in high-relief stucco decorations in the mannerist style, is the finest of any building from 16th-century Rome. Although the State Rooms are closed to the public, the richly decorated courtyard and a handful of galleries of paintings are open.

Museo di Arte Ebraico della Comunità Israelitica de Roma. Lungotevere Cenci (Tempio). ☎ **06/687-5051.** Admission 8,000L ($5.10) adults and children. June–Aug, Mon–Fri 9:30am–12:30pm; Sept–May, Mon–Thurs 9:30am–1pm and 3–5pm, Fri 9:30am–1:30pm. Bus: 56 or 60.

This museum of Hebraic art houses a permanent exhibition of the Roman Jewish community. It contains Jewish ritual objects and scrolls from the 17th to the 19th century as well as copies of tombstones, paintings, prints, and documents that illustrate 2,000 years of Jewish history in Rome. The collection of silver ceremonial objects is important, as is a selection of ancient ceremonial textiles. The documents of Nazi persecution are of exceptional interest.

5 Near Piazza Navona & the Pantheon

Much of this area, along with the Campo de' Fiori & the Jewish Ghetto neighborhood, is covered on Walking Tour 3, "Renaissance Rome" (see Chapter 7, "Strolling Through Rome").

Piazza Navona. Bus: 64, 70, or 492.

Surely one of the most beautifully baroque sites in all of Rome is this ocher-colored gem, unspoiled by new buildings or even by traffic. The shape results from the ruins of the Stadium of Domitian, which lies underneath. Great chariot races were once held here, some rather unusual, such as the one in which the head of the winning horse was lopped off as it crossed the finish line and carried by runners to be offered as a sacrifice by the Vestal Virgins on top of the Capitoline Hill. In medieval times the popes used to flood the piazza to stage mock naval encounters. Today the most strenuous activities are performed by occasional fire-eaters, who go through their evening paces before an interested crowd of Romans and visitors.

Attractions Near Campo de' Fiori & Piazza Navona

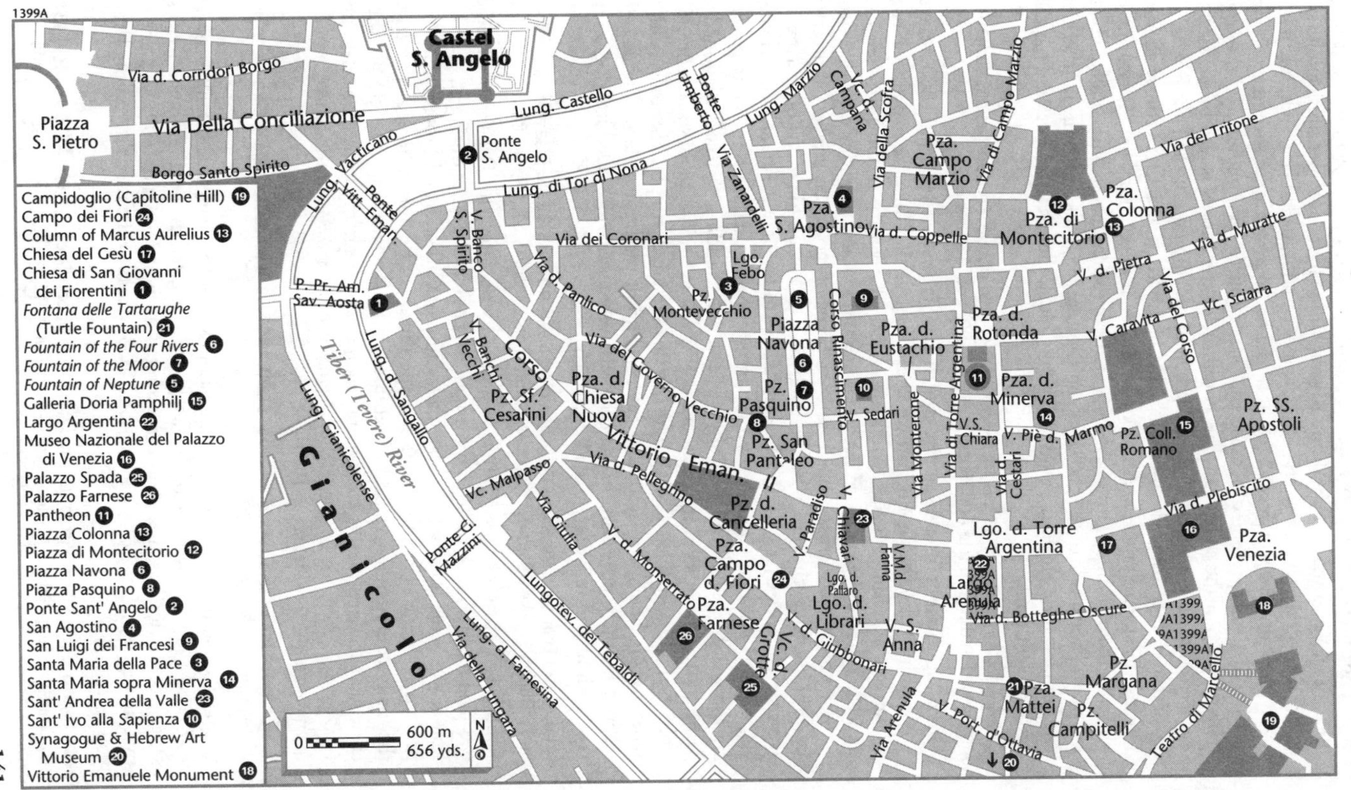

Beside the twin-towered facade of the **Church of Saint Agnese** (17th century), the piazza boasts several other baroque masterpieces. The best known, in the center, is Bernini's ✪ **Fountain of the Four Rivers,** whose four stone personifications symbolize the world's greatest rivers—the Ganges, Danube, della Plata, and Nile. It's fun to try to figure out which is which. (Hint: The figure with the shroud on its head is the Nile, so represented because the river's source was unknown at the time.) The fountain at the south end, the **Fountain of the Moor,** is also by Bernini and dates from the same period as the church and the Fountain of the Four Rivers. The **Fountain of Neptune,** which balances that of the Moor, is a 19th-century addition. During the summer there are outdoor art shows in the evening, but visit during the day—it's the best time to inspect the fragments of the original stadium, under a building on the north side of the piazza. If you're interested, walk out at the northern exit and turn left for a block. It's astonishing how much the level of the ground has risen since ancient times.

Sant'Ivo alla Sapienza. Corso del Rinascimento 40. No phone. Free admission. Sun 10am–noon. Closed mid-July to late Aug. Bus: 70, 81, 87, 90, 90B, 186, or 492.

One of Borromini's most distinctive churches, built between 1642 and 1660, St. Ivo's was crammed into the slightly claustrophobic courtyard of the Palazzo della Sapienza, a landmark that functioned as headquarters of the University of Rome between 1303 and 1935. Its steeple is capped with a bizarre and unique serpentine cone that twists its way upward to a cross-capped summit. Some of its aspects are best appreciated by professional architects, who are flabbergasted by combinations of convex and concave surfaces that couldn't be duplicated today. Their interactions create a high-energy symmetry that's based on an interlocking series of hexagons inspired by the wax hives built by a colony of bees. The building was commissioned by Urban VIII, a member of the Barberini family, whose family symbol was the bee. The only regularly scheduled visiting hours at this site are during Sunday mass. Otherwise, visiting hours vary according to the whim of the local prelates. Frankly, the exterior is much more fanciful than the relatively bare, white-sided interior, which is sometimes commandeered as a lecture hall.

San Luigi dei Francesi. Via Santa Giovanna d'Arco. ☎ **06/683-3818.** Free admission. Thurs 8am–12:30pm, Fri–Wed 8am–12:30pm and 3:30–7pm. Bus: 70, 81, 97, or 186.

Founded in 1518, but not completed until 70 years later, this Renaissance basilica was paid for by French bishops as the national church of France during an era when France was being torn apart by warring factions of Catholics and Protestants. Many prominent French Catholics requested specifically to be buried here, as proven by the many commemorative plaques. Inside, in the last chapel on the left, are three critically acclaimed works from Caravaggio's early years in Rome: the celebrated *Calling of St. Matthew* on the left, *St. Matthew and the Angel* in the center, and *The Martyrdom of St. Matthew* on the right.

San Agostino. Via della Scrofa 80. ☎ **06/6880-1962.** Free admission. Daily 8am–noon and 4:30–7:30pm. Bus: 81, 90, or 90B.

Originally commissioned by the archbishop of Rouen, France, and built between 1479 and 1483, this was one of the first churches erected during the Roman Renaissance. Its interior was altered and redecorated in the 1700s and 1800s. A painting by Caravaggio, *Madonna of the Pilgrims* (1605) hangs in the first altar on the left as you enter.

Santa Maria della Pace. Vicolo del Arco della Pace 5, off Via della Pace. ☎ **06/686-1156.** Free admission. Tues–Sat 10am–noon and 4–6pm, Sun 9–11am. Bus: 70, 81, 87, 90, 90B, 186, or 492.

According to legend, blood flowed from a statue of the Virgin above the altar after someone threw a pebble at it. This legend motivated Pope Sixtus IV to rebuild the church in the 1500s on the foundations of an even older sanctuary as a supplication to God to end some of the many armed conflicts the Vatican was engaged in at the time (hence its name, "Saint Mary of the Peace"). It was embellished in 1504 with the addition of a rather severe-looking cloister by Bramante, and again in 1656 with a lavish baroque facade. The interior contains Raphael's *Sibils,* painted in 1514, and Peruzzi's depiction of the *Madonna with Saints Bridget and Catherine.* The church is near Piazza Navona, and has been undergoing extensive renovations for years.

✪ **Pantheon.** Piazza della Rotonda. ☎ **06/6830-0230.** Free admission. July–Sept, daily 9am–6pm; Oct–June, Mon–Sat 9am–4pm, Sun 9am–1pm. Bus: 46, 62, 64, 170, or 492 to Largo di Torre Argentina; then walk up Via di Torre Argentina or Via dei Cestari.

Of all the great buildings of ancient Rome, only the Pantheon ("All the Gods") remains intact today. It was built in 27 B.C. by Marcus Agrippa, and later reconstructed by the emperor Hadrian in the first part of the 2nd century A.D. This remarkable building is among the architectural wonders of the world because of its dome and its concept of space.

The Pantheon was once ringed with white marble statues of Roman gods in its niches. Animals were sacrificed and burned in the center, and the smoke escaped through the only means of light, an opening at the top 27 feet in diameter. The Pantheon is 142 feet wide and 142 feet high. Michelangelo came here to study the dome before designing the cupola of St. Peter's (whose dome is 2 feet smaller than the Pantheon's).

Other statistics are equally impressive. The walls are 25 feet thick, and the bronze doors leading into the building weigh 20 tons each. The temple was converted into a church in the early 7th century, which helped save it from destruction.

About 125 years ago the tomb of Raphael was discovered in the Pantheon (fans still bring him flowers). Victor Emmanuel II, king of Italy, and his successor, Umberto I, are interred here.

Santa Maria Sopra Minerva. Piazza della Minerva 42. ☎ **06/679-3926.** Free admission. Daily 7am–noon and 4–7pm. Bus: 119.

This is one of the most culturally diverse and eclectic churches in Rome, a building that gracefully bridges the gap between the worlds of ancient Rome, the Gothic period, and the Renaissance. It's the only Gothic church of any substance in all of Rome. Founded in the 700s, it was built in its present form during many stages between 1280 and 1453. It lies only a few steps from the Pantheon, on the foundations of what was originally a temple to the goddess Minerva. The headquarters of Rome's Dominican order lie adjacent to this church, whose artistic and literary treasures include many icons of the high Renaissance, such as the body, the letters, and the religious writings of St. Catherine of Siena, and Michelangelo's statue of the Risen

Impressions

Simple, erect, severe, austere, sublime—shrine of all saints and temple of all gods, from Jove to Jesus—spared and blest by time; looking tranquility, while falls or nods arch, empire, each thing round thee, and man plods his way through thorns to ashes—glorious dome! Shalt thou not last?—Time's scythe and tyrant's rods shiver upon thee—sanctuary upon thee—sanctuary and home of art and piety—Pantheon prime of Rome.

—Byron, *Childe Harold's Pilgrimage*

Christ (1521). The church's many tombs and graves include those of hundreds of ordinary Roman citizens, as well as the tomb of the Dominican monk and painter, Fra Angelico. Plaques on the building's facade record the height of the waters of the Tiber during some of its worst floodings. The most disastrous of these occurred in 1598, when the level of the water rose 33 feet and drowned thousands. The whimsical baby elephant carrying a small obelisk in the piazza outside was designed by Bernini.

Piazza Colonna. Off Via del Corso. Bus: 81, 90, or 90B.

Its centerpiece is one of the most dramatic obelisks in town, the Column of Marcus Aurelius, a hollow bronze column rising 83 feet above the piazza. Built between A.D. 180 and 196, and restored (some say "defaced") in 1589 by a pope who replaced the statue of the Roman warrior on top with a statue of St. Paul, it's one of the ancient world's best examples of heroic bas-relief and one of the most memorable sights of Rome. Beside the piazza's northern edge rises the Palazzo Chigi, official residence of the Italian prime minister.

Chiesa del Gesù. Piazza del Gesù. ☎ **06/678-6341.** Free admission. Apr–Sept, daily 6am–12:30pm and 4–7pm; Oct–Mar, daily 6am–12:30pm and 4:30–7:15pm. Bus: 44, 46, 56, 60, 62, 64, 65, 70, 81, or 90.

Built between 1568 and 1584 by donations from a Farnese cardinal, the Chiesa del Gesù functioned for several centuries as the most potent and powerful church in the Jesuit order. Conceived as a bulwark against the perceived menace of the Protestant Reformation, it's sober, monumental, and very important to the history of the Catholic Counter-Reformation. The sheathing of yellow marble that covers part of the interior was added during the 1800s.

Palazzo Doria Pamphilj. Piazza Collegio Romano 2. ☎ **06/679-7323.** Gallery, 12,000L ($7.70) per person; apartments, 9,000L ($5.75) adults, 5,000L ($3.20) students and senior citizens. Tues and Fri–Mon 10am–1pm; private visits may be arranged. Bus: 44, 46, 56, 60, 61, 64, 65, 70, or 75.

Located off Via del Corso, this museum offers visitors a look at what it was really like to live in an 18th-century palace. Like many Roman palaces of the period, the mansion is partly leased to tenants (on the upper levels), and there are even shops on the street level, but all this is easily overlooked after you enter the grand apartments of the historic princely Doria Pamphilj family, which traces its lines to before the great 15th-century Genoese admiral Andrea Doria. The regal apartments surround the central court and gallery of the palace.

The 18th-century decor pervades the magnificent ballroom, drawing rooms, dining rooms, and even the family chapel. Gilded furniture, crystal chandeliers, Renaissance tapestries, and portraits of family members are everywhere. The Green Room is especially rich in treasures, with a 15th-century Tournay tapestry, paintings by Memling and Filippo Lippi, and a seminude portrait of Andrea Doria by Sebastiano del Piombo. The Andrea Doria Room is dedicated to the admiral and to the ship of the same name. It contains a glass case with mementos of the great maritime disaster of the 1950s.

Skirting the central court is a picture gallery with a memorable collection of frescoes, paintings, and sculpture. Most important among a number of great works are the portrait of Innocent X by Velázquez, called one of the three or four best portraits ever painted; *Salome* by Titian; and works by Rubens and Caravaggio. Notable also are *The Bay of Naples* by Pieter Brueghel the Elder and a copy of Raphael's portrait of Principessa Giovanna d' Aragona de Colonna (who looks remarkably like Leo-nardo's *Mona Lisa*). Most of the sculpture came from the Doria country estates.

It includes marble busts of Roman emperors, bucolic nymphs, and satyrs. Even without the paintings and sculpture, that gallery would be worth a visit just for its fresco-covered walls and ceilings.

6 Around Piazza di Spagna & Piazza del Popolo

Some of this area is covered on Walking Tour 2, "The Heart of Rome" (see Chapter 7, "Strolling Through Rome").

✪ **Spanish Steps (Piazza di Spagna).** Metro: Pz. di Spagna. Bus: 56, 60, 62, 81, 95, 492.

The Spanish Steps were the last part of the outside world that Keats saw before he died in a house at the foot of the stairs (see the "Keats-Shelley Memorial," below). The steps—filled in the spring with flower vendors, jewelry dealers, and photographers snapping pictures of tourists—and the square take their names from the Spanish Embassy, which used to have its headquarters here. Designed by Italian architect Francesco de Sanctis between 1723 and 1725, they were funded almost entirely by the French as a preface to the French national church, Trinità dei Monti, at the top. Unfortunately in recent years, even during tourist season, the steps have been vacant because of massive restorations. Work is underway to complete the project by the year 2000.

At the foot of the steps is a boat-shaped fountain designed by Pietro Bernini (not to be confused with his son, Giovanni Lorenzo Bernini, who proved to be a far greater sculptor). About two centuries ago, when the foreign art colony was in its ascendancy, the 136 steps were covered with young men and women who wanted to pose for the painters—men with their shirts unbuttoned to show off what they hoped was a Davidesque physique, and women consistently draped like Madonnas.

Keats-Shelley Memorial. Piazza di Spagna 26. ☎ **06/678-4235.** Admission 5,000L ($3.20). May–Sept, Mon–Fri 9am–1pm and 3–6pm; Oct–Apr, Mon–Fri 9am–1pm and 2:30–5:30pm. Metro: Pz. di Spagna.

At the foot of the Spanish Steps is this 18th-century house where Keats died of consumption on February 23, 1821, at the age of 25. "It is like living in a violin," wrote Italian author Alberto Savinio. Since 1909, when the building was bought by English and American aficionados of English literature, it has been a working library to honor Keats, Byron, and Shelley, who drowned off the coast of Viareggio with a copy of Keats in his pocket (both are buried in the Protestant Cemetery; see "Testaccio & South," later in this chapter). Mementoes inside range from the kitsch to the immortal, and are almost relentlessly laden with literary nostalgia. The apartment where Keats spent his last months, carefully tended by his close friend Joseph Severn, shelters a strange death mask of Keats as well as the "deadly sweat" drawing by Severn. For the full story on Keats and Shelley in Italy, pick up Neville Rogers's good little volume at the small bookstand.

Via dei Condotti. From Piazza di Spagna to Via del Corso.

Both its edges are lined with the kinds of designer-name shops that make virtually anyone salivate. Even if you don't consider yourself particularly materialistic, this

Impressions

There is a horrid Thing called the mal'aria that comes to Rome every summer, and kills one, and I did not care for being killed so far from Christian burial.

—Horace Walpole, letter to the Hon. Henry Seymour Conway, July 1740 homage to the good life *a l'Italiana* might change your mind. The stores and shopping in general are covered fully in "Shopping A to Z" in Chapter 8.

Mausoleo Augusteo (Augustus Mausoleum). Via di Ripetta and Piazza Augusteo Imperatore. Bus: 81, 90, or 90B.

This seemingly indestructible pile of bricks along Via di Ripetta has been here for 2,000 years and will probably remain for another 2,000. Like the larger tomb of Hadrian across the river, this was once a circular, marble-covered affair with tall cypress trees, symmetrical groupings of Egyptian obelisks, and some of the most spectacular ornamentation in Europe. Many of the emperors of the 1st century had their ashes deposited in golden urns inside this building, and it was probably due to the resultant crowding that Hadrian later decided to construct an entirely new tomb (today, the Castel Sant'Angelo) for himself in another part of Rome. After periods when it functioned as a Renaissance fortress, a bullfighting ring, and a private garden, the tomb was restored in the 1930s by Mussolini, who might have envisioned it as a burial place for himself. You cannot enter the mausoleum, but you should circumnavigate it along the four streets that encircle the exterior.

Ara Pacis (Altar of Peace). Via di Ripetta. ☎ **06/6710-3569.** Admission 4,000L ($2.55). Apr–Sept, Tues–Wed and Fri–Sun 9am–1:30pm, Tues and Sat 4–7pm; Oct–Mar, Tues–Wed and Fri–Sun 9am–1:30pm. Bus: 81, 90, or 90B.

In an airy glass-and-concrete building beside the eastern banks of the Tiber at Ponte Cavour rests a reconstructed treasure from the reign of Augustus. It was built by the Senate as a tribute to that emperor and the peace he had brought to the Roman world. You can see portraits of the imperial family—Augustus, Livia (his wife), Tiberius (Livia's son and the successor to the empire), even Julia (the unfortunate daughter of Augustus, exiled by her father for her sexual excesses)—on the marble walls. The altar was reconstructed from literally hundreds of fragments scattered in museums for centuries. A major portion came from the foundations of a Renaissance palace on the Corso. The reconstruction—quite an archeological adventure story in itself—was executed (and sometimes enhanced) by the Fascists during the 1930s.

✪ **Trevi Fountain (Fontana di Trevi).** Piazza di Trevi. Metro: Pz. Barberini.

As you elbow your way through the summertime crowds, you'll find it hard to believe that this little piazza was nearly always deserted before *Three Coins in the Fountain* brought the tour buses. Today it's a must on everybody's itinerary. To do it properly, hold your lira coin in the right hand, turn your back to the fountain, and toss the coin over your shoulder (being careful not to bean anyone behind you). Then the spirit of the fountain will see to it that you return to Rome some day—or that's the tradition, at least.

Actually, this is an evolution of an even older tradition of drinking from the fountain. Nathaniel Hawthorne (1804–64), in his novel *The Marble Faun,* wrote that anyone drinking this fountain's water "has not looked upon Rome for the last time." Because of pollution no one drank from it for years. Since the fountain has been restored in 1994 and is running again, the water is supposedly pure, owing to an electronic device that keeps the pigeons at bay. We'd still suggest that you skip a "Trevi cocktail" and have a mineral water at a café instead.

Supplied by water from the Acqua Vergine aqueduct, and a triumph of the baroque style, the fountain was based on the design of Nicolo Salvi (who is said to have died of illness contracted while supervising the project) and completed in 1762. The design centers around the triumphant figure of Neptunus Rex, standing on a shell chariot drawn by winged steeds and led by a pair of tritons. Two allegorical figures in the side niches represent good health and fertility.

Attractions Near the Spanish Steps & Piazza del Popolo

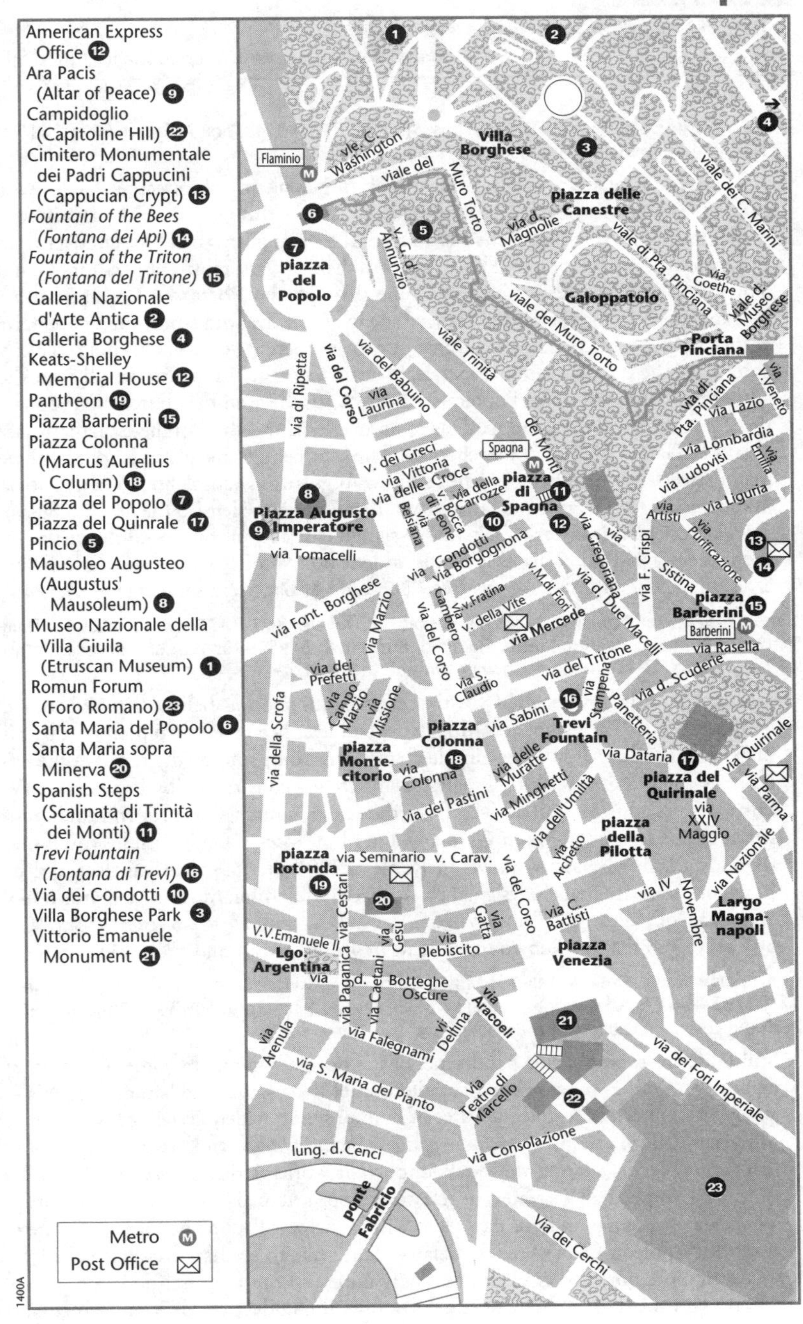

Impressions

Italy: A paradise inhabited with devils.
—Sir Henry Wotton, letter to Lord Zouche, June 1592

Piazza del Popolo. Metro: Flaminio. Bus: 90, 90B, 95, 490, 495, or 926 (or tram no. 119 or 225) to Pzle. Flaminio; then walk through the city gate.

The "people's square" owes its present look to Napoleon's architect, Valadier, who added the elliptical arms and end fountains to enclose this piazza, which already contained the 3,200-year-old **obelisk** of Ramses II that Augustus had brought over from Egypt in the 1st century B.C. This square was the first sight most 19th-century Grand Tourists saw when they arrived in Rome through the **Porta del Popolo,** with a Bernini facade facing the piazza. If they rode in at Carnival time, they might also have witnessed gruesome public executions. Just to your left as you come through the city gate from the Metro stop at Piazzale Flaminio on the other side you'll find the Church of Santa Maria del Popolo (see below). Just beyond the church are the stairs that rise through the **Pincio** gardens to an overlook and the Borghese Gardens (see "Parks & Gardens," later in this chapter). The south end of the piazza is split by three major streets: Via di Ripetta on the right (to Augustus's Mausoleum), Via del Corso in the middle (to Piazza Venezia), and Via Babuino on the left (to the Spanish Steps). Two almost identical Carlo Rainaldi–designed churches sit on the corners between these streets, and on either side of the trident lie two of Rome's more fashionable cafés, the Rosati and the Canova (see "The Café & Bar Scene" in Chapter 9).

Santa Maria del Popolo. Piazza del Popolo 12. ☎ **06/361-0836.** Free admission. Daily 7am–12:30pm and 4–7pm. Metro: Flaminio. Bus: 90, 90B, 95, 490, 495, or 926 (or tram no. 119 or 225) to Pzle. Flaminio; then walk through the city gate.

During the early days of the Christian church this site was believed to be haunted by the ghost of Nero, who, according to legend, had been secretly buried here by his nurse and mistress. In 1099 a simple chapel was built, supposedly to drive the demons away, and in the 1500s a majestic church was constructed by Pope Sixtus IV. Funds for its construction derived from the sale of church sinecures and the imposition of taxes on churches in Germany and other foreign lands. Inside, you'll find the oldest stained-glass windows in Rome (1509), an apse that was designed by Bramante, separate chapels designed by Raphael and Bernini, frescoes by Pinturicchio, and a pair of paintings (*The Crucifixion of St. Peter* and *The Conversion of St. Paul*) by Caravaggio that are known to students of art history around the world.

✪ **Galleria Borghese.** Piazzale del Museo Borghese, off Via Pinciano, in the Villa Borghese. ☎ **06/854-8577.** Admission 4,000L ($2.55). Tues–Sat 9am–2pm, Sun 9am–7pm. Bus: 910 from the Termini or 56 from Pz. Barberini.

Still under restoration, this handsome villa is normally home to some of the finest paintings in Rome—a representative collection of Renaissance and baroque masters—along with important sculpture. Three of Bernini's most widely acclaimed works grace the ground-floor rooms: *The Rape of Persephone, David,* and *Apollo and Daphne* (his finest piece). Among the other important works is the *Conquering Venus* by Antonio Canova, Italy's greatest neoclassic sculptor. Actually, this early 19th-century work created a sensation in its day because its model was Pauline Bonaparte Borghese, sister of Napoleon (if the French dictator didn't like to see his sister half naked, he was even more horrified at Canova's totally nude version of himself).

The second floor, which normally houses the collection of Renaissance and baroque paintings, is closed for restoration, and may be for a long time. The impressive paintings are more or less on semipermanent display at San Michele a Ripa, Via di San Michele 22 (☎ **06/58431**), in the Trastevere district on the other end of town. The display of canvases is almost too rich for one visit. If you're pressed for time, concentrate on three works by Raphael (especially the young woman holding a unicorn in her lap, and the *Deposition from the Cross*). There are also works by Caravaggio (1571–1610), leader of the realists, including his *Madonna of the Palafrenieri.* Rubens indulges in his favorite theme, the elders lusting after Susanna, and Titian is represented by four works, including his *Sacred and Profane Love.* Admission to the paintings is included in your Galleria Borghese ticket, and it's open Monday to Friday from 9:30am to 1pm and 4 to 8pm, and on Saturday from 9:30am to 1pm.

After visiting the gallery, you may want to join the Italians in their strolls through the **Villa Borghese** (see "Parks & Gardens," later in this chapter), replete with zoological gardens and small bodies of water.

Galleria Nazionale d'Arte Moderna. Viale delle Belle Arti 131. ☎ **06/322-4151.** Admission 8,000L ($5.10) adults, free for children 17 and under. Tues–Sat 9am–7pm, Sun 9am–1pm. Bus: 19 or 30.

The National Gallery of Modern Art is in the Villa Borghese Gardens, a short walk from the Etruscan Museum. With its neoclassical and romantic paintings and sculpture, it's a dramatic change from the glories of the Renaissance and the Imperial period. Its 75 rooms also house Italy's largest collection of 19th- and 20th-century artists. Included are important works of Balla, Boccioni, de Chirico, Morandi, Manzù, Marini, Burri, Capogrossi, and Fontana, and a large collection of Italian optical and pop art. Look for Modigliani's *La Signora dal Collaretto* and his large *Nudo.* Several important sculptures, including one by Canova, are on display in the museum's gardens.

The gallery also houses a large collection of foreign artists, including the French impressionists Degas, Cézanne, and Monet, and the post-Impressionist van Gogh. Surrealism and expressionism are well represented in works by Klee, Ernst, Braque, Miró, Kandinsky, Mondrian, and Pollock. You'll also find sculpture by Rodin. The collection of graphics, the storage rooms, and the department of restoration can be visited by appointment Tuesday to Friday.

✪ **Museo Nazionale di Villa Giulia (Etruscan).** Piazzale di Villa Giulia 9. ☎ **06/322-6571.** Admission 8,000L ($5.10) adults, free for children 17 and under and for seniors 60 and over. Tues–Sat 9am–7pm, Sun 9am–1pm. Metro: Flaminio. Bus: 19, 30, 225, or 926.

A 16th-century papal palace in the Villa Borghese Gardens shelters this priceless collection of art and artifacts of the mysterious Etruscans, who predated the Romans. Known for their sophisticated art and design, the Etruscans left a legacy of sarcophagi, bronze sculptures, terra-cotta vases, and jewelry, among other items.

If you have time only for the masterpieces, head for Sala 7, which has a remarkable 6th century B.C. *Apollo* from Veio (clothed, for a change). The other two widely acclaimed pieces of statuary in this gallery are *Dea con Bambino* (a goddess with a baby) and a greatly mutilated, but still powerful, *Hercules* with a stag. In the adjoining room, Sala 8, you'll see the lions' sarcophagus from the mid–6th century B.C. which was excavated at Cerveteri, north of Rome.

Finally, one of the world's most important Etruscan art treasures is the bride and bridegroom coffin from the 6th century B.C. (in Sala 9), also dug out of the tombs of Cerveteri. Near the end of your tour, another masterpiece of Etruscan art awaits you in Sala 33: the *Cista Ficoroni,* a bronze urn with paw feet, mounted by three figures, which dates from the 4th century B.C.

Gore Vidal's Roma

Gore Vidal, the author of 22 novels, including the acclaimed multivolume fictional chronicle of American history (*Burr* in 1973 and *Lincoln* in 1984, among them), and the recent memoir *Palimpsest,* really began to discover Rome in 1948. He'd just published his first bestseller, *The City and the Pillar,* the first novel of any consequence about male homosexuality. He headed for Rome and the Excelsior Hotel, just as expatriates still do today. The bar here along Via Veneto was the center for rich foreigners (as it is today). Later he moved to the Eden Hotel (which is back in business again, and better than ever following a major overhaul in 1995). He was joined by playwright Tennessee Williams, whom Vidal called "The Glorious Bird," and Rome and its "golden boys" of that era were ready to be plucked. Later the writers would compare notes from the night before over breakfast at the Doney on Via Veneto, while being observed by such visitors as Orson Welles.

Vidal viewed Rome after 1948 and throughout the 1960s and 1970s as a "sexual paradise." This was the pre-AIDS era when sex was "spontaneous and untroubled," according to Vidal. The orgies in his flat became famous throughout the Roman underground. Young men and women were eager to participate. Although Vidal later gave up his Roman flat of many years and moved to Ravello, he's still a frequent visitor to the city. However, Vidal finds the Rome of today "sullen, with mephitic air, and full of crime of every sort. Currently the Poles are thought to be the most murderous of recent arrivals, while prostitution is either very expensive or antiseptic, and, between AIDS and knives, too dangerous to be bothered with."

In the winter of 1962 Vidal, along with his longtime companion, Howard Auster, rented a ground-floor apartment on Rome's Via Giulia. Although they were to move elsewhere later, into an apartment overlooking the Tiber, "Gore & Howard" were always to live near Campo de' Fiori. They could always be seen shopping at this open-air market in their search for the freshest of ingredients (Vidal was particularly addicted to fresh peas).

Later, Rome served Vidal as he gathered research notes and—if you believe in that sort of thing—literary inspiration from the ruins of the Capitoline Hill and the stones of the city's ancient forums. The novel that emerged, *Julian,* was judged

7 Around Via Veneto & Piazza Barberini

Via Veneto. Metro: Pz. Barberini.

Although this most famous of Roman streets may have passed its *la dolce vita* heyday in the golden 1950s, it remains a prime target for sightseers. The street cuts through the center of the gardens of what used to be one of the most princely villas in Rome, the 1662 Villa Ludovisi. In 1885 Prince Boncompagni Ludovisi built a glorious estate on Via Veneto, but was forced to sell it to pay the taxes. The buyer was Margherita, widow of King Umberto I. Today the palace, renamed the Villa Margherita, is the most famous building along the street and is the site of the heavily guarded American Embassy.

Major hotels and restaurants line the avenue, none more famous than the Hotel Excelsior, former haunt of movie stars such as Elizabeth Taylor in the 1950s era of "Hollywood on the Tiber" (see "Near Via Veneto & Piazza Barberini" in Chapter 4). Sharing space with hotels, restaurants, and cafés like the Caffè de Paris a critical success for its reinterpretation of the lives of the emperors during the Roman empire's final days. Urbane, knowledgeable, and uncommonly difficult to write, it examined Rome from the point of view of aristocratic, well-educated classicists who blamed the demise of their civilization squarely on the camp of the unwashed, uneducated rabble—that is, the Christians. Few other modern novels so evocatively portray the nostalgia of the ancient Romans' long-ago loss of empire, and few others breathe life so effectively into the value system of the pre-Christian era.

Later, Vidal emulated the travel patterns of the ancient emperors, retreating from the city's heat and midsummer smells to a windy and panoramic clifftop near Ravello, on the Amalfi Drive. There, he says, he can gaze over waters and coastlines whose geography is inextricably linked with the origin of many of the ancient Roman myths and fables.

When in Rome today, Vidal prefers to eat regularly at Da Fortunato al Pantheon, Pantheon 55 (☎ 06/679-2788), near Piazza della Rotonda. The place is overrun by politicians from the nearby Parliament buildings. Everyone flocks here for the "perfect" risotto, or, if it's Saturday, the "perfect" tripe. You might opt for their grilled sea bass instead. It's said that this restaurant can grant your "maddest" out-of-season culinary fantasy, such as strawberries in winter.

Vidal, who was asked by Fellini to play himself in *Roma*, when questioned in the film as to why he chose to live in Rome, he responded: "Now the world has begun to dream of the world's end through nuclear war or overpopulation or pollution—take your pick—so what better place to watch the last act than in a city that calls itself Eternal?"

That, more or less, is what Vidal told movie audiences. But he later admitted that the "real reason" he enjoys Rome is because he enjoys human-scale village life. He felt that many Roman shops in the old neighborhoods were pretty much as they were 2,000 years ago. For his living room in Rome, he prefers the piazza in front of the Pantheon, following in the footsteps of George Eliot, Pietro Macagni, Stendhal, and Thomas Mann. He calls these former luminaries "our friendly ghosts—eternal presences—for the time being!"

(see "The Café & Bar Scene" in Chapter 9) are the headquarters of banks, insurance companies, and publishers.

Today middle-age tourists revisiting Rome wonder what became of that *la dolce vita* atmosphere captured in Fellini's 1960 film. On weekends Roman officials close the street to traffic to make it more alluring, but as a nightlife center, Via Veneto has had its day. One London critic reported: "What male visitors get today are bimbos on the doors of grotesquely expensive nightclubs, who entice them in to atrocious floorshows, terrible food, and sleazy company."

Cimitero Monumentale dei Padri Cappucini. In the Church of the Immaculate Conception, Via Vittorio Veneto 27. ☎ **06/487-1185.** Free admission (donation expected). Daily 9am–noon and 3–6pm. Metro: Pz. Barberini.

Qualifying as one of the most horrifying sights in all Christendom, this is a cemetery of skulls and crossbones woven into mosaic "works of art" just a short walk from Piazza Barberini. To make this allegorical dance of death, the bones of more than 4,000 Capuchin brothers were used. Some of the skeletons are intact, draped with

Impressions

Rome reminds me of a man who lives by exhibiting to travellers his grandmother's corpse.

—James Joyce, letter to Stanislaus Joyce, September 1906

Franciscan habits. The creator of this chamber of horrors? The tradition of the friars is that it was the work of a French Capuchin. Their literature suggests that the cemetery should be visited keeping in mind the historical moment of its origins, when Christians had a rich and creative cult for their dead, when great spiritual masters mediated and preached with a skull in hand. Those who have lived through the days of crematoriums and other such massacres may view the graveyard differently, but to many who pause to think, this macabre sight of death has a message. It's not for the squeamish. The entrance is halfway up the first staircase on the right of the church.

Piazza Barberini. Metro: Pz. Barberini. Bus: 56, 60, 62, 95.

The piazza lies at the foot of several Roman streets, among them Via Barberini, Via Sistina, and Via Vittorio Veneto. It would be a far more more pleasant spot were it not for the heavy traffic swarming around its principal feature, Bernini's **Fountain of the Triton.** For more than three centuries the strange figure sitting in a vast open clam has been blowing water from his triton. Off to one side of the piazza is the clean, aristocratic side facade of the Palazzo Barberini, named for one of Rome's powerful families. The Renaissance Barberini reached their peak when a son was elected pope (Urban VIII). This Barberini pope encouraged Bernini and gave him great patronage.

As you go up Via Vittorio Veneto, look for the small fountain on the right-hand corner of Piazza Barberini, which is another of Bernini's works, the small **Fountain of the Bees.** At first they look more like flies, but they are the bees of the Barberini, the crest of that powerful family complete with the crossed keys of St. Peter above them (the keys were always added to a family crest when a son was elected pope).

Galleria Nazionale d'Arte Antica. Via delle Quattro Fontane 13. ☎ **06/481-4430.** Admission 8,000L ($5.10) adults, free for children 17 and under and for seniors 60 and over. Tues–Sat 9am–2pm, Sun 9am–1pm. Metro: Pz. Barberini.

The Palazzo Barberini, right off Piazza Barberini, is one of the most magnificent baroque palaces in Rome. It was begun by Carlo Maderno in 1627 and completed in 1633 by Bernini, whose lavishly decorated rococo apartments, called the Gallery of Decorative Art, are open to the public. The palace today houses the Galleria Nazionale.

On the first floor of the palace, a splendid array of paintings includes works from the 13th to the 16th century, most notably a *Mother and Child* by Simone Martini, and works by Filippo Lippi, Andrea Solario, and Francesco Francia. Il Sodoma has some brilliant pictures here, including *The Rape of the Sabines* and *The Marriage of St. Catherine.* One of the best-known paintings is Raphael's beloved *La Fornarina,* the baker's daughter who was his mistress and who posed for his Madonna portraits. Titian is represented by *Venus and Adonis.* Other artists exhibited include Tintoretto, El Greco, and Holbein the Younger. Many visitors come here just to see the magnificent Caravaggios, including *Narcissus.*

The bedroom of Princess Cornelia Costanza Barberini and Prince Giulio Cesare Colonna di Sciarra still stands just as it was on their wedding night, and many household objects are displayed in the decorative art gallery. In the chambers, which have frescoes and hand-painted silk linings, you can see porcelain from Japan and Bavaria, canopied beds, and a wooden baby carriage.

Le Quattro Fontane. At the corner of Via delle Quattro Fontane and Via del Quirinale. Metro: Pz. Barberini.

The unexpected presence of these fountains at the intersection of two narrow, traffic-clogged streets provides newcomers with the kind of aesthetic shock that's only possible in a truly great city. Composed of four symmetrical fountains built into the outside corners of four identical buildings, they were conceived as part of the Renaissance redevelopment of Rome ordained by Pope Sixtus IV between 1585 and 1590. The two female fountains represent either Juno and Diana or Strength and Fidelity (depending on your point of view); the two male fountains stand for the Tiber and the Nile. The site, incidentally, is close to the pinnacle of the Quirinale Hill, one of the seven summits on which ancient Rome was originally built.

Piazza del Quirinale. Metro: Pz. Barberini.

Until the end of World War II the palace on this piazza was the home of the king of Italy, and before that it was the residence of the pope. Despite its origins during the Renaissance, when virtually every important architect in Italy worked on some aspect of its sprawling premises, it's rich in associations to ancient emperors and deities. The colossal statues of the *dioscuri* Castor and Pollux, which now form part of the fountain in the piazza, were found in the nearby great Baths of Constantine, and in 1793 Pius VI had the ancient Egyptian obelisk moved here from the Mausoleum of Augustus. The sweeping view of Rome from the piazza is itself worth the trip, and the palace, crowning the highest of the seven ancient hills of Rome, is open to the public on Sunday from 9am to 1pm. Admission is free, but a passport or similar ID is required to enter.

8 Near the Termini

Basilica di Santa Maria Maggiore. Piazza di Santa Maria Maggiore. ☎ **06/483194.** Free admission. Daily 7am–7pm. Metro: Termini.

This great church, one of the four major basilicas of Rome, was originally founded by Pope Liberius in A.D. 358 but was rebuilt by Pope Sixtus III in A.D. 432–440. Its campanile, erected in the 14th century, is the loftiest in the city. Much doctored in the 18th century, the church's facade is not an accurate reflection of the treasures inside. The basilica is especially noted for the 5th-century Roman mosaics in its nave, as well as for its coffered ceiling, said to have been gilded with gold brought from the New World. In the 16th century Domenico Fontana built a now-restored "Sistine Chapel." In the following century Flaminio Ponzo designed the Pauline (Borghese) Chapel in the baroque style. The church contains the tomb of Bernini, Italy's most important sculptor and architect during the baroque era in the 17th century. Ironically, the man who changed the face of Rome with his elaborate fountains is buried in a tomb so simple it takes a sleuth to track it down (to the right near the altar). Restoration of the 1,600-year-old church has begun and is scheduled for completion in the year 2000.

Santa Maria degli Angeli. Piazza della Repubblica 12. ☎ **06/488-0812.** Free admission. Daily 7:30am–12:30pm and 4–6pm. Metro: Pz. della Repubblica.

On this site, which adjoins the National Roman Museum near the railway station, once stood the "tepidarium" of the 3rd-century Baths of Diocletian. But in the 16th

Attractions Near Via Veneto & Termini

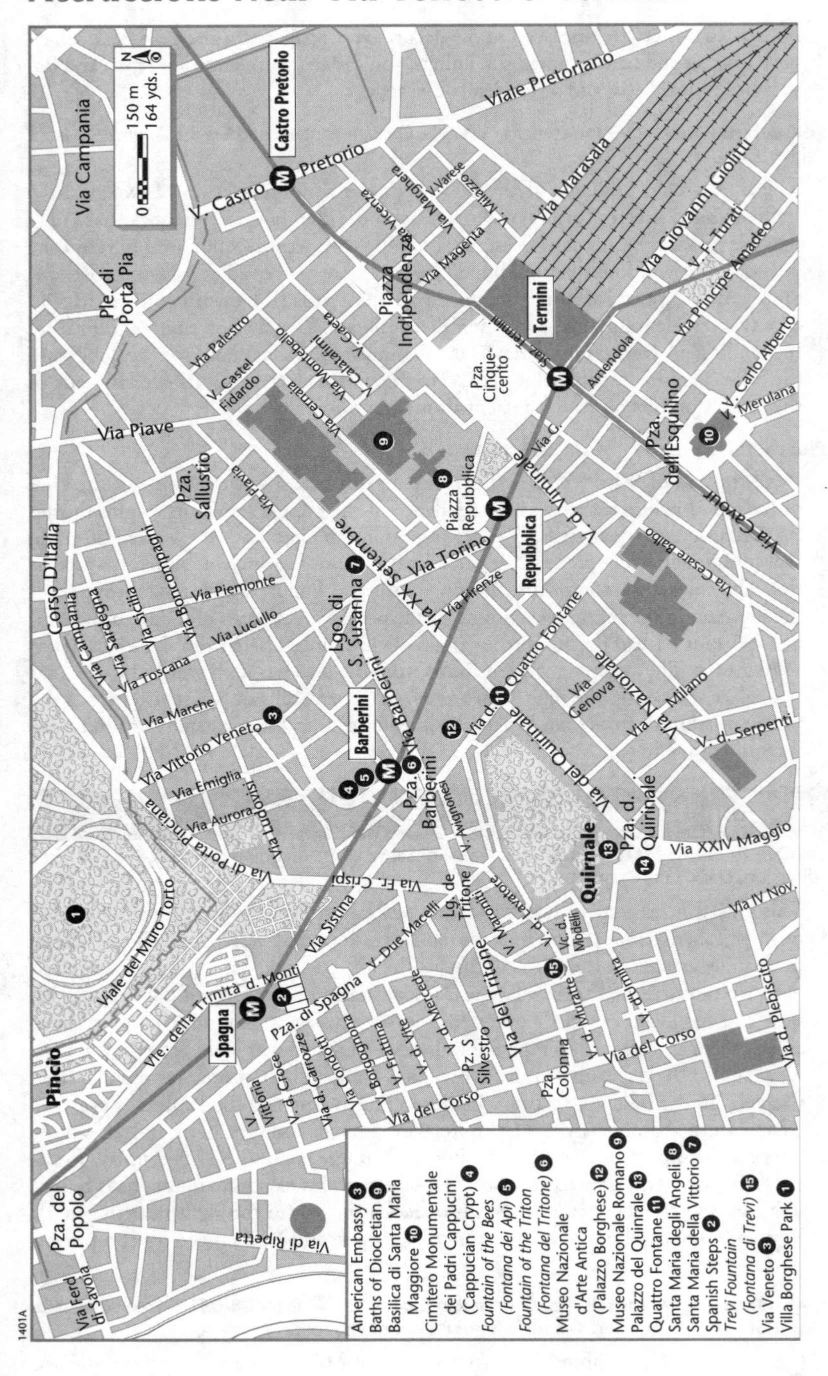

1401A

Impressions

Turn all the pages of history, but Fortune never produced a greater example of her own fickleness than the city of Rome, once the most beautiful and magnificent of all that ever were or will be. . .not a city in truth, but a certain part of heaven.

—Poggio Bracciolini (1380–1459)

century Michelangelo—nearing the end of his life—converted the grand hall into one of the most splendid churches in Rome. Surely the artist wasn't responsible for "gilding the lily"—that is, putting *trompe-l'oeil* columns in the midst of the genuine pillars. The church is filled with tombs and paintings, but its crowning treasure is the genuine statue of St. Bruno by the great French sculptor Jean-Antoine Houdon. His sculpture is larger than life and about as real.

✪ **Museo Nazionale Romano (National Roman Museum).** Via Enrico de Nicola 79. ☎ **06/488-2298.** Admission 12,000L ($7.70). Tues–Sat 9am–2pm, Sun and holidays 9am–1pm. Metro: Pz. della Repubblica.

Located near Piazza dei Cinquecento, which fronts the railway station, this museum occupies part of the 3rd-century A.D. Baths of Diocletian and a section of a convent that may have been designed by Michelangelo. It houses one of Europe's finest collections of Greek and Roman sculpture and early Christian sarcophagi.

The Ludovisi Collection is the apex of the museum, particularly the statue of the Gaul slaying himself after he has done in his wife (a brilliant copy of a Greek original from the 3rd century B.C.). Another prize is a one-armed Greek *Apollo.* A galaxy of other sculpted treasures includes *The Discus Thrower of Castel Porziano* (an exquisite copy), *Aphrodite of Cirene* (a Greek original), and the so-called *Hellenistic Ruler,* a Greek original of an athlete with a lance. A masterpiece of Greek sculpture, *The Birth of Venus,* is in the Ludovisi throne room. *The Sleeping Hermaphrodite* (Ermafrodito Dormiente) is an original Hellenistic statue. You can stroll through the cloister, filled with statuary and fragments of antiquity, including a fantastic mosaic.

Santa Maria della Vittoria. Via XX Settembre 17. ☎ **06/482-6190.** Daily 6:30am–noon and 4:30–6pm. Metro: Pz. della Repubblica. Bus: 16, 36, 37, or 60.

Although far from being the largest baroque church in Rome, it's one of the most ostentatiously decorated, loaded with contrasting shades of marble, gilded stucco, and flickering candles. The Capella Cornaro (fourth opening on the left), contains one of the most frequently photographed baroque sculptures in the world, Bernini's controversial and highly theatrical *Ecstacy of St. Theresa,* where with a bit of imagination, you might doubt that the saint's ecstacy is entirely spiritual. Gazing down on her, with a smile that might be either sadistic or tender, is an angel about to pierce her with a golden arrow. Surrounding the emotionally charged setting, like members of the audience in a theater, are statues of the chapel's donor and eight members of his family. The church itself was built between 1608 and 1620, and restored in 1991.

9 The Catacombs of the Appian Way

Of all the roads that led to Rome, **Via Appia Antica (Appian Way)**—built in 312 B.C.—was the reigning leader. It eventually stretched all the way from Rome to the seaport of Brindisi, through which trade with the colonies in Greece and the East was funneled. According to Christian tradition, it was on the Appian Way that an escaping Peter encountered the vision of Christ, which caused him to go back into the city to face subsequent martyrdom.

Along the Appian Way, patrician Romans built great monuments above the ground and Christians met in the catacombs beneath the earth—and you can visit the remains of both. In some dank, dark grottoes (never stray too far from either your party or one of the exposed lightbulbs), you can still discover the remains of early Christian art. Only someone wanting to write a sequel to *Quo Vadis?* would visit all the catacombs, but of those open to the public, the Catacombs of St. Callixtus and those of St. Sebastian are the most important.

Of the Roman monuments on Via Appia Antica, the most impressive is the **Tomb of Cecilia Metella,** within walking distance of the catacombs. The cylindrical tomb honors the wife of one of Julius Caesar's military commanders from the Republican era. Why such an elaborate tomb for such an unimportant person in history? Cecilia Metella happened to be singled out for enduring fame because her tomb remained and the others decayed.

Catacombe di San Sebastiano (Tomb of St. Sebastian). Via Appia Antica 136. ☎ **06/788-7035.** Admission 8,000L ($5.10) adults, 4,000L ($2.55) children 6–15, free for children 5 and under. Wed–Mon 9am–noon and 2:30–5:30pm. Bus: 118 from near the Colosseo Metro station.

Today the tomb of the martyr is in the church built above the site, but his original tomb was in the catacombs under the church. From the reign of the emperor Valerian to the reign of the emperor Constantine, the bodies of Saint Peter and Saint Paul were hidden in these catacombs. The big church was built here in the 4th century. None of the catacombs, incidentally, is a grotto; all are dug from *tufo,* a soft volcanic rock. This is the only Christian catacomb in Rome that's always open. The tunnels here, if stretched out, would reach a length of 7 miles. In the tunnels and mausoleums are mosaics and graffiti, along with many other pagan and Christian objects from centuries even before the time of Constantine.

Catacombe di San Callisto (Catacombs of St. Callixtus). Via Appia Antica 110. ☎ **06/513-6725.** Admission 8,000L ($5.10) adults, 4,000L ($2.55) children 6–15, free for children 5 and under. Thurs–Tues 8:30am–noon and 2:30–5pm (to 5:30pm in summer). Bus: 218 from San Giovanni in Laterano to Fosse Ardeatine.

"The most venerable and most renowned of Rome," said Pope John XXIII of these funerary tunnels. The founder of Christian archeology, Giovanni Battista de Rossi (1822–94), called them "catacombs par excellence." They are the first cemetery of the Christian community of Rome, burial place of 16 popes in the 3rd century. They bear the name of St. Callixtus, the deacon whom Pope St. Zephyrinus put in charge of them and who was later elected pope (217–22) in his own right. The cemeterial complex is made up of a network of galleries stretching for nearly 12 miles, structured in five different levels, and reaching a depth of about 20 meters. There are many sepulchral chambers and almost half a million tombs. Paintings, sculptures, and epigraphs (with such symbols as the fish, the anchor, and the dove) provide invaluable material for the study of the life and customs of the ancient Christians and the story of their persecutions.

Entering the catacombs, you see at once the most important crypt, that of the nine popes. Some of the original marble tablets of their tombs are still preserved. The next crypt is that of St. Cecilia, the patron of sacred music. This early Christian martyr received three ax strokes on her neck, the maximum allowed by Roman law, which failed to kill her outright. Farther on you'll find the famous Cubicula of the Sacraments, with its 3rd-century frescoes. The catacombs were dug from the middle of the 2nd century up until the middle of the 5th century as cemeteries and places of worship—never private dwellings.

10 Testaccio & South

Only a city as ancient as Rome could boast an entire neighborhood built atop a rubbish heap where almost every pot shard is a valuable reminder of antiquity.

The area east of the Tiber and just west of Pyramide functioned as Rome's dockyards. In A.D. 55 Nero ordered that Rome's thousands of broken amphorae and terra-cotta roof tiles be stacked in a carefully designated pile. (Its name, Monte Testaccio, derived from *testae,* the ancient word for "pot shards.") Over the centuries the mound grew to a height of around 200 feet, then compacted to form the centerpiece for **Testaccio,** one of the city's most unusual neighborhoods. Eventually, houses were built on the terra-cotta mound, and caves were dug into its mass for the storage of wine and foodstuffs (thanks to the porosity of the terra-cotta, a constant temperature of 50°F is maintained throughout the year).

Because of this natural refrigeration, the neighborhood also began to attract dozens of simple, blood-soaked slaughterhouses. Laborers were paid part of their meager salaries with the *quanto quarto* (fifth quarter) of each day's slaughter (that is, the tail, the feet, the intestines, and the offal), which otherwise had no commercial value. With a history of transforming these organs into edible and flavorful food, the neighborhood cooks in Testaccio take much of the credit for developing the flavorful tripe and oxtail dishes that form an integral part of the Roman working-class diet to this day. One of the neighborhood's best and earthiest restaurants, Cecchino dal 1887, is recommended separately (see Chapter 5, "Dining").

Today the district is rustic, unglamorous, and working-class, but with a crude kind of charm that its aficionados compare to an unspoiled and relatively "undiscovered" version of Trastevere. A pivotal crossroads of the district lies at the intersection of Via Caio Cestio and Via Nicola Zabaglia.

Pyramid of Caius Cestius. Piazzale Ostiense. Metro: Piramide. Bus: 30.

Dating from the 1st century B.C., the Pyramid of Caius Cestius, about 120 feet high, looks as if it belongs to the Egyptian landscape. It was constructed during the "Cleopatra craze" in architecture that swept across Rome. The pyramid can't be entered, but it's fun to circle and photograph. Who was Caius Cestius? A rich magistrate in Imperial Rome whose tomb is more impressive than his achievements.

Protestant Cemetery. Via Caio Cestio 6. ☎ **06/574-1141.** Admission free, but a 1,000L (65¢) offering is customary. Apr–Sept, Tues–Sun 9am–6pm; Oct–Mar, Tues–Sun 9am–5pm. Metro: Piramide. Bus: 13, 27, 30b, 57, or 318.

Near Porta San Paola, in a setting of cypress trees, lies the old cemetery where John Keats is buried. In a grave nearby, Joseph Severn, his "deathbed companion," was interred beside him six decades later. Dejected, and feeling his reputation as a poet diminished by the rising vehemence of his critics, Keats asked that the following epitaph be written on his tombstone: "Here lies one whose name was writ in water." A great romantic poet Keats certainly was, but a prophet, thankfully not.

Percy Bysshe Shelley, author of *Prometheus Unbound,* drowned off the Italian Riviera in 1822, before his 30th birthday. His ashes rest alongside those of Edward John Trelawny, fellow romantic and man of the sea. Trelawny maintained—but this was not proved—that Shelley may have been murdered, perhaps by petty pirates bent on robbery.

Basilica di San Paolo Fuori le Mura (St. Paul Outside the Walls). Via Ostiense. ☎ **06/541-0341.** Free admission. Basilica, daily 7am–6pm; cloisters, daily 9am–12:45pm and 3–6pm. Metro: San Paolo Basilica. Bus: 4, 11, 23, 170, or 673.

The Basilica of St. Paul, whose origins go back to the time of Constantine, is the fourth great patriarchal church of Rome. It burned in 1823 and was subsequently rebuilt. This basilica is believed to have been erected over the tomb of St. Paul. From the inside its windows may appear at first to be stained glass, but they're actually translucent alabaster. With its forest of single-file columns and its mosaic medallions (portraits of the various popes), it's one of the most streamlined and elegantly decorated churches in Rome. Its single most important treasure is a 12th-century candelabrum designed by Vassalletto, who is also responsible for the remarkable cloisters—in themselves worth the trip "outside the walls." They contain twisted pairs of columns enclosing a rose garden. The Benedictine monks and students sell a fine collection of souvenirs, rosaries, and bottles of Benedictine in the gift shop every day except Sunday and religious holidays.

11 In Trastevere

This most Roman of Roman neighborhoods is covered in detail on Walking Tour 4, "Trastevere" (see Chapter 7, "Strolling Through Rome"), but here are the full write-ups of the major sights to get you started.

Santa Maria in Trastevere. Piazza di Santa Maria in Trastevere. ☎ **06/581-4802.** Free admission. Daily 7:30am–12:30pm and 4–7pm. Bus: 56, 60, 75, 170, or 710 to Viale Trastevere.

This Romanesque church at the picturesque center of Trastevere was originally built around A.D. 350 and is considered one of the oldest churches in Rome. The body was added around 1100 and the portico in the early 1700s. The restored mosaics in the apse date from around 1140, and below them are the 1293 mosaic scenes from the life of Mary by Pietro Cavallini. The faded mosaics on the facade are 12th or 13th century, and the octagonal fountain in the piazza is an ancient Roman original restored and added to in the 17th century by Carlo Fontana.

Santa Cecilia in Trastevere. Piazza di Santa Cecilia. ☎ **06/589-9289.** Admission: Church (including the fresco), free, but a donation is expected; excavations below the church, 12,000L ($7.70). Main church, daily 10am–noon and 4–6pm; fresco, Tues and Fri 10–11am. Bus: 56, 60, 75, 170, or 710 to Viale Trastevere.

A cloistered and still-functioning convent with a fine garden, Santa Cecilia contains a difficult-to-visit fresco by Cavallini in its inner sanctums, and a late 13th-century baldacchino by Arnalfo di Cambio over the altar. The church is built on the reputed site of Cecilia's long-ago palace, and for a fee you can descend under the church to inspect the ruins of some Roman houses as well as peer through a gate at the highly stuccoed grotto underneath the altar.

GIANICOLO (JANICULUM HILL)

From many vantage points in the Eternal City the views are panoramic. Scenic gulpers, however, have traditionally preferred the outlook from the Janiculum Hill (across the Tiber), not one of the "Seven Hills" but certainly one of the most visited (and a stopover on many bus tours). The view is at its best at sundown, or at dawn, when the skies are often fringed with mauve. The Janiculum was the site of a battle between Guiseppe Garibaldi and the forces of Pope Pius IX in 1870—an event commemorated today with statuary. To reach the Gianicolo, take bus no. 41 from Ponte Sant'Angelo.

12 Around Vatican City

In the middle of the Tiber's major bend on its way through the city is the site of one of the most famous executions of the Renaissance, **Piazza San Angelo.** There, in

Attractions in Trastevere

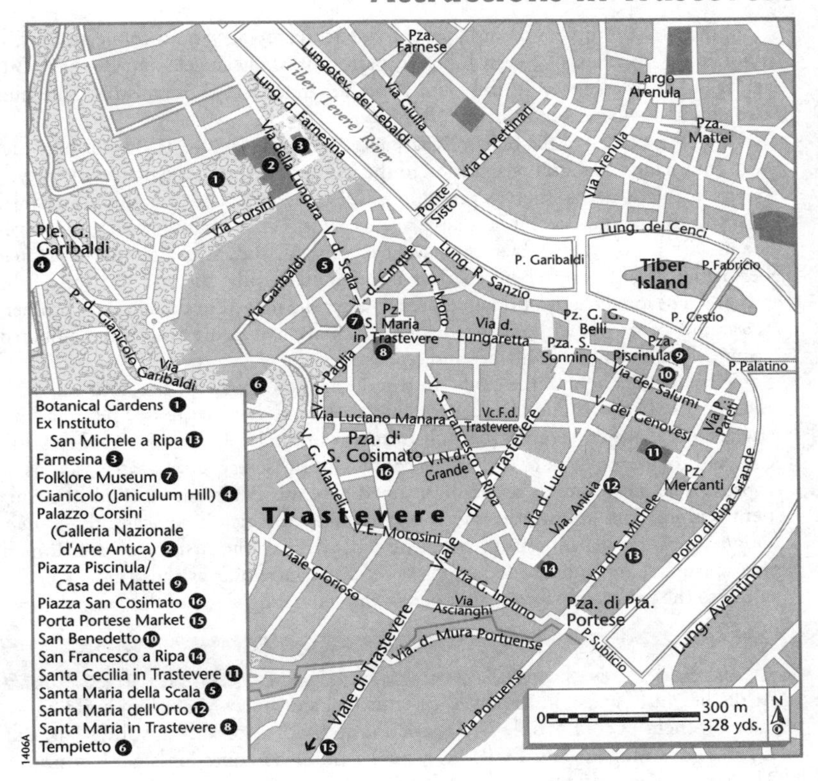

1599, Beatrice Cenci and several members of her family were beheaded on orders of Pope Clement VIII. Their crime? Plotting the successful death of their very rich and very brutal father. Their tale later inspired a tragedy by Shelley and a novel by a 19th-century Italian politician named Francesco Guerrazzi.

Stretching across the river north of the piazza is the **Ponte Sant'Angelo.** The trio of arches in the river's center is basically unchanged since the bridge was built around A.D. 135; the arches that abut the river's embankments were added late in the 19th century as part of a flood-control program. On December 19, 1450, so many pilgrims gathered on this bridge (which at the time was lined with wooden buildings) that about 200 of them were crushed to death. Since the 1960s the bridge has been reserved exclusively for pedestrians who can stroll across and admire the statues designed by Bernini as they head toward the Castel Sant'Angelo at the bridge's northern end.

Castel Sant'Angelo. Lungotevere Castello 50. ☎ **06/687-5036.** Admission 8,000L ($5.10), free for children 17 and under and for seniors 60 and over. Daily 9am–1pm. Closed the second and last Tues of each month. Metro: Ottaviano. Bus: 23, 46, 49, 62, 64, 87, 98, 280, or 910.

This overpowering structure, in a landmark position on the Tiber, was originally built in the 2nd century A.D. as a tomb for the emperor Hadrian; it continued as an imperial mausoleum until the time of Caracalla. If it looks like a fortress, it should—that was its function in the Middle Ages, built over the Roman walls and linked to the Vatican by an underground passageway that was much used by the fleeing popes, who escaped from unwanted visitors like Charles V during his sack of the city in 1527.

In the 14th century it became a papal residence, enjoying various connections with Boniface IX, Nicholas V, even Julius II, patron of Michelangelo and Raphael. But its legend rests largely on its link with Pope Alexander VI, whose mistress bore him two children—Cesare and Lucrezia Borgia.

Of all the women of the Italian Renaissance, Lucrezia (1480–1519) is the only one who commands universal recognition in the Western world, her name a virtual synonym for black deeds, such as poisoning. But popular legend is highly unreliable: Many of the charges biographers have made against her (such as incestuous involvements with her brother and father) may have been only successful attempts to blacken her name. In addition to being part of an infamous family, she was a patron of the arts and a devoted charity worker, especially after she moved to Ferrara. Her brother, Cesare, of course, is without defense—a Machiavellian figure who is remembered accurately as a symbol of villainy and cruel spite.

Today the highlight of the castle is a trip through the Renaissance apartments with their coffered ceilings and lush decoration. Their walls have witnessed plots and intrigues that make up some of the arch-treachery of the High Renaissance. Later you can go through the dank cells that once rang with the screams of Cesare's victims of torture. The most famous figure imprisoned here was Benvenuto Cellini, the eminent sculptor and goldsmith, remembered chiefly for his classic, candid *Autobiography.* Now an art museum, the castle halls display the history of the Roman mausoleum, along with a wide-ranging selection of ancient arms and armor. You can climb to the top terrace for another one of those dazzling views of the Eternal City.

13 EUR—Mussolini's Marble Suburb

At the height of Mussolini's power, he launched a complex of modern buildings—many of them in cold marble—to dazzle Europe with a scheduled world's fair. But Il Duce got strung up, and **EUR** ("ay-your")—the area in question—got hamstrung. The new Italian government that followed inherited the uncompleted project and decided to turn it into a center of government and administration. It has also developed into a residential section of fairly deluxe apartment houses. Most of the cold granite edifices fail to escape the curse of *Il Duce moderno,* but the small "city of tomorrow" is softened considerably by a man-made lagoon, which you can row across in rented boats.

Italy's great modern architect, Milan-born Pier Luigi Nervi, designed the **Palazzo dello Sport** on the hill. One of the country's most impressive modern buildings, it was the chief site of the 1960 Olympics. Another important structure is the **Palazzo dei Congressi** in the center, an exhibition hall with changing displays of industrial shows that's well worth a stroll. You'll also spot architecture reminiscent of Frank Lloyd Wright, and a building that evokes the design of the United Nations in New York.

For still another look at Mussolini's architectural achievements, head across the river from EUR to the **Foro Italico.** Shades of 1932! This complex of sports stadiums blatantly honors Il Duce. At the entrance to the forum an obelisk bears the name MVSSOLINI so firmly engraved that to destroy the lettering would be to do away with the monument. It stands defiantly. Visitors on a sunny day walk across the mosaic courtyard with DVCE imbedded repeatedly in the pavement. The big attraction of this freakish site is the "Stadium of Marbles," encircled with 50 marble nude athletes—draped discreetly so as not to offend the eyes of the Golden Madonna on the hill beyond. Take bus no. 1 from Piazza della Repubblica.

Impressions

Brickwork I found thee, and marble I left thee! their Emperor vaunted;
"Marble I thought thee, and brickwork I find thee!" the Tourist may answer.
—Arthur Hugh Clough, *Amours de Voyage* (1849)

Museo della Civiltà Romana. Piazza Giovanni Agnelli. ☎ **06/592-6135.** Admission 5,000L ($3.20) adults and children. Tues and Thurs 9am–1:30pm and 4–7pm, Wed and Fri–Sat 9am–1:30pm, Sun 9am–1pm. Metro: Linea B to EUR Fermi.

This museum of Roman civilization houses Fiat-sponsored reproductions that recapture life in ancient Rome. Its major exhibition is a plastic representation in miniature of what ancient Rome looked like at the apex of its power. You'll see the Circus Maximus, the intact Colosseum, the Baths of Diocletian, and lots more—breathing life and a real feel of city layout to the few broken columns and sketchy foundations you see in the forums.

14 Parks & Gardens

The **Villa Borghese** park in the heart of Rome is 3½ miles in circumference. One of the most elegant parks in Europe, it was created by Cardinal Scipione Borghese in the 1600s. Umberto I, king of Italy, acquired it in 1902 and presented it to the city of Rome, renaming it Villa Umberto I. However, Romans preferred their old name, which has stuck. A park of landscape vistas and wide-open "green lungs," the greenbelt is crisscrossed by roads, but you can escape from the traffic and seek a shaded area—usually pine or oak—to enjoy a picnic or simply relax. In the northeast of the park is a small zoo, and the park is also home to two of the top museums in Rome, the Galleria Borghese with its Renaissance and baroque masterpieces and the Villa Giulia Etruscan museum, as well as the fine national gallery of modern art (see "Around Piazza di Spagna & Piazza del Popolo," earlier in this chapter).

The **Villa Doria Pamphilj,** behind the Vatican, acquired from Princess Orietta Doria Pamphilj, was opened to the public in 1971. (The princess is descended from the world-famous naval commander Andrea Doria.) The park is about half as large as Central Park in New York, but it's more than twice the size of the Villa Borghese, filling a sad emptiness in the Roman capital by providing some much-needed green space. At one time the park belonged to Pope Innocent X, who planted it with exotic shrubbery, trees, and flowers. Take bus no. 23, 30, 32, 49, 51, or 64.

15 Especially for Kids

Children usually enjoy wandering around the **Colosseum** and the **Roman Forum** (see "The Forum, the Colosseum & the Heart of Ancient Rome," earlier in this chapter), as well as the climb to the top of the dome of St. Peter's Basilica. The **Fun Fair (Luna Park),** along Via delle Tre Fontane (☎ **06/592-5933**), at EUR, is one of the largest in Europe. It's known for its "big wheel" at the entrance, and there are merry-go-rounds, miniature railways, and shooting galleries, among other attractions. Admission is free, but you pay for each ride. It's closed Tuesday.

The **Teatro delle Marionette degli Accettella,** appearing at the Teatro Mongiovino, Via Giovanni Genocchi 16 (☎ **06/513-9405**), has performances for children on Saturday and Sunday (except in July and August) at 4:30pm. Tickets are 12,000L ($7.70) for adults and children.

The **Puppet Theater** on Pincio Square (☎ **06/860-1733**) in the Villa Borghese gardens has performances nearly every day. While there, you might also like to take your children through the **Villa Borghese** park (it's closed to traffic). Children enjoy the fountain displays and the lake, and there are many wide spaces in which they can play. You can rent boats at the **Giardino del Lago,** and explore the **zoo** at Viale del Giardino Zoologico 20 (☎ **06/321-6564**). It's open Monday to Friday from 8:30am to 5pm and on Saturday and Sunday from 8:30am to 6pm (it closes an hour earlier in winter). Admission is 10,000L ($6.40) for adults, free for small children. Take bus no. 19 or 30.

At 4pm on any day, you can take your child to the **Quirinale Palace,** Piazza del Quirinale, the residence of the president of Italy. There's a military band and a parade at that time, as the guards change shifts.

16 Organized Tours

Because of the sheer volume of artistic riches in Rome, some visitors prefer to begin their stay with an organized tour. While few things can really be covered in any depth on these "overview tours," they're sometimes useful for getting the feel for the geography of a complicated city. One of the leading tour operators (among the zillions of possibilities) is **American Express,** Piazza di Spagna 38 (☎ **06/67641**). It's open Monday to Friday from 9am to 5:30pm and on Saturday from 9am to 12:30pm. Of the many tour operators functioning in Rome, American Express is the one whose tours are the most closely geared to the American language and American visitors.

One of the most popular tours is a 4-hour orientation tour of Rome and the Vatican, which departs most mornings at 9:30am and costs 60,000L ($38.40) per person. Another 4-hour tour, which focuses on the Rome of antiquity (including visits to the Colosseum, the Roman Forum, the ruins of the Imperial Palace, and the Church of San Pietro in Vincoli), costs 50,000L ($32). Of the many excursions offered to sites outside the city limits of Rome, the most popular is a 5-hour bus tour to Tivoli to visit the Villa d'Este and its spectacular gardens and the ruins of the Villa Adriana, all for the price of 63,000L ($40.30) per person.

If your time in Italy is rigidly limited, you might opt for 1-day excursions to points farther afield on tours that are marketed by (but not conducted by) American Express. Although rushed and far too short to expose the many-layered majesty of these destinations, a series of 1-day tours is offered to Pompeii, Naples, and Sorrento for 132,000L ($84.50) per person, to Florence for 162,000L ($103.70), and to Capri for 184,000L ($117.75). Lunch is included on these full-day trips, but you'll need a lot of stamina—each departs from Rome around 7am and returns sometime after 9 or 10pm.

17 Catching a Soccer Match & Outdoor Activities

SOCCER

Soccer (*calcio*) is one of the three or four all-consuming passions of thousands of Romans. Rome boasts two intensely competitive teams, Lazio and Roma, which play either against each other or against visiting teams from other parts of the world every Sunday afternoon. Matches are held at the **Stadio Olimpico,** Foro Italico dei Gladiatori (☎ **06/36851**), originally built by Mussolini as a nationalistic (Fascist) statement. Thousands of tickets are sold during the 2 or 3 hours before each game. The players usually take a break during June, July, and August, beginning the season with something approaching pandemonium in September.

OUTDOOR ACTIVITIES

BIKING The traffic is murderous and the pollution might make your head spin, but there are quiet times (early morning and Sunday) when a spin beside the Tiber or through the Borghese Gardens might prove highly appealing. You can find bike-rental stands on Viale della Pineto in the Villa Borghese and at the following Metro stops: Flaminio, Largo San Silvestro, Largo Argentina, and Piazza di Spagna.

BOWLING One of the city's largest bowling complexes, whose hordes of participants provide a spectacle almost more interesting than the game itself, is **Bowling Roma,** Viale Regina Margherita 181 (☎ **06/855-1184**), off Via Nomentana.

GOLF Rome boasts several courses, which will usually welcome members of other golf clubs. Each, of course, will be under the greatest pressure on Saturday and Sunday, so as a nonmember it would be best to schedule your arrival for a weekday.

One of the capital's best courses, with its clubhouse in a villa built during the 1600s and fairways designed by Robert Trent Jones, is the **Country Club Castelgandolfo,** Via Santo Spirito 13, Castelgandolfo (☎ **06/931-2301**). An older, more entrenched, and more prestigious course is the **Circolo del Golf Roma,** Via Appia Nuova 716/A (☎ **06/780-3407**). About 8½ miles from the city center is the **Olgiata Golf Club**, Largo Olgiata 15, off Via Cassia (☎ **06/3088-9141**).

HORSEBACK RIDING The most convenient of Rome's several riding clubs is the **Associazione Sportiva Villa Borghese,** Via del Galoppatoio 23 (☎ **06/320-0487**). Other stables are in the **Circolo Ippico Olgiata,** Largo Olgiata 15 (☎ **06/3088-8792**), off Via Cassia, and the **Società Ippica Romana,** Via del Monti della Farnesina 18 (☎ **06/324-0591**). Tack and equipment are English style.

JOGGING Not only does jogging provide a moving view of the city's monuments, but it might improve your general health as well. Beware of the city's heat, however, and the speeding traffic. Several possible locations include the park of the **Villa Borghese,** where the series of roads and pathways provide a verdant oasis within the city's congestion. The best places to enter the park are at Piazza del Popolo or at the top of Via Veneto. The **Cavalieri Hilton,** Via Cadlolo 101, Monte Mario (☎ **06/35091**), has a jogging path (measuring a third of a mile) through the trees and flowering shrubs of its landscaping. The grounds that surround the **Villa Pamphilij** contain three running tracks, although they might either be locked or in use by local teams. Certain stretches of the Lungotevere sidewalk along the river provide almost uninterrupted courses for runners. A final possibility, not recommended after dark, is the rounded premises of the **Circus Maximus.** Built by the ancient Romans, and now reduced to dust and grandiose rubble, the outward perimeter (ringed with roaring traffic) measures about a half mile.

SWIMMING One of the busiest all-year pools is in the **Roman Sport Center,** Via del Galoppatoio 33 (☎ **06/320-1667**), adjacent to the parking lot in the Villa Borghese. Open to the public, it contains two large swimming pools, squash courts, a gym, and saunas. In another part of town, the **Piscina della Rose,** Viale America (☎ **06/592-6717**), is an Olympic-size pool open to the public (and crowded with teenagers and *bambini*) between June and September. More sedate, set in lushly landscaped gardens, and open to nonresidents, is the pool at the **Cavalieri Hilton,** Via Cadlolo 101 (☎ **06/35091**) in Monte Mario.

TENNIS The best tennis courts are at private clubs, usually in the suburbs. Players are highly conscious of proper tennis attire, so be prepared to don your most sparkling whites and your best manners. One of the best-known clubs is **Tennis Club Parioli,** Largo Uberto de Morpurgo 2, Via Salaria (☎ **06/8620-0882**), open daily from 8am to noon only.

7 Strolling Through Rome

Visitors with very limited time might want to concentrate on Walking Tour 1, "Rome of the Caesars," and Walking Tour 2, "The Heart of Rome." Those with more time can explore "Renaissance Rome" and "Trastevere." Many of the major sights along these routes, especially on Walking Tours 2 to 4, are covered fully in Chapter 6. These tours serve both to string the sights together—for those who have limited time or want more structure to their visit—and to cover some of the other, less well known sights along the way.

WALKING TOUR 1
Rome of the Caesars

Start: Via Sacra, in the Roman Forum.
Finish: Circus Maximus.
Time: 5½ hours.
Best Times: Any sunny day.
Worst Times: After dark, or when the place is overrun with tour groups.

This tour tries to incorporate the most central of the monuments that attest to the military and architectural grandeur of ancient Rome. As a whole, they comprise the most famous and evocative ruins in the world, despite such drawbacks as the roaring traffic that's the bane of the city's civic planners, and a general dustiness and heat that might test even the hardiest amateur archeologists.

After the collapse of Rome and during the Dark Ages, the forums and many of the other sites on this tour were lost to history, buried beneath layers of debris, their marbles mined by medieval buildiers, until Mussolini set out to restore the grandeur of Rome by reminding his compatriots of their glorious past.

THE ROMAN FORUM

The more westerly of the two entrances to the Roman Forum is at the corner of Via dei Fori Imperiali and Via Cavour, adjacent to Piazza Santa Maria Nova. The nearest Metro is the Colosseo stop.

As you walk down into the Forum along a masonry ramp, you'll be heading for Via Sacra, the ancient Roman road that ran through the Forum connecting the Capitoline Hill, to your right, with the Arch of Titus (1st century A.D.), off to your left. The Roman Forum

Walking Tour—Rome of the Caesars

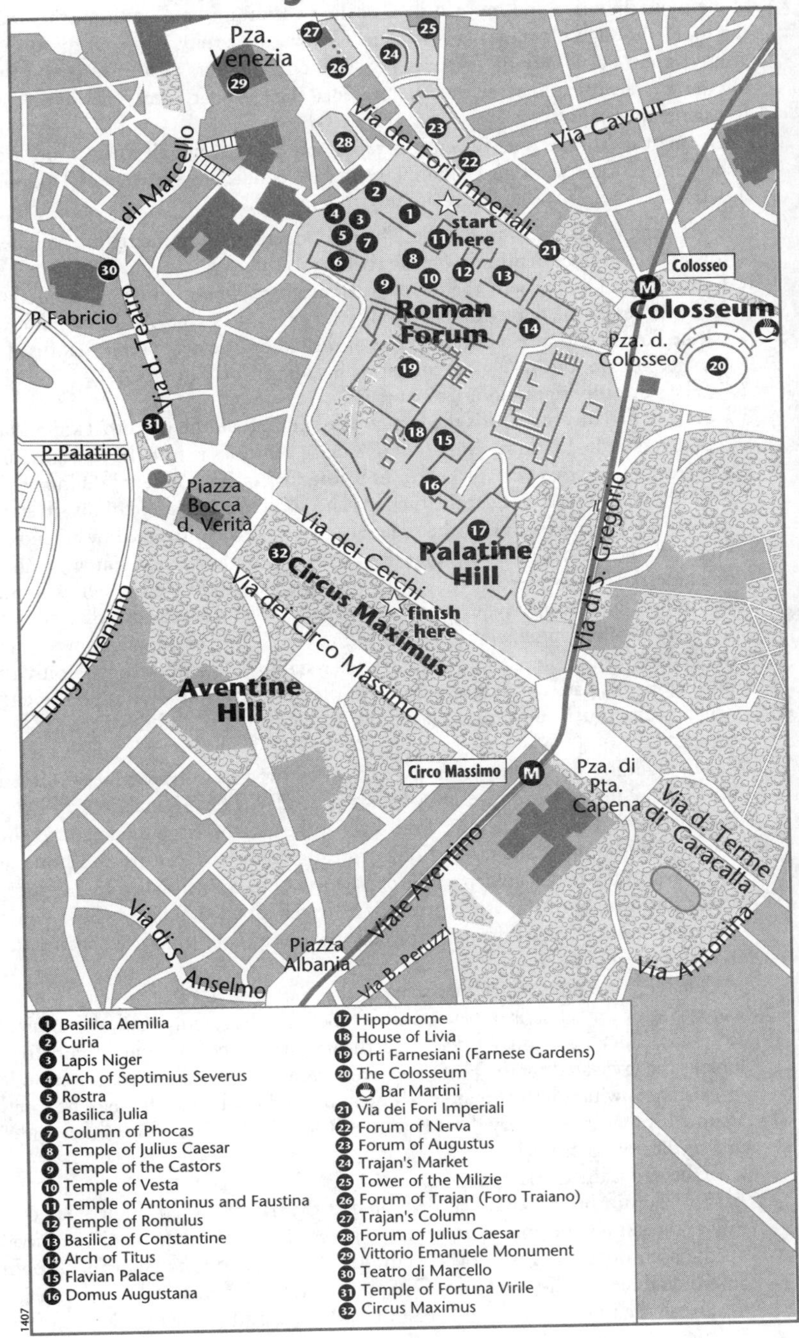
Pza. Venezia
Via dei Fori Imperiali
Via Cavour
di Marcello
start here
finish here
Colosseo
Colosseum
Pza. d. Colosseo
Roman Forum
P.Fabricio
Via d. Teatro
P.Palatino
Piazza Bocca d. Verità
Via dei Cerchi
Palatine Hill
Via di S. Gregorio
Circus Maximus
Via dei Circo Massimo
Lung. Aventino
Aventine Hill
Circo Massimo
Pza. di Pta. Capena
Via d. Terme di Caracalla
Viale Aventino
Via di S. Anselmo
Piazza Albania
Via B. Peruzzi
Via Antonina
1 Basilica Aemilia
2 Curia
3 Lapis Niger
4 Arch of Septimius Severus
5 Rostra
6 Basilica Julia
7 Column of Phocas
8 Temple of Julius Caesar
9 Temple of the Castors
10 Temple of Vesta
11 Temple of Antoninus and Faustina
12 Temple of Romulus
13 Basilica of Constantine
14 Arch of Titus
15 Flavian Palace
16 Domus Augustana
17 Hippodrome
18 House of Livia
19 Orti Farnesiani (Farnese Gardens)
20 The Colosseum
Bar Martini
21 Via dei Fori Imperiali
22 Forum of Nerva
23 Forum of Augustus
24 Trajan's Market
25 Tower of the Milizie
26 Forum of Trajan (Foro Traiano)
27 Trajan's Column
28 Forum of Julius Caesar
29 Vittorio Emanuele Monument
30 Teatro di Marcello
31 Temple of Fortuna Virile
32 Circus Maximus
1407

is the more dignified and more austere of the two forums you'll visit on this walking tour. Although it consists mostly of artfully evocative ruins scattered confusingly around a sun-baked terrain, it represents almost 1,000 years of Roman power during the severely disciplined period that preceded the legendary decadence of the later Roman emperors.

During the Middle Ages, when this was a cow pasture and all these stones were underground, there was a dual column of elm trees connecting the Arch of Titus with the Arch of Septimius Severus (A.D. 200), to your right.

Arriving at Via Sacra, turn right. The random columns on the right as you head toward the Arch of Septimius Severus belong to the:

1. **Basilica Aemilia,** formerly the site of great meeting halls and shops, all maintained for centuries by the noble Roman family who gave it its name. At the corner nearest the Forum entrance are some traces of melted bronze decoration that fused to the marble floor during a great fire set by invading Goths in A.D. 410.

   The next important building is the:

2. **Curia,** or Senate house—it's the large brick building on the right that still has its roof. Romans had been meeting on this site for centuries before the first structure was erected, and that was still centuries before Christ. The present building is the fifth (if one counts all the reconstructions and substantial rehabilitations) to stand on the site. Legend has it that the original building was constructed by an ancient king with the curious name of Tullus Hostilius. The tradition he began was a noble one indeed, and our present legislative system owes much to the Romans who met in this hall. Unfortunately, the high ideals and inviolate morals that characterized the early Republican senators gave way to the bootlicking of imperial times, when the Senate became little more than a rubber stamp. Caligula, who was only the third emperor, had his horse appointed to the Senate (it was a life appointment), which pretty much sums up the state of the Senate by the middle of the 1st century A.D.

   The building was a church until 1937, when the Fascist government tore out the baroque interior and revealed what we see today. The original floor of Egyptian marble and the tiers that held the seats of the senators have miraculously survived. In addition, at the far end of the great chamber we can see the stone on which rested the fabled golden statue of Victory. Originally installed by Augustus, it was disposed of in the 4th century by a fiercely divided Senate, whose Christian members convinced the emperor that it was improper to have a pagan statue in such a revered place.

   Outside, head down the Curia stairs to the:

3. **Lapis Niger,** the remains of black marble blocks that reputedly mark the tomb of Romulus. They bask today under a corrugated metal roof. Go downstairs for a look at the excavated tomb. There's a stone here with the oldest Latin inscription in existence, which unfortunately is nearly unintelligible. All that can be safely assumed is that it genuinely dates from the Rome of the kings, an era that ended in a revolution in 510 B.C.

   Across from the Curia, the:

4. **Arch of Septimius Severus** was dedicated at the dawn of the troubled 3rd century to the last decent emperor who was to govern Rome for some time. The friezes on the arch depict victories over Arabs and Parthians by the cold but upright Severus and his two dissolute sons, Geta and Caracalla. Severus died on a campaign to subdue the unruly natives of Scotland, and at the end of the first decade of the 3rd century Rome unhappily fell into the hands of the young Caracalla, chiefly remembered today for the baths he had built.

Walk around to the back of the Severus arch, face it, and look to your right. There amid the rubble can be discerned a semicircular stair that led to the famous:

5. **Rostra,** the podium from which dictators and caesars addressed the throngs of the Forum below. One can just imagine the emperor, shining in his white toga surrounded by imperial guards and distinguished senators, gesticulating grandly like one of the statues on a Roman roofline. The motley crowd falls silent, the elegant senators pause and listen, the merchants put down their measures, even the harlots and unruly soldiers lower their voices in such an august presence. Later emperors didn't have much cause to use the Rostra, making their policies known through edict and assassination instead.

Now, facing the colonnade of the Temple of Saturn, once the public treasury, and going to the left, you'll come to the ruins of the:

6. **Basilica Julia,** again little more than a foundation. The basilica gets its name from Julius Caesar, who dedicated the first structure in 46 B.C. Like many buildings in the Forum, the basilica was burned and rebuilt several times, and the last structure dated from those shaky days after the Gothic invasion of 410. Throughout its history it was used for the hearing of civil court cases, which were conducted in the pandemonium of the crowded Forum, open to anyone who happened to pass by. The building was also reputed to be particularly hot in the summer, and it was under these sweaty and unpromising circumstances that Roman justice, the standard of the world for a millennium, was meted out.

Walking back down the ruined stairs of the Basilica Julia and into the broad area whose far side is bounded by the Curia, you'll see the:

7. **Column of Phocas.** Probably lifted from an early structure in the near vicinity, this was the last monument to be erected in the Roman Forum, and it commemorates the Byzantine emperor Phoca's generous donation of the Pantheon to the pope of Rome, who almost immediately transformed it into a church.

Now make your way down the middle of the Forum nearly back to the ramp from which you entered. The pile of brick with the semicircular indentation that stands in the middle of things was the:

8. **Temple of Julius Caesar,** erected some time after the dictator was deified. Judging from the reconstruction, it was quite an elegant building. As you stand facing the ruins, with the entrance to the Forum on your left, you'll see on your right three columns originally belonging to the:

9. **Temple of the Castors.** This temple perpetuated the legend of Castor and Pollux, who appeared out of thin air in the Roman Forum and were observed watering their horses at the fountain of Juturna (still visible today), just as a major battle against the Etruscans turned in favor of Rome. Castor and Pollux, the heavenly twins—and the symbol of the astrological sign Gemini—seem a favorite of Rome.

The next major monument is the circular:

10. **Temple of Vesta,** wherein dwelt the sacred flame of Rome, and the Atrium of the Vestal Virgins. A vestal virgin was usually a girl of good family who signed a contract for 30 years. During that time she lived in the ruin we're standing in right now. Of course, back then it was an unimaginably rich marble building with two floors. There were only six Vestal Virgins at a time during the imperial period, and even though they had the option of going back out into the world at the end of their 30 years, few did. The cult of Vesta came to an end in 394, when a Christian Rome secularized all its pagan temples. A man standing on this site before then would have been put to death immediately.

Stand in the atrium with your back to the Palatine and look beyond those fragmented statues of the former vestals to the:

11. **Temple of Antoninus and Faustina.** It's the building with the freestanding colonnade just to the right of the ramp where you first entered the Forum. Actually, just the colonnade dates from imperial times; the building behind it is a much later church dedicated to San Lorenzo.

 After you inspect the beautifully proportioned Antoninus and Faustina temple, head up Via Sacra away from the entrance ramp toward the Arch of Titus. Pretty soon, on your left, you'll see the twin bronze doors of the:

12. **Temple of Romulus.** It's the doors themselves that are really of note here—they're the original Roman doors, and swing on the same massive hinges they were originally mounted on in A.D. 306. In this case, the temple is not dedicated to the legendary cofounder of Rome, but to the son of its builder, the emperor Maxentius, who gave his son the name Romulus in a fit of antiquarian patriotism. Unfortunately for both father and son, they competed with a general who deprived them of their empire and lives. That man was Constantine, who, while camped outside Rome during preparations for one of his battles against Maxentius, saw the sign of the Cross in the heavens with the insignia *In hoc signo vinces* (in this sign shall you conquer). Raising the standard of Christianity above his legions, he defeated the emperor Maxentius and became the first Christian emperor.

 At the time of Constantine's victory (A.D. 306), the great:

13. **Basilica of Constantine** (marked by those three gaping arches up ahead on your left) was only half finished, having been started by the unfortunate Maxentius. However, Constantine finished the job and affixed his name to this, the largest and most impressive building in the Forum. To our taste, the more delicate, Greek-influenced temples are more attractive, but you have to admire the scale and the engineering skill that erected this monument. The fact that portions of the original coffered ceiling are still intact is amazing. The basilica once held a statue of Constantine so large that his little toe was as wide as an average man's waist. You can see a few fragments from this colossus—the remnants were found in 1490—in the courtyard of the Conservatory Museum on the Capitoline Hill. As far as Roman emperors went, Christian or otherwise, ego knew no bounds.

 From Constantine's basilica, follow the Roman paving stones of Via Sacra to the:

14. **Arch of Titus,** clearly visible on a low hill just ahead. Titus was the emperor who sacked the great Jewish temple in Jerusalem, and the bas-relief sculpture inside the arch shows the booty of the Jews being carried in triumph through the streets of Rome, while Titus is crowned by Victory, who comes down from heaven for the occasion. You'll notice in particular the candelabrum, for centuries one of the most famous pieces of the treasure of Rome. In all probability it lies at the bottom of the Busento River in the secret tomb of Alaric the Goth.

Palatine Hill

When you've gathered your strength in the shimmering hot sun, head up the Clivus Palatinus, the road to the palaces of the Palatine Hill. With your back to the Arch of Titus, it's the road going up the hill to the left.

It was on the Palatine Hill that Rome first became a city. Legend tells us that the date was 753 B.C. The new city originally consisted of nothing more than the Palatine, which was soon enclosed by a surprisingly sophisticated wall, remains of which can still be seen on the Circus Maximus side of the hill. As time went on and Rome grew in power and wealth, the boundaries were extended and later enclosed by the Servian Wall. When the last of the ancient kings was overthrown (510 B.C.), Rome had already extended over several of the adjoining hills and valleys. As Republican times progressed, the Palatine became a fashionable residential district. So it remained until Tiberius—who, like his predecessor, Augustus, was a bit too modest to really call himself "emperor" out loud—began the first of the monumental palaces that were to cover the entire hill.

It's difficult today to make sense out of the Palatine. The first-time viewer might be forgiven for suspecting it to be an entirely artificial structure built on brick arches. Those arches, which are visible on practically every flank of the hill, are actually supports that once held imperial structures. Having run out of building sites, the emperors, in their fever, simply enlarged the hill by building new sides on it.

The road goes on only a short way, through a small sort of valley filled with lush, untrimmed greenery. After about 5 minutes (for slow walkers), you'll see the ruins of a monumental stairway just to the right of the road. The Clivus Palatinus turns sharply to the left here, skirting the monastery of San Bonaventura, but we'll detour to the right and take a look at the remains of the:

15. Flavian Palace. As you walk off the road and into the ruins, you'll be able to discern that there were once three rooms here. But it's impossible for anyone but an archeologist to comprehend quite how splendid these rooms were. The entire Flavian Palace was decorated in the most lavish of colored marbles and gold. Much of the decoration survived as late as the 18th century, when the greedy duke of Parma removed most of what was left. The room closest to the Clivus Palatinus was called the Lararium, and held statues of the divinities that protected the imperial family. The middle room was the grandest of the three. It was the imperial throne room, where sat the ruler of the world, the emperor of Rome. The far room was a basilica, and as such was used for miscellaneous court functions, among them audiences with the emperor. This part of the palace was used entirely for ceremonial functions. Adjoining these three rooms are the remains of a spectacularly luxurious peristyle. You'll recognize it by the hexagonal remains of a fountain in the middle. Try, if you can, to imagine this fountain surrounded by marble arcades planted with mazes and equipped with mica-covered walls. On the opposite side of the peristyle from the throne room are several other great reception and entertainment rooms. The banquet hall was here, and beyond it, looking over the Circus Maximus, are a few ruins of former libraries. Although practically nothing remains except the foundations, every now and again you'll catch sight of a fragment of colored marble floor in a subtle, sophisticated pattern.

The imperial family lived in the:

16. Domus Augustana, the remains of which lie toward the Circus Maximus, slightly to the left of the Flavian Palace. The new building that stands here—it looks old to us, but in Rome it qualifies as a new building—is a museum (usually closed). It stands in the absolute center of the Domus Augustana. In the field adjacent to the stadium well into the present century stood the Villa Mills, a gingerbread Gothic villa of the 19th century. It was quite a famous place, owned by a rich Englishman who came to Rome from the West Indies. The Villa Mills was the scene of many fashionable entertainments in Victorian times, and it's interesting to note, as H. V. Morton pointed out, that the last dinner parties that took place on the Palatine Hill were given by an Englishman. At any of several points along this south-facing belvedere of the Palatine Hill, you'll be able to see the faraway oval walls of the Circus Maximus. Continue with your exploration of the Palatine Hill by heading across the field parallel to the Clivus Palatinus until you come to the north end of the:

17. Hippodrome, or Stadium of Domitian. The field was apparently occupied by parts of the Domus Augustana, which in turn adjoined the enormous stadium. The

Impressions

One of those miserable ruins which refused to disintegrate, a spot fit only for lame cats to seek refuge from small boys.

—H. V. Morton, *A Traveller in Rome*

stadium itself is worth examination, although sometimes it's difficult to get down inside it. The perfectly proportioned area was usually used for private games, staged for the amusement of the imperial family. As you look down the stadium from the north end, you can see, on the left side, the semicircular remains of a structure identified as Domitian's private box. Some archeologists claim that the "stadium" was actually an elaborate sunken garden.

The aqueduct that comes up the wooded hill used to supply water to the Baths of Septimius Severus, whose difficult-to-understand ruins lie in monumental poles of arched brick at the far end of the stadium.

Returning to the Flavian Palace, leave the peristyle on the opposite side from the Domus Augustana and follow the signs for the:

18. House of Livia. They take you down a dusty path to your left. Although legend says that this was the house of Augustus's consorts, it actually was Augustus's all along. The place is notable for some rather well-preserved murals showing mythological scenes. But more interesting is the aspect of the house itself—it's smallish, and there never were any great baths or impressive marble arcades. Augustus, even though he was the first emperor, lived simply compared to his successors. His wife, Livia, was a fiercely ambitious aristocrat who divorced her own husband to marry the emperor (the ex-husband was made to attend the wedding, incidentally) and, according to some historians, was the true power behind Roman policy between the death of Julius Caesar and the ascension of Tiberius. She even controlled Tiberius, her son, since she had engineered his rise to power through a long string of intrigues and poisonings.

After you've examined the frescoes in Livia's parlor, head up the steps that lead to the top of the embankment to the north. Once on top, you'll be in the:

19. Orti Farnesiani (Farnese Gardens), the 16th-century horticultural fantasy of a Farnese cardinal. They're constructed on top of the Palace of Tiberius, which, you'll remember, was the first of the great imperial palaces to be built on this hill. It's impossible to see any of it, but the gardens are cool and nicely laid out. You might stroll up to the promontory above the Forum and admire the view of the ancient temples and the Capitoline heights off to the left.

You've now seen the best of the Forum and the Palatine. To leave the archeological area, you should now continue walking eastward along the winding road that meanders steeply down from the Palatine Hill to Via di San Gregorio. When you reach the roaring traffic of that busy thoroughfare, walk north toward the bulk of what some Romans consider the most potent symbol of their city:

20. The Colosseum. Its crumbling, oval bulk is the greatest monument of ancient Rome, and visitors are impressed with its size, its majesty, and its ability to conjure up the often cruel entertainments that were devised inside for the pleasure of the Roman masses. Either visit it now or return later.

TAKE A BREAK On a hill in back of the landmark Colosseum is the **Bar Martini,** Piazza del Colosseo 3A (☎ 06/700-4431). Have your coffee or cool drink outside at one of the tables and absorb one of the world's greatest architectural views: that of the Colosseum itself. A pasta dish costs 8,000L ($5.10); a sandwich, 3,000L to 5,000L ($1.90 to $3.20). Service is daily from 8:30am to midnight.

The Imperial Forums

Begun by Julius Caesar as an answer to the overcrowding of Rome's older forums during the days of the Empire, the imperial forums were at the time of their construction flashier, bolder, and more impressive than the old Roman Forum, and as such represented the unquestioned authority of the Roman emperors at the height of their absolute power. After the collapse of Rome and during the Dark Ages, they, like many other ancient monuments, were lost to history, buried beneath layers of debris until Mussolini, in an egomaniacal attempt to draw comparisons between his Fascist regime and the glory of ancient Rome, helped to restore the grandeur of Rome by reminding his compatriots of their glorious imperial past.

With your back to the Colosseum, walk westward along the:

21. Via dei Fori Imperiali, keeping to the right side of the street. It was Mussolini who issued the controversial orders to cut through centuries of debris and junky buildings to reveal many archeological treasures and carve out this boulevard linking the Colosseum to the grand 19th-century monuments of Piazza Venezia. The vistas over the ruins of Rome's imperial forums from the northern side of the boulevard makes for one of the most fascinating walks in Rome.

Some of the rather confusing ruins you'll see from the boulevard include the shattered remnants of the colonnade that once surrounded the Temple of Venus and Roma. Next to it, you'll see the back wall of the Basilica of Constantine. Shortly, on the street's north side, you'll come to a large outdoor restaurant, where Via Cavour joins the boulevard. Just beyond the small park across Via Cavour are the remains of the:

22. Forum of Nerva, best observed from the railing that skirts it on Via dei Fori Imperiali. It was built by the emperor whose 2-year reign (A.D. 96–98) followed that of the paranoid Domitian. You'll be struck by just how much the ground level has risen in 19 centuries. The only really recognizable remnant is a wall of the Temple of Minerva with two fine Corinthian columns. This forum was once flanked by that of Vespasian, which is now, however, completely gone. It's possible to enter the Forum of Nerva from the other side, but you can see it just as well from the railing.

The next forum you approach is the:

23. Forum of Augustus, built to commemorate the emperor's victory over the assassins Cassius and Brutus in the Battle of Philippi (42 B.C.). Fittingly, the temple that once dominated this forum—whose remains can still be seen—was that of Mars Ultor, or Mars the Avenger, in which stood a mammoth statue of Augustus which has unfortunately completely vanished. You can enter the Forum of Augustus from the other side (cut across the wee footbridge).

Continuing along the railing, you'll see next the vast semicircle of:

24. Trajan's Market, Via IV Novembre 95 (☎ 06/679-0048), whose teeming arcades stocked with merchandise from the far corners of the Roman world long ago collapsed, leaving only a few ubiquitous cats to watch after things. The shops once covered a multitude of levels, and you can still wander around many of them. In front of the perfectly proportioned semicircular facade—designed by Apollodorus of Damascus at the beginning of the 2nd century—are the remains of a great library, and fragments of delicately colored marble floors still shine in the sunlight between stretches of rubble and tall grass.

While the view from the railing is interesting, Trajan's Market is worth the descent below street level. To get there, follow the service road you're on until you reach the monumental Trajan's Column on your left, where you turn right and go up the steep flight of stairs that leads to Via Nazionale. At the top of the stairs, about half a block farther on the right, you'll see the entrance to the market. It's open Tuesday to Saturday from 9am to 7pm and on Sunday from 9am to 1pm. Admission is 3,750L ($2.40) for adults, 2,500L ($1.60) for students, and free for children 17 and under and for seniors 60 and over.

Before you head down through the labyrinthine passageways, you might like to climb the:

25. **Tower of the Milizie,** a 12th-century structure that was part of the medieval headquarters of the Knights of Rhodes. The view from the top (if it's open) is well worth the climb.

From the tower, you can wander where you will through the ruins of the market, and admire the sophistication of the layout and the sad beauty of the bits of decoration that still remain. When you've examined the brick and travertine corridors, head out in front of the semicircle to the site of the former library; from here, scan the retaining wall that supports the modern road and look for the entrance to the tunnel that leads to the:

26. **Forum of Trajan (Foro Traiano),** entered on Via IV Novembre near the steps of Via Magnanapoli. Once through the tunnel, you'll emerge in the newest and most beautiful of the imperial forums, designed by the same man who laid out the adjoining market. There are many statue fragments and pedestals that bear still-legible inscriptions, but more interesting is the great Basilica Ulpia, whose gray marble columns rise roofless into the sky. You wouldn't know it to judge from what's left, but the Forum of Trajan was once regarded as one of the architectural wonders of the world. Constructed between 107 and 113, it was designed by the Greek architect Apollodorus of Damascus.

Beyond the Basilica Ulpia is:

27. **Trajan's Column,** which is in magnificent condition, with intricate bas-relief sculpture depicting Trajan's victorious campaign (although from your vantage point you'll only be able to see the earliest stages). The emperor's ashes were kept in a golden urn at the base of the column. If you're fortunate, someone on duty at the stairs next to the column will let you out there. Otherwise, you'll have to walk back the way you came.

The next stop is the:

28. **Forum of Julius Caesar,** the first of the imperial forums. It lies on the opposite side of Via dei Fori Imperiali, the last set of sunken ruins before the Victor Emmanuel monument. While it's possible to go right down into the ruins, you can see everything just as well from the railing. This was the site of the Roman stock exchange, as well as of the Temple of Venus, a few of whose restored columns stand cinematically in the middle of the excavations.

On to the Circus Maximus

From here, retrace your last steps until you're in front of the white Brescian marble monument around the corner on Piazza Venezia, where the:

29. **Vittorio Emanuele Monument** dominates the piazza. The most flamboyant landmark in Italy, it was constructed in the late 1800s to honor the first king of Italy. It has been compared to everything from a frosty wedding cake to a Victorian typewriter. An eternal flame burns at the Tomb of the Unknown Soldier. The interior of the monument has been closed to the public for many years.

Keep close to the monument and walk to your left, in the opposite direction from Via dei Fori Imperiali. You might like to pause at the fountain that flanks one of the monument's great white walls and splash some icy water on your face. Stay on the same side of the street, and just keep walking around the monument. You'll be on Via del Teatro Marcello, which takes you past the twin lions that guard the sloping stairs and on along the base of the Capitoline Hill.

Keep walking along this street until you come to the:

30. Teatro di Marcello, on your right. You'll recognize the two rows of gaping arches, which are said to be the models for the Colosseum. Julius Caesar is credited with starting the construction of this theater, but it was finished many years after his death (in 11 B.C.) by Augustus, who dedicated it to his favorite nephew, Marcellus. A small corner of the 2,000-year-old arcade has been restored to what presumably was the original condition. Here, as everywhere, there are numerous cats stalking around the broken marble.

The bowl of the theater and the stage were adapted many centuries ago as the foundation for the Renaissance palace of the Orsini family. The other ruins belong to old temples. To the right is the Porticus of Octavia, dating from the 2nd century B.C. Note how later cultures used part of the Roman structure without destroying its original character. There's another good example of this on the other side of the theater. There you'll see a church with a wall that completely incorporates part of an ancient colonnade.

Keep walking along Via del Teatro Marcello away from Piazza Venezia for 2 more long blocks, until you come to Piazza della Bocca della Verità. The first item to notice in the attractive piazza is the rectangular:

31. Temple of Fortuna Virile. You'll see it on the right, a little off the road. Built a century before the birth of Christ, it's still in magnificent condition. Behind it is another temple, dedicated to Vesta. Like the one in the Roman Forum, it's round, symbolic of the prehistoric huts where continuity of the hearthfire was a matter of survival.

About a block to the south you'll pass the facade of the Church of Santa Maria in Cosmedin, set on Piazza della Bocca della Verità. Even more noteworthy, a short walk to the east, is the:

32. Circus Maximus, whose elongated oval proportions and ruined tiers of benches might remind you of the setting for *Ben Hur*. Today a formless ruin, the victim of countless raids on its stonework by medieval and Renaissance builders, the remains of the once-great arena lie directly behind the church. At one time 250,000 Romans could assemble on the marble seats, while the emperor observed the games from his box high on the Palatine Hill.

The circus lies in a valley formed by the Palatine Hill on the left and the Aventine Hill on the right. Next to the Colosseum, it was the most impressive structure in ancient Rome, located certainly in one of the most exclusive neighborhoods. Emperors lived on the Palatine, while the great palaces of patricians sprawled across the Aventine, which is still a rather nice neighborhood. For centuries the pomp and ceremony of imperial chariot races filled this valley with the cheers of thousands.

When the dark days of the 5th and 6th centuries fell on the city, the Circus Maximus seemed a symbol of the complete ruination of Rome. The last games were held in 549 on the orders of Totilla the Goth, who had seized Rome in 547 and established himself as emperor. He lived in the still-glittering ruins on the Palatine and apparently thought that the chariot races in the Circus Maximus would lend credence to his charade of empire. It must have been a pretty miserable show, since the decimated population numbered something like 500 when Totilla recaptured the city. The Romans of those times were caught between Belisarius, the imperial general from Constantinople, and Totilla the Goth, both of whom fought bloodily for control of Rome. After the travesty of 549, the Circus Maximus was never used again, and the demand for building materials reduced it, like so much of Rome, to a great dusty field.

To return to other parts of town, head for the bus stop adjacent to the Church of Santa Maria in Cosmedin, or walk the length of the Circus Maximus to its far end and pick up the Metro to Termini or anywhere else in the city that appeals to you.

WALKING TOUR 2
The Heart of Rome

Start: Palazzo del Quirinale.
Finish: Piazza Santi Apostoli.
Time: 3½ hours.
Best Times: Sunday mornings.
Worst Times: Morning and afternoon rush hours on weekdays.

This walking tour will lead you down narrow, sometimes traffic-clogged streets that have witnessed more commerce and religious fervor than any other neighborhood in Rome. Be prepared for glittering and very unusual shops that lie cheek by jowl with churches that date back to A.D. 500.

Begin in the monumental, pink-toned:

1. **Piazza del Quirinale.** Crowning the highest of the seven ancient hills of Rome, this is where Augustus's Temple of the Sun once stood (the steep marble steps that now lead to Santa Maria d'Aracoeli on the Capitoline Hill once serviced this spot), and part of the fountains in the piazza were built from the great Baths of Constantine, which also stood nearby. The palace, today home to the President of Italy, is open to the public only on Sunday mornings.

   You can admire a view overlooking Rome from the piazza's terrace, then meander along the curiously lifeless streets that surround it before beginning your westward descent along Via della Dataria and your northerly descent along Via San Vincenzo to one of the most famous waterworks in the world, the:

2. **Trevi Fountain.** Supplied by water from the Acqua Vergine aqueduct, and a triumph of the baroque style, it was based on the design of Nicolo Salvi (who is said to have died of illness contracted during his supervision of the project) and completed in 1762. On the southwestern corner of the fountain's piazza you'll see a somber, not particularly spectacular-looking church (Chiesa S.S. Vincenzo e Anastasio) with a strange claim to fame. In it are contained the hearts and intestines of several centuries of popes. This was the parish church of the popes when they resided at the Quirinal Palace on the hill above, and for many years each pontiff willed those parts of his body to the church. According to legend, the church was built on the site of a spring that burst from the earth after the beheading of St. Paul, at one of three sites where his head is said to have bounced off the ground.

   If you must, throw a coin or two into the fountain to ensure your return to Rome, then walk around to the right of the fountain along streets whose names will include Via di Stamperia, Via del Tritone, and Via F. Crispi. These lead to a charming street, Via Gregoriana, whose relatively calm borders and quiet apartments flank a narrow street that inclines upward to one of the most spectacular public squares in Italy:

Walking Tour—The Heart of Rome

3. **Piazza della Trinità dei Monti.** Partly because of its position at the top of the Spanish Steps (which you'll descend in a moment), partly because of its soaring Egyptian obelisk and its lavish allegiance to perfect baroque symmetry, it's one of the most theatrical points of convergence in Italy. Flanking the piazza are buildings that have played a pivotal role in French politics for centuries, including the Church of Trinità dei Monti, begun by the French monarch Louis XII in 1502, and restored during Napoléon's occupation of Rome in the early 1800s. The eastern edge of the square, adjacent to Via Gregoriana, is the site of the 16th-century Palazzetto Zuccaro, built for the mannerist painter Federico Zuccaro with doorways and window openings fashioned into deliberately grotesque shapes inspired by the mouths of sea monsters. (It lies between Via Gregoriana, Via Sistina, and Piazza Trinità dei Monti.) In this building, at the dawn of the French Revolution, David painted the most politicized canvas in the history of France, *The Oath of the Horatii* (1784), which became a symbol of the Enlightenment then sweeping through the salons of Paris. Today the palazzetto is owned by the German Institute for Art History.

   Begin your meandering descent of the most famous staircase in the world, the:

4. **Spanish Steps (Scalinata della Trinità dei Monti),** an azalea-flanked triumph of landscape design that takes its name (its English name, at least) from the Spanish Embassy, which was in a nearby palace during the 19th century. The Spanish, however, had nothing to do with the construction of the steps. Designed by Italian architect Francesco de Sanctis between 1723 and 1725, they were funded almost entirely by the French as a preface to the above-mentioned French national church, Trinità dei Monti.

   The Spanish Steps are at their best in spring, when they're filled with flowers that seem to cascade down into Piazza di Spagna, a piazza designed like two interconnected triangles. Ongoing restoration has made this a much less desirable place to hang out—especially for the young—than it was in years past. It's interesting to note that in the early 19th century the steps were famous for the sleek young men and women who lined the travertine steps flexing muscles and exposing ankles in hopes of attracting an artist and being hired as a model.

   The boat-shaped Barcaccia fountain, in the piazza at the foot of the steps, was designed by Bernini's father at the end of the 16th century.

   There are two nearly identical houses at the foot of the steps on either side. One is the home of Babington's Tea Rooms (our "Take a Break," below); the other is the house where the English romantic poet John Keats lived—and died. That building contains the:

5. **Keats-Shelley Memorial (Casina Rossa),** at Piazza di Spagna 26. Keats died here on February 23, 1821, at the age of 25, during a trip he made to Rome to improve his failing health. Since 1909, when the building was bought by well-intentioned English and American aficionados of English literature, it has been a working library established in honor of Keats and Shelley, who drowned off the coast of Viareggio with a copy of Keats in his pocket. Mementoes inside range from the kitsch to the immortal, and are almost relentlessly laden with literary nostalgia.

TAKE A BREAK Opened in 1893 by Miss Anna Maria Babington, Babington's Tea Rooms, Piazza di Spagna 23 (☎ 06/678-6027), has been serving homemade scones and muffins—along with a good cuppa—ever since, based on her original recipes. Celebrities and thousands of tourists have stopped off here to rest in premises inspired by England's Victorian age. Prices are high, however.

In the past, the Piazza di Spagna area was a favorite of English lords, who rented palaces hereabouts and parked their coaches on the street. Americans predominate in the 20th century, especially since the main office of American Express is right on Piazza di Spagna and dispenses all those letters (and money) from home. Much to the dismay of many Romans, the piazza is also home to a McDonald's. To the extreme southern edge of the square—flanked by Via Due Macelli, Via Propaganda, and Piazza di Spagna—is an odd vestige of the Catholic church's sense of missionary zeal, the:

6. **Collegio di Propoganda Fide.** It was established in 1627 as the headquarters of a religious organization devoted to the training of young missionaries, and later grew into one of the most important centers for missionary work in the world. Owned and administered by the Vatican, and therefore exempt from most of the laws and legalities of Italy, it contains design elements by two of the 17th century's most bitter artistic rivals, Bernini and Borromini.

   The street that runs east-west as the logical continuation of the descent of the Spanish Steps is one of the most celebrated venues for style and materialism in Italy:

7. **Via Condotti,** lined with the bounty of the Italian fashion industry. Even the least materialistic will enjoy window shopping along this impressive line-up of the most famous names in international fashion. *Note:* Via Condotti is only the most visible of several upscale shopping streets in the neighborhood. For more of the same kind of temptation, detour onto a smaller but equally glamorous parallel street, Via della Croce, 2 blocks to the north, and wander at will amid the bounty. Make it a point, however, to eventually return to Via Condotti for the continuation of this walking tour.

   Via Condotti ends at a shop-lined plaza, Largo Goldoni, where your path will fork slightly to the right onto Via Tomacelli. Staying on the right-hand (northern) edge of the street, turn right at the second intersection into Piazza Augusto, site of the:

8. **Mausoleo Augusteo (Augustus Mausoleum).** Once covered with marble and cypress trees, this tomb housed the ashes of many of the emperors of the 1st century all the way up to Hadrian (who built what is now Castel Sant'Angelo across the river for his own tomb). The imperial remains stayed intact within this building until the 5th century, when invading barbarians smashed the bronze gates and stole the golden urns, probably emptying the ashes on the ground outside. The tomb was restored by Mussolini, and while you cannot enter the mausoleum itself, you can walk around it.

   At the mausoleum's southwestern corner (Largo San Rocco), veer northwest until you reach the edge of the Tiber, stopping for a view of a bizarre, almost surreal compendium of ancient archeological remnants restored, and in some cases enhanced, by Mussolini. It sits in an airy glass-and-concrete building beside the eastern banks of the Tiber at Ponte Cavour. Inside is one of the treasures of antiquity, the:

9. **Ara Pacis (Altar of Peace),** built by the Senate as a tribute to Augustus and the peace he had brought to the Roman world. Look closely at the marble walls for portraits of Augustus's imperial family. Mussolini collected the few fragments of this monument that were scattered in museums thoughout the world and gave his archeological engineers a deadline for digging out the bulk of the altar, which remained underground—below the water table and forming part of the foundation of a Renaissance palace on the Corso. Fearful of failing Il Duce, the engineers hit

upon the idea of chemically freezing the water surrounding the altar and simply chipping the relic out in huge chunks of ice, building new supports for the palace overhead as they went.

After your contemplation of the fragments of another civilization's history, proceed southward along Via Ripetta, cross over Piazza di Porto di Ripetta, then fork left, walking southeast along Via Borghese for a block until you reach the austerely dignified entrance to the:

10. **Palazzo Borghese (Borghese Palace).** Although many of the art treasures that once graced its interior now form part of the Galleria Borghese collections (for details, see "Around Piazza di Spagna & Piazza del Popolo" in Chapter 6), this huge and somewhat disjointed *palazzo* retains its status as the modern-day Borghese family's seat of power and prestige. Bought from another family in 1605 by the cardinal destined to become Pope Paul V, it was later occupied by Paolina Borghese, Napoléon's sometimes scandalous sister, a noted enemy of opera composer Rossini. Regrettably, the palace is not open to the public, as it carefully guards its status as one of the most prestigious private homes in the world.

From your vantage point, walk in a westerly direction along Via Fontanella Borghese back to a square you've already visited, Largo Goldoni, the western terminus of Via Condotti. The busy avenue on your right is one of the most richly stocked treasure troves of Italian merchandise in Rome:

11. **Via del Corso.** When compared to the many meandering streets with which it merges, its rigidly straight lines are unusual. In the 18th century residents of Rome commandeered the street to race everything from horses to street urchins, festooning the windows of buildings on either side of the narrow street with banners and flags. Although today its merchandise is not as chic (or as expensive) as what you'll find along Via Condotti (see above), it's well worth more than a few glances to see what's up in the world of Italian fashion.

Walk south along Via del Corso's western edge, turning right (west) after 1 block into Piazza San Lorenzo in Lucina. The severely massive building on the piazza's northern edge is the:

12. **Palazzo Ruspoli,** a 16th-century testament to the wealth of a Florentine family, the Rucellai. Family members commissioned the same architect (Bartolommeo Ammannati) who designed parts of the Pitti Palace in Florence to build their Roman headquarters. Today the building belongs to a private foundation, although it's occasionally open for temporary, but infrequently scheduled exhibitions. The entrance is at Via del Corso 418A, although your best vantage point will be from Piazza San Lorenzo in Lucina. On the piazza's southern edge rises the:

13. **Chiesa di San Lorenzo in Lucina.** Most of what you'll see today was rebuilt around 1650, although if you look carefully, the portico and most of the bell tower have survived almost unchanged since the 1100s. According to tradition, this church was built on the site of the mansion of Lucina, a prosperous Roman matron who salvaged the corpses of Christian martyrs from prisons and amphitheaters for proper burials. The church was founded by Sixtus III, who reigned for 8 years beginning in A.D. 432. Inside, look for the tomb of the French painter Poussin (1594–1665), which was carved and consecrated on orders of the French statesman Chateaubriand in 1830.

After your visit, retrace your steps back to Via del Corso and walk southward until you reach the venerable perimeter of:

14. **Piazza Colonna.** Its centerpiece is one of the most dramatic obelisks in town, the Column of Marcus Aurelius, a hollow bronze column rising 83 feet above the piazza. Built between A.D. 180 and 196, and restored (some say "defaced") in 1589

by a pope who replaced the statue of the Roman warrior on top with a statue of St. Paul, it's one of the ancient world's best examples of heroic bas-relief and one of the most memorable sights of Rome. Beside the piazza's northern edge rises the Palazzo Chigi, official residence of the Italian prime minister.

Continue walking west from Piazza Colonna into another square a few steps to the east and you'll find yourself in a dramatic piazza designed by Bernini:

15. **Piazza di Montecitorio.** This was the site during ancient times of the cremations of the Roman emperors. In 1792 the massive obelisk of Psammetichus II, originally erected in Egypt in the 6th century B.C., was placed here as the piazza's centerpiece. Brought to Rome by barge from Heliopolis in 10 B.C., it was unearthed from a pile of rubble in 1748 at a site close to the Church of San Lorenzo in Lucina. The Palazzo di Montecitorio which rises from the piazza's northern edge is the modern-day site of the Italian legislature (the Chamber of Deputies) and is closed to the public.

Retrace your steps back to Via del Corso, then walk south, this time along its eastern edge. Within 6 blocks, just after crossing over Via dell'Umilità, you'll see the solid stone walls of the namesake church of this famous shopping boulevard:

16. **Chiesa San Marcello al Corso.** Originally founded in the 4th century, and rebuilt in 1519 after a disastrous fire, it was ornamented in the late 1600s with a baroque facade by Carlo Fontana. A handful of ecclesiastical potentates from the 16th and 17th centuries, many resting in intricately carved sarcophagi, are contained inside.

After your visit, return to the piazza in front of the church, then continue walking for half a block south along Via del Corso. Turn left (eastward) onto Via S.S. Apostoli, then turn right onto Piazza S.S. Apostoli, and conclude this tour with a visit to a site that has witnessed the tears of the penitent since the collapse of the Roman Empire, the:

17. **Chiesa S.S. Apostoli.** Because of alterations to the site, especially a not-very-harmonious rebuilding that began in the early 1700s, there's very little to suggest the ancient origins of this church of the Holy Apostles. It was founded in the dim, early days of the Roman papacy, sometime between A.D. 556 and 561, by Pope Pelagius as a thanksgiving offering for the short-term defeat of the Goths at a battle near Rome. The most interesting parts of this ancient site are the fluted stone columns at the end of the south aisle, in the Cappella del Crocifisso; the building's front portico, added in the 1300s, which managed to incorporate a frieze from ancient Rome; and one of the first works executed by Canova, a painting near the high altar completed in 1787, shortly after his arrival in Rome. The church is open daily from 6:30am to noon and 4 to 7pm.

WALKING TOUR 3
Renaissance Rome

Start: Via della Conciliazione (Piazza Pia).
Finish: Galleria Doria Pamphilj.
Time: 4 hours, not counting a tour of the Castel Sant'Angelo and visits to the Palazzo Spada and the Palazzo Pamphilj.
Best Times: Early and mid-mornings.
Worst Times: After dark.

The threads that unify this tour are the grandiose tastes of Rome's Renaissance popes and the meandering river that has transported building supplies, armies, pilfered treasures from other parts of Europe, and such famous personages as Cleopatra and Mussolini into Rome. Slower and less powerful than many of Italy's other rivers (such as the mighty Po, which irrigates the fertile plains of Lombardy and the north), the Tiber varies, depending on the season, from a sluggish ribbon of sediment-filled water only 4 feet deep to a 20-foot-deep torrent capable of flooding the banks that contain it.

The last severe flood to destroy Roman buildings occurred in 1870. Since then, civic planners have built mounded barricades high above its winding banks, a development that has diminished the river's visual appeal. The high embankments, as well as the roaring traffic arteries that parallel them, obscure views of the water along most of the river's trajectory through Rome. In any event, the waters of the Tiber are so polluted that many modern Romans consider their concealment something of a benefit.

Begin your tour at Piazza Pia. (Don't confuse Piazza Pia with nearby Piazza Pio XII.) Piazza Pia is the easternmost end of Rome's most sterile and impersonal boulevard:

1. **Via della Conciliazione.** Conceived by Mussolini as a monumental preface to the faraway dome of St. Peter's Basilica, its construction required the demolition of a series of medieval neighborhoods between 1936 and 1950, rendering it without challenge the most disliked avenue in Rome.

   Walk east toward the massive and ancient walls of the:

2. **Castel Sant'Angelo.** Originally built by the emperor Hadrian in A.D. 135 as one of the most impressive mausoleums in the ancient world, it was adapted for use as a fortress, a treasure vault, and a pleasure palace for the Renaissance popes. Visit its interior, noting the presence near the entrance of architectural models showing the castle at various periods of its history. Note the building's plan (a circular tower set atop a square foundation), and the dry moats (used today for impromptu soccer games by neighborhood kids), which long ago were the despair of many an invading army.

   After your visit, walk south across one of the most ancient bridges in Rome:

3. **Ponte Sant'Angelo.** The trio of arches in the river's center is basically unchanged since the bridge was built around A.D. 135; the arches that abut the river's embankments were added late in the 19th century as part of a flood-control program. On December 19, 1450, so many pilgrims gathered on this bridge (which at the time was lined with wooden buildings) that about 200 of them were crushed to death. Today the bridge is reserved exclusively for pedestrians, since vehicular traffic was banned in the 1960s. On the southern end of the bridge is the site of one of the most famous executions of the Renaissance:

4. **Piazza San Angelo.** Here, in 1599, Beatrice Cenci and several members of her family were beheaded on orders of Pope Clement VIII. Their crime? Plotting the successful death of their very rich and very brutal father. Their tale later inspired a tragedy by Shelley and a novel by a 19th-century Italian politician named Francesco Guerrazzi.

   From the square, cut southwest for 2 blocks along Via Paola (crossing the busy traffic of Corso Vittorio Emmanuele in the process) onto:

5. **Via Giulia.** Laid out during the reign of Pope Julius II (1503–13), its straight edges were one of Renaissance Rome's earliest examples of urban planning. Designed to facilitate access to the Vatican, it was the widest, straightest, and longest inner-city street in Rome at the time of its construction. Its edges housed the 16th-century homes of such artists as Raphael, Cellini, and Borromini, and the architect Sangallo. Today the street is lined with some of the most spectacular antiques stores

Walking Tour—Renaissance Rome

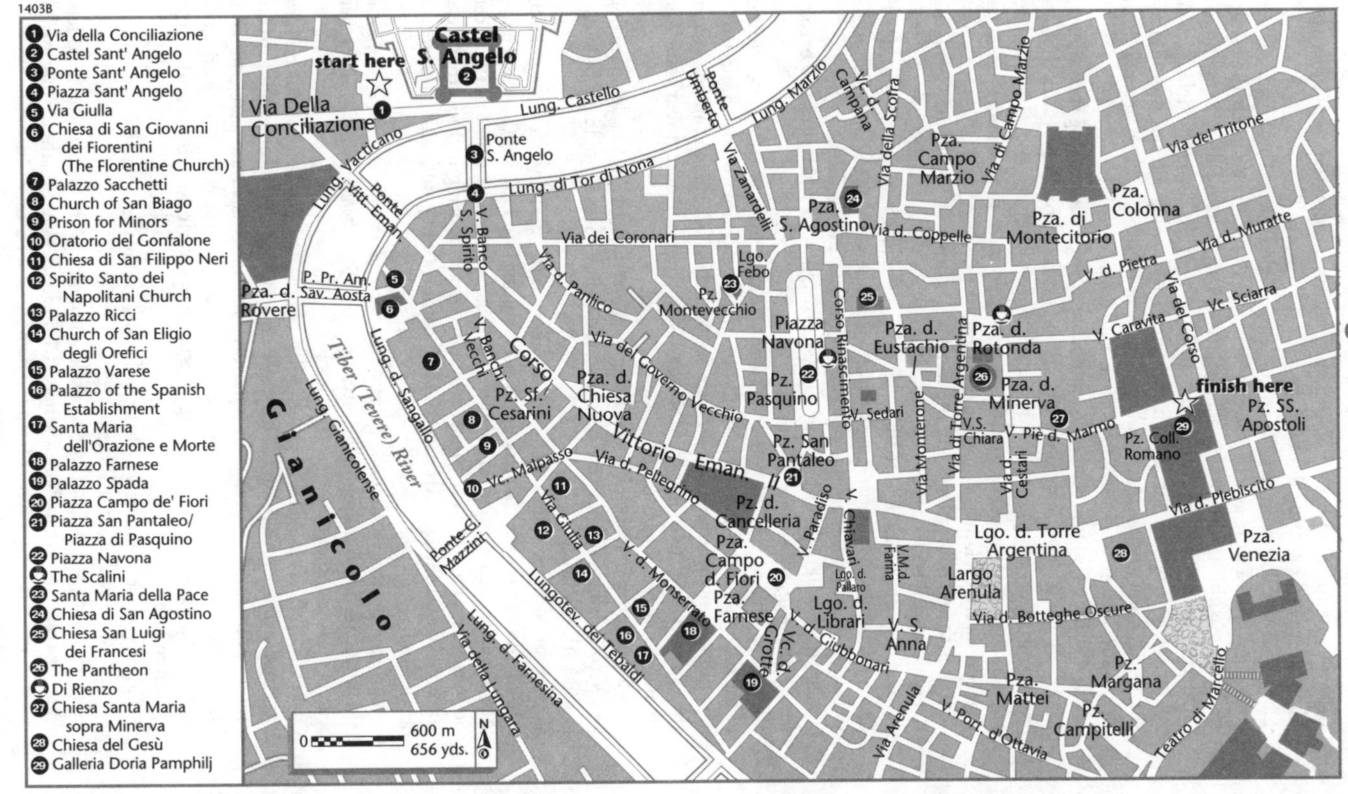
1403B
1 Via della Conciliazione
2 Castel Sant' Angelo
3 Ponte Sant' Angelo
4 Piazza Sant' Angelo
5 Via Giulla
6 Chiesa di San Giovanni dei Fiorentini (The Florentine Church)
7 Palazzo Sacchetti
8 Church of San Biago
9 Prison for Minors
10 Oratorio del Gonfalone
11 Chiesa di San Filippo Neri
12 Spirito Santo dei Napolitani Church
13 Palazzo Ricci
14 Church of San Eligio degli Orefici
15 Palazzo Varese
16 Palazzo of the Spanish Establishment
17 Santa Maria dell'Orazione e Morte
18 Palazzo Farnese
19 Palazzo Spada
20 Piazza Campo de' Fiori
21 Piazza San Pantaleo/ Piazza di Pasquino
22 Piazza Navona
The Scalini
23 Santa Maria della Pace
24 Chiesa di San Agostino
25 Chiesa San Luigi dei Francesi
26 The Pantheon
Di Rienzo
27 Chiesa Santa Maria sopra Minerva
28 Chiesa del Gesù
29 Galleria Doria Pamphilj
Castel S. Angelo
start here
finish here
Via Della Conciliazione
Pz. SS. Apostoli
Pza. Venezia
Piazza Navona
Tiber (Tevere) River
Gianicolo
0
600 m
656 yds.
N

in Rome. At the terminus of Via Paola, the first building on Via Giulia you're likely to see is the soaring dome of the:

6. **Chiesa di San Giovanni dei Florentini (Florentine Church)**, designated as the premier symbol of the city of Florence in papal Rome. Its design is the result of endless squabblings between such artistic rivals as Sansovino, Sangallo, and Maderno, each of whom added embellishments of his own. Michelangelo had submitted a design for the church, although his drawing did not prevail during the initial competition. Although most of the building was completed during the 1620s, Lorenzo Corsini added the facade during the 1700s.

   Now walk in a southeasterly direction along Via Giulia, making special note of houses at no. 82 (built in the 1400s, it was offered by Pope Julius II to the Florentine community), no. 85 (the land it sits on was once owned by Raphael), and no. 79 (built in 1536 by the architect Sangallo as his private home, it was later snapped up by a relative of Cosimo de' Medici).

   In less than 3 short blocks, on the northwest corner of Vicolo del Cefalo, rises the symmetrical bulk of the:

7. **Palazzo Sacchetti.** Completed by Vasari in the mid-1500s, it was built for the Sacchetti family, a Florence-based family of bankers and merchants who moved to Rome after they lost an epic power struggle with the Medicis.

   Continue walking south along Via Giulia. On your right rises the baroque facade of the unpretentious:

8. **Church of San Biagio.** Although its front was added in the early 1700s, it's one of the oldest churches in Rome, rebuilt from an even earlier model around 1070. The property of an Armenian Christian sect based in Venice, the church is named after an early Christian martyr (St. Biagio), a portion of whose throat is included among the sacred objects inside.

   Walk another short block south along Via Giulia. Between Via del Gonfalone and Vicolo della Scimia are the barred windows of what was originally built early in the 19th century as a:

9. **Prison for Minors.** This, along with another nearby building (at Via Giulia 52, a few blocks to the south, which was built during the mid-1600s) incarcerated juvenile delinquents, political prisoners, debtors, common rogues, and innocent victims of circumstance for almost a hundred years. During its Industrial Revolution heyday, armed guards supervised all comings and goings along this section of Via Giulia.

   Turn right onto Vicolo della Scimia and descend toward the Tiber. On your left, at no. 18, is a building used since the early 1500s as a guildhall for the flag-bearers of Rome, the:

10. **Oratorio del Gonfalone.** The guild of flag-bearers had, by the time this building was constructed, evolved into a charitable organization of concerned citizens and a rather posh social and religious fraternity. The frescoes inside were painted in 1573 by Zuccari. Restored during the early 1980s, they today form a backdrop for concerts held inside. The building is usually open Monday to Saturday from 9:30am to noon.

    Walk to the very end of Vicolo della Scimia and make a hard left onto Vicolo Prigioni, which will eventually lead back to Via Giulia.

    At this point, as you continue to walk south along Via Giulia, you'll notice a swath of trees and a curious absence of buildings flanking the corner of Via Moretta. In 1940 Mussolini ordered the demolition of most of the buildings along Via Moretta for the construction of a triumphal boulevard running from east to west. His intention—which was never fulfilled—was to link together the nearby

Ponte Mazzini with Corso Vittorio Emmanuele. One building that suffered was the:

11. **Chiesa di San Filippo Neri,** whose baroque facade sits near the corner. Originally funded during the early 1600s by a wealthy but ailing benefactor in hopes of curing his gout, the church retains only its facade—the rest of the building was demolished. Where choirs once sang and candles burned during masses, there is now a market for fruits and vegetables.

About another block to the south, on your right, rises the bulk of the:

12. **Spirito Santo del Napolitani Church.** Once one of the headquarters of the Neapolitan community in Rome, the version you see today is a product of a rebuilding during the 1700s, although parts of the foundation were originally constructed during the 1300s.

Slightly farther to the south, at Via Giulia 146, rises the:

13. **Palazzo Ricci,** one of the many aristocratic villas that once flanked this historic street. For a better view of its exterior frescoes, turn left from Via Giulia into Piazza Ricci to admire this building from the rear.

Returning to Via Giulia, walk south for a block, then turn right onto Via Barchetta. At the corner of Via di San Eligio, notice the:

14. **Church of San Eligio degli Orefici,** which was designed, according to popular belief, by Raphael in 1516. Completed about 60 years later, it was dedicated to (and funded by) the city's gold- and silversmiths.

Return to Via Giulia and notice, near its terminus, the:

15. **Palazzo Varese,** Via Giulia 16, built as an aristocratic residence in the Tuscan style; and, at Via Giulia 151, the:

16. **Palazzo of the Spanish Establishment.** Constructed in anticipation of the 1862 visit of Elizabeth, queen of Spain, for the occasion of her charitable visit to Rome, it was designed by Antonio Sarti.

Continue walking south along Via Giulia, past the faded grandeur of at least another half-dozen palazzi. These will include the Palazzo Cisterno (from about 1560), at no. 163; Palazzo Baldoca/Muccioli/Rodd (about 1700), at no. 167; and Palazzo Falconieri (about 1510), at no. 1.

Opposite the corner of Via dei Farnesi rise the walls of one of the most macabre buildings in Rome, the church of:

17. **Santa Maria dell'Orazione e Morte.** Built around 1575, and reconstructed about 160 years later, it was the property of an order of monks whose job it was to collect and bury the unclaimed bodies of the indigent. Notice the depictions of skulls decorating the church's facade. During the Renaissance, underground chambers lined with bodies led from the church to the Tiber, where barges carried the corpses away. Although these vaults are not open to the public, the church's interior decoration carries multiple reminders of the omnipresence of death.

After exiting the church, notice the covered passageway arching over Via Giulia. Built in 1603, and designed by Michelangelo, it connected the:

18. **Palazzo Farnese,** whose rear side rises to your left, with the Tiber and a series of then-opulent gardens and villas that no longer exist. The Palazzo Farnese was designed by Sangallo and Michelangelo, among others, and has housed dignitaries ranging from Pope Paul III to Queen Christina of Sweden. Today the French Embassy, it's closed to the public. For the best view of the building, cut west from Via Giulia along any of the narrow streets (Via Mascherone or Via dei Farnesi will do nicely) to reach Piazza Farnese.

To the southwest is a satellite square, Piazza Quercia, at the southern corner of which rises the even more spectacular exterior of the:

19. Palazzo Spada, Capo di Ferro 3. Built around 1550 for Cardinal Gerolamo Capo di Ferro, its ornate facade is stuccoed in high-relief in the mannerist style. Although the State Rooms are closed to the public, the courtyard and several galleries are open.

From here, walk 2 blocks north along either Vicolo del Grotte or Via Balestrari till you reach one of the most famous squares of Renaissance Rome:

20. Piazza Campo de' Fiori. During the 1500s this square was the geographic and cultural center of secular Rome, with inns and the occasional burning at the stake of religious heretics. Today the campo hosts a morning open-air food market every day except Sunday.

After your visit, continue to walk northward for 3 meandering blocks along the narrow confines of Via Baullari to:

21. Piazza San Pantaleo / Piazza di Pasquino, whose interconnected edges are the site of both the Palazzo Massimo (to the east) and the Palazzo Braschi (Museo di Roma) to the north. The Palazzo Massimo (currently home to, among other things, the Rome campus of Cornell University) was begun as a private home in 1532 and designed with an unusual curved facade that corresponded to the narrow confines of the street. Regrettably, because it's open to the public only 1 day a year (March 17), it's viewed as a rather odd curiosity from the Renaissance by most passersby. More accessible is the Palazzo Braschi, built during the late 1700s by Pope Pius IV Braschi for his nephews. Severe and somewhat drab, it was the last palace ever built in Rome by a pope. Since 1952 it has contained the exhibits of the Museo Roma, a not very well funded entity whose visiting hours and future are uncertain.

Continue walking north for 2 blocks until you reach the southernmost entrance of the most thrilling square in Italy:

22. Piazza Navona. Originally laid out in A.D. 86 as a stadium by the emperor Domitian, stripped of its marble in the 4th century by Constantine, and then embellished into the lavish baroque form you'll see today during the Renaissance, it has witnessed as much pageantry and heraldic splendor as any other site in Rome. The fact that it's reserved exclusively for pedestrians adds enormously to its charm, but makes parking in the neighborhood around it almost impossible.

Wander around the confines of this baroque beauty, stopping to:

TAKE A BREAK Established in 1882, **Tre Scalini**, Piazza Navona 30 (☎ 06/687-9148), is the most famous rendezvous point on the square. Literally hundreds of people go here every day to sample its tartufi (ice cream disguised with a coating of bittersweet chocolate, cherries, and whipped cream). There are simpler versions of gelato as well.

After your refreshment, head for the piazza's northwestern corner, adjacent to the startling group of heroic fountains at the square's northern edge, and exit onto Via di Lorenesi. Walk westward for 2 crooked blocks, forking to the left onto Via Parione until you reach the edge of one of the district's most charming churches:

23. Santa Maria della Pace. According to legend, blood flowed from a statue of the Virgin above the altar after someone threw a pebble at it. This legend motivated Pope Sixtus IV to rebuild the church in the 1500s on the foundations of an even older sanctuary. For generations after that, its curved porticos, cupola atop an octagonal base, and frescoes by Raphael helped make it one of the most fashionable churches for aristocrats residing in the surrounding palazzos.

After admiring the subtle curves that counterbalance one another throughout this place, retrace your steps back to the welcoming confines of Piazza Navona, then exit from it at its northernmost (narrow) end. Walk across the broad expanse of Via Zanardelli to its northern edge, then head east for 2 blocks to Piazza San Agostino, on whose northern flank rises the:

24. **Chiesa di San Agostino.** Built between 1479 and 1483, originally commissioned by the archbishop of Rouen, France, it was one of the first churches erected in Rome during the Renaissance. Its interior was altered and redecorated in the 1700s and 1800s. A painting by Caravaggio, *Madonna of the Pilgrims* (1605), hangs over the first altar on the left, as you enter.

After your visit, continue walking east along Via Zanardelli, turning south in about a block onto Via della Scrofe. Be alert to the fact that this street will change its name, in rapid order, to Largo Toniolo and Via Dogana, but regardless of how it's marked, walk for about 2 blocks south until, on the right, you'll see a particularly charming church, the:

25. **Chiesa di San Luigi dei Francesi,** which has functioned as the national church of France in Rome since 1589. Subtly carved into its facade is a stone salamander, the symbol of the Renaissance French monarch François I. Inside are a noteworthy series of frescoes by Caravaggio depicting *The Martyrdom of St. Matthew.*

Continue walking south for less than a block along Via Dogana, then turn left for a 2-block stroll along the Salita dei Crescenzi. Suddenly, at Piazza della Rotonda, there will emerge a sweeping view of one of our favorite buildings in all of Europe:

26. **The Pantheon.** Rebuilt by Hadrian around A.D. 125, it's the best-preserved ancient monument in Rome, a remarkable testimony to the skill of ancient masons, whose partial use of granite helped ensure the building's longevity. Originally dedicated to all the gods, it was transformed into a church (Santa Maria ad Martyres) by Pope Boniface IV in A.D. 609. Many archeologists find the building's massive, slightly battered dignity thrilling. Its flattened dome is the widest in the world, exceeding the width of the dome atop St. Peter's by about 3 feet.

TAKE A BREAK For contemplating the glory of the Pantheon, Di Rienzo, Piazza della Rotunda 8–9 (☎ 06/686-9097), is the most ideal café in Rome. Here you can sit at a table enjoying a pick-me-up while you view not only one of the world's premier ancient monuments, but also the lively crowd of people who come and go on this square, one of the most interesting in Rome.

After your coffee, walk southward along the eastern flank (Via Minerva) of the ancient building. That will eventually lead you to Piazza di Minerva. On the square's eastern edge rises the massive and severe bulk of a site that's been holy for more than 3,000 years:

27. **Chiesa di Santa Maria Sopra Minerva.** Beginning in 1280, early Christian leaders ordained that the foundation of an already ancient temple dedicated to Minerva (goddess of wisdom), be reused as the base for Rome's only Gothic church. Unfortunately, architectural changes and redecorations during the 1500s and the 1900s stripped this building of some of its original allure. Despite that, the roster of ornaments inside—including an awe-inspiring collection of medieval and Renaissance tombs—creates an atmosphere that's something akin to a religious museum.

After your visit, exit Piazza di Minerva from the square's easternmost edge, following Via del Gesù in a path that proceeds eastward, then meanders to the south.

Continue walking southward until you eventually cross over the roaring traffic of Corso Vittorio Emanuele II / Via del Plebiscito. On the southern side of that busy avenue, you'll see a church that for about a century after the Protestant Reformation was one of the most influential in Europe, the:

28. **Chiesa del Gesù.** Built between 1568 and 1584 with donations from a Farnese cardinal, this functioned for several centuries as the most potent and powerful church in the Jesuit order. Conceived as a bulwark against the perceived menace of the Protestant Reformation, it's sober, monumental, and historically very important to the history of the Catholic Counter-Reformation. The sheathing of yellow marble that covers part of the interior was added during the 1800s.

After your visit, cross back over the roaring traffic of Via del Plebiscito, walk eastward for 2 blocks, and turn left (north) onto Via de Gatta. Pass through the first piazza (Piazza Grazioli), then continue northward to Piazza del Collegi Romano, site of the entrance to one of Rome's best-stocked museums, the:

29. **Galleria Doria-Pamphilj,** Piazza del Collegio Romano 1. It's described fully under "Palazzo Doria-Pamphilj" in "Near Piazza Navona & the Pantheon" in Chapter 6.

WALKING TOUR 4
Trastevere

Start: Isola Tiberina.
Finish: Palazzo Corsini.
Time: 3 hours, not counting museum visits.
Best Times: Daylight hours during weekday mornings, when the outdoor food markets are open, or early on a Sunday, when there's very little traffic.
Worst Times: After dark.

Not until the advent of the Fellini films (whose grotesqueries seemed to reflect many of the scenes you're likely to see in this neighborhood) did Trastevere emerge as a world-famous district of Rome. Set on the western bank of the Tiber, away from the bulk of Rome's most-visited monuments, Trastevere (whose name translates as "across the Tiber") seems a world apart from the ethics, mores, and architecture of the rest of Rome. Its residents have traditionally been considered less extroverted and more suspicious than the Romans across the river.

Because only a fraction of Trastevere has been excavated, it remains one of Rome's most consistently unchanged medieval neighborhoods, despite a trend toward gentrification. Amply stocked with dimly lit and very ancient churches, crumbling buildings angled above streets barely wide enough for a Fiat, and highly articulate inhabitants who have stressed their independence from Rome for many centuries, the district is the most consistently colorful of the Italian capital.

Be warned that street crime, pickpockets, and purse snatchers seem more plentiful here than in Rome's more frequently visited neighborhoods, so leave your valuables behind and be alert to what's going on around you.

Your tour begins on the tiny but historic:

1. **Isola Tiberina.** Despite its location in the heart of Rome, it has always been a refuge for the sick, and a calm and sun-flooded backwater. The oldest bridge in Rome, the Ponte Fabricio, built in 62 B.C., connects the island to the Tiber's eastern bank. The church at the island's eastern end, San Bartolomeo, was built during the 900s by the Holy Roman Emperor Otto III, although dozens of subsequent rebuildings have removed virtually everything of the original structure. The complex of buildings at the island's western end contain the hospital of

Walking Tour—Trastevere

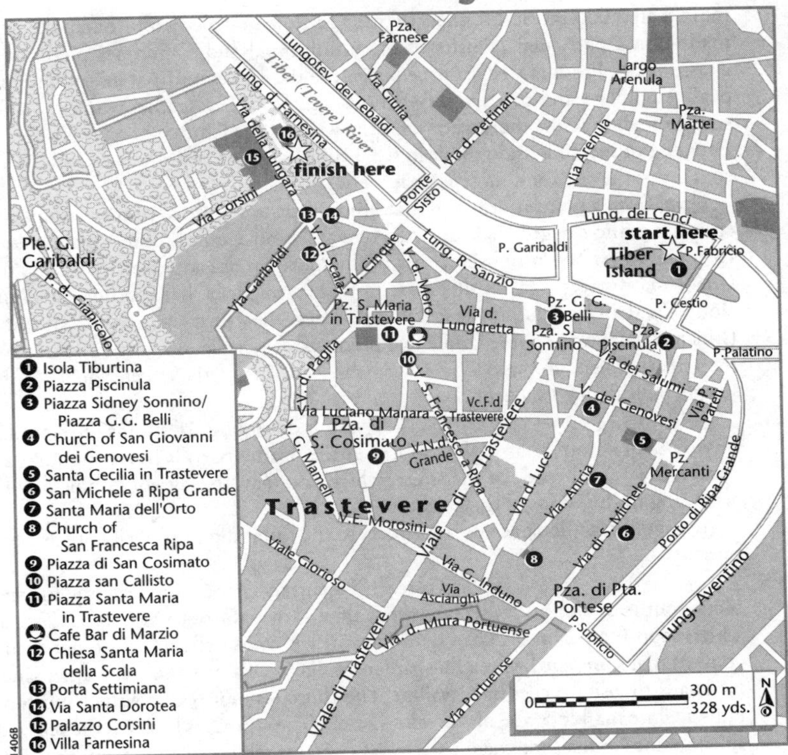

Fatebenefratelli, whose foundations and traditions date back to the ancient world (the island was associated with the healing powers of the god Aesculapius, son of Apollo).

Walk south along the bridge (Ponte Cestio) that connects the island to the western bank of the Tiber. After crossing the raging traffic, which runs parallel to the riverbanks, continue south for a few steps. Soon, you'll reach:

2. Piazza Piscinula. Named after the Roman baths *(piscina)* that once stood here, the square contains the tiny but ancient Church of San Benedetto, whose facade was rebuilt in a simplified baroque style during the 1600s. It's classified as the smallest Romanesque church in Rome and supposedly is built on the site where St. Benedict, founder of the Benedictine order, lived as a boy. Directly opposite the church rises the intricate stonework of the Casa dei Mattei. Occupied during the Renaissance by one of the city's most powerful and arrogant families (the Mattei), it was abondoned as unlucky after several family members were murdered during a brawl at a wedding held inside. In reaction, the family moved to more elegant quarters across the Tiber.

Exit the piazza at the northwest corner, walking west along either the narrow Via Gensola or the somewhat wider Via della Lungaretta. In about 2 jagged blocks you'll reach the first of a pair of connected squares:

3. Piazza Sidney Sonnino (named after the Italian minister of foreign affairs during World War I); a few hundred feet to the north, facing the Tiber, is Piazza G. G. Belli, with a statue commemorating Giuseppe Gioacchino Belli (1791–1863), whose more than 2,000 satirical sonnets (written in Roman dialect) on Roman life have made him a particular favorite of the uninhibited and sometimes pugnacious Trasteverans. From one edge of the piazza rise the 13th-century walls of the Torre degli Anguillara and the not-very-famous church of St. Agatha, whereas on the southern edge, across the street, stand the walls of the Church of San Crisogono. Founded in the 500s and rebuilt in the 1100s (when its bell tower was added), it contains stonework and mosiacs that merit a visit.

Now, from a point near the southernmost expanses of these connected squares, cross the traffic-clogged Viale di Trastevere and head southeast into a maze of narrow alleyways. We propose at this point that you ask a passerby for Via dei Genovesi, as street signs in this maze of piazzas might be hard to find. Walking along Via dei Genovesi, traverse Via della Luce, then turn right onto Via Anicia (which was named after the family that produced the medieval leader Pope Gregory the Great). Then, at Via Anicia 12, on the west side of the street, you'll see the simple but dignified walls of the:

4. **Church of San Giovanni dei Genovesi.** Built during the 1400s for the community of Genoa-born sailors who labored at the nearby port, it has a tranquil garden on the opposite side of the street, which you may or may not be able to visit according to the whim of the gatekeeper.

After your visit, look across Via Anicia to the forbidding rear walls and ancient masonry of:

5. **Santa Cecilia in Trastevere.** (To reach its entrance, continue walking another block southeast along Via dei Genovesi, then turn right onto Via Santa Cecilia, which soon funnels into Piazza dei Mercanti.) A cloistered and still-functioning convent that's preceded with a fine garden, Santa Cecilia contains in its inner sanctum hard-to-visit frescoes by Cavallini. The church is more easily visited and contains a white marble statue of the saint herself. The church is built on the reputed site of Saint Cecilia's long-ago palace and contains sections dating from the 12th to the 19th century.

St. Cecilia, who proved of enormous importance in the history of European art as a symbol of the struggle of the early church, was a Roman aristocrat—and one of the wealthiest women in Rome—condemned for her faith by a Roman prefect around A.D. 300. According to legend, her earthly body proved extraordinarily difficult for Roman soldiers to slay, affording the saint ample opportunity to convert bystanders to the Christian cause as she bled slowly to death over a period of 3 days.

TAKE A BREAK About half a dozen cafés lie near this famous church. Any of them will serve frothy cups of cappuccino, tasty sandwiches, ice cream, and drinks.

After your refreshment, take the opportunity to wander randomly down three or four of the narrow streets outward from Piazza dei Mercanti. Of particular interest might be Via del Porto, which stretches south to the Tiber. A port—the largest in Rome—once flourished at this street's terminus (Porto di Ripa Grande). During the 1870s redesign of the riverfront, when the embankments were added, the port was demolished.

Your exploration of this riverfront area has fortuitously brought you adjacent to a superb collection of paintings. To reach it from the river, retrace your steps northward along Via del Porto, turning left onto Via di San Michele. At no. 22, inside a stucco-covered, peach-colored building that never manages to loose its bureaucratic anonymity despite its age, you'll see a new and somewhat oddly configured collection of paintings whose presence in Trastevere is the result of an unexpected bureaucratic glitch in the city's administration of its museums:

6. **San Michele a Ripa Grande.** The paintings you'll see inside were for many years stored on the second floor of the Borghese Gallery, in another part of Rome. Although their presence here was originally envisioned as strictly temporary, the site was unexpectedly redefined as semipermanent just before press time. For more details, see the "Galleria Borghese" under "Around Piazza di Spagna & Piazza del Popolo" in Chapter 6.

   After your perusal of the artworks, turn north onto Via Madonna dell'Orto, a narrow street that intersects Via di San Michele. One block later, at the corner of Via Anicia, you'll see the baroque:

7. **Santa Maria dell'Orto,** which was originally founded by the vegetable gardeners of Trastevere during the early 1400s, when the district provided most of the green vegetables for the tables of Rome. Famous for the obelisks that decorate its corniches (added in the 1760s) and for the baroque gilding inside, it's one of the district's most traditional churches. There's a risk that it might be closed for renovation at the time of your visit, although a view of the facade is undeniably charming nonetheless.

   Now walk southwest along Via Anicia. In 2 blocks the street funnels into Piazza di San Francesco d'Assisi. On your left, notice the ornate walls of the:

8. **Church of San Francesco a Ripa.** Built in the baroque style, and attached to a medieval Franciscan monastery, the church contains a mannerist statue by Bernini depicting Ludovica Albertoni. It's the last known work Bernini ever sculpted, and supposedly one of his most mystically transcendental.

   Exit from Piazza di San Francesco d'Assisi and walk north along Via San Francesco a Ripa. After traversing the feverish traffic of Viale di Trastevere, take the first left onto a tiny street with a long name, Via Natale del Grande Cardinale Merry di Val. (Its name is sometimes shortened to simply "Via Natale," if it's marked at all on your map.) This funnels into:

9. **Piazza di San Cosimato,** known for its busy food market, which operates every weekday from early morning until around noon. On the north side of the square lies the awkwardly charming church of San Cosimato, sections of which were built around A.D. 900; it's closed to the public.

   Exit from the piazza's north side, heading up Via San Cosimato (its name might not be marked). This will lead into:

10. **Piazza di San Callisto.** Much of the real estate surrounding this square, including the 17th-century Palazzo San Callisto, belongs to the Vatican. The edges of this piazza will almost imperceptibly flow into one of the most famous squares of Rome:

11. **Piazza di Santa Maria in Trastevere.** The Romanesque church that lends the piazza its name (Santa Maria in Trastevere) is the most famous building in the entire district. Originally built around A.D. 350 and thought to be one of the oldest churches in Rome, it sports a central core that was rebuilt around 1100 and an entrance and portico that were added in the 1840s. The much-restored mosaics on both the facade and in the interior, however, date from around 1200. Its sense of timelessness is enhanced by the much-photographed octagonal fountain in front and the hundreds of pigeons.

TAKE A BREAK Try one of the many cafés that line this famous square. Although any would be suitable, a good choice might be the **Café Bar di Marzio,**

Piazza di Santa Maria in Trastevere 14B, where rows of tables, both inside and out, offer an engaging view of the ongoing carnival of Trastevere.

After your refreshment, walk to the church's north side, toward its rear. Stretching from a point beginning at its northwestern edge is an ancient square, Piazza di San Egidio, with its own drab and rather nondescript 16th-century church (Chiesa di San Egidio) set on its western edge. Use it as a point of reference for the left-hand street that funnels from its base in a northeasterly direction, Via della Scala.

The next church you'll see on your left, just after Vicolo della Scala, is:

12. **Santa Maria della Scala,** a 17th-century baroque monument that belongs to the Discalced Carmelite order of nuns. The interior contains works by Caravaggio and his pupils. There's also a pharmacological oddity in the annexes associated with the building. They include a modern pharamacy as well as a room devoted to arcane jars and herbal remedies that haven't changed very much since the l8th century.

In about 5 evocative blocks you'll reach a triumphal archway that marks the site of one of the ancient Roman portals to the city, the:

13. **Porta Settimiana.** Although during the 3rd century it was a vital link in the Roman defenses of the city, its partially ruined masonry provides little more than poetic inspiration today. Much of its appearance dates from the age of the Renaissance popes, who retained it as a site marking the edge of the ancient Aurelian wall. The narrow medieval-looking street leading off to the right is:

14. **Via Santa Dorotea.** Site of a rather drab church (Chiesa San Dorotea, a few steps from the intersection with Via della Scala), the street also marks a neighborhood that, according to legend, was the home of La Forinara, the baker's daughter. She was the mistress of Raphael, and he painted her as the Madonna, causing a scandal in his day.

Return to Via della Scala (which at this point has changed its name to Via della Lungara) and continue walking north. After Via Corsini, the massive palace on your left is the:

15. **Palazzo Corsini,** Via della Lungara 10. Built in the 1400s for a nephew of the pope, it was acquired by Queen Christina of Sweden, the fanatically religious monarch who abdicated the Protestant throne of Sweden for a life of devotion to Catholic causes. Today it houses some of the collection of the National Gallery of Ancient Art, plus European paintings of the 17th and 18th centuries. It's open Tuesday to Sunday from 9am to 2pm.

After your visit, cross Via della Lungara, heading east toward the Tiber, for a look at what was once the most fashionable villa in Italy, the:

16. **Villa Farnesina.** It was built between 1508 and 1511 by a Sienese banker, Agostino Chigi (Il Magnifico), who was believed to be the richest man in Europe at the time. After his death in 1520, the villa's frescoes and carvings were partially sacked by German armies in 1527. After years of neglect, the building was bought by the Farnese family, after whom it is named today, and in the 18th century, by the Bourbons of Naples. Graced with sculpture and frescoes (some by Raphael and his studio), it now belongs to the Italian government, and is the home of the National Print Cabinet (Gabinetto Nazionale delle Stampe), whose collections are open for view only by appointment. The public rooms, however, are open Monday to Saturday from 9am to 1pm, and also on Tuesday afternoon from 3 to 5:30pm.

8 Shopping

Rome offers shoppers temptations of every kind. This section will try to give you focus so that when you feel the urge—which sometimes overcomes even the most stalwart of visitors—you'll be ready. You may well find charming shops and stores offering excellent value as you venture off the beaten track; what follows here is a description of certain streets known throughout Italy for their elegant shops. Be forewarned: The rents on these famous streets are very high, and some of those costs will almost certainly be passed on to the consumer. Nonetheless, a stroll down some of these streets usually presents a cross section of the most sought-after wares in Italy.

Cramped urban spaces and a sophisticated sense of taste have encouraged most Italian stores to elevate the boutique philosophy to its highest levels. Lack of space usually restricts an establishment's goods to one particular style, degree of formality, or mood. So browse at will, and let the allure of the shop window (particularly when shopping for fashions) communicate the mood and style of what you're likely to find inside.

Caveat: We won't pretend that Rome is Italy's finest shopping center (Florence, Venice, and Milan are), nor that its shops are unusually inexpensive—many of them aren't. But even on the most elegant of Rome's thoroughfares, there are values mixed in with the costliest items.

1 The Shopping Scene

Bring your pocket calculator with you and keep in mind that stores are often closed between 1 and 4pm.

SHIPPING Shipping can be a problem, but—for a price—any object can be packed, shipped, and insured. For major purchases, you should buy an all-risks insurance policy to cover damage or loss in transit. Since these policies can be expensive, check into whether using a credit or charge card to make your purchase will provide automatic free insurance.

TAX REBATES ON PURCHASES IN ITALY Visitors to Italy are sometimes appalled at the high taxes and add-ons that seem to influence so many of the bottom-line costs of going to Italy. Those taxes, totaling as much as 19% to 35% for certain goods, apply to big-ticket purchases of more than 525,000L ($336) but can be refunded if you plan ahead and perform a bit of sometimes tiresome paperwork. When you make your purchase, be sure to get a receipt from the vendor. When you leave Italy, find an Italian Customs agent at the point of your exit from the country. The agent will want to see the item you've bought, confirm that it's physically leaving Italy, and stamp the vendor's receipt.

You should then mail the stamped receipt (keeping a photocopy for your records) back to the original vendor. The vendor will, sooner or later, send you a check representing a refund of the tax you paid at the time of your original purchase. Reputable stores view this as a matter of ordinary paperwork and are very businesslike about it. Less honorable stores might lose your receipts. It pays to deal with established vendors on purchases of this size.

MAJOR SHOPPING STREETS

Via Borgognona It begins near Piazza di Spagna, and both the rents and the merchandise are chic and very, very expensive. Like its neighbor, Via Condotti, Via Borgognona is a mecca for wealthy, well-dressed shoppers from around the world. Its architecture and its storefronts have retained their baroque or neoclassical facades.

Via Condotti Easy to find because it begins at the base of the Spanish Steps, Via Condotti is the poshest upper-bracket shopping street in Rome, and the best example in Europe of a certain kind of avidly elegant consumerism. Even the incursion in recent years of a sampling of less elegant stores hasn't diminished the allure of this street as a consumer's playground for the rich and the very, very rich.

Via Frattina It begins at Piazza di Spagna and runs parallel to Via Condotti. Part of its length is closed to traffic. The concentration of shops is denser, although some claim that its image is slightly less chic and that prices are lower than on Via Condotti. Via Frattina is usually thronged with shoppers who appreciate the lack of motor traffic.

Via del Corso It doesn't attempt the stratospheric image (or prices) of Via Condotti or Via Borgognona, and its styles tend to be aimed at younger consumers. There are, however, some gems scattered amid the shops selling jeans and sporting equipment. This street was lucky enough to have most automobile traffic diverted for some of its length. The most interesting shops are on the section nearest the fashionable cafés of Piazza del Popolo.

Via Sistina Beginning at the top of the Spanish Steps and running from Trinità dei Monti into Piazza Barberini, Via Sistina's shops are small, stylish, and based on the personalities of their owners. Pedestrian traffic is not as dense as it is on the other streets on this list.

Via Francesco Crispi Most shoppers reach this street by following Via Sistina one long block from the top of the Spanish Steps. Within a block of the intersection of these two streets are several shops well suited for unusual and not very expensive gifts. It's convenient to combine a visit to this street with Via Sistina.

Via Nazionale Its layout reeks of 19th-century grandeur and ostentatious beauty, but its traffic is horrendous and crossing it involves a good sense of timing and a strong understanding of Italian driving patterns. It begins at Piazza della Repubblica and runs down almost to Piazza Venezia. You'll find an abundance of leather stores—more reasonable than in many other parts of Rome—and a welcome handful of stylish boutiques.

Rome Shopping

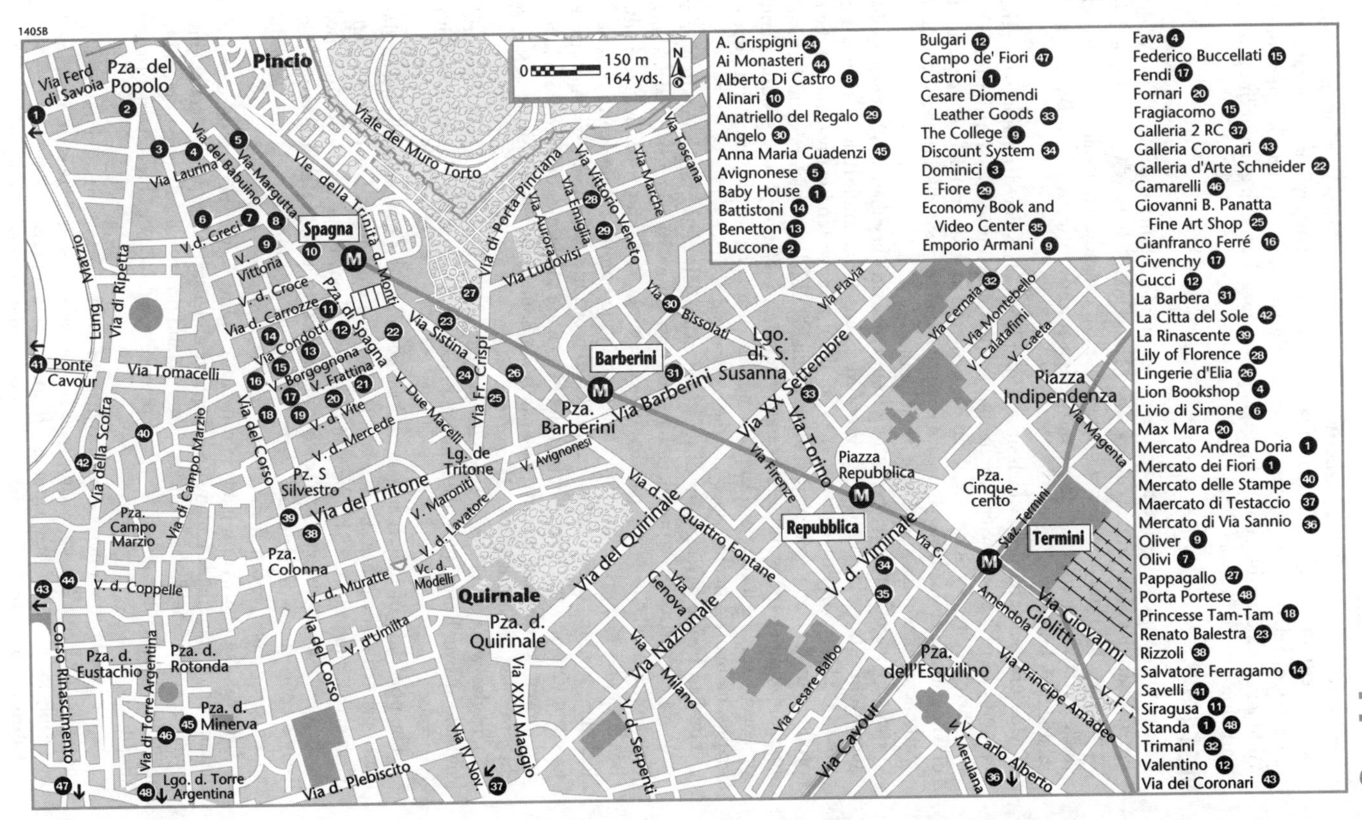

Via Vittorio Veneto & Via Barberini Evocative of *La Dolce Vita* fame and (now-diminished) fortunes, Via Veneto is filled these days with luxury hotels and cafés and an array of relatively expensive stores selling shoes, gloves, and leather goods. Although it's a desirable address by day, this street can be rough at night (muggings), and motor traffic is always both dense and noisy.

BEST BUYS

The Italian aesthetic has exerted more power on the definition of beauty for Westerners than that of any other culture, and because of the Italians' consummate skill as manufacturers and designers, it's no surprise that consumers from all over the world flock to Italy's shops, trade fairs, and design studios to see what's new, hot, and salable back home.

Most obvious is **fashion,** which since World War II has played a major part in the economy of Milan, whose entrepreneurs view Rome as a principal distribution center. There are literally hundreds of famous designers for both men and women, most of whom make eminently stylish garments. Materials include silks, leathers, cottons, synthetics, and wools, often of the finest quality.

Italian design influences everything from typewriter keyboards to kitchen appliances to furniture. The Italian studios of Memphis-Milan and Studio Alchimia are two of the leaders in this field, and many of their products (and many copies of their products by derivative companies) are now highly visible in machines and furnishings throughout the world. You can preview many of Italy's new products and designs by reading a copy of *Domus,* a monthly magazine that reports, with photographs, on many different aspects of the country's design scene.

Food and wine never go out of style, and many gourmets bring home to North America the gastronomic products that somehow always taste better in Italy. Many Roman shops sell chocolates, pastries, liqueurs, wines, and limited-edition olive oils. Be alert to restrictions against importing certain food products into North America, including anything fresh, such as fruit, and also prosciutto. Italian wines include many excellent vintages, and bottles of liqueurs (which are sometimes distilled from herbs and flowers) make unusual gifts. You can bring home only 1 liter of wine or spirits duty free—if, of course, you're 21 or over.

The **glassware** of Italy (and especially of Venice) is famous throughout the world and sold all over Rome. It's fragile enough to look into shipping it directly home with insurance.

The **porcelain** of Italy is elegant and sought after, but we personally prefer the hand-painted rustic plates and bowls of thick-edged **stoneware.** Done in strong and clear glazes, and influenced by their rural origins, the bowls and plates are often used at the most formal dinners for their originality and style. The **tiles** and **mosaics** of Italy are virtually without equal in the world, whether used individually as drink coasters or decorative ornaments, or in groups set into masonry walls.

Lace was, for many years, made in convents by nuns. Venice became the country's headquarters. Handmade Italian lace is exquisite and justifiably expensive, crafted into a wide array of tablecloths, napkins, clothing, and bridal veils. Beware of machine-made imitations, although with a bit of practice you'll soon be able to recognize the shoddy copies.

Paper goods, stationery, elegantly bound books, prints, and engravings are specialties of Italy. The engravings you find amid stacks of dozens of others will invariably look stately when hanging—framed—on a wall back home.

Fabrics, especially silk, are made near Lake Como, in the foothills of the Italian Alps. Known for their supple beauty and their ability to hold color for years (the thicker the silk, the more desirable), these silks are rivaled only by the finest of India, Thailand, and China. Their history in Italy goes back to the era of Marco Polo, and possibly much earlier.

Finally, Rome is the home to a **religious objects** industry. Centered around the streets near the Church of Santa Maria Sopra Minerva are dozens of shops selling pictures, statues, and reliefs of most of the important saints, the Madonna, Jesus, and John the Baptist.

2 Shopping A to Z

ANTIQUES

Some visitors to Italy come for its treasure trove of salable antiques alone. But long gone are the postwar days when you found priceless treasures for pocket change. The prices of almost all antiques have risen to alarming levels as increasingly wealthy Europeans have outbid one another in frenzies of acquisitive lust. You might remember that any dealer who risks the high rents of central Rome to open an antiques store is probably acutely aware of the value of almost everything ever made, and will probably recognize anything of value long before his or her clients. Beware of fakes, insure anything you buy and have shipped, and for larger purchases, keep your paperwork in order for your eventual tax refund.

If you love antiques, one street you should frequent is **Via dei Coronari.** Buried in an ancient section of Campo Marzio (near Piazza Navona), Via dei Coronari is an antiquer's dream: There are more than 40 antiques stores within 4 blocks, literally lined with inlaid secretaries, gilded consoles, vases, urns, chandeliers, breakfronts, marble pedestals, chaises, refectory tables, candelabra—you name it. The entrance to the street is just north of Piazza Navona. Turn left outside the piazza, past the excavated ruins of Domitian's Stadium, and the street will be just ahead of you.

Via del Babuino is another major street for antiques in Rome, with some of the most prestigious stores found here, including Alberto di Castro (our favorite store for prints—see "Art," below), but many others as well, including **Cesare Lampronti,** Via del Babuino 67 (☎ **06/679-5800**), and **Granmercato Antiquario Babuino,** Via del Babuino 150 (☎ **06/323-5686**).

Galleria Coronari. Via dei Coronari 59. ☎ **06/686-9917.**

The Galleria Coronari is a desirable shop that might be used as a starting point for browsing through many other shops nearby. Many of its antiques are nostalgia-laden bric-a-brac, small enough to fit into a suitcase, including jewelry, dolls, paintings, and ornate picture frames from the 19th century. Also represented is furniture from the 18th, 19th, and early 20th centuries, and such oddities as a completely furnished dollhouse, accurate even down to the miniature champagne bottles in the miniature pantry. Open Monday from 3:30 to 7:30pm and Tuesday to Saturday from 10am to 1pm and 3:30 to 7:30pm.

ART

Alberto di Castro. Via del Babuino 71. ☎ **06/361752.**

Alberto di Castro is one of the largest dealers in antique prints and engravings in Rome. You'll find rack after rack of depictions of everything from the Colosseum to the Pantheon, each evocative of the best architecture in the Mediterranean world, priced between $25 and $1,000, depending on the age and rarity of the engraving. Open Monday from 3:30 to 7:30pm and Tuesday to Saturday from 10am to 1pm and 3:30 to 7:30pm.

Galleria d'Arte Schneider. Rampa Mignanelli 10. ☎ **06/678-4019.**

Located a few steps from one of the ramps leading into the side of the Spanish Steps, near the Hassler Hotel, this is one of the best-established and most enduring art galleries in Rome. Launched in 1953 by Robert Schneider, an American-born professor of languages, it specializes in lesser-known sculpture and paintings by Italians or foreign residents of Rome. Among the artists whose work has been promoted early in their careers by this gallery are Dimitre Hadzi, George d'Almeida, Paolo Buggiani, and Mirko Balsedella. Surprisingly, within the world of Italian art galleries, the frequently changing inventories here are relatively affordable, ranging in price from 1,000,000L to 10,000,000L ($640 to $6,400). The building that contains the gallery, incidentally, was designed in the 19th century by a Danish sculptor to serve as a refuge for artists ever after. Today the day-to-day operations of the gallery are conducted by Mr. Schneider's charming wife, Dolores. The gallery keeps no set hours, and some days it doesn't open at all—so call first. When they do open it's only Monday to Saturday from 4:30 to 7:30pm. Always closed in August.

Giovanni B. Panatta Fine Art Shop. Via Francesco Crispi 117. ☎ **06/679-5948.**

In business since 1890, this store is up the hill toward the Villa Borghese. Here you'll find excellent prints in color and black-and-white, covering a variety of subjects from 18th-century Roman street scenes to astrological charts. Also, there's a good selection of reproductions of medieval and Renaissance art—attractive and reasonably priced as well. Open on Monday from 3:30 to 7:30pm and Tuesday to Saturday from 9:15am to 1pm and 3:30 to 7:30pm.

BOOKSTORES

Economy Book and Video Center. Via Torino 136. ☎ **06/474-6877.**

Catering to the expatriate English-speaking communities of Rome, this bookstore sells only English-language books (both new and used, paperback and hardcover), greeting cards, and videos. Staffed by British, Australian, or American workers, it lies about a block from the Piazza della Repubblica Metro station, and bus lines no. 64 and 70. It's open in summer, Monday to Friday from 9am to 8pm and on Saturday from 9am to 2pm; in winter, on Monday from 3 to 8pm and Tuesday to Saturday from 9am to 8pm.

The Lion Bookshop. Via del Babuino 181. ☎ **06/322-5837.**

The Lion Bookshop is the oldest English-language bookshop in town, specializing in literature, both American and English. It also sells children's books and photographic volumes on both Rome and Italy. A vast choice of English-language videos is for sale or rent. The store is open Monday to Saturday from 9:30am to 1:30pm and 3:30 to 7:30pm (closed in August).

Rizzoli. Largo Chigi 15. ☎ **06/679-6641.**

Rizzoli has one of the largest collections of Italian-language books in Rome. If your native language happens to be French, English, German, or Spanish, the endless shelves of this large bookstore will have a section to amuse, enlighten, and entertain you. Open Monday to Saturday from 9am to 2pm and 2:30 to 7:30pm and on Sunday from 10:30am to 1:30pm and 4 to 8pm.

DEPARTMENT STORES

La Rinascente. Piazza Colonna, Via del Corso 189. ☎ **06/679-7691.**

This upscale department store offers clothing, hosiery, perfume, cosmetics, and other goods. It also has its own line of clothing (Ellerre) for men, women, and children.

This is the largest of the Italian department-store chains, and its name is seen frequently on billboards and newspaper ads throughout the country. Open on Monday from 2 to 7:30pm and Tuesday to Saturday from 9:30am to 7:30pm.

Standa. Corso Francia 124. ☎ **06/333-8719.**

Standa could not be considered stylish by any stretch of the imagination, but some visitors find it enlightening to wander—just once—through the racks of department-store staples to see what an average Italian household might accumulate. Other branches are at Corso Trieste 200, Via Trionfale (without number), Via Cola di Rienzo 173, Viale Regina Margherita (without number), and Viale Trastevere 60. All branches are open on Monday from 3:30 to 7:30pm and Tuesday to Saturday from 9am to 1pm and 2:30 to 7:30pm.

DISCOUNT SHOPPING

Certain stores that can't move their merchandise at any price often consign their unwanted goods to discounters. In Italy, the original labels are usually still inside the garment (and you'll find some very chic labels strewn in with mounds of garments bearing less enviable names). Know in advance, however, that these garments couldn't be sold at higher prices in more glamorous shops, and some garments are either the wrong size, the wrong "look," or have a stylistic mistake.

Discount System. Via del Viminale 35. ☎ **06/482-3917.**

Discount System sells men's and women's wear by many of the big names (Armani, Valentino, Nino Cerruti, Fendi, and Krizia). Even if an item isn't from a famous designer, it often comes from a factory that produces some of the best quality Italian fashion. However, don't give up hope: If you find something you like, know that it will be priced at around 50% of its original price tag in its original boutique, and it just might be a cut-rate gem well worth your effort. Open on Monday from 3:30 to 7:30pm and Tuesday to Saturday from 9:30am to 1pm and 3:30 to 7:30pm.

EYEGLASSES

La Barbera. Via Barberini 74. ☎ **06/483628.**

This place has been in business since 1837 and has a substantial reputation in the field of optical equipment. The store also carries a full spectrum of related wares: cameras, film, binoculars, opera glasses, and microscopes. You can have prescription glasses reproduced in 48 hours. For those once-fashionable hangouts on Via Veneto and Piazza del Popolo, take a look at Barbera's collection of sunglass frames—more than 5,000 varieties. Open on Monday from 3:30 to 7:30pm and Tuesday to Saturday from 9am to 7:30pm.

FASHION

See also "Department Stores," "Discount Shopping," "Leather," "Lingerie," and "Shoes."

FOR MEN

Angelo. Via Bissolati 34. ☎ **06/474-1796.**

Angelo is a custom tailor for discerning men and has been featured in such publications as *Esquire* and *GQ.* He employs the best cutters and craftspeople, and his taste in style and design is impeccable. Custom shirts, suits, dinner jackets, even casual wear, can be made on short notice. A suit, for instance, takes about 8 days. If you haven't time to wait, Angelo will ship anywhere in the world. Open Monday to Friday from 9:30am to 1pm and 3:30 to 7:30pm and on Saturday from 9:30am to 1pm.

Emporio Armani. Via del Babuino 119. ☎ **06/322151.**

This store stocks relatively inexpensive menswear crafted by the couturier who has dressed perhaps more stage and screen stars than any other designer in Italy. The designer's more expensive line—sold at sometimes staggering prices that are nonetheless up to 30% less than what you'd pay in the United States—is a short walk away at Giorgio Armani, Via Condotti 77 (☎ 06/699-1460). Both branches are open on Monday from 3 to 7pm, Tuesday to Friday from 10am to 7pm, and on Saturday from 9am to 7pm.

Valentino. Via Condotti 13. ☎ **06/678-3656.**

This is a swank emporium for the men's clothing of the acclaimed designer. Here you can become the most fashionable man in town, but only if you can afford those high prices. Valentino's women's haute couture is sold around the corner in an even bigger showroom at Via Bocca di Leone 15 (☎ 06/679-5862). Both stores are open on Monday from 3 to 7pm and Tuesday to Saturday from 10am to 7pm.

For Women

Benetton. Via Condotti 18. ☎ **06/679-7982.**

Despite the gracefully arched ceiling and its prized location, this branch of the worldwide sportswear distributor charges about the same prices as branches at less glamorous addresses. Famous for woolen sweaters, tennis wear, blazers, and the kind of outfits you'd want to wear on a private yacht, this company has suffered (like every other clothier) from inexpensive copies of its designs. The original, however, is still best for guaranteed quality. Open on Monday from 3:30 to 7:30pm and Tuesday to Saturday from 10am to 7:30pm.

Gianfranco Ferré. Via Borgognona 42B. ☎ **06/679-0050.**

Here you'll find the women's line by this famous designer whose clothes have been called "adventurous." Open on Monday from 3:30 to 7:30pm and Tuesday to Saturday from 9:30am to 1:30pm and 3:30 to 7:30pm.

Givenchy. Via Borgognona 21. ☎ **06/678-4058.**

This is the Roman headquarters of one of the great designer names of France, a company known since World War I for its couture. In its Roman branch, the company emphasizes ready-to-wear garments for stylish women with warm Italian weather in mind. Open on Monday from 3 to 7pm and Tuesday to Saturday from 10am to 7pm.

Max Mara. Via Frattina 48 (at Largo Goldoni). ☎ **06/679-3638.**

Max Mara is one of the best outlets in Rome for women's clothing. The fabrics are appealing and the alterations are free. Open on Monday from 3:30 to 7:30pm and Tuesday to Saturday from 10am to 2pm and 3:30 to 7:30pm.

Renato Balestra. Via Sistina 67. ☎ **06/679-5424.**

Rapidly approaching the stratospheric upper levels of Italian fashion is Renato Balestra, whose women's clothing exudes a lighthearted elegance. This branch carries a complete line of the latest Balestra ready-to-wear designs for women. The company's administrative headquarters and the center of its couture department is nearby, at Via Ludovici 35 (☎ 06/482-1723), although advance appointments are recommended here. Stop in at the Via Sistina branch for an idea of the designer's style before launching yourself into a dialogue with Balestra's couture department, if only to save costs. Both outlets are open on Monday from 3 to 7pm, Tuesday to Friday from 10am to 7:30pm, and on Saturday from 9am to 7pm.

For Children

Baby House. Via Cola di Rienzo 117. ☎ **06/321-4291.**

Baby House offers what might be the most label-conscious collection of children's and young people's clothing in Italy. With an inventory of clothes suitable for children and adolescents to age 15, they sell clothing by Valentino, Bussardi, and Laura Biagiotti, whose threads are usually reserved for adult, rather than juvenile, playtime. Open on Monday from 3:30 to 7:30pm and Tuesday to Saturday from 9am to 1pm and 3:30 to 7:30pm.

Benetton. Via Condotti 19. ☎ **06/679-7982.**

Benetton isn't as expensive as you might expect. This store is the outlet for children's clothes (from infants to age 12) of the famous sportswear manufacturer. You can find rugby shirts, corduroys and jeans, and accessories in a wide selection of colors and styles. Open on Monday from 3:30 to 7:30pm and Tuesday to Saturday from 10am to 7:30pm.

The College. Via Vittoria 52. ☎ **06/678-4073.**

The College has everything you'll need to make adorable children more adorable. Part of the inventory is reserved for adult men and women, but the majority is intended for the infant and early adolescent offspring of the store's older clients. There's another branch at Via Condotti 47 (☎ 06/678-4036) that sells only clothes for women, not for children or men. Both branches maintain the same hours: on Monday from 3:30 to 7:30pm and Tuesday to Saturday from 9:30am to 1pm and 3:30 to 7:30pm.

Sportswear

Oliver. Via del Babuino 61. ☎ **06/3600-1906.**

Specializing exclusively in sportswear for men and for women, this is the least expensive line of clothing offered by the otherwise chillingly expensive designer Valentino. His clothing is easy to wear and casually stylish, with warm-weather climates in mind. Open on Monday from 3 to 7pm and Tuesday to Saturday from 10am to 7:30pm.

Food

Castroni. Via Cola di Rienzo 196. ☎ **06/687-4383.**

This place carries a bountiful array of unusual foodstuffs from throughout the Mediterranean. If you want herbs from Apulia, peperoncino oil, cheese from Val d'Aosta, or that strange brand of balsamic vinegar whose name you can never remember, Castroni will probably have it. Large, old-fashioned, and filled to the rafters with the abundance of agrarian Italy, it also carries certain foods considered exotic in Italy but commonplace in North America, such as taco shells and corn curls. Open Monday to Saturday from 8am to 2pm and 3:30 to 8pm.

Gifts

Anatriello del Regalo. Via Frattina 123. ☎ **06/678-9601.**

This store is known for stocking an inventory of new and antique silver, some of it among the most unusual in Italy. All the new items are made by Italian silversmiths, in designs ranging from the whimsical to the severely formal and dignified. Also on display are antique pieces of silver from England, Germany, and Switzerland. Open on Monday from 3:30 to 7:30pm and Tuesday to Saturday from 9am to 1pm and 3:30 to 7:30pm.

A. Grispigni. Via Francesco Crispi 59. ☎ **06/679-0290.**

This store has a large assortment of leather-covered boxes, women's purses, compacts, desk sets, and cigarette cases. Many items are inlaid with gold, including Venetian wallets and Florentine boxes. Open on Monday from 3:30 to 7pm and Tuesday to Saturday from 9:30am to 1pm and 3:30 to 7pm.

JEWELRY

Since the days when the ancient Romans imported amethysts and pearls from the distant borders of their empire, and when the great trading ships of Venice and Genoa carried rubies and sapphires from Asia, the Italians have always collected jewelry. Styles range from the most classically conservative to neo-punk-rock frivolous and part of the fun is shopping for styles you might never have considered to be truly your own.

Bulgari. Via Condotti 10. ☎ **06/679-3876.**

Bulgari is the capital's most prestigious jeweler and has been since the 1890s. The shop window, on a conspicuously affluent stretch of Via Condotti, is a bit of a visual attraction in its own right. Bulgari designs combine classical Greek aesthetics with Italian taste. Over the years Bulgari has followed changes in style, yet clings to tradition as well. Prices range from affordable to "the sky's the limit." Open on Monday from 3 to 7pm and Tuesday to Saturday from 10am to 7pm.

E. Fiore. Via Ludovisi 31. ☎ **06/481-9296.**

In this store near Via Veneto, you can choose a jewel and have it set according to your specifications. Or make your selection from a rich assortment of charms, bracelets, necklaces, rings, brooches, corals, pearls, and cameos. Also featured are elegant watches, silverware, and goldware. Fiore also does expert repair work on your own jewelry and watches. Open Monday to Saturday from 9am to 7pm (closed August).

Federico Buccellati. Via Condotti 31. ☎ **06/679-0329.**

One of the best gold- and silversmiths in Italy, Federico Buccellati sells neo-Renaissance creations that will change your thinking about the way gold and silver are designed. Here you'll discover the Italian tradition and beauty of handmade jewelry and hollowware whose principles sometimes hark back to the designs of Renaissance goldmaster Benvenuto Cellini. Open Tuesday to Saturday from 10am to 1:30pm and 3 to 7pm.

LEATHER

Italian leather is among the very best in the world, and at its best can attain butter-soft textures more pliable than cloth. You'll find hundreds of leather stores in Rome, many of them excellent.

Cesare Diomedi Leather Goods. Via Vittorio Emanuele Orlando 96–97. ☎ **06/488-4822.**

Located in front of the Grand Hotel, this store offers one of the most outstanding collections of leather goods in Rome. And leather isn't all you'll find in this small, two-story shop with a winding staircase. There are many other distinctive items, such as small gold cigarette cases and jeweled umbrellas, that make this a good stopping-off point for that last gift. Upstairs is a wide assortment of elegant leather luggage and accessories. Open Monday to Saturday from 9am to 1pm and 3:30 to 7:30pm.

Fendi. Via Borgognona 36A–39. ☎ **06/679-7641.**

The House of Fendi is mainly known for its leather goods, but it also has furs, stylish purses, ready-to-wear clothing, and a new men's line of clothing and accessories.

Gift items, home furnishings, and sports accessories are also sold here, all emblazoned with an "F." Open on Monday from 3:30 to 7:30pm and Tuesday to Saturday from 9:30am to 7:30pm; closed Saturday afternoon July to September.

Gucci. Via Condotti 8. ☎ **06/679-0405.**

Gucci, of course, is a legend. An established firm since 1900, it sells high-class leather goods, such as suitcases, handbags, wallets, shoes, and desk accessories. It also has departments complete with elegant men's and women's wear, including tailored shirts, blouses, and dresses, as well as ties and scarves of numerous designs. *La bella figura* is alive and well at Gucci, and prices have never been higher. Among the many temptations is Gucci's own perfume. Open on Monday from 3 to 7pm and Tuesday to Saturday from 10am to 7pm.

Pappagallo. Via Francesco Crispi 115. ☎ **06/678-3011.**

This is a suede and leather factory; the staff at this "parrot" makes their own goods, including bags, wallets, and suede coats. The quality is fine, and the prices are most reasonable. Open on Monday from 3:30 to 7:30pm and Tuesday to Saturday from 9am to 1pm and 3:30 to 7:30pm.

LINGERIE

Brighenti. Via Frattina 7–8. ☎ **06/679-1484.**

Brighenti sells strictly *lingerie di lusso,* or perhaps better phrased, *haute corseterie.* The shop is amid several famous neighbors on Via Frattina. Open on Monday from 3:30 to 7:30pm and Tuesday to Saturday from 9am to 1pm and 3:30 to 7:30pm; closed August.

Princesse Tam-Tam. Via Frattina 72. ☎ **06/679-2524.**

This is the exclusive distributor in Rome for a line of French women's undergarments that, considering their quality and style, and the store's location on one of the most spectacularly desirable shopping streets of Rome, are less expensive than you might have thought. Inventories include brassières, panties, slips and half-slips, and some of the most appealing women's pajamas in Italy. Some have touches of lace, but most items are crafted from cotton. Open on Monday from 3 to 7:30pm and Tuesday to Saturday from 10am to 1pm and 3 to 7:30pm.

Lengerie D'Elia. Via Sistina 119. ☎ **06/488-1909.**

This place offers delicately beautiful lingerie and negligées, all the original designs of Luisa Romagnoli. Most of the merchandise sold here is of shimmery Italian silk; other items, to a lesser degree, are of fluffy cotton or frothy nylon. Highly revealing garments are sold either ready-to-wear or custom-made. Open on Monday from 3:30 to 7:30pm and Tuesday to Sunday from 9am to 1pm and 3:30 to 7:30pm.

MARKETS

Piles of fresh vegetables arranged above ancient pavements in the streaming Italian sunshine is a sight few foreign visitors can resist. Here's a rundown on the Roman markets known for the freshest produce, the most colorful and uninhibited merchants, and the longest-running traditions.

Campo de' Fiori. Piazza Campo de' Fiori. Bus: 44, 46, 62, 70, 81, 90, 90B, or 492.

During the Renaissance this neighborhood contained most of the inns that pilgrims and merchants from other parts of Europe would use for lodgings. Today its battered and slightly shabby perimeter surrounds about a hundred merchants who arrange their produce every day into artful tapestries of Italian bounty. Most of the stalls are open Monday to Saturday from 7am to 1:30pm.

Mercato Andrea Doria. Via Andrea Doria. Metro: Ottaviano.

After a visit to this open-air festival of bounty, you might never again want to shop in a local supermarket. Set near the Vatican, on a large, sun-baked stretch of pavement between Via Tunisi and Via Santamaura, the merchandise includes meats, poultry, eggs, dairy products, wines, an endless assortment of *frutta e verdura,* and even some scruffy-looking racks of secondhand clothing. It's open Monday to Saturday from 7am to 1pm.

Mercato dei Fiori. Via Trionfale. Metro: Ottaviano.

Most of the week this vast covered market sells flowers only to retail florists, who resell them to consumers. Every Tuesday, however, the industrial-looking premises is open to the public, who crowd in for access to exotic, Mediterranean flowers at bargain-basement prices. Open to the public Tuesday from 10:30am to 1pm.

Mercato delle Stampe. Largo della Fontanella di Borghese. Bus: 44, 46, 62, or 64.

Virtually everything that's displayed in the dozens of battered kiosks here is dog-eared and evocatively ragtag. You'll find copies of engravings, books, magazines from the the 1960s or earlier, and prints and engravings that are either worthless or worthwhile, depending on their provenance. If your passion is the printed word, this is your place, and bargaining for value is part of the experience. Vendors remain in place Monday to Saturday from 7am to 1pm.

Mercato di Testaccio. Piazza Testaccio. Metro: Piramide.

Because their stalls are covered from the wind, rain, and dust of the rest of Rome, the vendors here are able to retain an air of permanence about their set-ups that most outdoor markets simply can't provide. Inside you'll find fishmongers, butchers, cheese sellers, a wide array of dairy products, and the inevitable fruits and vegetables of the Italian harvest. It's open Monday to Saturday from 7:30am to 1:30pm.

Mercato di Via Sannio. Via Sannio. Metro: San Giovanni in Laterano.

If you like street fairs loaded with items that verge on the junky, but which contain occasional nuggets of value or eccentric charm, this is the market for you. Regrettably, rare or unusual items are getting harder to find here, as every antiques dealer in Italy seems to have combed through the inventories long before your arrival. Despite that, you'll find some ragtag values in the endless racks of clothing that await cost-conscious buyers. Open Monday to Saturday from 8am to 1pm.

Porta Portese. Via Portuense and Via Ippolito Nievo. Bus: 170 or 280.

This is the largest and most famous *mercato delle pulci (*flea market) in Rome, a Sunday-morning staple that many Romans consider much, much more interesting and colorful than attending church. Vendors are likely to sell merchandise ranging from secondhand paintings of madonnas (the Italian market is glutted with these) to termite-eaten wooden Il Duce medallions. There are also pseudo-Etruscan hairpins, bushelsful of rosaries, television sets that haven't transmitted an image since 1965, books printed early in the l9th century, and rack after rack of secondhand (or never-sold) clothing. Serious shoppers can often ferret out a good buy in a setting that has thrived here since the end of World War II. By 10:30am the place is full of people, including vendors who sometimes arrive before dawn to get a desirable place to set up shop. As you would at any street market, beware of pickpockets. It's open only on Sunday, from 7am to 1pm.

Offbeat Shopping

- **Galleria 2 RC**, Via dei Delfini 16 (☎ 06/6992-2414), has the best print studio in Rome, a collection of beautifully reproduced works from famous artists. It's almost as good as owning the real thing.
- **Avignonese,** Via Margutta 16 (☎ 06/361-4004), can be counted on to come up with unusual and tasteful objects for the home. Each object, from lamps to terra-cotta boxes, appears unique and specially crafted.
- **Alinari,** Via d'Albert 16A (☎ 06/679-2923), takes its name from the famed Florentine photographer of the 19th century. Original prints of Alinari are almost as prized as paintings in national galleries. Photographs by him are sold here, a record of how Rome looked a century ago.
- **Olivi,** Via del Babuino 136 (☎ 06/3600-0064), is called "The Old Curiosity Shop of Rome." Professor Olivi is a whiz when it comes to knowing Roman history and collecting a treasure trove of old prints.
- **Fava,** Via del Babuino 180 (☎ 06/361-0807), recaptures the era when Neapolitans sold 17th- and 18th-century pictures of the eruptions of Vesuvius, once highly sought by collectors. Many of these "volcanic paintings" of yesterday—so eagerly purchased by Britishers in particular—can still cause a conflagration today. Really unusual art from the attics of yesterday.
- **Livio di Simone,** Via San Giacomo 23 (☎ 06/3600-1732), carries unusual suitcases (in many shapes and sizes) in which hand-painted canvas has been sewn into the bags. Every one is chic and lovely.
- **Battistoni,** Via Condotti 61A (☎ 06/678-6241), sells the finest men's shirts in the world. After having said that, as Marlene Dietrich once noted, you don't need to sell the shop anymore. In addition, they also hawk a men's cologne, called Marte (Mars), for the "man who likes to conquer."
- **Siragusa,** Via delle Carrozze 64 (☎ 06/679-7085), is more like a museum than a shop, specializing in unusual jewelry, based on ancient carved stones or archeological pieces. Handmade chains, for example, often hold coins and beads discovered in Asia Minor that date from the 3rd to the 4th century B.C.

MOSAICS

Savelli. Via Paolo VI 27. ☎ **06/6830-7017.**

This company specializes in the manufacture and sale of mosaics, an art form as old as the Roman Empire itself. Many of the objects in the company's gallery were inspired by ancient originals discovered in thousands of excavations throughout the Italian peninsula, including those at Pompeii and Ostia. Others, especially the floral designs, depend on the whim and creativity of the artists. Objects include tabletops, boxes, and vases. The cheapest mosaic objects begin at around $125, and are unsigned products crafted by students at a school for artists that's partially funded by the Vatican. Objects made in the Savelli workshops that are signed by the individual artists (and that tend to be larger and more elaborate) range from $500 to as much as $25,000. The outlet also contains a collection of small souvenir items such as keychains and carved statues. Open Monday to Saturday from 9am to 6:30pm and on Sunday from 9:30am to 1:30pm.

RELIGIOUS ART & FASHION

Anna Maria Guadenzi. Piazza della Minerva 69A. ☎ **06/679-0431.**

Set in a neighborhood loaded with purveyors of religious art and icons, this shop claims to be the oldest of its type in Rome. If you collect depictions of the Mother of Jesus, paintings of the saints, exotic rosaries, chalices, small statues, or medals, you can feel secure knowing that thousands of pilgrims have spent their money here before you. Whether you view its merchandise as a devotional aid or as bizarre kitsch, this shop has it all. Open on Monday from 3:30 to 7:30pm and Tuesday to Saturday from 9am to 1pm and 3:30 to 7:30pm; closed August 10 to 20.

Gamarelli. Via Santa Chiara 34. ☎ **06/6880-1314.**

Few laypeople ever really think about how or where a clergyman might clothe himself for mass, but in the Eternal City, the problem is an almost universal obsession. If you're looking for a gift for your parish priest, or a nephew who has decided to take the vows, head to this store that's known as the "Armani" of the priestly garment biz. Established 200 years ago, it employs a battalion of embroiderers, usually devout Catholics in their own right, who wield needles and either purple, scarlet, or gold threads like the legendary swords of the Counter-Reformation. The inventories are so comprehensive that priests, bishops, and cardinals from around the world consider the place a worthwhile stopover during their pilgrimages to Rome. The store does not stock any garments for nuns. It's open Monday to Friday from 8:30am to 1pm and 3:30 to 7:30pm.

SHOES

Dominici. Via del Corso 14. ☎ **06/361-0591.**

An understated facade a few steps from Piazza del Popolo shelters an amusing and lighthearted collection of men's and women's shoes in a rainbow variety of vivid colors. The style is aggressively young-at-heart, and the children's shoes are adorable. Open on Monday from 3:30 to 8pm and Tuesday to Saturday from 9:30am to 1pm and 3:30 to 8pm.

Fragiacomo. Via Condotti 35. ☎ **06/679-8780.**

Here you can buy shoes for both men and women in a champagne-colored showroom with gilt-touched chairs and big display cases. Open on Monday from 3:30 to 7:30pm and Tuesday to Saturday from 9:30am to 1:30pm and 3:30 to 7:30pm.

Lily of Florence. Via Lombardia 38 (off Via Vittorio Veneto). ☎ **06/474-0262.**

This famous Florentine shoemaker now has a shop in Rome, with the same merchandise that made the outlet so well known in the Tuscan capital. Colors come in a wide range, the designs are stylish, and leather texture is of good quality. Shoes for both men and women are sold here, and American sizes are a feature. Open Monday to Saturday from 9:30am to 7:30pm.

Salvatore Ferragamo. Via Condotti 73–74. ☎ **06/679-8402.**

Salvatore Ferragamo sells elegant and fabled footwear, plus women's clothing and accessories, ties, and ready-to-wear in an atmosphere full of Italian style. The name became famous in America when such screen stars as Pola Negri and Greta Garbo began appearing in Ferragamo shoes. There are always many customers waiting to enter the shop; management allows them in small groups. Figure on a 30-minute wait outside. Open Monday to Saturday from 10am to 7pm.

SILVER

Fornari. Via Frattina 133. ☎ **06/678-0105.**

In the mid-1990s one of Rome's most prestigious purveyors of silver and luxury goods was reconfigured and redefined after a family dispute altered the older and more distinguished format forever. The newest manifestation lies a short walk from the old setting, in a two-story showroom filled with silver, lamps, porcelain, crystal, furniture, and gift items from many different manufacturers throughout Italy and Europe. Virtually anything can be shipped to private homes or wedding receptions anywhere in the world. Open on Monday from 3 to 7pm and Tuesday to Saturday from 10am to 1pm and 3 to 7:30pm; closed August.

TOYS

La Città del Sole. Via della Scrofe 65. ☎ **06/687-5404.**

Other than the branch in Milan, this is the largest and best stocked of any of the stores in its 40-member chain. It specializes in amusements for children and adults, with a wide range of toys and games that don't require computers to operate. Many of the games are configured in English, others in Italian, and include the raw materials for the kind of pastimes that a family or inmates of a college dorm could spend time pursuing. Examples include role-playing games, battlefield strategy games, family games, and children's games that will challenge a young person's gray matter and probably drive their parents crazy. Also for sale are such rainy-day distractions as miniature billiards tables and tabletop golf sets. Open on Monday from 3:30 to 7:30pm and Tuesday to Saturday from 10am to 7:30pm.

WINES & LIQUORS

Ai Monasteri. Piazza delle Cinque Lune 76. ☎ **06/6880-2783.**

Italy produces a staggering volume of wines, liqueurs, and after-dinner drinks, and here you'll find one of the city's best selections. It offers a treasure trove of liquors (including liqueurs and wines), honey, and herbal teas made in monasteries and convents all over Italy. You can buy excellent chocolates and other candies here as well. The shop will ship some items home for you. You make your selections in a quiet atmosphere, reminiscent of a monastery, just 2 blocks from Piazza Navona. Open Monday to Wednesday and on Friday and Saturday from 9am to 1pm and 4:30 to 7:30pm, and on Thursday from 9am to 1pm and 5 to 8pm; closed August.

Buccone. Via Ripetta 19. ☎ **06/361-2154.**

This is a historic wine shop, right near Piazza del Popolo. Its selection of wines and gastronomic specialties is among the finest in Rome. Open Monday to Saturday from 9am to 1:30pm and 4 to 8pm.

Trimani. Via Goito 20. ☎ **06/446-9661.**

Trimani, established in 1821, sells wines and spirits from Italy, among other offerings. Purchases can be shipped to your home. It collaborates with the Italian wine magazine *Gambero Rosso,* organizing some lectures about wine where devotees can improve their knowledge and educate their tastebuds. Open Monday to Saturday from 8:30am to 1:30pm and 3:30 to 8pm and on Sunday from 10am to 1:30pm and 4 to 7:30pm.

9 Rome After Dark

When the sun goes down, lights across the city bathe palaces, ruins, fountains, and monuments in a theatrical white light. There are few things quite as pleasurable as a stroll past the solemn pillars of old temples, or the cascading torrents of **Renaissance fountains** glowing under the blue-black sky. Of the fountains, the Naiads (Piazza della Repubblica), the Tortoises (Piazza Mattei), and of course, the Trevi are particularly alluring. The **Capitoline Hill** is panoramically lit at night (behind the Senatorial Palace is a fine view of the **Roman Forum**). If you're staying across the Tiber, **Piazza San Pietro** (in front of St. Peter's Basilica) is particularly impressive at night, when the tour buses and crowds have departed. And a combination of illuminated architecture, Renaissance fountains, and, frequently, sidewalk stage shows and art expositions is at **Piazza Navona.** If you're ambitious and have a good sense of direction, try exploring the streets west of Piazza Navona, which look like a stage set when they're lit at night.

There are no inexpensive nightclubs in Rome, so be duly warned. Another important warning: Between mid-June and late-August, central Rome abandons all hope of gaining access to worthwhile discos, since any of them worth their salt move to seaside venues in either Ostia or Fregene. If it's midsummer and you're dying to go dancing, phone any of the clubs in this survey and calls will be rerouted to the new, temporary seaside venue. Whether or not you'll consider the westward trek worth the trouble is another matter. You might opt instead for a bout of evening urban strolls and barhopping instead. Other clubs close at different times each year, so it's hard to keep up-to-date. Always have your hotel check to see if a club is operating before you make a trek to it. Furthermore, many of the legitimate nightclubs, besides being expensive, are frequented by hookers plying their trade.

But remember that for many Romans, a night on the town means dining late at a trattoria. The local denizens like to drink wine and talk after their meal, even when the waiters are putting chairs on top of empty tables.

For information about events in Rome, pick up a copy of ***This Week in Rome,*** which is distributed free at the tourist office and often is available at hotel reception desks. It spotlights seasonal entertainment and documents events of special interest.

Even if you don't speak Italian, you can generally follow the listings of special events and evening entertainment featured in ***La Repubblica,*** one of the leading Italian newspapers. ***TrovaRoma,*** a special weekly entertainment supplement—good for the coming week—is published in this paper on Thursday.

1 The Performing Arts

MAJOR COMPANIES

Rome's premier cultural venue is the Teatro dell'Opera (see below), where standards may not be as high as at Milan's legendary La Scala, but where performances are stellar nevertheless. The outstanding local troupe is the **Rome Opera Ballet** (see below).

Rome doesn't have a major center for classical music concerts, although performances of the most important orchestra, the **RAI Symphony Orchestra,** most often take place at the RAI Auditorium as well as at the Academy of St. Cecilia (see below).

Rome is also a major stopover for international stars. Rock headliners often perform at **Stadio Flaminio, Foro Italico,** and at two different places in the EUR, the **Palazzo della Civilità del Lavoro** and the **Palazzo dello Sport.** Most of the concerts are at the Palazzo dello Sport. Instead of trying to call these venues, contact a ticket agent, **Orbis,** Piazza Esquilino 37 (☎ **06/474-4776**), which not only will let you know what's happening in Rome at the time of your visit, but will also sell you a ticket to the performance. The Orbis box office is open Monday to Friday from 9:30am to 1pm and 4 to 7:30pm and on Saturday from 10am to 1pm.

CLASSICAL MUSIC

Academy of St. Cecilia. Via della Conciliazione 4. ☎ **06/678-0742.** Tickets 25,000L–80,000L ($16–$51.20). Bus: 30.

Concerts given by the orchestra of the Academy of St. Cecilia usually take place at Piazza di Villa Giulia, site of the Etruscan Museum, from the end of June to the end of July; in winter they're held in the concert hall on Via della Conciliazione. Depending on circumstances, the organization sometimes selects other addresses in Rome for its concerts, including a handful of historic churches, when available.

Teatro Olimpico. Piazza Gentile da Fabriano. ☎ **06/323-4890.** Tickets 20,000L–80,000L ($12.80–$51.20), depending on the event.

Large and well publicized, this echoing stage hosts a widely divergent collection of singers, both classical and pop, who perform according to a schedule that sometimes changes at the last minute. Occasionally the space is devoted to chamber orchestras or visits by foreign orchestras.

OPERA

Teatro dell'Opera. Piazza Beniamino Gigli 1. ☎ **06/481601.** Tickets 20,000L–260,000L ($12.80–$166.40).

If you're in the capital for the opera season, usually from the end of December until June, you may want to attend a performance at the historic Rome Opera House, located off Via Nazionale. In the summer the venue switches to Piazza di Siena. Nothing is presented here in August.

BALLET & DANCE

Performances of the **Rome Opera Ballet** are given at the Teatro dell'Opera (see above). The regular repertoire of classical ballet is supplemented by performances of internationally acclaimed guest artists, and Rome is on the agenda for major troupes from around the world. Also, watch for announcements in the weekly entertainment guides to Rome about venues other than the Teatro dell'Opera, including the Teatro Olimpico or even open-air ballet performances. Both modern (such as the Alvin Ailey dancers) and classical dance troupes appear frequently in Rome. Check the entertainment guides to see what's happening at the time of your visit.

DINNER THEATER

Fantasie di Trastevere. Via di Santa Dorotea 6. ☎ **06/588-1671.** Cover 35,000L ($22.40) including the first drink, 75,000L–80,000L ($48–$51.20) including dinner.

In this unusual place you'll be instantly immersed in the bravura and gaiety of uninhibited Roman nightlife. The setting is the "people's theater," where the famous actor, Petrolini, made his debut. You dine on hearty regional cuisine while you're entertained by some two dozen folk singers and musicians performing in regional attire, making it a festive affair. Some of their songs are old Roman and Neapolitan favorites; others are esoteric. Meals are served daily beginning at 8pm, and piano bar music is offered from 8:30 to 9:30pm, followed by the show, lasting from 9:30 to 10:30pm.

2 The Club & Music Scene

NIGHTCLUBS

Alien. Via Vellertri 13–17. ☎ **06/841-2212.** Cover (including the first drink) 30,000L–38,000L ($19.20–$24.30).

In a setting devoted to celebrating hi-tech, futuristic rows of exposed pipes and ventilation ducts, you'll find a deliberatly bizarre space-age view of future shock, bathed in strobe lights and electronic music. Dull moments in any evening are punctuated with a cabaret-esque master or mistress of ceremonies whose brief interludes of cabaret or comedy accent a diet of very new-wave music. Open Monday to Sunday from 11pm to 6am.

Alpheus. Via del Commercio 36. ☎ **06/574-7826.** Cover (including the first drink) 15,600L ($10).

One of Rome's largest and most energetic nightclubs contains three sprawling rooms, each with a different musical sound and an ample number of bars. You'll find areas devoted to Latin music packed with Spanish-speaking Catholics eager for a break from too constant an exposure to Rome's churches, other areas playing rock, and an area devoted to jazz. Live bands come and go, and there's enough cultural variety in the crowd to keep virtually anyone amused throughout the course of the evening. Open Tuesday to Sunday from 10:30pm to 4am.

Arciliuto. Piazza Monte Vecchio 5. ☎ **06/687-9419.** Cover (including the first drink) 35,000L ($22.40).

One of the most romantic candlelit spots in Rome is reputedly the former studio of Raphael. Guests enjoy a musical salon ambience, listening to both a guitarist and a lutenist. The evening's presentation also includes Neapolitan love songs, old Italian madrigals, even current hits from New York's Broadway or London's West End. The setting and atmosphere are intimate. Drinks run 10,000L ($6.40). Highly recommended, it's hard to find, but it's within walking distance of Piazza Navona. Open Monday to Saturday from 10pm to 2am; closed July 20 to September 3.

Black Out. Via Saturnia 18. ☎ **06/7049-6791.** Cover (including the first drink) 10,000L–15,000L ($6.40–$9.60).

Counterculture, blasé, and clinging to musical models of the punk-rock and UK-Indie culture of faraway London, Black Out occupies an industrial-looking site that opens between 1am and 4am only on Friday and Saturday. Whenever it can manage, a live band is presented Thursday—very late. It's one of the best sites in town for a view of counterculture alienation and rage as interpreted by modern Italian youth. Recorded music (Friday and Saturday) includes punk, retro, rhythm and blues, grunge, and whatever else happens to be in fashion at the moment of your arrival. The Thursday-night live acts, when presented at all, can be just about anything.

La Cabala / The Blue Bar / Hostaria dell'Orso. Via dei Soldati 25. ☎ **06/686-4221.** Cover: Blue Bar, none; La Cabala (including the first drink), 15,000L–35,000L ($9.60–$22.40).

During the heyday of *la dolce vita,* these premises were the most talked-about evening venue of Rome, attracting elegant Italians and well-heeled foreigners throughout the 1950s and 1960s. Today the spotlight has shifted to other venues, although many Romans continue to view the place with affection and nostalgia. The setting is a 14th-century palazzo, near Piazza Navona, which began its life as a simple inn. Clients who have used its dining and/or overnight facilities through the ages have included Dante, Rabelais, Montaigne, Goethe, and thousands of other, less well-documented scholars and pilgrims.

Today the establishment contains three separate areas: In the cellar, the Blue Bar is a moody but mellow enclave featuring cocktails and music from two pianists and a guitarist. Drinks run 15,000L to 35,000L ($9.60 to $22.40). On street level is a formal restaurant serving international cuisine, the Hostaria dell'Orso, charging 25,000L to 50,000L ($16 to $32) for main courses. Menu items include spigolo in cartoccio con frutti di mar (sea bass cooked in a paper bag, garnished with shellfish) and spaghetti in cartoccio with lobster and risotto served with scampi and radicchio. One floor above street level is La Cabala, a disco that attracts a well-dressed, over-25 crowd. Some clients visit all three areas during a night on the town, although no one will mind if you decide to patronize only the disco or only the bar. The restaurant serves dinner Monday to Saturday from 7:30pm to midnight. The Blue Bar and La Cabala are open Monday to Saturday from 10:30pm to 3 or 4am, depending on business. All three floors are closed on Sunday. If you plan to dine here, reservations are recommended.

Club Picasso. Via Monte di Testaccio 63. ☎ **06/574-2975.** Free Tues–Thurs; 15,000L ($9.60) Fri–Sat (including the first drink).

Everything about this place was inspired by a large, gregarious nightclub in a place like Los Angeles, where R&B, rock, and funk blare out across a crowd that loves to dance, dance, dance. Don't expect only a crowdful of teeny-boppers, as clients here include 20-year-olds to 50-year-olds (who remember some of the music as original to their college years), with lots of high-energy people-watchers in between. Beer begins at 10,000L ($6.40). A bouncer at the door maintains strict provisions against anyone who looks like troublemaking is part of his or her agenda. Open Tuesday to Saturday from 10pm to 4am.

Folkstudio. Via Frangipane 42. ☎ **06/487-1063.** Tickets 10,000L–20,000L ($6.40–$12.80), plus a one-time membership fee of 5,000L ($3.20).

Very little about this place has changed since it was founded in 1962. It prides itself on a battered and well-used venue that resembles "an old underground cantina" from the earliest days of the hippie era. The PA system and lighting aren't very sophisticated, but the ambience is refreshing and can be fun, and the musical acts

Major Concert & Performance Halls

Rome Opera House (Teatro dell'Opera)	☎ 06/481601
Academy of St. Cecilia	☎ 06/678-0742
Teatro Olimpico	☎ 06/323-4890

manage to draw some surprisingly likable performers of old-fashioned soul music, gospel, funk, and folk, as well as traditional music from such countries as Ireland. From time to time a musician might even break into a recital of poetry that's more or less gracefully interspersed with the music. Some kind of act is presented Tuesday to Sunday from 9:30 to 11pm. No drinks are served inside, as the place considers itself a concert hall rather than a nightclub, but several bars and cafés in the neighborhood sell bottles of beer and whisky in plastic cups to go, and no one at Folkstudio will object if you carry them in with you. The place is closed from early July until late September.

Gilda. Via Mario de' Fiori 97. ☎ **06/678-4838.** Cover (including the first drink) 40,000L ($25.60).

Gilda is an adventurous combination of nightclub, disco, and restaurant known for the glamorous acts it books. Past performances have included Diana Ross and splashy, Paris-type revues, often with young women from England and the United States. The artistic direction assures first-class shows, a well-run restaurant, three bars, and the latest disco music played between the live musical acts. The restaurant and pizzeria open at 9:30pm and occasionally present shows. An international cuisine is featured, with meals costing from 35,000L ($22.40). The nightclub opens at midnight, presenting music of the 1960s as well as modern recordings, and closes at 4am. There's also an attractive piano bar on the premises called Swing, featuring Italian and Latin American music.

The Gossip Café. Via Romagnosi 11A. ☎ **06/361-1348.** Cover (including the first drink): Tues–Thurs, 15,000L ($9.60); Fri–Sat, 15,000L ($9.60) for women, 25,000L ($16) for men.

The Gossip Café, formerly Divina, is a chic rendezvous, a relaxing piano bar, and a raging disco. The owners are the same, but the look has been updated. The tables are smaller and are clustered around an expanded dance floor. You can still have a romantic evening, but you can also find a trendy spot to dance the night away. It's open Tuesday to Saturday from 11pm to either 4 or 5am. *Note:* It's important to call for a reservation, as some nights are by invitation only, at which time you can't get in unless you're a "friend of the club" (frequent patron).

Heaven. Via di Porta Ardeatina 118A, Ostiense. ☎ **06/522-0560.** Cover (including the first drink) 38,000L ($24.30).

Its enormous dance floor, flashing lights, and cheerful music emulates more than most other clubs the upbeat disco ambience of the 1970s and 1980s. Come here for what usually turns out to be an uncomplicated rendezvous in a setting that includes such musical themes as garage, house, and old-fashioned rock 'n' roll. Live bands intersperse their music with recorded imports. Open Tuesday to Saturday from 11pm to 4am.

Magic Fly. Via Bassanello 15, Cassia-Grottarossa. ☎ **06/3326-8956.** Cover (including the first drink) 10,000L–30,000L ($6.40–$19.20).

Small-scale, and somewhat cramped when it really begins to rock, this club is more elegant than the norm, and lies outside the ring road that encircles the center of Rome, about 3 miles northeast of the city's center. It changes its sound depending on the night of the week, and might include Latin salsa and merengue, American-style rock, or British new wave, according to a schedule that most of underground, late-night Rome seems to understand instinctively. Throughout the place, there's often a sense of posh that encourages many of the men to wear neckties. Transportation to the place is invariably a taxi. Open Wednesday to Saturday from 11pm to dawn.

Radio Londra. Via Monte Testaccio. No phone. Cover 10,000L ($6.40).

More than any other club on this list of recommendations, this one revels in the counterculture ambience of punk rock, inspired, as its name would imply, by the chartreuse-haired, nose-pierced devotees so common in London. There's no phone, and very few rules inside, except for an emphasis on allowing clients to look and act as weird and freaky as possible. Drinks begin at around 5,000L ($3.20) each. It's open Wednesday to Sunday from midnight till dawn.

Yes, Brazil. Via San Francesco a Ripa 103. ☎ **06/581-6267.** No cover.

This is one of Rome's most animated and popular Latin music nightspots. Set in Trastevere in the dimly lit recesses of a building erected in the 1500s, it manages to incorporate mobs of Italians and South Americans who dip and sway to dance steps that usually manage to be some derivation of Brazil's most famous dance, the samba. There's live music every night of the week, a point of honor at a club that keeps its dependence on recorded music to a minimum. It's open every night from 9:30pm to 2am. No cover is imposed, and beer ranges in price from 8,000L to 10,000L ($5.10 to $6.40); a whisky and soda goes for 12,000L ($7.70).

CABARET

Da Ciceruacchio. Via del Porto 1 (on Piazza dei Mercanti). ☎ **06/580-6046.**

This Trastevere restaurant was once a sunken jail—the ancient vine-covered walls date from the days of the Roman Empire. Folkloric groups are presented throughout the evening, especially singers of Neapolitan songs, accompanied by guitars and harmonicas—a rich repertoire of old-time favorites, some of them with bawdy lyrics. Featured here are charcoal-broiled steaks and chops, along with lots of local wine. Bean soup is a specialty. The grilled mushrooms are another good opening, as is the spaghetti with clams. For a main course, we'd recommend scampi with curry or charcoal-broiled meats. You can dine here Tuesday to Sunday from 8pm to midnight for 35,000L to 60,000L ($22.40 to $38.40).

Da Meo Patacca. Piazza dei Mercanti 30. ☎ **06/5833-1086.**

Da Meo Patacca, in Trastevere, would have pleased Barnum and Bailey. On a gaslit piazza from the Middle Ages, it serves bountiful self-styled "Roman country" meals to flocks of tourists. The atmosphere is one of extravaganza—primitive, colorful, theatrical in a carnival sense. It's good fun if you're in the mood. From the huge open-spit oven and the charcoal grill, many hastily turned out platters are served. Downstairs is a vast cellar with strolling musicians and singers. The restaurant has a tavern theme and is decked out with wagon wheels, along with garlands of pepper and garlic. And many offerings are as adventurous as the decor—wild boar, wild hare, and quail—but there are also corn on the cob, pork and beans, thick-cut sirloins, and chicken on a spit. Come here for the general fun and entertainment—not for refined cuisine. Expect to spend 60,000L ($38.40) and up for a meal here. In summer, you can dine at outdoor tables. It's open daily from 8 to 11:30pm.

JAZZ, SOUL & FUNK

Alexanderplatz. Via Ostia 9. ☎ **06/3974-2171.** Club membership (valid for 3 months) 12,000L ($7.70).

At this leading jazz club, you can hear jazz (not rock) Monday to Saturday from 9pm to 2am, with live music beginning at 10:15pm. A whisky begins at 10,000L ($6.40). There's also a restaurant, with a good kitchen, which serves everything from pesto alla genovese to gnocchi alla romana to Japanese cuisine. Full meals cost 35,000L to 40,000L ($22.40 to $25.60).

Big Mama. Vicolo San Francesco a Ripa 18. ☎ **06/581-2551.** Club membership (a one-time charge) 20,000L ($12.80). No cover for minor shows; 20,000L–30,000L ($12.80–$19.20) for big acts.

Big Mama is a hangout for jazz and blues musicians where you're likely to meet the up-and-coming jazz stars of tomorrow. But sometimes the big names appear as well. The entrance fee depends on what's being presented. Drinks range from 5,000L to 12,000L ($3.20 to $7.70). Closed July to September, the club is open Monday to Saturday from 9pm to 1:30am.

Fonclea. Via Crescenzio 82A. ☎ **06/689-6302.** No cover Sun–Fri; 10,000L ($6.40) Sat.

Fonclea offers live music every night—jazz, Dixieland, rock, rhythm and blues, and funk. This is basically a cellar jazz establishment that attracts a wide spectrum of Roman life. The music starts at 9:15pm and usually lasts until 12:30am. The club is open nightly from 7pm to 2am (to 3:30am on Friday and Saturday). There's also a restaurant that features grilled meats, salads, and crêpes. A meal starts at 35,000L ($22.40), but if you want dinner it's best to reserve a table, as the club becomes crowded after 10:30pm. Drinks run 5,000L to 12,000L ($3.20 to $7.70). Closed July and August.

Music Inn. Largo dei Fiorentini 3. ☎ **06/6880-2220.** Cover 15,000L ($9.60).

The Music Inn is among the leading jazz clubs of Rome. Some of the biggest names in jazz, both European and American, have performed here. It's open Thursday to Sunday from 8pm to 2am. Closed in July and August.

Notorious. Via San Nicolà de Tolentino 22. ☎ **06/474-6888.** Cover (including the first drink) 40,000L ($25.60).

Notorious really isn't. It's one of the most popular discos in the city, and the music is always recorded. Some of the most beautiful people of Rome show up in these crowded confines, often in their best disco finery. But show up late—it's more fashionable. It's open Tuesday to Saturday from 11pm to 4am.

Saint Louis Music City. Via del Cardello 13A. ☎ **06/474-5076.** Cover (including club membership) 7,000L ($4.50).

This is another leading jazz venue. In large, contemporary surroundings, it doesn't necessarily attract the big names in jazz; what you get instead are young and sometimes very talented groups beginning their careers. Many celebrities have been known to patronize the place. Soul and funk music are performed on occasion. You can also enjoy meals at a restaurant on the premises, which cost 35,000L ($22.40) and up. Drinks range from 8,000L to 12,000L ($5.10 to $7.70). It's open Tuesday to Sunday from 9pm to 2am.

GAY & LESBIAN CLUBS

Angelo Azzuro. Via Cardinal Merry del Val 13. ☎ **06/580-0472.** Cover (including the first drink) 10,000L ($6.40) Fri and Sun; 20,000L ($12.80) Sat.

Angelo Azzuro is a gay "hot spot," deep in the heart of Trastevere, which is open Friday, Saturday, and Sunday from 11pm to 4am. No food is served, nor is live music presented. Men dance with men to recorded music, and women are also invited to patronize the club. Friday is for women only. Additional libations cost 10,000L ($6.40) each.

The Hangar. Via in Selci 69. ☎ **06/488-1397.**

Established in 1984 by an expatriate, Louisiana-born American, John, and his Italian partner, Gianni, this is the premier gay bar in Rome. It's set on one of Rome's oldest streets, adjacent to the Roman Forum in the house on the site of the palace inhabited by the emperor Nero's deranged wife, Messalina. (Her ghost is rumored to inhabit the premises.) Each of the establishment's two bars has its own independent sound system.

Women are welcome any night except Monday, when videos and entertainment for gay men are featured. The busiest nights are Saturday, Sunday, and Monday, when as many as 500 patrons cram inside. Beer starts at 6,000L ($3.85); whisky, at 10,000L ($6.40). It's open Wednesday to Monday from 10:30pm to 2:30am. The Hangar is closed 3 weeks in August.

Joli Coeur. Via Sirte 5. ☎ **06/8621-5827.** Cover (including the first drink) 10,000L ($6.40).

Open only on Saturday and Sunday nights from 10:30pm to 2am, this bar caters to gay women. Saturday night is reserved for women only, although Sunday the crowd can be mixed. A fixture in the city's lesbian nighttime scene, it attracts women from around Europe during its very limited opening hours. Information about Joli Coeur (which translates as "Pretty Heart") is offered at The Hangar (see above), because of the difficulties in reaching Joli Coeur directly. After the obligatory first drink, subsequent libations cost 10,000L ($6.40) and up.

L'Alibi. Via Monte Testaccio 44. ☎ **06/574-3448.** Cover 10,000L ($6.40) Thurs; 12,000L ($7.70) Wed and Fri–Sun. Bus: 20N or 30N from Largo Argentina near the Piramide.

L'Alibi, in the Testaccio sector, away from the heart of Rome, is a year-round venue on many a gay man's agenda. The crowd, however, tends to be mixed, both Roman and international, straight and gay, male and female. One room is devoted to dancing. It's open Wednesday to Sunday from 11pm to 5am. Drinks run 10,000L ($6.40).

3 The Café & Bar Scene

It seems there's nothing Romans like to do better than sit and talk over their favorite beverage—usually wine or coffee. So it's not surprising that there are a variety of places in which you, too, can enjoy these pleasures.

CAFES

ON VIA VENETO

The most famous of the cafés of Rome are on Via Vittorio Veneto. While they line the streets from Piazza Barberini all the way to the Pincian Gate, the best are near the latter landmark. The most famous are Harry's Bar and the Caffè de Paris.

This area, once exclusive and expensive—now only expensive—is still a much-visited part of town, with stores selling jewelry and airline tickets.

Those old enough to remember the 1950s may recall Marcello Mastroianni fighting off the paparazzi here in *La Dolce Vita.* You'll probably spend at least one night on Via Veneto. Few visitors want to miss it.

Caffè de Paris. Via Veneto 90. ☎ **06/488-5284.**

The Caffè de Paris rises and falls in popularity, depending on the decade. In the 1950s it was a haven for the fashionable; it's now a popular restaurant in summer where you can occupy a counter seat along a bar or a table inside. However, if the weather's right, the tables spill right out onto the sidewalk and the passing crowd walks through. Coffee starts at 6,000L ($3.85) if you sit outside but only 1,200L (75¢) if you stand at the bar. A whisky and soda goes for 12,000L ($7.70). Open Thursday to Tuesday from 8am to 1am.

Harry's Bar. Via Veneto 50. ☎ **06/484643.**

Harry's Bar is the choicest watering spot along this gilded street. It has no connection to the world-famous Harry's Bars in Florence, Venice, Paris, and other cities. In many respects, the Roma Harry's is the most elegant of them all, with tapestry walls, elaborate wood paneling, curvy plastering, and sconces.

You can have excellent, but outrageously priced, food here as well, taking your meal in summer (if you prefer) at one of the sidewalk tables. In back is a small dining room, which serves some of the finest food in central Rome; meals go for 90,000L to 100,000L ($57.60 to $64). A whisky costs 9,000L to 12,000L ($5.75 to $7.70). The restaurant is open Monday to Saturday from 12:30 to 3pm and 7:30pm to 12:30am. The bar is open Monday to Saturday from 11:30am to 1:30am; closed August 1 to 10.

On Piazza del Popolo

The fashion-conscious denizens of Rome, known as the *bella gente,* or Beautiful People, are seldom seen on Via Veneto anymore. Instead some of them make a point to be seen (especially after midnight) in Piazza del Popolo. There's an element of excitement in the air here—the feeling that something interesting is just about to happen. The little outdoor tables of the two leading sidewalk cafés sprawl far and wide. They're surrounded by expensive Italian sports cars, elegant women with German accents, and men in leather pants.

Café Rosati. Piazza del Popolo 4–5. ☎ **06/322-5859.**

The chicest place to go for a drink has been in business since 1923. Originally it was more or less an ice-cream parlor. Light food items are available, but most people order a drink, a beer, or a dish of ice cream. You can sit out front at one of the tables spreading into the piazza. There's a constant stream of low, growling Maseratis cruising slowly by while young Italian men in silk shirts hang from the car windows, eying sleek blondes. Drinks are more expensive, of course, if you select a table. But who wants to stand at the bar? Whisky at a table starts at 10,000L ($6.40). Open daily from 7:30am to 1am. Food is served in the restaurant daily from noon to 4pm.

Canova Café. Piazza del Popolo. ☎ **06/361-2231.**

Although the management has filled the interior of this café with boutiques selling expensive gift items, including luggage and cigarette lighters, many Romans still consider this *the* place to be on Piazza del Popolo. The Canova has a sidewalk terrace for pedestrian-watching, plus a snack bar, a restaurant, and a wine shop inside. In summer you'll have access to a quiet courtyard whose walls are covered with ivy and where flowers grow in terra-cotta planters. Expect to spend 1,300L (85¢) for a coffee at the stand-up bar; if you order at a table, coffee costs 5,300L ($3.40). A meal is offered for around 18,000L ($11.50). Food is served daily from noon to 3:30pm and 7 to 11pm, but the bar is open daily from 7am to midnight or 1am.

In Trastevere

Just as Piazza del Popolo lured the chic crowd from Via Vittorio Veneto, several cafés in Trastevere, across the Tiber, threaten to do the same for Popolo. Fans who saw Fellini's *Roma* know what Piazza di Santa Maria in Trastevere looks like. The square—filled with milling throngs in summer—is graded with an octagonal fountain and a church dating from the 12th century. On the piazza, despite a certain amount of traffic, children run and play, and occasional spontaneous guitar fests are heard when the weather's good.

Café-Bar di Marzio. Piazza di Santa Maria in Trastevere 18B. ☎ **06/581-6095.**

This warmly inviting place, which is strictly a café (not a restaurant), has both indoor and outdoor tables at the edge of the square with the best view of its famous fountain. Whisky begins at 9,000L ($5.75), and a coffee goes for 3,000L ($1.90). It's open Tuesday to Saturday from 7am to 2am.

Near the Pantheon

Despite the allures of Trastevere, many visitors to the Eternal City now view Piazza della Rotonda, at the Pantheon, as the "living room" of Rome. (It's also much easier to get to, and there always seem to be more taxis available than in the narrow streets of somewhat remote Trastevere.) The neighborhood around the Pantheon (which many visitors consider their favorite building anywhere in Europe) is especially popular on a summer night.

Caffè Sant'Eustachio. Piazza Sant'Eustachio 82. ☎ **06/686-1309.**

Strongly brewed coffee is one of the elixirs of Italy, and many Romans will walk many blocks for what they consider a superior brew. One of the most talked-about espresso shops, Sant'Eustachio, is on a small square near the Pantheon, where the city water supply comes from a source outside Rome that the emperor Augustus funneled in with an aqueduct in 19 B.C. Rome's most experienced judges of espresso claim that the water plays an important part in the coffee's flavor, although steam forced through ground Brazilian coffee roasted on the premises has an effect as well. Purchase a ticket from the cashier for as many cups of coffee as you want, and leave a small tip of 200L (15¢) for the counterman when he gives you your receipt. Coffee costs 1,400L (90¢) if you're standing, 3,000L ($1.90) at a table. Open Tuesday to Friday and on Sunday from 8:30am to 1am, and on Saturday from 8:30am to 1:30am.

Di Rienzo. Piazza della Rotonda 8–9. ☎ **06/686-9097.**

This is the most desirable café here, and in fair weather you can sit at one of the sidewalk tables (if you can find one that's available). In cooler weather you can retreat inside the elegant café, whose walls are inlaid with the same type of marble found on the floor of the Pantheon. Many types of pasta appear on the menu, as does risotto alla pescatora (fisher's rice) and several meat courses such as roast veal. Coffee costs 4,000L ($2.55) at a table or 1,200L (75¢) at the bar. The restaurant is open daily from 7am to either 1 or 2am.

On the Corso

Café Alemagna. Via del Corso 181. ☎ **06/678-9135.**

Alemagna is a monumental café usually filled with busy shoppers. On the premises is just about every kind of dining facility a hurried resident of Rome could want, including a stand-up sandwich bar with dozens of selections available from behind a glass case, a cafeteria, and a sit-down area with waiter service. The decor includes high coffered ceilings, baroque wall stencils, glove lights, crystal chandeliers, and black stone floors. Pastries start at 1,700L ($1.10); coffee, at 1,300L to 1,600L (85¢ to $1). It's open daily from 7am to 10pm.

Near the Spanish Steps

Antico Caffè Greco. Via Condotti 86. ☎ **06/679-1700.**

This café has been reputed for many years to be both the place of origin and the relay point for much of the gossip of Rome's most glamorous shopping district. The Greco is considerably older than the other cafés mentioned; in fact, it has been serving drinks in its front-room bar since 1760. Over the years it has attracted such notables as Goethe, Stendhal, and D'Annunzio. Lying half a block from the foot of the Spanish Steps, it still retains a 19th-century atmosphere. The waiters wearing black tailcoats seat you at small marble tables. Beyond the carved wooden bar are four or five small, elegant rooms whose walls are covered with silk and hung with oil paintings in gilded frames. The house specialty is a paradiso, made with lemon and orange, costing 10,000L ($6.40), and light sandwiches are also available. The café is open Monday to Saturday from 8am to 9pm, but closed for 10 days in August (days vary).

Near Piazza Colonna

Giolitti. Via Uffici del Vicario 40. ☎ **06/699-1243.**

For devotees of gelato (addictively tasty ice cream), Giolitti is one of the city's most popular nighttime gathering spots—in the evening, it's thronged with strollers with a sweet tooth. To satisfy that craving, try a whipped cream–topped Giolitti cup of gelato. The ice cream costs 3,500L ($2.20) and up. Some of the sundaes look like Vesuvius about to erupt. If you sit at a table and order one, the cost is from 8,000L ($5.10). Good-tasting snacks are also served during the day.

Many people take gelato out to eat on the streets, whereas others enjoy it in the post-Empire splendor of the salon inside. You can have your *coppa* from 7am to 2am Tuesday to Sunday. There are many excellent, smaller gelateria throughout Rome, wherever you see the cool concoction advertised as *produzione propria* (homemade).

Near Piazza Navona

Bar della Pace. Via della Pace 3–5. ☎ **06/686-1216.**

The Bar della Pace, located near Piazza Navona, has elegant neighbors, such as Santa Maria della Pace, a church with sybils by Raphael and a cloister designed by Bramante. The bar dates from the beginning of this century, with wood, marble, and mirrors forming its decor. It's open Tuesday to Sunday from 11am to 2:30am. A whisky begins at 10,000L ($6.40).

Hemingway. Piazza delle Coppelle 10. ☎ **06/686-4490.**

Hemingway is hidden behind a discreet door off one of the most obscure piazzas in Rome. Inside, the owners have re-created a 19th-century decor beneath soaring vaulted ceilings that shimmer from the reflection of various glass chandeliers. An interior room repeats in scarlet what the first room did with shades of emerald. Evocations of a Liberty-style salon are strengthened by the sylvan murals and voluptuous portraits of reclining odalisques. Assorted painters, writers, and creative dilettantes occupy the clusters of overstuffed armchairs and listen to classical music. Drinks begin at 10,000L ($6.40). Open in summer, daily from 9pm to 2am; in winter, Monday and Wednesday to Saturday from 9pm to 2am.

WINE BARS

The fermented fruits of the vine have played a prominent role in Roman life since the word *bacchanalian* was first invented—and that was very early indeed.

Enoteca Fratelli Roffi Isabelli. Via della Croce 76B. ☎ **06/679-0896.**

This is one of the best places to taste the wines of Italy. A stand-up drink in its darkly antique confines might be the perfect ending to a visit to the nearby Spanish Steps. Set behind an unflashy facade, this place is the best repository in this chic shopping district for Italian wines, brandies, and grappa. You can opt for a postage-stamp table in back or else stay at the bar with its impressive display of wines, which are stacked on shelves in every available corner. A glass of wine costs 4,000L to 12,000L ($2.55 to $7.70), depending on its quality; grappa begins at 6,000L ($3.85). Open daily from 11am to midnight.

IRISH PUBS

The two most popular Irish pubs in Rome draw mostly English-speaking expatriates. You can always see a cluster of disoriented local teenagers here and there, but their Italian is drowned in the sea of English, Scottish, Irish, Canadian, Australian, and sometimes American accents. If you want to mingle with people who speak your language, try one of these places. Both near Piazza di Santa Maria Maggiore, they may be a little difficult to find, but once you've found one, someone will direct you, or even walk with you, to the other.

Druid's Den. Via San Martino ai Monti 28. ☎ **06/488-0258.**

The popular Druid's Den is open daily from 5pm to 12:30am. Here, while enjoying a pint of beer at 7,000L ($4.50), you can listen to Irish music and dream of Eire. A group of young Irishmen one night even did an Irish jig in front of the delighted Roman spectators. The "den" is near Piazza di Santa Maria Maggiore and the train station.

Fiddler's Elbow. Via dell'Olmata 43. ☎ **06/487-2110.**

Fiddler's Elbow, near Piazza di Santa Maria Maggiore and the railway station, is reputedly the oldest pub in the capital. It's open daily from 4:30pm to 12:30am. A pint of Guinness is 7,000L ($4.50); sometimes, however, the place is so packed you can't find room to drink it.

4 Movies

Pasquino Cinema. Vicolo del Piede 19, Piazza di Santa Maria in Trastevere. ☎ **06/580-3622.** Bus: 56 or 60 from Via Vittorio Veneto or 170 from Stazione Termini.

This is a small theater showing English-language films of fairly recent vintage interspersed with some classics and art-house favorites. Phone the theater if you want to know what's playing. It's on a little street, just a block from Piazza di Santa Maria in Trastevere. In fact, it makes quite a pleasant evening to catch a show at Pasquino, then have a drink or cappuccino afterward at one of the cafés on the square, where you can admire the village atmosphere, the fine architecture, and the scene around the fountain. Tickets to the theater cost 9,000L ($5.75). There are usually four screenings daily between 4 and 11pm.

10 Side Trips from Rome

Rome is surrounded by a countryside that has delighted Romans and foreigners for hundreds of years. The attractions are varied—beaches, ancient temples, Renaissance palaces—and all are within an easy trip distance. While we've indicated possible public transportation below, here's where a rental car really comes in handy. (See Chapter 3 for information on renting a car.)

Unless you're rushed beyond reason, allow at least 3 days to take a look at the attractions in the environs of Rome.

1 Tivoli

20 miles E of Rome

An ancient town, Tivoli's origins predate those of Rome itself. At the height of the empire, "Tibur," as it was called, was a favorite retreat for the rich. Horace, Catullus, Sallust, Maecenas, and a few emperors (notably Hadrian) maintained lavish villas here near the woods and waterfalls. It was popular enough to warrant a Roman road, Via Tiburtina, whose modern descendant funnels trucks and tour buses into today's Tivoli. During the Middle Ages Tivoli achieved a form of independence, which was to last through its rise in fortunes during the Renaissance. This latter period saw real-estate investment by several of the wealthier princes of the church, especially Cardinal Ippolito d'Este. By the late 19th century Tivoli had been incorporated into the new kingdom of Italy and its former privileges of independence passed into history.

ESSENTIALS

GETTING THERE Take Metro Linea B to the end of the line, the Rebibbia station. After exiting the station, catch an Acotral bus the rest of the 30-minute ride to Tivoli. Generally buses depart about every 20 minutes. Service is daily from 5:30am to 11pm; a one-way ticket costs 2,300L ($1.45).

By Car Expect about an hour's drive with traffic on Via Tiburtina.

VISITOR INFORMATION For tourist information, go to Piazza Garibaldi (☎ **0774/21249**). Open Monday to Saturday from 9am to 6pm and on Sunday from 9am to 2pm.

Side Trips from Rome

SEEING THE PALACES & GARDENS

✪ **Villa Adriana (Hadrian's Villa).** Via di Villa Adriana. ☎ **0774/530203.** Admission 8,000L ($5.10) adults, free for children 17 and under and for seniors 60 and over. Daily 9am–sunset (about 6:30pm Apr–Oct, 4pm Nov–Mar). Bus: 2 or 4 from Rebibbia to the Villa Adriana.

Below the foothills on which Tivoli is built lies a gently sloping plain, the site of the Villa Adriana, built in A.D. 135. Today the ruins cover slope after slope of the rolling terrain—fully 180 acres. Hadrian was a widely traveled and highly cultured man; he was also something of an amateur architect, and he personally designed a large part of the villa. It was built as a heaven on earth in which to spend a long and luxurious retirement surrounded by a court that numbered in the hundreds. Having traveled extensively as a general, Hadrian had seen much of the world, and he sought to re-create in his villa at Tibur those sights that most pleased him. Hadrian did not wish to build replicas of just rooms, or even palaces he had seen: He reconstructed entire valleys complete with the temples that had made them famous (the Canopus on the estate is one example). Much of the ruin is readily recognizable, and it's easy to wander around the hot baths and the cold baths and experience a real sense of the villa as it once was. In addition to the Poekile, the Lyceum, the valley of Tempe (named after a vale in Thessaly), the Academy, and the Canopus (a replica of a sacred canal linking the Nile to the Temple of Serapis), there was even an Inferno. (This last attraction is in an olive grove lying in a portion of the villa that hasn't yet been excavated, so it's hard to visit.)

Hadrian didn't live long enough to enjoy the full pleasure he expected from the villa; he died of a painful and undiagnosed illness 3 years after its completion. Legend has it that he was able to perform miracles on his deathbed—restoring sight to the blind and that sort of thing.

✪ **Villa d'Este.** Piazza Trento, Viale delle Centro Fontane. ☎ **0774/312070.** Admission 8,000L ($5.10) adults when the water jets are set at full power, 5,000L ($3.20) adults at other times; free for children 17 and under and for seniors 60 and over. Nov–Jan, daily 9am–4pm; Feb, daily 9am–5pm; Mar and Oct, daily 9am–5:30pm; Apr and Sept, daily 9am–6:30pm; May–Aug, daily 9am–6:45pm. Bus: 2 or 4 from Rebibbia to near the villa entrance.

The Villa d'Este was named after the 16th-century cardinal who transformed it from a government palace (it had been built in the 13th century as a Benedictine convent) into a princely residence that remained in the cardinal's family until 1918.

The 16th-century frescoes and decorations are attractive but unexceptional. The garden on the sloping hill beneath is another story. It's a perfect fairy tale of the Renaissance, using water as a medium of sculpture, much the way the ancients used marble—there are fountains in every imaginable size and shape. Pathways are lined with 100 fountains, and stairs are flanked with cascades on either side. There are fountains you can walk under, fountains you can walk over, and long reflecting pools with surreal trees in between. The fountains have names—*Owl and Bird*, the *Oval Fountain*, *Fountain of Glass*—and in centuries past, might possibly have concealed practical jokes. The Renaissance aristocracy were immensely amused by a shot of water in someone else's eye.

Villa Gregoriana. Largo Sant'Angelo. ☎ **0774/334522.** Admission 2,500L ($1.60). Daily 9am to 1 hour before sunset. Bus: 2 or 4 from Rebibbia to near the villa entrance.

The gardens were built by Pope Gregory XVI in the 19th century. Whereas the Villa d'Este dazzles with artificial glamour, the Villa Gregoriana relies on nature. At one point on the circuitous walk carved along a slope, visitors stand and look out onto the most spectacular waterfall (Aniene) at Tivoli. The track to the bottom of the banks of the Annio is studded with grottoes, and balconies open onto the chasm.

From one of the belvederes is a panoramic view of the Temple of Vesta on the hill. The only problem is that if you do make the full journey, you may need to summon a helicopter to lift you back up again—the climb is fierce.

WHERE TO DINE

Albergo Ristorante Adriano. Via di Villa Adriana 194. ☎ **0774/535028.** Main courses 20,000L–40,000L ($12.80–$25.60); fixed-price menu 75,000L ($48). AE, DC, MC, V. Mon–Sat 12:30–2:30pm and 8–10pm, Sun 12:30–2:30pm. Bus: 2 or 4 from Rebibbia or Tivoli. ITALIAN.

This place might be the perfect stopover before or after you visit Hadrian's Villa. At the bottom of the villa's hill, in a stucco-sided building a few steps from the ticket office, it offers terrace dining under plane trees in summer or indoor dining in a high-ceilinged room with terra-cotta walls, neoclassical moldings, and Corinthian pilasters painted white. The food is home-style cooking—nothing fancy. Roman menus include roast lamb, saltimbocca, a variety of veal dishes, deviled chicken, a selection of salads and cheeses, and simple desserts. They are especially proud of their homemade pasta dishes.

Le Cinque Statue. Via Quintillio Varo 1. ☎ **0774/335366.** Reservations recommended. Main courses 10,000L–20,000L ($6.40–$12.80). AE, DC, MC, V. Sat–Thurs 12:30–3pm and 7:30–10pm. Closed Aug 15–Sept 7. Bus: 2 or 4 from Rebibbia or Tivoli. ROMAN.

Established in the 1950s in a building from the 1920s, this restaurant takes its name from the quintet of old carved statues, including Apollo Belvedere and gladiators, that decorate it. This comfortable restaurant is maintained by a single hardworking Italian family, who prepare an honest and unpretentious cuisine without a lot of fuss and bother. Everything is accompanied by the wines of the hill towns of Lazio. Begin with a pastiche of mushrooms, or make a selection from their varied antipasto offerings. Try rigatoni with fresh herbs, tripe fried Roman style, or a mixed fry of brains and vegetables. All the pasta is freshly made on the premises. They also have a wide variety of ice creams and fruits.

2 Palestrina

24 miles E of Rome

Like Tibur, ancient Preneste (as Palestrina was called) was a superb holiday spot. It was the favorite of Horace and Pliny, and even Hadrian, who maintained a villa here.

ESSENTIALS

GETTING THERE Buses leave every 30 to 45 minutes during the day from Rome; departures are from Via Castro Pretorio (take the Metro to the stop at Castro Pretorio to catch the bus). It takes about an hour to reach Palestrina.

By Car Take either Via Prenestina (much less trafficked than Via Tiburtina), or the autostrada (A2) and get off at Valmontana; the latter route is much quicker.

WHAT TO SEE & DO

The town was really known for the great **Temple of Fortuna Primigenia,** which covered most of the hill where Palestrina stands today. In its inner sanctum was an oracle, to which thousands journeyed regularly from Rome over the ancient stone road. As it was the fashion for emperors to enlarge and beautify temples and public facilities, the Temple of Fortuna grew to gigantic proportions. However, it fell into rapid decay at the end of the 4th century, when pagan temples were ordered closed by the Christian imperial government. During the Middle Ages it was a stronghold for a string of families—the physical situation on top of Mount Ginestro was perfect—the last of which, the Barberini, erected a palace at the summit of the temple. The vast sanctuary was almost forgotten until World War II, when Allied bombers made runs on Palestrina and uncovered the ruins with exploding bombs.

Today Palestrina consists of a modern town at the foot of Mount Ginestro, the excavated levels of the temple on the slopes above, the Palazzo Barberini at the highest point of the temple, and a tangle of medieval streets on the crown of the mountain.

Museo Nazionale Archeologico di Palestrina. Palazzo Barberini. ☎ **06/953-8100.** Admission 4,000L ($2.55) adults, free for children 17 and under and for seniors 60 and over. Daily 9am to 1 hour before sunset. Follow the signs from the center to the top of the town.

The Barberini museum houses a collection of Etruscan artifacts, a mosaic of the Nile at flood from the Fortuna sanctuary (an intricate piece on the top floor of the museum), and a view of the surrounding countryside that certainly makes you feel like a Renaissance prince or princess.

WHERE TO STAY & DINE

Albergo Ristorante Stella (Restaurant Coccia). Piazza della Liberazione 3, Palestrina, 00036 Roma. ☎ **06/953-8172.** Fax 06/957-3360. 27 rms, 2 suites. A/C TV TEL. 90,000L ($57.60) double; 150,000L ($96) suite. AE, DC, V. Free parking.

A buff-colored contemporary hotel and restaurant, the Stella is in the commercial district of town on a cobblestone square filled with parked cars, trees, and a small fountain. It was renovated in 1995, although the bedrooms remain rather basic, but comfortable. The simple lobby is filled with warm colors and contains curved leather couches and autographed photos of local sports heroes.

The restaurant, serving a zesty Roman cuisine, is sunny, filled with a cluttered kind of modernity. Meals start at 40,000L ($25.60). There's a small bar where you might have an apéritif. The bar and restaurant are open daily from noon to 3pm and 7 to 9pm.

3 Castelli Romani

The name means "Roman castles," which they're not. The *castelli* are really a series of little hill towns, grouped on mountain slopes around two lakes. Some are extremely ancient, and all have been popular as holiday retreats at least since the days of the Roman Empire. The best way to visit the castelli is with a car, especially since many of the towns don't have enough to keep you occupied for more than an hour or so. Without a car, you'll have to take one of the many buses serving the castelli that leaves from the Subaugusta Metro stop, and this takes a lot of time.

MARINO

Marino, the closest to Rome (only 15 miles away), is about 4½ miles off Via Appia Nuova quite near Ciampino Airport. Much of Marino's original charm has fallen victim to modern builders, but the town is still the place to go each October during the grape harvest. At that time the town's fountains are switched from water to wine and everyone can drink for free.

ROCCA DI PAPA

This is the most attractive of the hill towns, and it lies only some 6 miles from Marino. The best road if you're driving is 217 to the junction with 218, where you make a left turn. Before the intersection, you'll be high on a ridge above Lake Albano—the views of the lake, the far woods, and the papal palace of Castel Gandolfo on the opposite mountain are superb. Just before Rocca di Papa is the entrance to the toll road to Monte Cavo. A temple of Jove once stood on top of this mountain, and before that, the tribes of the area met with King Tarquin (the Proud) before Rome was a republic. Atop the mountain is a restaurant with reasonable prices and a panoramic view of the surrounding Alban Hills and hill towns. Down below, Rocca di Papa is a tangle of old streets and churches. A legend of dubious origin claims that Hannibal once camped just below the town in a wooded hollow.

NEMI

From Rocca di Papa it's only a short drive to this tiny town clinging to a woody precipice above the lake of the same name. The ancient Romans knew these parts well. A temple to Diana once stood in the valley and the lake was called her "looking glass." If October is the time for Marino, May is the ideal time for Nemi, when a festival is held in honor of the local strawberries.

WHAT TO SEE & DO

Looking from any of the balconies in Nemi, you'll see what looks like an airplane hangar in the valley right by the lakeshore. This unprepossessing building has the important-sounding name of **Museo delle Navi,** Via di Diana (☎ **06/936-8140**), and until World War II it held the remains of two luxurious barges that floated in the lake during the reign of Caligula (assassinated A.D. 41). The boats, which were fitted out lavishly with bronze and marble, were sunk during the reign of Claudius (he succeeded the insane Caligula) and were entirely forgotten until Mussolini drained the lake in the 1930s. The barges were found, set up in a lakeside museum, and remained as a wonder of ancient Rome until the Nazis burned them (out of spite) during their retreat from Rome and environs. Today the museum houses mainly models of the ships and some of the metal and mosaic bits that survived the fire. Admission is 4,000L ($2.55) for adults, free for children 17 and under and for seniors 60 and over. It's open Monday to Saturday from 9am to 1:30pm and on Sunday from 9am to 1pm. To reach the museum, unless you're driving, you have to walk from the center of Nemi toward the lake.

The 15th-century **Palazzo Ruspoli,** a baronial estate, is the focal point of Nemi, but the hill town itself invites exploration—particularly the alleyways the local denizens call streets and the houses with balconies jutting out over the slopes. While darting through the Castelli Romani, try to time your schedule for lunch in Nemi.

WHERE TO DINE

La Taverna. Via Nemorense 13. ☎ **06/936-8135.** Reservations required. Main courses 13,000L–16,000L ($8.30–$10.25). AE, DC, MC, V. Thurs–Tues 12:30–2pm and 8–10pm. INTERNATIONAL.

Offering a large array of the dishes of the region, as well as a rustic atmosphere, La Taverna is worth the trouble it takes to get there. In April the *fragole* (wild strawberries) signs go out. Otherwise try fettuccine with mushrooms. For a main dish, we suggest the chef's specialty, arrosto di abbacchio e maiale (it consists of both a pork chop and grilled lamb). Fresh fish is also featured. If you want to have a Roman feast, accompany your main dish with large roasted mushrooms, priced according to size, and a small fennel salad. When finished, it's traditional to order Sambucca, a clear white liquor like anisette, "with a fly in it." The "fly" is a coffee bean—usually three of them—which you suck on for added flavor.

EN ROUTE TO CASTEL GANDOLFO

The road to Gandolfo leads us through a few "worth a visit" towns on the way. **Genzano,** on the other side of Lake Nemi, has views of the countryside and a 17th-century palace that belonged to the Sforza-Cesarini.

Ariccia is an ancient town that sent representatives to meet with Tarquin the Proud on top of Monte Cavo 2,500 years ago. After many centuries of changing hands, especially between medieval and Renaissance families, it has taken on a suburban look. The palace in the middle of town is still private and belongs to the Chigi family.

Albano practically adjoins Castel Gandolfo. It has a long history—this is the reputed site of Alba Longa, the so-called mother city of Rome, but it's quite built up in a modern way today. Trains going to Albano leave from Stazione Termini in Rome.

CASTEL GANDOLFO

Now we come to the summer residence of the pope. The papal palace, a 17th-century edifice designed by Carlo Maderno, stands practically on the foundations of another equally regal summer residence, the villa of the emperor Domitian. Unfortunately, the palace, the gardens, and the adjoining Villa Barberini can't be visited. You'll have to content yourself with the piazza out front with its church and fountain by Bernini.

FRASCATI

Lying 13 miles southeast of Rome, lying out on Via Tuscolana, this is the best known of the hill towns. Some 1,073 feet above sea level, Frascati is celebrated for its white wines. Golden vineyards cover the surrounding northern slopes of the outer crater ring of the Alban Hills. From its lofty perch you'll see a panoramic view of the countryside and the other small towns.

ESSENTIALS

GETTING THERE You can take an Acotral bus from the Anagnina station at the end of Metro Linea A in Rome. Buses leave on the 20-minute trip about every 30 minutes daily from 5am to 10:30pm, and a one-way ticket costs 1,500L (95¢).

By Car From the ring road around Rome (its southeast section), motorists head southeast along Route 215.

VISITOR INFORMATION Tourist information is available at Piazza Marconi 1 (☎ **06/942-0331**). Open April to October, Monday to Friday from 9am to 1pm and 4 to 7pm and on Saturday from 9am to 1pm and 3:30 to 6:40pm.

WHAT TO SEE & DO

At one time Frascati was the chicest mountain resort for Roman society, as wealthy patricians erected villas here, with elaborate gardens and high-spouting fountains. Later the town belonged mainly to the papacy. From that period dates the most important villa, the **Villa Aldobrandini,** Via Massala (☎ **06/942-0331**), which owes part of its look to Maderno, the designer of the facade of St. Peter's. To visit the gardens, which are open only in the morning, go to the tourist office (see above). Tickets are issued free.

About 3 miles past the villa, motorists can reach **Tuscolo,** a spot known to the ancients with an amphitheater dating from the 1st century B.C. From here, you'll enjoy one of the most-photographed views in all the castelli.

Villa Torlonia, bombed in World War II, has been converted into a public park, known for its Theater of the Fountains with dramatic water displays.

WHERE TO DINE

Cacciani Restaurant. Via Armando Diaz 13. ☎ **06/942-0378.** Reservations required Sat–Sun. Main courses 15,000L–25,000L ($9.60–$16). AE, DC, MC, V. Tues–Sun 12:30–3pm and 7:30–10:30pm. Closed Jan 7–19 and Aug 18–27. ROMAN.

The Cacciani is the choicest restaurant in Frascati, where the competition has always been tough (Frascati foodstuffs once attracted Lucullus, the epicurean). A large, modern restaurant in the center of town, with a terrace commanding a view of the valley, the Cacciani has drawn such long-ago celebrities as Clark Gable. The kitchen is exposed to the public, and it's fun just to watch the women wash the sand off the spinach. To get you started, we recommend the pasta specialties, such as fettuccine or rigatoni alla vaccinara (oxtail in tomato sauce). For a main course, the baby lamb with a special sauce of white wine and vinegar is always reliable. There's a large choice of wines, which are kept in a cave under the restaurant.

The owners, the Cacciani family, will arrange a combined visit to several of the wine-producing villas of Frascati along with a memorable meal at their elegant restaurant, on terms that can be arranged before your arrival if you call.

4 Ostia

16 miles SW of Rome

Ostia was the port of ancient Rome and a city in its own right. The currents and uneven bottom of the Tiber prevented Mediterranean shipping from going farther upstream, so merchandise was transferred to barges for the remainder of the trip. Ostia's fate was tied closely to that of the empire. At the peak of Rome's power, the city had 100,000 inhabitants—hard to imagine looking at today's ruins. Ostia was important enough to have had a theater (still standing in reconstructed form), numerous temples and baths, great patrician houses, and a large business complex. Successive emperors enlarged and improved the facilities, notably Claudius and Trajan, but by the time of Constantine (4th century A.D.), the tide was turning. The barbarian sieges of Rome in the 5th century spelled the end of Ostia.

Without the empire to trade with and Rome to sell to, the port quickly withered, reverting in a few centuries to a malarial swamp without a trace of Roman civilization. The excavations, still only partial, were started by the papacy in the 19th century, but the really substantial work took place between 1938 and 1942 under the Mussolini government.

ESSENTIALS

GETTING THERE Take the Metro Linea B to the Magliana station, at a cost of 1,500L (95¢) for a one-way ticket. At Magliana, change to the Lido train (for which you'll need to buy another 1,500L ticket). From there it's about a 20-minute ride to the Ostia Antica stop, then a short walk to the excavations.

By Car Drive out Via Ostiense heading for Route 8 (signposted LIDO DI ROMA OSTIA).

WHAT TO SEE & DO

Today a visit to ✪ **Ostia Antica,** Viale dei Romagnoli 717 (☎ **06/565-0022**), is one of the most history-laden afternoons you can spend near Rome. It's relatively secluded, and the ruins invite discovery. There are picnic spots beside fallen columns and near old temple walls, and it's even easy to reach (see "Essentials," above). While you're there, be sure to see the **museum,** which has a fine collection of statuary found in the ruins. Entrance to the grounds is 8,000L ($5.10), free for those 17 and under. It's open daily: 9am to 6pm April to September, and 9am to 5pm October to March.

The history of **Lido di Ostia,** the congested beachfront, goes back only to 1926, when the first highway linking Rome to the coast was built. Prior to that, it was a malaria-ridden waste, unvisited and unwanted. Because it's so easy to reach by Metro, the beach crowds can and do get quite heavy on weekends.

Our recommendation is that you don't join them—at any time. One Roman journalist recently wrote: "The notorious beaches here are dangerous to your health. Don't go near the murky, polluted waters unless it's your custom to swim in the canals of Venice."

Confine your swimming to hotel pools or public swimming pools in the Rome area; or, better yet, head for one of the beach resorts along any of the Italian coastlines. A good beach recommendation near Rome is Fregene, 23 miles west of Rome.

5 Cerveteri & Tarquinia

As Livy's Trojans landed in ancient Italy, so did the Etruscans. Who were they? We still don't know, and the many inscriptions they left behind—mostly on graves—are no help since the Etruscan language has never been deciphered. We deduce the date of their arrival on the west coast of Umbria at around 800 B.C.

Two former strongholds of the Etruscans can be visited today, Cerveteri and Tarquinia. (For Etruscan museums in Rome, see the Vatican's Etruscan Museum and the Etruscan Museum of the Villa Giulia, both in Chapter 6.)

CERVETERI

28 miles NW of Rome

Cerveteri is older than Rome and stands on the site of a major Etruscan stronghold called Caere. If you drive there, you'll pass through the rolling hills of the Roman countryside. You'll eventually see the city's medieval walls up in the hills on your right; on the left are the modern towers of Ladispoli, a rapidly growing seaside town.

ESSENTIALS

GETTING THERE The best way to reach Cerveteri is by car. Head out Via Aurelia, northwest of Rome, for a distance of 28 miles.

By Bus Take Metro Linea A in Rome to the Lepanto stop. From Via Lepanto, you can catch an Acotral coach to Cerveteri (☎ 06/324-4724); the trip takes about an hour and costs 4,900L ($3.15). Once at Cerveteri, it's a 1¼-mile walk to the necropolis—just follow the signs that point the way.

WHAT TO SEE & DO

It's the Etruscan heritage that brings visitors to Cerveteri today, for while the Caere of the living has long vanished, the Caere of the dead still exists in a relatively good state of preservation. Next to their city, the Etruscans built their major **Necropolis of Cerveteri** (☎ **06/994-0001**), a city of tombs. Most of the circular, dome-shaped graves date from the 7th century B.C., and several have been found completely intact, untouched since their doors were sealed 2,600 years ago. The necropolis lies on the other side of a small valley from the medieval battlements, and it's still surrounded by grape vineyards. There's no sound here except the rather ghostly moans of the wind in the pine trees. Only a portion of the necropolis is excavated, but it's quite extensive. You can climb in and out of the tombs, which are decorated inside as Etruscan homes were. Note the absence of the arch, an architectural innovation of the later Romans. The necropolis is open May to September, Tuesday to Sunday from 9am to 7pm (in other months, 9am to 3:30pm). Admission is 8,000L ($5.10).

Many of the treasures in the Villa Giulia in Rome came from Caere, and many other priceless pieces of that distant culture are on display at the **Museo Nazionale Cerite,** Piazza di Santa Maria Maggiore (☎ **06/994-1354**). It contains a rare collection of Etruscan pottery, among other exhibits. The museum is housed in Ruspoldi Castle, with its ancient walls and crenellations. It's open Tuesday to Sunday: from 9am to 7pm May to September, from 9am to 2pm October to April. Admission is free.

When you're through visiting the necropolis and the museum, it's pleasant to stroll around the twisting lanes of the town, pausing perhaps at the battlements to survey the vastness of the countryside. The Tyrrhenian Sea glitters in the sunshine, and Ladispoli rises like a dream city on the shore.

TARQUINIA

60 miles NW of Rome

An even more striking museum is at Tarquinia, near Civitavecchia, which was the port of Rome in the days of Trajan. The situation of Tarquinia is commanding, with a view of the sea. It's medieval in appearance, with its fortifications and nearly two dozen towers.

ESSENTIALS

GETTING THERE As for public transportation, the train is the preferred choice; a *diretto* train from the Stazione Termini takes 50 minutes.

By Bus Eight buses a day leave from the Via Lepanto Metro stop in Rome for the 2-hour trip to the neighboring town, Barriera San Giusto, which is 1 1/2 miles from Tarquinia. Bus schedules are available at the tourist office (see below). In Rome, call 06/85-6384 for information.

By Car Take Via Aurelia outside Rome and continue on the autostrada toward Civitavecchia. Bypass Civitavecchia and continue another 13 miles north until you see the exit signs for Tarquinia.

VISITOR INFORMATION Tourist information is available at the tourist office at Piazza Cavour (☎ **0766/856036**), 1 1/2 miles from Tarquinia. Open Monday to Friday from 8am to 2pm and 4 to 7pm.

WHAT TO SEE & DO

The ✪ **Tarquinia National Museum,** Piazza Cavour (☎ **0766/856036**), is housed in the Gothic-Renaissance Palazzo Vitelleschi, dating from 1439. It displays a large number of sarcophagi and Etruscan exhibits removed from the nearby necropolis. But the reason people drive all the way up here from Rome is to see a pair of winged horses that were removed from the front of a temple. This work by an unknown artist numbers among the greatest masterpieces of Etruscan art ever discovered. The museum is open Tuesday to Sunday: from 9am to 7pm May to October, and from 9am to 2pm in the off-season. Admission is 8,000L ($5.10) for adults, free for children 17 and under and for seniors 60 and over.

The same ticket you purchased to enter the museum also admits you to the **Etruscan Necropolis** (☎ **0766/856308**), the leading sightseeing attraction of

Tarquinia. You can reach the grave sites by taking a bus at the Barriera San Giusto and getting off at the Cimitero stop. Or it's about a 20-minute walk from the museum (inquire at the museum for directions).

The most important tombs here are chambers hewn out of rock containing well-preserved paintings. Actually, the necropolis covers more than 2½ miles of windswept ground, with hundreds upon hundreds of tombs—not all of which have been visited by the *tombaroli* (grave robbers). A guide shows you the most important tombs. The paintings give an intimate glimpse of the daily life of the Etruscans, including their customs, beliefs, and religion. One of the tombs most popular with tourists dates from the 5th century B.C. Paintings there depict guests at a banquet, lying on beds, waited on by naked ephebes. Colors include red and pale pink from iron oxide, blue from the dust of lapis lazuli, and black from charcoal. The necropolis is open Tuesday to Sunday: April to October from 9am to 1 hour before sunset, until 2pm November to March.

6 Viterbo

61 miles N of Rome

The 2,000 years that have gone into the creation of the city of Viterbo make it one of the most interesting day trips from Rome. While it traces its history back to the Etruscans, the bulk of its historical architecture dates from the Middle Ages and the Renaissance, when the city was a residence—and hideout—for the popes. The old section of the city is still surrounded by thick stone walls that once protected the inhabitants from papal (or antipapal, depending on the situation at the time) attacks.

ESSENTIALS

GETTING THERE From Rome take Metro Linea A to Flaminio. At the Flaminio station, follow the signs pointing to Roma Nord station. Once there, purchase a combined rail and bus ticket to Viterbo, costing 5,900L ($3.80) one-way. The train takes you to Saxa Rubra in just 15 minutes. At Saxa Rubra, take an Acotral bus for the 1½-hour trip to Viterbo. Especially if you're trying to see Viterbo on a day trip, it might be worth the extra money to take a taxi from Saxa Rubra the remainder of the way. Call 0761/332-8333 for transportaion information.

By Car Take Autostrada 2 north to the Orte exit.

VISITOR INFORMATION Tourist information is at Piazzale dei Caduti 16 (☎ **0761/304795**). Open Monday to Saturday from 8am to 2pm.

WHAT TO SEE & DO

The only way to see Viterbo properly is to wander through the narrow cobblestone streets of the medieval town, pausing in front of the antiquity-rich structures. **Piazza del Plebiscito,** dominated by the 15th-century town hall, impresses with the fine state of preservation of Viterbo's old buildings. The courtyard and fountain in front of the town hall and the 13th-century governor's palace are favorite meeting places for townfolk and visitors alike.

Just down Via San Lorenzo is **Piazza San Lorenzo,** the site of Viterbo's cathedral, which sits atop the former Etruscan acropolis. The **Duomo,** dating from 1192, is a composite of architectures, from its pagan foundations to its Renaissance facade to its Gothic bell tower. Next door is the 13th-century **Palazzo Papale,** built as a residence for the pope, but also serving as a hideout when the pope was in exile. It was also the site of three papal elections. The exterior staircase and the colonnaded loggia combine to make up one of the finest examples of civil Roman architecture from the Gothic period.

The finest example of medieval architecture in Viterbo is the **San Pellegrino Quarter,** reached from Piazza San Lorenzo by a short walk past Piazza della Morte. This quarter, inhabited by working-class Viterboans, is a maze of narrow streets, arched walkways, towers, steep stairways, and ornamental fountains.

Worth a special visit is the **Convent of Santa Maria della Verità,** dating from 1100. The church contains 15th-century frescoes by Lorenzo da Viterbo, student of Piero della Francesca.

Parco dei Mostri (Park of the Monsters). Villa delle Meraviglie, Bomarzo. ☎ **0761/924029.** Admission 10,000L ($6.40) adults, 6,000L ($3.85) children 6 and under. Daily 8am–dusk. Bus: 6 from Piazza Martiri d'Ungheria in Viterbo.

About 8 miles east of Bagnaia at Bomarzo lies the Park of the Monsters. Prince Vicino Orsini had it built in a deep valley that's overlooked by the Orsini Palace and the houses of the village. On the other side of the valley are stone cliffs. Prince Orsini's park, Bosco Sacro (Sacred Wood), is filled with grotesque figures carved from natural rock. The figures probably date from about 1560 (Annibale Caro, a Renaissance poet, refers to them in a letter he wrote in 1564). They rise mysteriously from the wild Latium landscape, covered with strangling weeds and moss. Nature and art have created a surrealistic fantasy; the Mouth of Hell (an ogre's face so big that people can walk into its gaping mouth), a crude Hercules slaying an Amazon, nymphs with butterfly wings, a huge tortoise with a statue on its shell, a harpy, a mermaid, snarling dogs, lions, and much, much more. If you need to refresh yourself after the excursion to the edge of madness, you'll find a snack shop near the entrance.

Villa Lante. Bagnaia. ☎ **0761/288008.** Admission (30-minute garden tour) 4,000L ($2.55). May–Aug, Tues–Sun 9am–7:30pm; Mar–Apr and Sept–Oct, Tues–Sun 9am–5:30pm; Nov–Feb, Tues–Sun 9am–4pm. Bus: 6 from Viterbo.

The English author Sacheverell Sitwell called Villa Lante, located in Bagnaia, a suburb of Viterbo, "the most beautiful garden in Italy." Indeed, it's a worthy contender with Villa d'Este at Tivoli for that title. Water from Monte Cimino flows down to the fountains of the villa, running from terrace to terrace until it reaches the central pool of the regal garden, with statues, stone banisters, and shrubbery. Two symmetrical Renaissance palaces make up the villa. The estate is now partly a public park, which is open during the day. The gardens that adjoin the villa, however, can only be visited on a guided tour. (The gatekeeper at the guard house will show you through, usually with a group that has assembled.) The interiors of the twin mansions can't be visited without special permission.

Appendix

A Basic Vocabulary

English	Italian	Pronunciation
Thank you	Grazie	graht-tzee-yey
Please	Per favore	*pehr* fah-*vohr*-eh
Yes	Si	See
No	No	noh
Good morning *or* **Good day**	Buongiorno	bwohn-*djor*-noh
Good evening	Buona sera	*Bwohn*-ah *say*-rah
Good night	Buona notte	*Bwohn*-ah *noht*-tay
How are you?	Come sta?	*koh*-may *stah*
Very well	Molto bene	*mohl*-toh *behn*-ney
Goodbye	Arrivederci	ahr-ree-vah-*dehr*-chee
Excuse me (to get attention)	Scusi	*skoo*-zee
Excuse me (to get past someone on the bus)	Permesso	pehr-*mehs*-soh
Where is? . . .	Dov'è? . . .	doh-*vey*? . . .
the station	la stazione	lah stat-tzee-*oh*-neh
a hotel	un albergo	oon ahl-*behr*-goh
a restaurant	un ristorante	oon reest-ohr-*ahnt*-eh
the bathroom	il bagno	eel *bahn*-nyoh
To the right	A destra	ah *dehy*-stra
To the left	A sinistra	ah see-*nees*-tra
Straight ahead	Avanti (*or* sempre diritto)	ahv-vahn-tee (*sehm*-preh dee *reet*-toh)
How much is it?	Quanto costa?	*kwan*-toh *coh*-sta?
The check, please	Il conto, per favore	eel kon-toh *pehr* fah-*vohr*-eh
When?	Quando?	*kwan*-doh
Yesterday	Ieri	ee-*yehr*-ree
Today	Oggi	*oh*-jee
Tomorrow	Domani	doh-*mah*-nee
Breakfast	Prima colazione	*pree*-mah coh-laht-tzee-*ohn*-ay

ENGLISH	ITALIAN	PRONUNCIATION
Lunch	Pranzo	*prahn*-zoh
Dinner	Cena	*chay*-nah
What time is it?	Che ore sono?	kay *or*-ay *soh*-noh
Monday	Lunedì	loo-nay-*dee*
Tuesday	Martedì	mart-ay-*dee*
Wednesday	Mercoledì	mehr-cohl-ay-*dee*
Thursday	Giovedì	joh-vay-*dee*
Friday	Venerdì	ven-nehr-*dee*
Saturday	Sabato	*sah*-bah-toh
Sunday	Domenica	doh-*mehn*-nee-kah

NUMBERS

1 **uno** (*oo*-noh)
2 **due** (*doo*-ay)
3 **tre** (tray)
4 **quattro** (*kwah*-troh)
5 **cinque** (*cheen*-kway)
6 **sei** (say)
7 **sette** (*set*-tay)
8 **otto** (*oh*-toh)
9 **nove** (*noh*-vay)
10 **dieci** (dee-*ay*-chee)
11 **undici** (*oon*-dee-chee)
20 **venti** (*vehn*-tee)
21 **ventuno** (vehn-*toon*-oh)
22 **venti due** (*vehn*-tee *doo*-ay)
30 **trenta** (*trayn*-tah)
40 **quaranta** (kwah-*rahn*-tah)
50 **cinquanta** (cheen-*kwan*-tah)
60 **sessanta** (sehs-*sahn*-tah)
70 **settanta** (seht-*tahn*-tah)
80 **ottanta** (oht-*tahn*-tah)
90 **novanta** (noh-*vahnt*-tah)
100 **cento** (*chen*-toh)
1,000 **mille** (*mee*-lay)
5,000 **cinque milla** (*cheen*-kway *mee*-lah)
10,000 **dieci milla** (dee-*ay*-chee *mee*-lah)

B Italian Menu Savvy

Abbacchio roast haunch or shoulder of lamb baked and served in a casserole and sometimes flavored with anchovies.

Agnolotti a crescent-shaped pasta shell stuffed with a mixture of chopped meat, spices, vegetables, and cheese; when prepared in rectangular versions, the same combination of ingredients is identified as ravioli.

Amaretti crunchy, very sweet, almond-flavored macaroons.

Anguilla alla veneziana eel cooked in sauce made from tuna and lemon.

Antipasti succulent tidbits served at the beginning of a meal (before the pasta), whose ingredients might include slices of cured meats, seafood (especially shellfish), and cooked and seasoned vegetables.

Aragosta lobster.

Arrosto roasted meat.

Baccalà dried and salted codfish.

Bagna cauda hot and well-seasoned sauce, heavily flavored with anchovies, designed for dipping raw vegetables; literally translated as "hot bath."

Bistecca alla fiorentina Florentine-style steaks, coated before grilling with olive oil, pepper, lemon juice, salt, and parsley.

Bocconcini veal layered with ham and cheese, and fried.

Bollito misto assorted boiled meats served on a single platter.

Braciola pork chop.

Bresaola air-dried spiced beef.
Bruschetta toasted bread, heavily slathered with olive oil and garlic and often topped with tomatoes.
Bucatini hollow, coarsely textured spaghetti.
Busecca alla milanese tripe (beef intestines) flavored with herbs and vegetables.
Cacciucco ali livornese seafood stew.
Calzone pizza dough rolled with the chef's choice of sausage, tomatoes, cheese, etc., then baked into a kind of savory turnover.
Cannelloni tubular dough stuffed with meat, cheese, or vegetables, then baked in a creamy white sauce.
Cappellacci alla ferrarese pasta stuffed with pumpkin.
Cappelletti small ravioli ("little hats") stuffed with meat or cheese.
Carciofi artichokes.
Carpaccio thin slices of raw cured beef, sometimes in a piquant sauce.
Cassatta alla siciliana a richly caloric dessert combining layers of sponge cake, sweetened ricotta cheese, and candied fruit, bound together with an icing of chocolate buttercream.
Cervello al burro nero brains in black-butter sauce.
Cima alla genovese baked filet of veal rolled into a tube-shaped package containing eggs, mushrooms, and sausage.
Coppa cured morsels of pork filet encased in sausage skins, served in slices.
Costoletta alla milanese veal cutlet dredged in breadcrumbs, fried, and sometimes flavored with cheese.
Cozze mussels.
Fagioli white beans.
Fave fava beans.
Fegato alla veneziana thinly sliced calves' liver fried with salt, pepper, and onions.
Focaccia ideally, concocted from potato-based dough left to rise slowly for several hours, then garnished with tomato sauce, garlic, basil, salt, and pepper drizzled with olive oil; similar to a high-pan, deep-dish pizza most popular in the deep south, especially Bari.
Fontina rich cows'-milk cheese.
Frittata Italian omelet.
fritto misto a deep-fried medley of whatever small fish, shellfish, and squid are available in the marketplace that day.
Frutti di mare seafood (literally, "fruits of the sea").
Fusilli spiral-shaped pasta.
Gelato (produzione propria) ice cream (homemade).
Gorgonzola one of the most famous blue-veined cheeses of Europe; strong, creamy, and aromatic.
Gnocchi dumplings usually made from potatoes (*gnocchi alla patate*) or from semolina (*gnocchi alla romana*), often stuffed with combinations of cheese, spinach, vegetables, or whatever combinations strike the chef's fancy.
Granita flavored ice, usually with lemon or coffee.
Insalata di frutti di mare seafood salad (usually including shrimp and squid) garnished with pickles, lemon, olives, and spices.
Involtini thinly sliced beef, veal, or pork, rolled, stuffed, and fried.
Minestrone a rich and savory vegetable soup usually sprinkled with grated parmesan cheese and studded with noodles.

Mortadella mild pork sausage, fashioned into large cylinders and served sliced; the original lunchmeat baloney (because its most famous center of production is Bologna).

Mozzarella a nonfermented cheese made from the fresh milk of a buffalo (or, if unavailable, from a cow), boiled and then kneaded into a rounded ball, served fresh.

Mozzarella con pomodori (*also* **caprese**) fresh tomatoes with fresh mozzarella, basil, pepper, and olive oil.

Nervetti a northern Italian antipasto concocted from chewy pieces of calves' foot or shin.

Osso buco beef or veal knuckle slowly braised until the cartilage is tender, and then served with a highly flavored sauce.

Pappardelle alle lepre pasta with rabbit sauce.

Pancetta herb-flavored pork belly, rolled into a cylinder and sliced—the Italian bacon.

Panettone sweet, yellow-colored bread baked in the form of a brioche.

Panna heavy cream.

Pansotti pasta stuffed with greens, herbs, and cheeses, usually served with a walnut sauce.

Parmigiano parmesan, a hard and salty yellow cheese usually grated over pastas and soups but also eaten alone; also known as *granna.*

Peperoni green, yellow, or red sweet peppers.

Pesci al cartoccio fish baked in a parchment envelope with onions, parsley, and herbs.

Pesto a flavorful green sauce concocted from basil leaves, cheese, garlic, marjoram, and (if available) pine kernels.

Piccata al marsala thin escalope of veal braised in a pungent sauce flavored with marsala wine.

Piselli al prosciutto peas with strips of ham.

Pizza specific varieties include: *capricciosa* (its ingredients depend on the whim of the chef and can vary widely depending on his or her culinary vision and the ingredients at hand), *margherita* (incorporates tomato sauce, cheese, fresh basil, and memories of the first queen of Italy, Marguerite di Savoia, in whose honor it was first concocted by a Neapolitan chef), *napoletana* (includes ham, capers, tomatoes, oregano, cheese, and the distinctive taste of anchovies), *quatro stagione* (translated as "four seasons" because of the array of fresh vegetables in it; it also contains ham and bacon), and *siciliana* (contains black olives, capers, and cheese).

Pizzaiola a process whereby something (usually a beefsteak) is covered in a tomato-and-oregano sauce.

Polenta thick porridge or mush made from cornmeal flour.

Polenta de uccelli assorted small birds roasted on a spit and served with polenta.

Polenta e coniglio rabbit stew served with polenta.

Polla alla cacciatore chicken with tomatoes and mushrooms cooked in wine.

Pollo all diavola highly spiced grilled chicken.

Ragù meat sauce.

Ricotta a soft and bland cheese made from cow's or sheep's milk.

Risotto Italian rice.

Risotto alla milanese rice with saffron and wine.

Salsa verde "green sauce," made from capers, anchovies, lemon juice and/or vinegar, and parsley.

Saltimbocca veal scallop layered with prosciutto and sage; its name literally translates as "jump in your mouth," a reference to its tart and savory flavor.
Salvia sage.
Scaloppina alla Valdostana escalope of veal stuffed with cheese and ham.
Scaloppine thin slices of veal coated in flour and sautéed in butter.
Semifreddo a frozen dessert; usually ice cream with sponge cake.
Seppia cuttlefish (a kind of squid); its black ink is used for flavoring in certain sauces for pasta, and also in risotto dishes.
Sogliola sole.
Spaghetti a long, round, thin pasta, variously served: *alla bolognese* (with ground meat, mushrooms, peppers, etc.), *alla carbonara* (with bacon, black pepper, and eggs), *al pomodoro* (with tomato sauce), *al sugo/ragù* (with meat sauce), and *alle vongole* (with clam sauce).
Spiedini pieces of meat grilled on a skewer over an open flame.
Stracciatella broth containing egg and cheese.
Strangolaprete small nuggets of pasta, usually served with sauce; the name is literally translated as "priest-choker."
Stufato beef braised in white wine with vegetables.
Tagliatelle flat egg noodles.
Tiramisù richly caloric dessert containing layers of triple-crème cheeses and rum-soaked sponge cake.
Tonno tuna.
Tortelli pasta dumplings stuffed with ricotta and greens.
Tortellini rings of dough stuffed with minced and seasoned meat and served either in soups or as a full-fledged pasta covered with sauce.
Trenette thin noodles served with pesto sauce and potatoes.
Trippe alla fiorentina beef tripe (intestines).
Vermicelli very thin spaghetti.
Vitello tonnato cold sliced veal covered with tuna-fish sauce.
Zabaglione/zabaione egg yolks whipped into the consistency of a custard, flavored with marsala, and served warm as a dessert.
Zampone pig's trotter stuffed with spicy seasoned port, boiled and sliced.
Zuccotto a liqueur-soaked sponge cake, molded into a dome and layered with chocolate, nuts, and whipped cream.
Zuppa inglese sponge cake soaked in custard sauce and rum.

C Glossary of Architectural Terms

Ambone a pulpit, either serpentine or simple in form, erected in an Italian church.
Apse the half-rounded extension behind the main altar of a church; Christian tradition dictates that it be placed at the eastern end of the church, the side closest to Jerusalem.
Atrium a courtyard, open to the sky, in an ancient Roman house; the term also applies to the courtyard nearest the entranceway of an early Christian church.
Baldacchino (*also* **ciborium**) a columned stone canopy, usually placed above the altar of a church; spelled in English as baldachin or baldaquin.
Basilica any rectangular public building, usually divided into three aisles by rows of columns; in ancient Rome, this architectural form was frequently used for places of public assembly and law courts; later, Roman Christians adapted the form for many of their early churches; in theological terms, a basilica is a Catholic church given special ceremonial privileges.

Caldarium the steam room of a Roman bath.
Campanile a bell tower, often detached, of a church.
Capital the top of a column, often carved and usually categorized into one of three different orders: Doric, Ionic, or Corinthian.
Cavea the curved row of seats in a classical theater; the most prevalent shape was that of a semicircle.
Cella the sanctuary, or most sacred interior section, of a Roman temple.
Chancel section of a church containing the altar.
Choir the part of the church between the nave and the altar where the choir sits or where music or ceremonies are performed.
Cornice the decorative flange that defines the uppermost part of a classical or neoclassical facade.
Cortile courtyard or cloisters ringed with a gallery of arches or lintels set atop columns.
Crypt a church's main burial place, usually located below the choir.
Cupola a dome.
Duomo cathedral (literally, "dome").
Forum the main square, and principal gathering place, of any Roman town, usually adorned with the city's most important temples and civic buildings.
Grotesques carved and painted faces, deliberately ugly, used by everyone from the Etruscans to the architects of the Renaissance; they're especially amusing when set into fountains.
Loggia a roofed porch, balcony, or gallery.
Lozenge an elongated four-sided figure which, along with stripes, was one of the distinctive signs of the architecture of Pisa.
Narthex the anteroom, or enclosed porch, of a Christian church.
Nave the largest and longest section of a church, usually devoted to sheltering and/or seating worshippers, and often divided by aisles.
Pietra dura richly ornate assemblage of semiprecious stones mounted on a flat decorative surface, perfected during the 1600s in Florence.
Portico a porch, usually crafted from wood or stone.
Putti plaster cherubs whose chubby forms often decorate the interiors of baroque chapels and churches.
Stucco colored plaster composed of sand, powdered marble, water, and lime, either molded into statuary or applied in a thin, concretelike layer to the exterior of a building.
Telamone a structural column carved into a standing male form; the female version is called a *caryatid.*
Terme Roman baths.
Transenna stone (usually marble) screen separating the altar area from the rest of an early Christian church.
Travertine known as the stone from which ancient and Renaissance Rome was built, it's known for its hardness, light coloring, and tendency to be pitted or flecked with black.
Tympanum the half-rounded space above the portal of a church, whose semicircular space usually showcases a sculpture.

Index

ACCOMMODATIONS

Restaurants and Cafés